Rising Titans, Falling Giants

A VOLUME IN THE SERIES

Cornell Studies in Security Affairs

Edited by Robert J. Art, Robert Jervis, and Stephen M. Walt

A list of titles in this series is available at cornellpress.cornell.edu.

Rising Titans, Falling Giants

*How Great Powers Exploit
Power Shifts*

JOSHUA R. ITZKOWITZ
SHIFRINSON

Cornell University Press

Ithaca and London

Cornell University Press gratefully acknowledges receipt of subventions from the Department of International Affairs at the George Bush School of Government & Public Service and the Melvin G. Glasscock Center for Humanities Research, both at Texas A&M University, which aided in the publication of this book.

First published 2018 by Cornell University Press

Printed in the United States of America

Library of Congress Cataloging-in-Publication Data

Names: Shifrinson, Joshua R. Itzkowitz, author.
Title: Rising titans, falling giants : how great powers exploit power shifts / Joshua R. Itzkowitz Shifrinson.
Description: Ithaca : Cornell University Press, 2018. | Series: Cornell studies in security affairs | Includes bibliographical references and index.
Identifiers: LCCN 2018002247 (print) | LCCN 2018002931 (ebook) | ISBN 9781501725067 (pdf) | ISBN 9781501725074 (epub/mobi) | ISBN 9781501725050 (cloth ; alk. paper)
Subjects: LCSH: United States—Foreign relations—Soviet Union. | Soviet Union—Foreign relations—United States. | Great powers—History—20th century. | Balance of power—History—20th century.
Classification: LCC E183.8.S65 (ebook) | LCC E183.8.S65 S5435 2018 (print) | DDC 327.73047—dc23
LC record available at https://lccn.loc.gov/2018002247

Contents

Acknowledgments

To paraphrase Lyle Lanley, a professor with an acknowledgments section is a bit like a mule with a spinning wheel: it's not clear how he got it, and danged if he knows how to use it. This book was a long time coming. While I was a graduate student at the Massachusetts Institute of Technology (MIT) casting about for research topics, the 2007–8 financial crisis was reaching its apogee. In its aftermath, concerns over the course and consequences of U.S. decline were ubiquitous, yet the discussion was disassociated from anything theoretically or historically informed. The seed of a topic was planted in my mind.

Barry Posen systematically encouraged my efforts as this project took shape and evolved. Whatever arguments I offer in this work are immeasurably better for his feedback; in this, he enjoyed some payback for the critique I offered on his papers and book manuscript while serving as his research assistant. He is a consummate scholar and a role model. Dick Samuels and Taylor Fravel, who also helped shepherd this project along from the beginning, deserve equal praise. Dick offered incisive suggestions. Taylor was generous with input and critique at every stage.

Besides these three scholars, John Mearsheimer, David Edelstein, Jasen Castillo, Kelly Greenhill, and Marc Trachtenberg had the biggest influence on the book. Along with Christopher Layne, Valerie Hudson, Andy Ross, Andrew Natsios, Gabriela Thorton, and Gregory Gause, John, David, and Kelly provided instrumental feedback that helped transform an early version of this work into a completed volume. I owe David and Jasen a particular debt for commenting on multiple drafts of several chapters, often on short notice. Marc, meanwhile, was generous with his time, insight, and patience as I tried to sort through the complicated set of historical questions surrounding great power behavior in the post-1945 world.

Of course, no book can be completed without the help, input, encouragement, and support of a wide range of friends and colleagues. I am sure there are omissions in this list, but I particularly want to thank Owen Cote, Steve Van Evera, Brendan Green, Phil Haun, Lindsey O'Rourke, Jennifer Erickson, Ahsan Butt, Keren Fraiman, Andrew Radin, Dan Altman, Peter Krause, Will Norris, Aila Matanock, Jon Lindsay, Miranda Priebe, David Weinberg, Sameer Lalwani, Cindy Williams, Joshua Rovner, Harvey Sapolsky, Colin Jackson, Alec Worsnop, Michele Margolis, Erica Dobbs, Rachel Wellhausen, Noel Anderson, Ben Freidman, Kentaro Maeda, Joseph Torigian, James Conran, Mark Bell, Toby Harris, Paul Staniland, Nicholas Miller, Chris Clary, Caitlin Talmadge, Kaija Schilde, Tara Maller, Alex Downes, Jack Levy, Rachel Stein, Aisha Ahmad, Will Inboden, Annie Tracey Samuel, Sarah Bush, Chad Levinson, Walter Ladwig, Stefanie Hlatky, Rob Litwak, Ethan Corbin, Jim Goldgeier, Keith Darden, Rachel Whitlark, Jessica Trisko-Darden, Austin Carson, Kyle Lascurettes, Julia Macdonald, Jeff Friedman, Sheena Chestnut-Greitens, Rose Kelanic, Jennifer Dixon, Christian Ostermann, Kent Portney, Simon Miles, Evan Braden Montgomery, Tim McDonnell, James Graham Wilson, Stacie Goddard, James McAllister, Erik Gartzke, Jeremi Suri, Manjari Miller, Steve Lobell, Hal Brands, Emily Sellars, Paul MacDonald, Joseph Parent, Dale Copeland, Larry Napper, Norrin Ripsman, Kevin Narizny, Kate Geohegan, Katy Powers, Simon Toner, Paul Avey, Jon Markowitz, Robert Reardon, Ryan Grauer, Patrick Porter, Tim Crawford, David Blagden, Eugene Gholz, Domonic Bearfield, Justin Bullock, John A. Thompson, Dan Lindley, Eric Lorber, Richard Maass, Jennifer Keister, Mike Beckley, Stacie Pettyjohn, and John Schuessler. Brendan, in particular, heroically read nearly every word of an earlier version of the manuscript and made the final product far better; Miranda, Jennifer, and Lindsey deserve medals for tolerating far too many of my rambling theoretical musings and historical digressions. In addition, Mary Sarotte and Jeff Engel were incredible resources on U.S.-Soviet relations in the late Cold War and systematically encouraging as I tried to play historian. I am deeply indebted to Michele and the entire Margolis family for putting me up during trips to the Reagan Library.

Key portions of this project were completed at the Woodrow Wilson International Center for Scholars, the Belfer Center for Science and International Affairs, George Washington University's Institute for Security and Conflict Studies, the Dickey Center for International Understanding at Dartmouth College, and the Cato Institute. Steve Walt, Steve Miller, and Sean Lynn-Jones are heroes for sitting through at least three different presentations of my early research at the Belfer Center. Charlie Glaser is a true mensch for offering feedback and being willing to bounce around ideas during my year at George Washington. Meanwhile, I could not have asked for a better environment for revising this work into a viable book than that provided by the Dickey Center, where Bill Wohlforth, Jennifer Lind, Ben Valentino, Dan Benjamin, Daryl Press, and Steve Brooks were wonderful friends and mentors. The final revisions to this volume were undertaken while I was a visiting scholar with the Cato Institute's Defense and Foreign Policy Studies Program, and I am immensely grateful to Chris Preble for his support. Along the way, I also received useful comments from scholars at the MIRTH Colloquium at the University of California; Southern Methodist University's Tower Center; Lehigh University's Department of International Relations; and the University of Chicago's Program on International Security Policy.

My undergraduate advisers—Robert Art, David Hackett Fischer, Seyom Brown, and Shai Feldman—encouraged students to ask big questions and offer big answers. I have tried to follow that motto and am grateful for their guidance. I also benefitted beyond measure from the terrific research assistance provided by Amber Stubblefield, Hannah Fletcher, Lowell Van Ness, and—above all—Julie Malinda Thompson. At Cornell University Press, I thank Steve Walt, Roger Haydon, and Nuno Monteiro for their insightful comments on the final manuscript.

The research in this book was generously supported by grants from the Tobin Project, the Scowcroft Institute for International Affairs, the Clements Center at the University of Texas, and the MIT Center for International Studies. Robert Holzweiss and Zachary Roberts at the George H. W. Bush Presidential Library and Daniel Linke at Princeton University went above and beyond the call of duty in facilitating access to many of the archival documents employed in this project. I cannot thank Nicholas Burns, Robert Hutchings, and Philip Zelikow enough for their openness in discussing their work in the George H. W. Bush administration; their insights significantly shaped the research.

Beyond the classroom, my life has been enriched by many good friends, all of whom made sure that the research for this book did not overwhelm my life. Sam Eaton and Martin Kaminski made me look forward to each of our many barbeque trips and the occasional hiking diversion. Andy Jaffe and I spent college carousing, and I am glad we have kept that spirit alive. Prem Trivedi and Dan Schleifstein have been among my closest friends for years and voices of reason every step of the way. Melissa and Dave Wreski are two of my favorite people in the world. Karin Schneider has been a source of wisdom for many years; I owe her a great deal.

Lastly, my family has always been a source of inspiration. My mother, Joan Itzkowitz, consistently shows what perseverance means. Zachary Itzkowitz Shifrinson put up with a cranky older brother for too many months. The good humor and calm that he communicated in numerous phone calls made the research process bearable. Finally, I am lucky beyond measure to have Stephen Shifrinson for a father. At every step, he encouraged me. At every moment of doubt, he supported me. He has been my biggest fan, and I hope he knows I am his. It is to him that I dedicate this book.

Rising Titans, Falling Giants

Introduction

Rising States and the Fate of Declining Great Powers

Sir Orme Sargent was worried. Watching the stunning growth of U.S. and Soviet power as World War II wound down, the future permanent under-secretary of state in the British Foreign Ministry could not help but recognize that the distribution of power was shifting against Great Britain by the day. With the war over, Britain—once arguably the strongest state in Europe, but now nearly bankrupt—would be far weaker than its rising U.S. and Soviet counterparts. A grim future awaited. European security, Sargent wrote in July 1945, "is to a large degree in the hands of the Soviet Union and the United States," as "there is a feeling that Great Britain is now a secondary Power and can be treated as such."[1] Unless British strength grew rapidly, the country was destined to find itself falling further in the ranks of the great powers and vulnerable to Soviet and U.S. machinations.

Sargent's fears proved largely unfounded. In the immediate postwar world, a rising United States and Soviet Union both tried to keep the United Kingdom a great power. The United States' efforts initially involved limited financial aid to keep Britain afloat, but eventually saw the United States provide extensive economic assistance to reconstruct Britain's economy via the Marshall Plan and offer military backing via the North Atlantic Treaty Organization (NATO).[2] Nor was the United States alone, as the Soviet Union adopted strikingly similar policies. From 1945 through mid-1947, Soviet leaders tried to reach a quid pro quo with Britain that would divide Europe between the two states and, as British strength continued to falter, upped the ante by offering Britain a military alliance.[3] Of course, Soviet efforts to support Britain did not last forever: by late 1947, Soviet leaders were denouncing British policies and trying to undermine Britain's postwar recovery. Nevertheless, U.S. and Soviet responses to Britain's decline were not nearly as bad as Sargent had feared. Although the Soviet Union eventually preyed on British weaknesses, both the United States and Soviet Union first attempted to support Britain in Europe and, by the close of the 1940s, the

United States was actively engaged in rebuilding British economic and military capabilities.

Neither Sargent's concerns nor the varying U.S. and Soviet responses are unique. Across time and space, states facing decline—defined simply as one great power's sustained loss of economic and military capabilities relative to one or more other powers—have feared the future and worried, as Dale Copeland observes, that "if they allow a rising state to grow, it will either attack them later with superior power or coerce them into concessions that compromise their security."[4] After all, states living in a competitive international system have to provide for their own security, seemingly giving them good reasons to prey on potential rivals as their relative power grows.[5] Thucydides, for example, famously attributed the Peloponnesian War to "the growth of Athenian power and the fear which this caused in Sparta."[6] Similarly, Wilhelmine Germany's leaders saw the rise of Russia as "an ever increasing nightmare," just as Soviet leaders late in the Cold War worried that the United States would use its increasing strength to try "to gain superiority over the Soviet Union."[7]

In practice, however, rising states differ wildly in their approaches to declining great powers. Witnessing another's decline, some rising states go for the jugular and challenge a declining state's strategic position. As the Soviet Union declined in the 1980s and early 1990s, for example, the United States exploited Soviet weaknesses. Indeed, thousands of declassified documents and dozens of interviews with former policymakers show that the United States systematically took advantage of Soviet problems, initially pressing for asymmetric diplomatic and military concessions before eventually facilitating the demise of the Soviet alliance network and hindering Soviet economic recovery.[8] Similarly, Germany attempted to supplant a weakening Great Britain as Europe's leading power before the First World War through diplomatic aggrandizement and a naval arms race;[9] a rising Prussia fought a declining France for dominance in Central Europe in 1870–71;[10] and European influence in North America was undermined throughout the 1800s by the emerging United States.[11] Yet at other times, states are not as power hungry. A rising Russia, for instance, allied itself with a weakening France before 1914;[12] Germany tethered its cart to Austria-Hungary's increasingly decrepit horse after the 1870s;[13] and the Soviet Union limited its competition with the United States as the latter's power seemed to wane in the 1970s.[14] In short, rising state strategies vary markedly: rising states sometimes prey on declining states in economic, military, and/or diplomatic affairs, but they may also support their waning peers, as well as prey or support with greater or lesser intensity.

What explains these behaviors? When dealing with a declining great power, what strategies do rising states adopt? When and why do some rising states act as the United States did toward the Soviet Union in the 1980s and early 1990s, adopting predatory strategies designed to further weaken declining great powers and push them down the great power ranks? Under what conditions do rising states pursue supportive strategies designed to slow or stop a declining state's relative losses? Put simply, what explains rising state strategy toward declining great powers?

The Argument in Brief

In this book, I develop a theory of rising state strategy—what I term "predation theory"—to understand and account for a rising state's predatory or supportive policies toward its declining peers. Contrary to what policymakers may fear and scholars may expect, I argue that rising states engage in the most intensive and brutal kinds of predation only if a rising state concludes that a declining state simultaneously (1) can give the riser little or no help in opposing other great power threats, and (2) lacks military options to keep the riser in check. In these circumstances, rising states seeking to maximize power in an uncertain world have an opportunity to gain all they can at a decliner's expense by weakening the decliner as quickly as possible. Conversely, rising states tend to adopt supportive strategies the more they can use the declining state to counter other threats—in fact, they are especially supportive when they both need a declining state's help against other great powers and have little to fear militarily from the declining state. Just as the pre–World War I era saw a growing Germany improve ties with Austria-Hungary while a surging Russia tried to come to France's defense, rising states in these situations have good reason to prevent a decliner from growing weaker, as efforts to prey on a militarily denuded decliner can leave a rising state bereft of allies and facing a powerful opposing coalition.

Significantly, a rising state's desire for partners and the threat posed by a decliner are not perceptual issues affecting individual states idiosyncratically. Although policymakers rarely have perfect information regarding the distribution of power, once a rising state's leaders conclude that power is moving in their favor and against a decliner, their responses tend to vary depending on (1) the distribution of power, geography, and political relationships in the international system, and (2) the declining state's own military tools. When decline occurs in an environment where geography, power, and politics mean that a declining state is unable to help a rising state against other states or is itself a major threat, the riser has good reasons to prey on the decliner: doing so weakens a potential challenger and positions the riser to better compete against other great powers. In the best-case scenario, preying on a declining state that is the only other great power around allows a rising state to become a hegemon and operate free of great power threats. Here, the declining state's ability to credibly threaten war is the only thing that can keep a rising state's predation in check—the more a declining state can impose significant costs on a rising state in defense of its interests, the less intensely a rising state is likely to pursue a predatory strategy. Take away a declining state's ability to penalize a rising state, however, and the riser can set to work eliminating the decliner as a great power. This, I argue later in the book, was a major driver of U.S. efforts to exploit the Soviet Union's decline late in the Cold War: as Soviet problems worsened and military options waned, U.S. competitiveness increased.

These calculations change when a rising state needs assistance against other great powers and a declining state is positioned to help. In these circumstances, supportive strategies are an attractive way to bid for the declining state's cooperation, to keep the decliner out of opposing coalitions, and to avoid fruitless competition or war with a prospective partner. Just as a surging Soviet Union offered to work with Britain after World War II largely to gain British assistance against the United States, support reflects an effort by rising states both to find partners to share the costs of opposing other great powers and to keep opposing coalitions as small as possible. Here, however, a declining state's efforts to defend itself are a double-edged sword, as a declining state that can provide security for itself can also pose problems for friend and foe alike. Instead, only if a declining state is unable to challenge others do rising states come to its assistance in earnest, with the goal of rebuilding a partner over which they can exert influence.

Ultimately, focusing on a rising state's need for help against other threats, a declining state's ability to meet this need, and the military problems posed by a decliner in the process grounds rising state strategy in a riser's self-interest. As a rising state's need for help and worries about the decliner wax and wane across time and space, so too does rising state policy change. Thus, although declining states sometimes find their international lives nasty and brutish, this is not always the case.

Why Study Responses to Great Power Decline?

The implications of this study are stark. Throughout the post-1945 era, worries about decline have been at the forefront of debates over U.S. foreign policy.[15] Reflecting the outsize role of the United States in world politics, few issues are more central to discussions of international security at the start of the twenty-first century as understanding what policies emerging great powers such as China will adopt if and as U.S. power wanes. And like the concerns voiced in ancient Athens, pre-1914 Germany, and the late Cold War Soviet Union, worries that future rising states will prey on a waning United States are alive and well.[16] These concerns are not surprising. As Fareed Zakaria observes, rising states have generally "expanded their political interests abroad" as their power has grown.[17] As a result, declining states tend to fear that risers will increase the political, economic, and military demands placed on them. These escalating demands can end up threatening a declining state's vital interests, leaving it in the position of either accepting challenges to its survival or vital interests, or risking war.[18]

As noted above, however, rising states are not always predators—in fact, they sometimes treat declining great powers with surprising moderation and support. Understanding why states respond to another state's decline with predatory or supportive strategies is therefore central to addressing declining states' concerns. This insight can subsequently help declining states position themselves to ensure their security as their power wanes. Knowing, for instance, that rising states tend to support decliners that can help counter other threats suggests novel policy options for strategists worried about U.S. decline: rather than trying to compete with all rising states, there are circumstances in which the United States might be better served by underscoring its use in containing rising states' other opponents. In contrast, knowing that rising states prey on decliners that are unable to provide assistance against other threats implies that the more the United States is the sole actor standing between a rising state and the riser's hegemony, the more the United States needs to have a credible threat of force to keep predation in check. This, in turn, would push against calls for reductions in the U.S. military.

Above all, this study should interest students of international security concerned with the politics of power shifts in particular, and great power cooperation and competition more generally. On one level, predation theory offers insights into the central debate in the study of power shifts— namely, the role of change in the distribution of power as a cause of great power war. A large body of research argues that major wars tend to occur when a fundamental shift in the distribution of power—especially a power transition—empowers one state and disadvantages others.[19] Conversely, a growing number of studies propose that state responses to power shifts are more variable, shaped by a range of domestic and structural conditions.[20] Notably, this burgeoning literature helps explain why empirical tests of the link between conflict and shifting power have yielded mixed results, with some power shifts resulting in great power conflict while others shifts occur peacefully.[21]

The argument developed in this book thus contributes to ongoing efforts to clarify the relationship between power shifts and state behavior. Although not focused on conflict per se, circumstances causing rising state predation should increase the chance of conflict. To say this is to acknowledge that international politics is competitive. Not only might rising states attack declining states as part of their predatory efforts, but declining states might use force against the growing threat presented by rising states. Even though— as chapter 1 elaborates—rising states generally avoid policies that are most likely to provoke war until they enjoy a large military advantage, the combined effect of rising state predation and declining state unease invites miscalculation and conflict. In contrast, situations that incentivize rising state support limit the risk of war as rising states—by definition—forgo aggression as part of their supportive efforts, thereby reducing pressure on declining states to lash out. Support does not remove conflict from the power shift equation, but it creates room for reassurance and conciliation to limit the risk of violence. In short, predation theory refines the relationship between power shifts and conflict by proposing that the central question is not whether states end up at war during a power shift, but why states adopt strategies that increase or decrease the chance of conflict at such times.

Yet beyond the politics of great power rise and decline, determining when and why rising states prey on or support declining great powers speaks to debates at the heart of international relations theory over the sources of cooperation and competition in world politics. For decades, realist theories of all stripes have been critiqued for appearing to overpredict international competition and understate cooperation; more recently, so-called offensive realist arguments have received special attention for seeming to describe a world in which cooperation is scarce and states are always ready to seize opportunities to increase their relative power.[22] However, despite portraying a world in which states are often interested in maximizing power and trumping one another, the realist tradition is significantly more ambiguous as to when states actually engage in power-seeking behaviors. The best that can be claimed is that even power-hungry states engage in what John Mearsheimer terms "calculated aggression"—biding their time until the moment is right to strike—without explaining what conditions allow aggrandizement.[23] Depending on how states calculate whether predation pays, in other words, both competition and cooperation are possible within realist frameworks.

The argument developed in this volume thus makes three contributions to the study of cooperation and competition in international relations. First and foremost, I build on existing scholarship to explain when and why rising states conclude that predation pays. As noted above, policymakers and scholars often suggest that rising states' growing relative power makes them the most likely candidates for further expansion, even though the evidence for this behavior is decidedly mixed. Hence, identifying when and why rising states prey clarifies the circumstances in which great powers writ large challenge other states. Second, the argument helps explain when and why supportive strategies emerge even within a realist framework. In doing so, this book joins other recent research in explaining the sources of cooperation in world politics by describing the strategies states pursue when they do not seek to expand, alongside the conditions under which they aid other states.[24] For example, knowing why the rising United States supported the declining Britain but challenged the waning Soviet Union or why the surging Germany backed Austria-Hungary but preyed on France and Britain tells us much about cooperation and competition among great powers in general.

Finally, predation theory raises the possibility of bridging divides among different theoretical traditions. It does this by showing how power maximization and cooperation can be the product of the same basic set of calculations, as whether states prey on a decliner or support and cooperate with it varies according to calculations of power and opportunity common to many realist arguments. At its root, the argument thereby helps reconcile disparate research on great power cooperation and contestation in the context of great power rise and decline.

Alternative Accounts of Rising State Strategy

My theory also challenges a series of scholarly and policy arguments used to explain state strategy toward declining states drawn from several theoretical traditions. Paradoxically, given that the topic is central to policy and scholarship, there is only a limited body of systematic research examining rising state strategy.[25] This absence is even more surprising given that numerous studies examine the sources of decline,[26] state efforts to grapple with their own decline,[27] and declining state options for managing rising states.[28]

If rising state strategy is addressed at all, it most often comes up as part of aforementioned efforts in hegemonic stability and power transition theories to explain why declining hegemons and rising challengers go to war with one another for leadership of the international system. Here, scholars argue that war is more likely if a rising state is a revisionist or dissatisfied actor seeking to overturn an international order maintained by a declining hegemon, and less likely if a rising state is a satisfied power pursuing a status quo course. These studies, however, suffer from two related problems. First, they provide few clues as to why rising states pursue a revisionist or status quo policy in the first place.[29] Second, they focus nearly exclusively on competition between a dominant state and a rising challenger, thereby missing the fact that great powers face different incentives for cooperation and competition when more than two great powers are present.[30]

Although not full-fledged theories, other approaches offer predictions to explain what great powers writ large may want as their relative power grows. As elaborated below, I use these competing arguments to develop a research agenda to check predation theory's explanatory power. Instead of differentiating between status quo and revisionist powers, for example, research on insecurity spirals and misperceptions suggests that rising state predation or support varies depending on the intensity of the security dilemma.[31] Because great powers merely seek security for themselves—a key assumption of defensive realist approaches to international relations, and a point of division between defensive and offensive realist theories—it is only when a rising state fears that a declining state's path to security threatens the riser that a rising state has reasons to prey.[32] Conversely, the less a declining state threatens a rising state—for example, by winding down arms races and adopting nonthreatening military positions—the less intense the security dilemma and the more rising and declining states can find ways of cooperating. Supportive strategies are thus possible if declining states take steps to reassure rising states by limiting the political and military threat they pose.[33]

Similarly, research on trade and international political economy suggests that economic interdependence can dampen competitive tendencies and incentivize cooperation as power shifts. Interdependence does this by creating domestic interest groups whose livelihood depends on the continual free flow of goods and services. Provided that rising and declining states are both willing to trade, domestic groups interested in exchange will lobby against competitive policies that upset these relationships, thereby acting as brakes on predation.[34] This behavior should be especially strong when rising states have reason to believe that economic exchange will continue in the future.[35] Seeking to continue economic exchange, rising states thereby support and cooperate with declining states out of economic self-interest.

Still a third approach relates rising state strategy to domestic ideologies in rising and declining states. Here, rising states that share with decliners similar conceptions of what Mark Haas terms "domestic political legitimacy"—liberal, conservative, socialist, etc.—are expected to pursue supportive rather than predatory strategies.[36] Conversely, states with disparate ideologies are likely to pursue a predatory course. Scholars offer a variety of mechanisms to explain these phenomena, including claims that support is normatively appropriate when states share similar ideologies; that support for ideological fellow travelers and predation toward ideological rivals reinforces a rising state's domestic legitimacy; and that support reflects the diminished threat perceptions that occur when states share similar ideologies. Yet, regardless of the specific cause, the expectation is that birds of a similar ideological feather flock together amid shifting power.

Finally, a related line of research explains predation or support by emphasizing the ideas held by policymakers in rising states. From this perspective, a rising state's growing capabilities are necessary but insufficient for predation—it also needs to be led by elites whose unifying ideology calls for expansion.[37] These ideas can take many forms. For example, Christopher Layne argues that U.S. leaders have long espoused liberal causes that have led the United States to pursue "an expansionist—indeed, hegemonic or even imperial—policy."[38] Likewise, Nathan Leites, in his seminal study of Soviet worldviews, describes Soviet ideology as seeking to spread communism abroad and ensuring that "no advance, no matter how small, should be neglected."[39] Scholars today, meanwhile, are actively debating whether Chinese elites are adopting a narrowly nationalist perspective that calls for foreign expansion.[40] The expectation, therefore, is that rising states led by elites with expansionist worldviews will tend to prey on declining states as power shifts. By implication, supportive strategies are possible if the ruling ideology itself calls for cooperation with other great powers.[41]

The Path Ahead: Testing Predation Theory in the Archives

The remainder of this book presents the hypotheses and causal logic of pre-dation theory, tests the argument against competing accounts, and offers im-plications for scholars and policymakers. Following this introduction, chap-ter 1 outlines a way of studying a rising state's strategic choices vis-à-vis a declining great power. It also elaborates on the logic of predation theory by highlighting the links among the decliner's ability to assist rising states against other great powers, its military options, and rising state strategy.

The majority of the book consists of a pair of case studies examining the great power declines attendant to the start and end of the Cold War. Look-ing back from the span of several decades, it is easy to forget that the dawn of the postwar era and the closing salvos of the Cold War were driven in large part by fundamental changes in the distribution of power, as first the United Kingdom and then the Soviet Union tumbled from the ranks of the great powers. These declines, as suggested above, compelled other, relatively ris-ing great powers such as the United States to respond to shifts in the distri-bution of power.

As with most qualitative research, the objective in the case studies is not to test the theory against the universe of cases, but to show the explanatory power of the theory in particularly salient and data-rich episodes. To this end, the case studies draw on extensive qualitative research—involving thousands of archival and other primary source documents, alongside doz-ens of policymaker interviews—and leverage intra-case variation in support of three tasks. First, using the comparative case method, I assess whether predation theory's variables correctly predicted the strategies actually adopted by states facing another's relative decline. Second, I evaluate the theory's causal logic through process tracing since, by showing the sequences of events through which strategies change, I am able to obtain unique pur-chase on the mechanisms at the heart of the argument.[42] Finally, case stud-ies allow me to evaluate predation theory against competing accounts. In support of this objective, I selected cases that have extreme values on the variables emphasized by one or more of the alternative arguments, and for which my theory and its competitors generally make discrete and different empirical predictions. Combined, the cases thus allow strong tests of my ar-gument against alternative accounts: if other arguments explain rising state behavior, they should do so in readily observable ways in these cases. Hence, the more the rising state strategy is accurately explained by my argument rather than its competitors, the more confidence we have in the theory.[43] Each chapter therefore compares my argument to alternative approaches, show-ing that predation theory provides greater insight into the course and out-come of the cases than its competitors. In the process, the research also makes stand-alone historiographic contributions by illustrating the process and logic through which great power decline has been addressed in the post-1945 world.

Within each case study, I assess three types of evidence for insight into the course and conduct of rising state strategy. The first consists of the military, diplomatic, and economic policies these states adopted toward decliners. Identifying these policies allows me to categorize rising state strategies according to their predatory or supportive nature. Second, I consider the debates leading to the adoption of these strategies, and the policies that were considered but rejected by policymakers—that is, those individuals charged with forming and executing state policy. This offers insight into what strategists hoped to achieve with their policies and helps me reconstruct the underlying drivers of state behavior. Finally, I pay attention to moments within the cases when declining states responded to these strategies by seeking some kind of change in rising states' policies. Evaluating whether and why rising states responded to declining state pressure at these critical junctions provides insights into what relatively rising states wanted from declining states, how far they were willing to go to achieve these objectives, and their reasons for doing so.

The book proceeds chronologically. Chapters 2 and 3 examine efforts by the United States and Soviet Union to address the decline of the United Kingdom in the early postwar period. Although emerging from World War II as one of the Big Three victors in the conflict and included as one of the "superpowers" in William T. R. Fox's original treatment of the subject, the United Kingdom soon tumbled out of the great power ranks.[44] In response, the United States backed Great Britain—eventually offering it extensive economic and military assistance—while the Soviet Union seemingly tried to expand in the resulting power vacuum. These responses should be difficult for my argument to explain: as chapter 2 emphasizes, not only are U.S. efforts to support the United Kingdom seemingly addressed by accounts emphasizing the countries' ideological affinity, economic interdependence, and shared security dilemma, but Soviet predation makes sense in light of these arguments as well.

Making extensive use of U.S. and British primary sources, chapter 3 qualifies these accounts. In fact, and in line with predation theory, I show that both the United States and the Soviet Union supported the United Kingdom in the immediate postwar period, as the two states worked to retain the United Kingdom as a potential ally. Moreover, these efforts intensified as British military options waned. Notably, this trend helps explain the origins of Cold War touchstones such as the Marshall Plan and NATO. Just as important, it uncovers evidence of an unexpectedly cooperative Soviet Union immediately after World War II, including proposals for an Anglo-Soviet alliance in the winter of 1946–47. Indeed, Soviet and U.S. policies were strikingly symmetrical—and supportive of Britain—until late 1947, when growing Anglo-American cooperation led Soviet leaders to conclude that

Britain would never be a Soviet partner and so prompted the Soviet Union to try to weaken the United Kingdom. In sum, the theory advanced in chapter 1 provides more insight into the episode than its competitors, accurately predicting the course and conduct of Soviet and U.S. policies toward Great Britain.

Chapters 4 and 5 then study U.S. foreign policy and the decline of the Soviet Union during the late Cold War. As chapter 4 explains, this is a uniquely important case with which to test my theory. Not only did the Soviet Union decline in dramatic fashion and make major military reductions in the process—offering extreme values on predation theory's explanatory variables—but the case is intrinsically significant. With the waning of Soviet power, the United States experienced such a rise in its relative position that it became the world's sole superpower, far and away the most dominant state in international affairs. Most importantly, the case provides an especially strong test of my argument against competing accounts. Not only does a large body of scholarship propose that the United States cooperated with the Soviet Union during the latter's decline by managing change in Europe to both sides' advantage, but my theory and its competitors often make sharply different predictions regarding the course and drivers of U.S. strategy.

Drawing on thousands of recently declassified American archival documents and dozens of interviews with most of the major U.S. policymakers involved in U.S.-Soviet relations at the time, I show instead in chapter 5 that U.S. strategy was consistently predatory throughout the period of Soviet decline. Far from cooperating with the Soviet Union, U.S. strategy was driven by a persistent desire to maximize U.S. advantages, dominate the Soviet Union, and bring about a world in which the United States would be free of constraints imposed by other great powers. In fact, and unique to my argument, U.S. strategy became markedly more predatory after the collapse of Soviet military power in Eastern Europe following the Revolutions of 1989–90 created a window of opportunity for the United States to directly undercut the Soviet position in Europe. Simply put, rather than conciliating a declining Soviet Union, the United States preyed on the Soviet Union once Soviet decline began, sometimes doing so quite intensely. Again, my theory outperforms competing accounts of rising state strategy.

Finally, the conclusion performs several tasks. After summarizing the evidence from previous chapters, I offer brief additional assessments of the theory by examining great power responses to the declines of Austria-Hungary and France in the late nineteenth and early twentieth centuries. These cases are instructive extensions of the argument. Not only were Austria-Hungary and France the great losers in Europe's game of great power politics before World War I (see Appendix 1), but examining responses to the French and Austro-Hungarian declines shows that predation theory explains rising state behavior in an era when competition among many great powers was endemic. Combined with the post-1945 case studies, these additional cases thus demonstrate that the theory can account for rising state strategy across a wide swath of diplomatic history. Subsequently, I present policy implications emerging from the study, before highlighting the significance of the research for international relations theory. Ultimately, the argument and evidence in this book provide a novel explanation for rising states' behavior toward declining great powers, one that helps illuminate key aspects of great power relations in the modern world. Questions surrounding the rise and decline of great powers lie at the heart of international relations theory, historical interpretation, and diplomatic practice, making this book relevant to several fields.

Predation Theory

Rising states sometimes attempt to crush declining great powers but, at other times, strive to keep decliners strong and capable. When and why do rising states adopt such predatory or supportive strategies? The prior chapter introduced the puzzle of rising state strategy toward declining great powers and the importance of explaining these behaviors. Here, I develop predation theory to explain why rising state strategies differ along two key dimensions: (1) whether rising states seek to further weaken declining states or help them remain great powers, and (2) the level of effort used in pursuit of these objectives.

In brief, I argue that rising states prey upon or support decliners with varying degrees of assertiveness depending on (1) the decliner's utility as a partner against other great powers (its strategic value) and (2) its military tools for securing its interests (its military posture) and thus its ability to threaten rising states. All things being equal, the more a declining state can help a rising state confront other great powers and the less militarily threatening it is during this process, the more likely a rising state is to adopt a supportive strategy. Rising states do so because support helps distribute the costs of opposing other great powers and keeps declining states out of enemy coalitions. Conversely, rising states tend to prey on decliners the less a decliner can help balance or weaken other great powers and the less able a decliner is to punish a rising state's efforts with force.

Defining and Identifying Decline

THE CONCEPT OF DECLINE

Decline refers to situations in which a great power begins to lose a large share of its capabilities relative to one or more other great powers over a sustained period of time.[1] By "great power," I mean a state with the resources to make a good showing in a fight with the strongest state in the international system.[2] In an anarchic world where war and competition are endemic, the relative capabilities at a state's disposal constitute the *ultima ratio* of its security.[3] Military capabilities are significant because they affect a state's ability to deter or defeat adversaries, but economic capabilities are particularly important: economic power affects the quality and size of a state's military and the ability to sustain military power into the future, by shaping the raw resources that the state can convert into military assets.[4] Therefore, decline occurs whenever a state begins to lose capabilities, especially economic capabilities, relative to one or more other states in such fashion as to indicate that the losses reflect a fundamental shift in strength.[5] By definition, this process also causes one or more other great powers to experience a relative rise even if their absolute resources stay constant—in systemic terms, they constitute rising states.[6]

This definition of decline offers a subtle but important distinction from standard usage. Analysts often equate decline with situations in which states surpass one another in some set of capabilities, with the canonical cases of decline in works such as Paul Kennedy's *The Rise and Fall of the Great Powers* often fitting this bill.[7] Equating decline with a power transition, however, makes limited theoretical sense. Since states seek power because power is a means of achieving security, it is the narrowing or widening of the power gaps separating states that matters for security rather than changes in states' ordinal rankings.[8] Tellingly, for example, Austria-Hungary declined throughout the nineteenth century despite starting the century already weaker than France, Britain, and Russia, just as the Soviet Union declined in the late Cold War although the United States was stronger than it throughout the postwar period.[9] An adviser to Napoleon III captured the issue while watching Prussia grow in the 1860s, noting that "a country's power can be diminished by the mere fact of *new* forces accumulating around it."[10] Decline thus occurs whenever there is a significant power shift between one or more major states in the system regardless of whether states overtake one another—weak states that grow weaker and strong states that become less dominant also decline.[11]

This approach is also agnostic as to the sources of decline. Particularly in policy discussions, analysts often treat decline as if it referred only to a state's absolute loss of capabilities—that is, as if a state woke up one day to discover its economy had shrunk by some large percentage.[12] In reality, decline can spring from many sources. One state's absolute losses may be a cause, but so too may be the slowing of one state's growth rate, the relatively faster growth of other countries, and costly foreign adventures or domestic initiatives that sap a state's resources.[13] Moreover, while it may be important to understand different types of decline, the specific type of decline should not matter much when explaining rising state behavior. On one level, different types of decline can occur simultaneously. For instance, the Soviet Union's decline reflected Soviet difficulties adapting to a postindustrial economy, exacerbated by costly blunders such as the invasion of Afghanistan and ill-advised domestic reforms; arguably, late Victorian Britain experienced similar problems in taking advantage of the Second Industrial Revolution while countries like Germany and the United States grew.[14] Equally important, because world politics is competitive, the key issue for state strategy is that a change in relative power is occurring rather than why the change is happening. Especially because states look at relative power when assessing threats, they are primarily concerned with the diminishing resources that other states can bring to bear—not the sources of relative weakness per se.

MEASURING DECLINE

Defined this way, decline is pervasive, and the modern world, as Robert Gilpin observed, is "strewn with the debris of former great powers."[15] To identify cases of postwar decline—and thus of relatively rising states—I first identified those countries qualifying as European great powers and then determined whether and when these states declined.[16] Building on the idea that great powers are states that can make a good showing in an all-out fight against the strongest state in the system, I define great powers by whether they possessed at least 10 percent of the capabilities—particularly economic capabilities—of all states in a region and at least 25 percent of the capabilities of the strongest state in that area.[17] Here, I used Angus Maddison's data on gross domestic product (GDP) for the period from 1950 onward, while relying on the Correlates of War National Material Capabilities (NMC) for the pre-1950 period.[18] Having established which states qualified as great powers, I next identified periods of decline by applying three criteria. First, great powers had to lose at least 5 percent of their share of capabilities relative to the other great powers within a ten-year period, compared to the average over the preceding ten years. Second, those losses had to be sustained for at least five consecutive years. Third, the time frame for decline ends when states either began sustained growth or left the ranks of the great powers.[19] Meanwhile, I collected data on finer-grained measures of power such as a state's technological skill, the health of its economic foundations, and its military power projection capabilities—reported in the individual cases— to check and refine judgments over whether and when decline occurred.

This approach indicates that the United States, Great Britain, and the Soviet Union all qualified as great powers in Europe at points in the postwar era, with the latter two countries declining after 1945 (table 1.1). Though problems were growing for some time, decline manifested itself rapidly in both cases as the states fell from the great power ranks in less than ten years. Both cases also led to the relative rise of other great powers: Britain's decline saw Soviet and U.S. power grow in relation to the United Kingdom,[20] while the decline of the Soviet Union caused a relative increase in U.S. power and the emergence of the United States as the world's sole superpower

Table 1.1 Declining European great powers, 1945–2008

State	Years of Decline	Relatively Rising State(s)	Change in Power and Result
United Kingdom	c. 1945/1946–1949/1950	United States, Soviet Union	*Britain exits the great powers.* Britain goes from having approximately 11–14 percent of European capabilities and 25–33 percent of the capabilities of the United States (the strongest state) in 1945–46, to having less than 10 percent of European capabilities and around 20–25 percent of U.S. capabilities in 1949–50. By the mid-1950s, Britain has 8 percent of European capabilities and barely 20 percent of U.S. capabilities.[a]
Soviet Union	c. 1983/1984–1991	United States	*Soviet Union exits the great powers.* The Soviet Union goes from having approximately 20 percent of European GDP in the early 1980s to having at most 17–18 percent by 1990–91. It also loses ground relative to the United States, going from having approximately 30 percent of U.S. strength in the early 1980s to having a maximum of 25 percent by 1991. After 1991, the Soviet Union's collapse left Russia with less than 15 percent of U.S. GDP.

[a]British strength rose briefly in 1946. However, this was a temporary aberration that likely reflected not British recovery but the different rates at which the United States, the Soviet Union, and Britain adjusted to peacetime conditions.

by 1991.[21] In short, of the three great powers that emerged in Europe following the Second World War, only the United States remained within fifty years.[22] This raises the question: if decline is pervasive, how do we study its consequences?

Rising State Strategy and Great Power Decline

Decline carries major security implications. Alliances can form and dissolve as states react to shifting power.[23] Arms races can develop as states try to keep up with their opponents. Above all, wars may erupt as states respond to changes in relative strength.[24] As policymakers in the Second French Empire, Wilhelmine Germany, post–World War II Britain, and the late Cold War Soviet Union all learned, decline thus gives rise to debates as to how declining states will provide security for themselves as resources grow comparatively scarce and they confront the prospect of being too weak to address external threats—or, as the French Empress Eugenie told a Prussian official while watching Prussia grow in the 1860s, "With a nation like yours as a neighbor, we are in danger of finding you in Paris one day unannounced. I will go to sleep French and wake up Prussian."[25]

As the Empress Eugenie suggested, the policies of relatively rising states play a major role in affecting declining state security: by exacerbating or reducing threats to a declining state, rising states can further imperil or improve a decliner's situation.[26] Accordingly, this book examines a relatively rising state's strategy toward a declining great power. As I define it, "rising state strategy" refers to the ends-means chain adopted by a rising state to structure its relationship with a declining great power using the economic, military, and political tools at its disposal. Rising state strategy is not a grand strategy in itself. Rather, it is one component of a rising state's overall approach to international politics that deals specifically with how a riser generally plans to treat a declining great power.[27] In the process, rising state strategy also accounts for a rising state's relations with other great powers and how its approach is likely to affect these other relationships. In short, rising state strategy offers a framework for identifying the priorities in a state's relationship with a declining great power and suggests policies to reach the desired outcomes.[28] In this section, I elaborate on the concept of rising state strategy and the ways in which strategy varies, before explaining below when and why rising states pursue different strategic options.

VARIATION IN RISING STATES' STRATEGY: GOALS AND MEANS

Rising state strategies vary along two dimensions: the goals a rising state pursues toward a declining state, and the means employed to attain these goals. In principle, of course, rising state strategies can be differentiated according to any number of criteria. Often, this involves classifying rising states by whether they pursue revisionist or status quo objectives toward the international system writ large, and whether they are willing to use force to attain these objectives.[29] Missing from the discussion, however, is a deductive approach to the strategies employed specifically toward declining powers. After all, rising states can hold revisionist or status quo goals while treating declining states more or less benignly; some way to capture variation in the benign or competitive nature of these strategies is necessary. Focusing on a rising state's basic preference for the declining state's place as a great power and the tools used to obtain that outcome helps address this issue.

Goals Rising state goals refer to a rising state's basic preference for a declining state's place among the great powers. Just as declining states fear that rising states may try to weaken them yet hope for a better outcome, so do rising states have two basic options (table 1.2).

First, a rising state can try to shift the distribution of power further against a decliner, undermining the declining state as a great power and ultimately hoping to push it from the great power ranks—pursuing what I term a predatory goal.[30] Predation does not necessarily mean snuffing out a declining state's existence as a sovereign actor. Rather, rising states focus on the

Table 1.2 Indicators of rising state goals

Predatory: rising states seek to weaken a declining state as a great power	Supportive: rising states seek to keep a declining state a great power
Policymakers emphasize benefits of growing stronger at the decliner's expense	Policymakers worry about letting the decliner fall farther
Diplomatic, economic, and military initiatives challenge the decliner	Initiatives reduce or moderate threats to the decliner
Policies exhaust or remove resources from the decliner	Policies reduce the resources the decliner must expend, or provide resources directly to the decliner
Opportunities to maximize power are embraced	Opportunities to maximize power are passed over

significant, but less ambitious, goal of exacerbating ongoing shifts in power and, eventually, removing the decliner from the game of high politics. Here, rising states design policies to challenge a declining state's territorial, economic, political, and military interests, requiring the decliner to work harder and consume more resources to protect itself or to surrender its interests, all while seeking ways to make the declining state's international position increasingly difficult. As Robert Jervis argues, this dynamic dominated the Cold War as both the United States and Soviet Union sought to bankrupt and undermine the other (although, as I show in chapter 5, it was only in the 1980s and early 1990s that the United States had opportunities to make this goal a reality).[31] The hallmark of predation, then, is that a rising state seeks changes to the distribution of power in its favor and to the decliner's detriment. Of course, rising states may not actually attain these objectives, and their efforts play only a limited role in harming a declining state's relative position. Nevertheless, rising states that pursue predation still seek to foster meaningful shifts in the distribution of power that improve their relative position and worsen that of the decliner.

Second, a rising state can pursue a supportive goal. In this case, a rising state seeks to slow or prevent additional losses to a declining state's power position and sustain the decliner as a great power. A rising state does this by limiting threats to the decliner, reducing the resources the decliner must use and the risks it must run to provide security for itself. The United States, for example, supported the United Kingdom after World War II by offering economic and military assistance against the Soviet Union, just as Wilhelmine Germany backed Austria-Hungary politically and militarily against Russia before 1914. Thus, policymakers pursuing supportive goals craft policies to prevent a declining state from slipping any further and, by definition, ignore calls to grow at a decliner's expense. These steps may not actually stop a declining state's fall, but they still leave the decliner better off than if it were operating on its own.

Means After deciding to weaken or sustain a declining state, rising states must still determine how to achieve their goals. This may not be easy, as states often have other objectives that demand time, resources, and attention. States therefore need to decide the level of effort and what tools to use to affect the declining state's position as a great power.

Accordingly, the second dimension of rising state strategy consists of what Kevin Narizny calls the "assertiveness" of their means.[32] Assertiveness refers to whether a rising state is willing to expend economic, military, and political resources while bearing the risks of attempting to bring about a large and immediate change in the declining state's position as a great power. In doing so, it reflects a rising state's answers to three questions on the relationship among its rise, its desire for the declining state's continuation as a great power, and any other interests the rising state may have. First, when a rising state encounters opposition from a declining state, does it modify its policies in accordance with the decliner's wishes? Supportive strategies require taking the decliner's wishes to heart; predatory strategies, by definition, do not. Second, is the rising state willing to accept a meaningful trade-off or to sacrifice other interests in pursuit of its preferred outcome vis-à-vis the decliner? Finally, is the rising state willing to engage in meaningful consultations with third parties and scope what tools and policies it adopts in its relationship with the decliner in accordance with their interests?

Using this framework, I distinguish between two basic types of means: those that are intense, and those that are limited. A rising state employs intense means when it uses tools optimized to cause (or prevent) a rapid, fundamental shift in the distribution of power that will seriously threaten (or help) the declining state's continuation as a great power. In such situations, a rising state implicitly or explicitly concludes that pursuing its goal vis-à-vis a decliner requires (1) systematically and meaningfully responding to a declining state's concerns when engaged in a supportive strategy, or bypassing a decliner's opposition when engaged in predation; (2) making large sacrifices to other values such as economic growth or diplomatic autonomy to affect the declining state's position; or (3) ignoring or sidestepping input from other actors. To be sure, the different domestic and international circumstances of individual states can lead them to adopt different economic, military, and diplomatic policies even when employing intense means. For instance, democracies may find it normatively unpalatable to wage war against a declining state, just as nuclear armed great powers may not go to war against other nuclear states.[33] All things being equal, however, states employ intense means when they use tools that challenge or reinforce the foundations of a declining state's political order; remove large swaths of strategically important territory from the decliner's control or help the decliner to keep them; initiate or end large-scale challenges to a declining state's core interests; and/or significantly increase or decrease the economic costs and military risks a declining state runs to obtain security.

Intense means, in short, are designed to cause or forestall major revision to the status quo even if these steps are costly to rising states and generate significant external opposition. Baldly stated, they represent hard-line policies that provide either significant assistance or threaten significant harm to declining states. Prussia's decision to go to war with France in 1870 epitomizes the approach, as Prussia furthered its rise and accelerated France's decline by upending Europe's existing distribution of power.

In contrast, limited means cause gradual changes that moderately improve or undermine a declining state's position. They thus reflect a situation in which a rising state is (1) hesitant to precipitate a crisis with a decliner when preying on it or responds with ambivalence to a decliner's concerns when pursuing support; (2) unwilling to accept significant trade-offs vis-à-vis other interests to aid or undermine a decliner; or (3) reluctant to ignore the concerns of other states in pursuit of its preferred outcome, such that other states meaningfully influence its policies. If intense means quickly and directly affect the status quo, then limited means are symbolic or low-cost actions that only slowly affect the decliner's position.

Limited means can manifest in several ways. When pursuing predation, rising great powers may seek to slow a declining state's growth rate through economic sanctions; cautiously promote secessionist movements or political opposition movements that can affect the decliner's domestic stability; question the decliner's credibility, prestige, or political legitimacy to reduce its influence over allies and security against opponents; engage in efforts such as arms races or asymmetric arms control that shift the military balance against the decliner; and challenge its control over areas of secondary importance or probe its willingness to fight over core areas. China's effort to expand its reach over the South and East China Seas while slowly expanding its military is arguably a present-day example of this approach: Chinese efforts are not challenging core U.S. interests or immediately upsetting the military balance, but they are causing the United States to work harder to maintain the extant power structure. When supporting a declining state, meanwhile, rising great powers reduce or avoid steps that challenge a decliner's control over territory; offer symbolic diplomatic concessions to signal their interest in the decliner's well-being to other states; provide the decliner with moderate financial aid to slow or prevent further economic losses; and limit or end military challenges to the decliner. In the process, rising states also pace their efforts to avoid antagonizing other great powers: they generally reduce even constrained efforts to help or harm declining states if others voice opposition, calculating that they can always renew their efforts at a later date. A classic example is British support for Austria-Hungary against a rising Prussia in the 1860s: although British strategists did not want Prussia to eliminate Austria-Hungary as a factor in European great power politics, they kept Britain officially neutral and restricted British backing to private diplomatic encouragement for Austria-Hungary and infrequent warnings to Prussia that Britain would disapprove of efforts to "destroy the present equilibrium of power."[34]

Combined, the different goals and means generate four ideal types of strategies that rising states can adopt (figure 1.1). First, rising states can pursue a Relegation strategy. Relegation represents the classic fear of a declining great power, as a rising state pursuing this strategy adopts a predatory goal and challenges a declining state with intense means. Here, rising states seek to quickly and directly revise the status quo at the decliner's expense—ideally pushing it from the great power ranks—by employing policies that significantly sap the declining state's resources and dramatically undercut its capabilities.[35] The United States, for example, pursued Relegation toward the United Kingdom at various points in the nineteenth century, fighting a war and risking several militarized crises to evict Britain from North America.[36] En route to unifying Germany and establishing a preeminent role in continental Europe, Bismarckian Prussia adopted a similar course with France in the early 1870s, inaugurating a war, seizing French territory, and imposing a hefty financial indemnity to cripple the French economy.[37] Relegation thus encompasses policies such as waging war against a declining state, contesting the decliner's control over large swaths of economically or strategically important territory, targeting its allies, diplomatically isolating the state, and waging economic warfare. Again, states may choose different tools based on their particular circumstances, but the unifying theme is that these policies are designed to have a large and immediate negative influence on a declining state's well-being.

If Relegation represents a decliner's worst fear, then a Strengthening strategy represents its ideal outcome. Strengthening emerges when rising states actively support a decliner by taking steps to sustain or improve its position. To do this, rising states significantly reduce the costs a decliner needs to pay and the risks it must take to provide security for itself by putting their own security on the line and offering the decliner protection against other states, regular diplomatic backing, and large-scale economic assistance or other economic benefits. They also sustain these policies even if other actors voice opposition. These concessions are not cheap, so a rising state making these choices is signaling others that the declining state's continued survival is of major importance.[38] The German effort to back Austria-Hungary before 1914 even at the risk of war with Russia epitomizes this approach.[39]

Between Relegation and Strengthening are two middle-of-the-road strategies in which states pursue predatory or supportive courses in slow, deliberate fashion. I refer to these as Weakening and Bolstering strategies, respectively. Rising states that adopt Weakening strategies seek to undermine a declining state as a competitor through the use of limited means that gradually shift the distribution of power against the decliner. Put differently, weakening strategies see rising states try to move the distribution of power in their favor without incurring large strategic costs (such as risking war with a declining state) or making large immediate gains, while backing down from even these efforts if other states oppose their actions. To do so, a rising state tries to slowly revise the status quo at a decliner's expense by, for instance, engaging the decliner in an arms race, targeting its secondary interests, imposing economic sanctions to slow the declining state's growth, challenging its prestige and credibility, and engaging the decliner in diplomatic standoffs. These steps take a salami tactic-like approach to predation: they are unlikely to significantly harm a declining state in the short term, but they create conditions for a rising state to make large cumulative gains through incremental changes to the status quo.[40] American efforts against the Soviet Union in the early-mid 1980s illustrates the type: by delegitimating the Soviet political system, pursuing an arms buildup, and increasing economic strains on the Soviet economy, U.S. strategists hoped to undermine the foundations of Soviet strength.[41] This strategy may also be on display today, as many analysts worry that China's efforts to expand its military and revise the territorial

Rising state goals

	Predatory	Supportive
Intense	Relegation Example: nineteenth-century Anglo-American relations	Strengthening Example: pre-1914 German-Austrian relations
Limited	Weakening Example: U.S. policy toward the Soviet Union, 1980s	Bolstering Example: Anglo-Austrian relations, 1860s

Rising state means

Figure 1.1. Ideal types of rising state strategies.

status quo in East Asia represent incremental attempts to reduce U.S. strength in the region.[42]

Finally, states can pursue a Bolstering strategy. The objective here is to prevent a declining state from slipping further down the great power ranks, but to do so without incurring large costs or exposing oneself to others' ire. Rising states that use Bolstering thus move judiciously to maintain the status quo in the declining state's favor while constantly looking over their shoulders to assess others' reactions and to determine whether other interests are being sacrificed. Accordingly, a rising state is likely to offer a decliner diplomatic, political, and economic support on an ad hoc and inconsistent basis. Unsurprisingly, this approach is unlikely to be of much comfort to a declining state seeking external help, thereby creating the potential for contestation between rising states that want to proceed slowly and declining states that seek immediate assistance. Britain's ambivalent assistance to Austria-Hungary against Prussia in the 1860s mentioned above illustrates this strategy.

Predation Theory: Mechanisms and Logic

In this book, I develop what I call predation theory to explain when and why rising states adopt these different strategies toward their declining peers. My argument starts from the proposition that states exist in a self-help world and so rely primarily on their own means to ensure their survival as sovereign actors.[43] For many states, this means that they will seek to grow their relative power and, if possible, become the sole great power around—the hegemon. In anarchy, power is the *ultima ratio* for settling conflicts of interest by increasing the odds of victory in wartime and shaping bargains over conflicting interests in peace.[44] States in anarchy thus often face strong incentives to maximize power by increasing their capabilities and limiting those of their peers as each seeks to become the sole great power standing.

This does not mean, however, that states engage in an all-out frenzy to gain power no matter the cost and risk to themselves. Not only might there be other states that need to be kept from expanding, but maximizing power invites retaliation from other actors.[45] A state looking to expand must therefore carefully assess whether the benefits of expansion outweigh the risks involved. If the prospective benefits do not exceed the costs, then states—as John Mearsheimer puts it—tend to "wait for a more propitious moment" to grow.[46]

All things being equal, states thus prefer to expand by expending as little of their blood and treasure as possible. This has two consequences. First, a state interested in keeping other great powers in check while trying to gain for itself will want other actors to incur the risks and costs of confronting threats.[47] Ideally, this process will weaken several actors—the targeted great power(s) and the state(s) helping against the target—simultaneously, improving one's relative position. A state interested in maximizing power therefore often needs partners to which it can pass or at least share the costs of confronting other great powers in peacetime and that can serve as allies in wartime.[48] In fact, a state may need to cooperate with other states to use them as janissaries against competitors, dividing competitors' attention and sharing the strategic burden. Second, a rising state seeking to prey on a declining state still needs to calculate whether international conditions are favorable for a campaign against the decliner. In short, any given rising state is poised on a knife's edge and compelled to constantly calculate the costs and risks of preying on or supporting a decliner as it affects the rising state's own pursuit of greater power.

Building on this base, I argue that a rising state's choice of strategy depends on how that strategy fits into a rising state's ability to expand while constraining others from doing the same. Two variables—the declining state's *strategic value* to the riser and the decliner's *military posture*—drive this calculation. Strategic value affects whether a rising state pursues a predatory or supportive course by determining whether, on balance, it is more advantageous to a rising state's own security to keep the decliner as a great power or eliminate it from the great power ranks. Military posture, meanwhile, shapes the assertiveness of the rising state's predatory or supportive efforts by clarifying the security problems it faces from employing limited or intense means when pursuing either goal.

The remainder of this section elaborates what I mean by declining state strategic value and posture, and explains their importance for shaping risers' goals and means. The following section shows how strategic value and military posture together predict when and why risers pursue the different strategies discussed above.

STRATEGIC VALUE AND PREDATION OR SUPPORT

The decliner's strategic value reflects whether a rising state can use the decliner to weaken other great powers. Since a state can be rising while there are still other great powers that can imperil its security, it often wants to cooperate with other states and share the costs of addressing these threats.[49] Under such circumstances, a declining state may be an attractive partner that a rising state can employ against opponents at lower cost and risk than if it faced these threats alone.

Still, rising states do not always need declining states as partners, and not all decliners are poised to help. Instead, whether a declining state has strategic value depends on four criteria (table 1.3). First is whether there are states aside from the decliner that can harm a riser's security. This is largely a product of the polarity of the system in which rise and decline occurs.[50] In general, the presence of other great powers in a multipolar system means that a rising state will want to share the costs of containing or overcoming external threats to its security.[51] Under these conditions, a rising state is liable

Table 1.3 Determinants of declining state strategic value

Are other great powers present?

Is the declining state geographically positioned to help against other great power threats?

Does the decliner have the potential to assist against other threats?

Is the decliner politically available to help against other great powers?

to seek assistance from others wherever it can be obtained, including from a declining state.[52] In pre-1914 Europe, for example, the fact that Germany faced threats from both Russia and France meant that a declining Austria-Hungary was a valuable German partner; similarly, Britain was willing to set aside colonial rivalry with France to obtain French help against Germany.[53]

Conversely, bipolar systems make the declining state itself the principal threat to a rising state's security. When power shifts in bipolarity—causing one of two great powers to rise and the other to decline—the absence of other prospective challengers means that the riser does not need the decliner's help to obtain security. In fact, a rising state's security can be substantially improved if it eliminates the only other great power around and becomes a hegemon.[54] Hence, if the presence of several potential threats in multipolarity incentivizes rising states to consider working with decliners out of strategic self-interest, bipolarity primes rising states to compete for dominance.

Besides the presence or absence of other great powers, a declining state must also be geographically positioned to help a rising state against other great powers. Geography is one of the basic "structural modifiers" that affect whether and to what extent states influence one another.[55] Nevertheless, scholars have long debated what the relevant geographic features influencing international politics entail. Proponents of offense-defense theory, for instance, argue that distant states are generally less threatening to other great powers than states located nearby.[56] In contrast, scholars such as Mearsheimer propose that distance in itself is no impediment to competition; instead, only insular states separated from others by large water barriers face difficulties conquering and thus competing with other states.[57] Still others argue that insularity is a net boon to states: far from precluding great power expansion, insularity helps states compete by inhibiting counterbalancing and encouraging continental states to invite insular powers onshore as allies.[58]

These debates aside, what matters for rising states is less whether a decliner is an insular actor or located far from the rising state in absolute terms, and more the decliner's proximity to other great powers.[59] All things being equal, the closer a declining state is to other great powers, the more likely it can help a rising state against other competitors by threatening other states with war, engaging them in political disputes, or serving as a staging area for the rising state's forces. This logic applies both to continental powers (which can threaten others with a land invasion) and insular powers (which can serve as a base for naval, air, and land forces). Indeed, the fact that insular states may be able to deploy forces in several directions against multiple great powers may make them especially useful in opposing a rising state's other competitors. Collectively, these activities tend to absorb others' attention and limit the effort and resources they muster against the rising state.

Alternatively, a declining state that is comparatively far away or isolated from other great powers is less useful to a rising state. In this situation, a riser is unlikely to see a way to employ a decliner against other great power challengers owing to the decliner's comparative remove. Not only might a distant state not pose much of a challenge to other great powers and attract little attention, but it might not be easy to play an isolated decliner off against other states in a competitive international arena.[60] A related situation occurs when a declining state is effectively isolated from other states but proximate to a rising state. Here, not only is the decliner of little use against other threats, but it is also particularly well placed to challenge the riser, either alone or in conjunction with other states.

The importance of a declining state's relative geographic location was on display as a rising Wilhelmine Germany evaluated its strategic options in the run-up to World War I. Seeking help against Russia, German leaders saw a declining Austria-Hungary as a potential ally. Although Austria-Hungary abutted both Germany and Russia, German policymakers calculated that Austria-Hungary's geographic reach allowed it to abet German strategic ambitions by forcing Russia to divide its attention between Germany and Austria-Hungary. By the same token, however, German strategists viewed a waning France as a major challenger. This makes sense: located due west of Germany and with no other great powers around it, France was unable to assist Germany against Russia—or other prospective threats—and, free of having to hedge against other great powers, was able to focus its energies on opposing Germany. The result was the perennial problem of a two-front war that drove much of German strategy before 1914.

Third, a declining state needs to have the long-term potential to assist the riser against other threats. This is not to say that a decliner needs to currently have military forces to help against other threats. In fact, there are sometimes strategic or budgetary reasons why a declining state may be militarily denuded. Rather, a decliner needs to have the latent potential—the organizational skill, technological capacity, and economic foundation—so that the riser will conclude that if it comes to the decliner's assistance, the decliner can help it against other great powers.[61] American policymakers confronted with Britain's decline in the early Cold War faced precisely this situation, discussing how any program for European economic recovery that would help balance the Soviet Union "must embrace, or be linked to, some sort of plan for dealing with the economic plight of Britain."[62] Baldly stated, a rising state must conclude that a decliner can be rebuilt to serve a useful purpose. Otherwise, a riser would simply be throwing resources down a rabbit hole, and the decliner liable to collapse quickly if challenged.

Finally, a declining state must be politically available as a partner: it cannot be firmly aligned with a rising state's opponent(s), and there must be some political support within the declining state for cooperation with the riser.[63] In the competitive world of international politics, states make short-term calculations about which states are more or less threatening at any given time. Although a rising state may hope that a declining state will eventually defect from an opponent's coalition, it tends to focus on the strategic reality at hand and treat the decliner as an opponent as well.

High Strategic Value and Support When all of these criteria are met—that is, there are other great powers present and a declining state is well-positioned geographically, has the long-term potential, and is politically available to help confront these actors—a declining state has high strategic value, and rising states tend to pursue supportive strategies. There are three mechanisms driving this behavior. First, support is an effective way of using the declining state to contain and weaken other great powers. Supportive strategies can sustain the decliner as a stronger great power compared to what would otherwise be the case, compelling other states to focus on balancing the decliner.[64] This works to a rising state's advantage: at minimum, it protects a riser from other challengers by using the decliner as a diversion and security glacis; at best, it can weaken both the decliner and other great powers, creating opportunities for the riser's expansion.

Second, support prevents other states from employing the decliner against the riser. Clearly, if a rising state wants to use the decliner against other great powers, it needs to avoid steps that push the decliner into the arms of other actors. After all, not only might a strategically valuable state be useful to other great powers in opposing a rising state, but other great powers might aid a decliner to foreclose a riser's own strategic options.[65] Edward Gulick captured this basic insight long ago, noting that failure to preserve alignment options may "mean a failure to establish a workable balance."[66] Prussian-Austrian relations in the late 1800s illustrate the dynamic: despite having gone to war with Austria-Hungary in 1866, Prussia subsequently repaired Prusso-Austrian relations out of concern that neglecting to back Austria would foster a Franco-Austrian alliance and isolate Prussia.[67]

Finally, supportive strategies minimize unwanted competitions. If a declining state can assist a rising state against other states, then the last thing a riser should want is to provoke the decliner into arming or lashing out in a preventive conflict.[68] Hence, a key driver of Chinese foreign policy at the start of China's growth in the 1970s was to ensure good relations with the United States so the latter would focus on the Soviet Union rather than

27

China.[69] A related risk is that a declining state may inaugurate a wider conflict that harms a riser by provoking other great powers: even if a riser
wants to use a decliner to weaken other states, it may still worry that the
decliner will start a fight that escalates and imperil the riser.[70] Although there
is no guarantee that support will foreclose unwanted competitions, it makes
this result more likely by reducing actions that might trigger conflict between
the riser and the decliner, and by providing the riser leverage to restrain the
decliner's risky behavior.[71]

Low Strategic Value and Predation When some or all of the above conditions
are absent, however, a declining state has low strategic value and rising states
generally pursue predatory strategies. Three mechanisms again underlie
this response. First, when a rising state cannot use a decliner against other
states, predation improves the rising state's relative position. In multipolarity,
preying on a state with low strategic value can enable a riser's continued
growth by weakening prospective competitors. Before and after the Franco-
Prussian War, for example, a rising Prussia/Germany successfully preyed
on an isolated France, allowing Prussia/Germany to consolidate its strategic
position in Europe.[72] Equally important, a rising state in bipolarity whose
only competitor is declining may be able to live in a world free of great
power threats if it eliminates the declining state as a competitor—successful
predation in bipolarity allows a rising state to become hegemonic. Thus, as
noted earlier, the ancient Spartans feared that a rising Athens was out to
dominate ancient Greece by undercutting Sparta, thereby setting the stage
for the Peloponnesian War.

Relatedly, predation limits dangers to a rising state if conflict erupts. At
the most general level, weakening a low-value declining state reduces the likelihood of it successfully attacking the riser either alone or in concert with
others. This has a second-order benefit, as it frees the riser to focus on other,
potentially more threatening, states. One of the drivers of U.S. efforts to evict
European states from North America, for instance, was concern that European powers might contain or invade the United States by partnering with
other states in the Western Hemisphere.[73] Similarly, analysts discussing the
rise of China occasionally worry that China might try to neutralize Japan to
prevent it from contributing to an anti-China coalition.[74]

Finally, preying on a declining state with low strategic value denies the
decliner as an ally to others. Logically, if a rising state cannot use a decliner
against other great powers, then it has good reason to prevent other states
from gaining or keeping the decliner as a partner for themselves. Of course,
this effort may provoke other states into aiding the decliner. German expansion before 1914, for example, led a declining France and a relatively rising
Russia to make common cause, just as worries about Soviet expansion as
British power waned after 1945 spurred U.S. assistance to the United King-

dom.[75] Nevertheless, so long as it does not precipitate war, predation can pay as it limits the strength of a real or possible opposing bloc.

MILITARY POSTURE AND RISING STATE ASSERTIVENESS

Strategic value helps explain rising state strategy by identifying circumstances in which states that want power determine that preying on or supporting a declining state will help them attain that objective. However, it leaves a crucial question unanswered: how assertively should rising states pursue predation or support? There are potential costs to a riser from utilizing both intense and limited means. Like other states, decliners often want to maximize power and may therefore lash out to secure their long-term position. Preying on a decliner too intensely and too soon therefore risks triggering a costly conflict.[76] Similarly, intensely supporting a decliner may lead to a rising state's ensnarement in foreign adventures undertaken by an emboldened partner, trigger conflicts with other states by suggesting the formation of a powerful and aggressive coalition, and risk betrayal by and confrontation with the decliner.[77] Limited means, however, can have their own problems. For example, failing to intensely prey on a declining state at a propitious moment may foreclose a rising state's shot at becoming a hegemon. Meanwhile, limited efforts to support a strategically valuable decliner can cause the riser to lose the decliner as a partner if the declining state is preyed on by other powers or is backed by a rival state. Given these dilemmas, rising states need to calibrate their assertiveness to minimize the costs and adverse consequences involved.

The declining state's military posture accounts for this remaining variation in rising state strategy (figures 1.2 and 1.3). Military posture refers to a state's extant military capabilities in the most likely or salient theater of reference.[78] These capabilities involve more than simple troop numbers or raw measures of military potential.[79] Rather, posture reflects what one study terms "quantitative measurements and qualitative indicators" of military strength to describe how the forces at a state's disposal are trained, positioned, equipped, and deployed for the military scenario at hand.[80] Thus, for a state seeking to protect far-flung colonies, military posture involves weighing the quantity and quality of its naval and expeditionary forces and its ability to sustain these units in distant fields of operation. Conversely, states contemplating major war with other great powers will tend to be evaluated on their ability to field capable land forces, deploy air and naval units that support or supplement land forces, and sustain these units with the aim of deterring opponents in peacetime or fighting to stalemate (or victory) in wartime. Similarly, for a country trying to protect its homeland, posture involves deploying sufficient ground, air, naval, and—in certain instances— nuclear forces to deter or blunt an attack or to impose such costs that an aggressor decides the game is no longer worth the effort. Posture, in sum, is a baseline assessment of the quality and quantity of a state's existing forces and their ability to perform required military missions in an envisioned domain.[81]

Military postures, like other aspects of military power, can be categorized along different dimensions with varying degrees of complexity.[82] In the normal course of international politics, however, leaders are unlikely to pay as much attention to the specifics of how opposing militaries are structured, trained, or equipped in all domains as they are to whether one side is likely to make a good overall showing if a particular conflict erupts. I therefore distinguish between declining states with *robust* and those with *weak* military postures. A state has a robust posture if it possesses the military tools to deter an attack on a given interest if an opponent challenges it, or to impose meaningful costs—up to and including wartime victory—on an adversary if deterrence fails.[83] In antiquity, for example, a major constraint on the strategy of rising Athens was the strength of the Spartan army and the threat this posed to Athenian ambitions.[84] Similarly, strategists late in the Cold War regularly worried about the dangers of a clash between a rising United States and declining, but still militarily potent, Soviet Union.[85] Robust postures are thus defined by certain common traits (table 1.4). First, robust militaries have the freedom to maneuver to address an adversary's moves—obviously, a military that cannot get to a fight is not very useful. Second, they have the skills, numbers, training, command and control arrangements (i.e, leadership), and equipment to reliably perform a range of missions. Logically, militaries that surrender after the first shot is fired or that meet armored attacks with cavalry charges do not pose much of a problem for other great powers. Third, robust militaries have stable lines of communication that help them sustain combat power.

Finally, and if a state is armed with nuclear weapons, robust postures see conventional and nuclear forces well integrated for direct and—especially—extended deterrence. This last point requires some explanation. Nuclear weapons are excellent tools to ensure a state's physical survival, as the consequences of being struck with nuclear weapons raises the stakes for states contemplating aggression against another's homeland. However, nuclear weapons are less useful for threatening other states or protecting interests beyond a state's borders. As both the United States and Soviet Union learned during the Cold War, it is difficult to make extended deterrence credible without linking nuclear commitments to conventional military options.[86] Robustly postured nuclear states thus hold a diverse, capable, and well-integrated array of conventional and nuclear military tools for extended deterrence, as well as the ability to inflict unacceptable damage if an opponent threatens one's homeland.

Conversely, a state has a weak posture when it lacks the military capabilities to deter an attack or impose meaningful costs on an opponent if conflict

Table 1.4 Indicators of military posture

Robust: states can defend their interests and threaten to harm challengers	Weak: states are unable to defend themselves or impose large costs on potential challengers
Forces have the freedom to maneuver and get to a fight	Forces are unable to deploy (or deploy in a timely manner)
Numerous, well-equipped forces	Poorly equipped, inferior forces
Forces capable of a variety of missions	Forces narrowly trained, or inappropriately trained for missions at hand
Military units are reliable	Military units have limited will to fight
Good staying power and reliable lines of communication	Inability to sustain and reinforce combat power in the field

erupts. States in this situation may be unable to deploy troops to address a threat; field forces that lack staying power, proper training and leadership, or which are otherwise ill equipped to deal with the challenge at hand; or be unable to credibly threaten nuclear retaliation. Case in point, chronic underfunding, training and equipment shortfalls, and internal dissent in the Austro-Hungarian army caused many diplomats before 1914 to conclude that the force was unlikely to perform well in wartime. This, in turn, led German decision makers to fret about their ally and Russian policymakers to sense an opportunity for aggrandizement.[87] More recently, the collapse of British military power after World War II—epitomized by Britain's 1947 decision to withdraw from Greece and Turkey—led Dean Acheson (later the U.S. secretary of state) to see the United States as "met at Armageddon": U.S. leaders feared Soviet expansion in the resulting power vacuum.[88] In short, if robust postures suggest that states can make a good wartime showing with the forces on hand, weak postures indicate that a state is likely to crumple at the first clash of arms.

Importantly, military posture operates largely independent of strategic value, as the factors that drive strategic value have little bearing on a state's extant military capabilities. Strategic value is mostly an inherent feature of states, whereas military posture is largely a policy choice. For instance, neither a state's political availability nor the presence of other great powers determines the size and quality of its forces. Nor does a state's geographic position drive posture. For instance, the United Kingdom maintained a robust posture for continental operations before World War I—prepared to deploy the highly trained British Expeditionary Force at the outbreak of hostilities—only to gut the British army and virtually foreclose the possibility of a continental commitment in the interwar period; holding geography constant, posture can vary.[89]

Above all, military posture is different than a state's long-term potential. At root, posture reflects a state's decision to invest in its military or, put differently, its willingness to convert latent strength into actualized capabilities through military allocations. Just as these decisions may give relatively weak states disproportionately robust militaries, so states with significant latent potential may adopt weak military positions. Despite having a smaller economy than the United States throughout the Cold War, for instance, the Soviet Union converted a higher proportion of its resources into military assets, affording it rough military parity with the U.S. during much of that contest. In contrast, present-day Germany—despite having the fourth largest economy in the world—has limited its military investments and accepted a comparatively feeble military.[90] Of course, a state that is in the process of falling out of the ranks of great powers will eventually find itself unable to maintain a robust military.[91] Declining states can devote a growing portion of their resources to military affairs to keep pace with rising states, but over time the emergence of more powerful peers will foreclose a decliner's ability to field a comparatively potent military. Except for the exceptional situation in which a decliner is exiting the great powers, however, a state's decision to embrace a robust or weak posture is at base a political decision separate from the factors driving strategic value.[92]

THE IMPORTANCE OF POSTURE

A declining state's military posture has important consequences for rising state behavior. Robust postures matter because they make rising states run scared. For predatory states, maximizing power at the expense of a declining state that can defend itself risks pushing the decliner into launching a preventive war or, more generally, exacerbating tensions with a decliner that eventually leads to conflict.[93] Yet states interested in supporting a declining great power also face problems. On one level, a declining state that pumps resources into a robust military can more readily turn on and attack even its allies. Equally important, states with robust postures can easily threaten other great powers; a riser risks becoming ensnared in undesired conflicts by either provoking third parties into arming or lashing out themselves.[94] Put simply, because a robust declining state can provide security for itself, there is no need for rising states to pull the decliner's strategic chestnuts out of the fire. Even states interested in supporting a decliner have reason and opportunity to see how the situation evolves.

Weak postures, in contrast, clarify and reduce the risks of using intense means vis-à-vis declining states. First, the likelihood and consequences of a war initiated by a decliner go down, as other states are likely to easily defeat an attack and the decliner recognizes as much.[95] The risk of provoking third parties into arming and initiating preventive action themselves—potentially ensnaring a riser—diminishes for the same reason. At the same time, weak postures signal that remaining on the sidelines is no longer feasible. With a decliner unable to defend itself, rising states need to move expeditiously to either prevent it from being lost as a partner or preclude other states from unilaterally gaining from the decliner's weakness. After all, the fact that other rising states can have their own designs on a decliner means that a supportive riser may need to intensify its assistance to win the declining state's cooperation.[96] Likewise, predatory states may need to preempt other predators or—if preemption invites conflict with other states—work with other predators to ensure an equal division of the spoils. Overall, weak postures send a strong message that the time is nigh for states to either prey intensely on a decliner and get while the getting is good, or to intensely support the decliner before it is too late.

Shaping Strategy: The Interaction of Strategic Value and Posture

In tandem, the decliner's strategic value and posture explain when and why different rising state strategies tend to emerge (figure 1.2). They also generate a series of process predictions describing how rising states calculate the costs and benefits of predation, and when these calculations change.

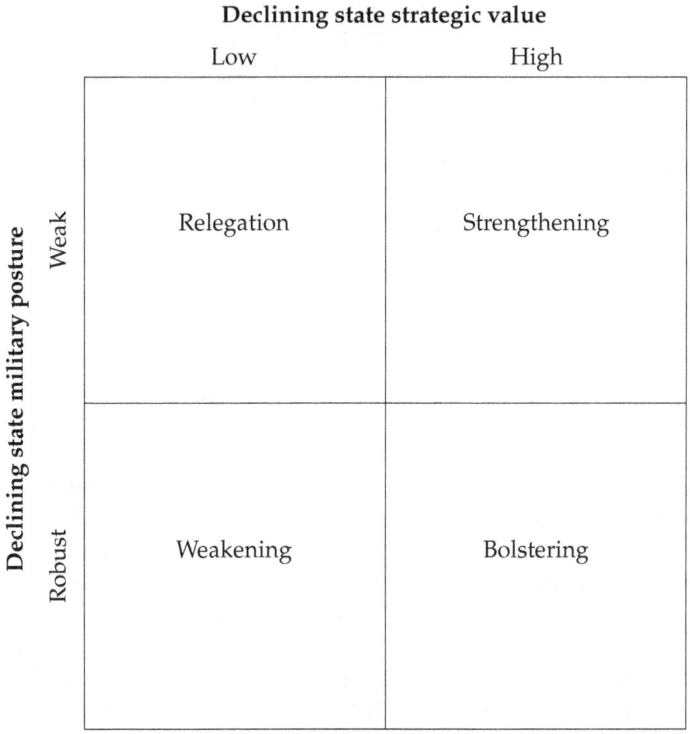

Declining state strategic value

	Low	High
Weak	Relegation	Strengthening
Robust	Weakening	Bolstering

Declining state military posture

Figure 1.2. Strategic value, posture, and rising state strategies.

RELEGATION STRATEGIES: LOW STRATEGIC VALUE
AND WEAK POSTURES

Relegation strategies occur when a declining state has low strategic value and a weak military posture. Because great powers tend to maximize power, a declining state that lacks strategic value presents an inviting target for a rising state, as predation can eliminate a potential challenger and hinder others from using the decliner to stymie the riser's own growth. In fact, successful predation against a declining state that is the riser's only major challenger may allow the riser to become a hegemon and operate free of great power threats. The risks of predation, meanwhile, are also minimized: although declining states may threaten to use force to check a rising state's ambitions, the decliner's weak military posture in this scenario renders the threat of force moot.[97]

In such circumstances, rising states generally conclude that they can benefit from power maximization and pay few costs along the way.[98] A rising state is thus freed to pursue Relegation and push the decliner down the great power ranks as assertively as possible. It can do this, for example, by diplomatically isolating the decliner, attacking the declining state, detaching or attacking the decliner's principal allies, and/or engaging in economic warfare. The incentive to quickly undercut a declining state is augmented by the possibility that the riser may have a limited window of opportunity to gain at the decliner's expense: although the declining state is militarily vulnerable today, it may recover or find powerful patrons in the future.[99] The result is a nightmare for a declining state, as a rising rival with both motive and opportunity to expand offers the decliner no quarter, choosing intense means to rapidly reduce its position.

WEAKENING STRATEGIES: LOW STRATEGIC VALUE
AND ROBUST POSTURES

Weakening strategies are used when a declining state lacks strategic value yet still has a robust military. In this case, rising states see predation as attractive for undermining a rival power and moving closer to hegemony. At the same time, a riser cannot ignore the reality that a declining state can still use force to keep predation in check. Particularly dangerous is the possibility of the declining state launching a preventive war or adopting hard-line policies that escalate into a military clash; without a large military advantage over the decliner, a rising state may be unable to defeat the decliner, or able to win only a Pyrrhic victory.[100] A rising state therefore constrains its assertiveness so long as the declining state can retaliate, employing limited policies to gradually revise the status quo at the decliner's expense.[101] If successful, these efforts can eventually exhaust the declining state so that it either falls from the great power ranks or atrophies to the point where its military strength is near collapse and Relegation becomes feasible. Weakening strategies thereby position risers to compete with declining states over the long haul, while in the interim avoiding steps that might lead a declining state to lash out in ways that hinder the riser's continued growth.

BOLSTERING STRATEGIES: HIGH STRATEGIC VALUE AND ROBUST POSTURES

Rising states adopt Bolstering strategies when a declining state has high strategic value and a robust posture. All things being equal, rising states that see strategic value in a decliner are likely to use support to obtain its help in distracting and weakening other great powers. When a declining state has a robust military posture, however, all things are not equal. Although a decliner's military strength makes it an effective counter against other great powers, it also means that rising states must worry that too much support might embolden the decliner into foreign adventures that can entrap its supporters or betray and challenge the rising state itself.[102] A related problem involves the reactions of third parties: intensely aiding a militarily potent decliner can signal the formation of a powerful and aggressive coalition, giving other countries an incentive to counterbalance and exposing a rising state to additional potential conflicts.

Rising states therefore tend to respond with Bolstering strategies. Bolstering avoids making life harder for a declining state and may even involve moderate efforts to stabilize its relative position. The focus here is on keeping the decliner capable of countering other threats, while also ensuring that relations are sufficiently warm that the decliner focuses its energies on states other than the riser in ways that are acceptable to the riser. That said, rising state efforts are constrained in such situations to providing limited assistance that minimize a riser's exposure to the decliner's misbehavior or a hostile response by other great powers.[103] Bolstering is therefore cooperation on the cheap, as a rising state does nothing to harm a decliner and only as much to help as is necessary to keep the declining state focused on other threats.[104] This approach thus solves two problems facing a rising state: it both facilitates the decliner's availability as a possible future ally and buys the rising state time for the decliner's threat of force to wane.

STRENGTHENING STRATEGIES: HIGH STRATEGIC VALUE AND WEAK POSTURES

Finally, Strengthening strategies are adopted when a declining state has high strategic value but a weak military posture. In these circumstances, rising states work intensely to sustain—and potentially even rebuild—a declining state's strength. Rising states can pursue this outcome by transferring resources, offering diplomatic guarantees, and even allying with the decliner. In other words, rising states opt for policies that make life substantially easier for the declining state than would otherwise be the case. This strategy is feasible because declining great powers are still great powers for a reason: although declining, they are still more capable than most other states and may be able to recover lost ground.[105] Of course, a rising state's efforts are unlikely to go so far that the decliner recovers to the point where it can again threaten the rising state, but they minimally prevent a decliner from falling any further.

Assisting a declining state in this way is not cheap. To intensely back a decliner, rising states must expend their own resources to protect, sustain, and/or reconstitute the decliner's capabilities, potentially even putting their own security on the line by promising to come to the decliner's aid if it is attacked (especially as the decliner regains strength). Despite the costs, however, Strengthening can pay. On one level, Strengthening is an attractive way for a rising state to secure a proxy to use against other great powers. The strategy can also give rising states influence over a declining state's policies.[106] With the decliner's military options limited and with other great powers around, a declining state needs protection, and a rising state can attempt to set conditions for its support to ensure that the decliner abets the riser's objectives while minimizing the risk of the decliner's manipulating or entrapping the riser.[107] Finally, risers can expect to pay a large penalty if they fail to act: other states may come to the decliner's assistance to gain it as a partner, or the declining state may collapse and leave a rising state isolated.[108] Collectively, this situation means that a rising state can doubly benefit from Strengthening, as a riser not only gains the decliner's help against other great powers, but blocks other actors from doing the same.

SHIFTS IN STRATEGY

To be clear, these strategies are not static, one-time deals. As the decliner's strategic value and military posture change, so too does rising state behavior (figure 1.3).[109] In particular, the former can increase or decrease as rising state capabilities change, other challengers emerge or disappear, and as the decliner's own strength and political availability vary. For example, Great Britain had low strategic value to the rising United States throughout much of the 1800s, but greater value in the twentieth century as a proxy first against Germany and later the Soviet Union.[110] Likewise, German growth before 1914 reinforced a declining France's value to Britain, just as Austria was of limited use to Germany before the 1860s but became increasingly valuable due to changes in Germany's threat environment and shifts in Austrian politics before World War I.[111]

Shifts in posture, meanwhile, reflect states' willingness to invest in their militaries and—in certain circumstances—the rise of other great powers. Political conditions in rising and declining states can result in growth or cuts

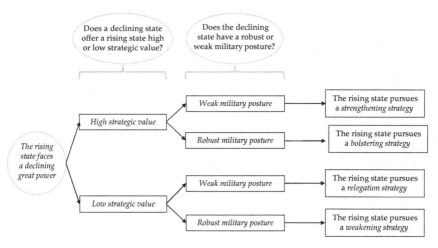

Figure 1.3. Rising state decision making and strategy.

to military forces that affect the decliner's net military capacity. Austro-Hungarian political disunity before 1914, for instance, deprived the Austrian military of adequate funding in the years before World War I. At a time when the other European powers were arming, the result was a military that punched below Austria's potential weight.[112] In addition, the emergence of states whose economic power exceeds that of a decliner can reinforce this dynamic over time by requiring the decliner to either accept a weakening military position or allocate a growing share of resources to military purposes. The late Cold War Soviet Union, for example, struggled to keep pace militarily with the surging United States as Soviet defense spending grew from an estimated 11–13 percent to nearly 18 percent of Soviet gross national product (GNP) during the 1980s; even so, Soviet leaders increasingly doubted their country's ability to sustain the existing military balance in the future.[113] France experienced a similar phenomenon before 1914: confronted with a rising Germany, French strategists endeavored—unsuccessfully—to find the people, funding, and technology to match German military power.[114] As noted above, eventually even a committed decliner may be unable to keep up militarily with relatively rising states. Until that point is reached, however, declining states can have a large say in their fate by adjusting their military policies as circumstances change.

CONNECTING STRUCTURE AND STRATEGY

One might wonder whether great powers and their leaders are aware of systemic conditions and, as the preceding discussion proposes, make cost-benefit analyses before they act. After all, it is an open question whether structural theories of international politics can be used as theories of foreign policy.[115] Absent what Gideon Rose terms a "transmission belt" linking external circumstances with state calculations, it seems difficult to claim that rising states focus on systemic circumstances—additional factors can intrude into the decision-making process.[116]

In practice, two mechanisms correct for this possibility. First, the unique nature of great power decline provides clear signals that states must begin thinking in strategic cost-benefit terms. As long as states and their leaders are reasonably concerned with their security—considering it among the most important goals they can pursue—they have profound incentives to monitor shifts in power. When major changes in the distribution of power occur, states therefore have a strong impetus to evaluate what these changes mean for their security, to get the calculus right, and to act as predicted.[117] Otherwise, a state is liable to find itself under duress from other states eager to ensure their own well-being.[118]

Not all states, however, successfully calculate the reactions of other great powers. Germany's behavior, for example, may have hastened its encirclement before 1914, just as Soviet policy spurred a massive counterbalancing coalition during the Cold War.[119] Still, even rising states that miscalculate often encounter strong international responses that push them to behave in line with the argument. For a state that is overly predatory, conflict and the decliner's loss as a partner are likely to correct excessively aggrandizing behavior. For an overly supportive state, pressures from other great powers will reveal that the rising state is forgoing opportunities to have its way in world politics and thus move it toward predation. Put simply, states that miscalculate encounter constraints and opportunities as they act, and tend to adjust their strategies accordingly. Some states—like Wilhelmine Germany and the Soviet Union—may still ignore these pressures, but they are likely to be the exception rather than the rule.

Testing the Argument

In sum, I argue that a declining state's strategic value and its military posture together determine whether a rising state will adopt a strategy involving predatory or supportive goals and use limited or intense means to pursue these objectives. Accordingly, the case studies in subsequent chapters test predation theory against the competing arguments described in the introduction. The cases do so primarily by examining the strategies adopted in response to two great power declines in postwar Europe: Great Britain's decline from approximately 1945 to 1949 and the Soviet Union's decline in the period 1983–91. The first episode is the closest we have to a modern case of decline in which relatively rising states could use the decliner to counter other great power threats: though often overlooked, Great Britain was considered one of the superpowers at the end of World War II, with the ability to abet or hinder Soviet and U.S. postwar plans. American and Soviet policy toward Britain therefore provides a good venue to assess whether rising states support decliners with high strategic value. Meanwhile, few analysts would dispute that the Cold War saw the United States and Soviet Union compete for dominance in Europe. Hence, the Soviet Union's decline should be among the clearest examples of situations in which a rising state is unlikely to value a decliner and engage in predation. That said, I also step back in the conclusion to briefly examine the German, British, and Russian responses to the declines of Austria-Hungary and France in the late nineteenth and early twentieth centuries. These final empirical sketches showcase my argument's generalizability by looking at an additional set of cases in a different historical period.

Four features of the British and Soviet cases make them attractive for evaluating predation theory. First, they offer strong tests of my argument against alternative explanations.[120] As shown in the following chapters, predation theory and its competitors generally make different predictions—ones that are often both unique and certain—as to the course and conduct of great power politics in the cases. Second, and relatedly, the cases should be difficult for predation theory to explain insofar as many of the alternative approaches seem to provide powerful accounts of rising state behavior in the cases.[121] For example, scholars such as Mark Haas, Christopher Layne, Andrew Kydd, and Dale Copeland have separately sought to explain U.S. strategy toward the declining Soviet Union using ideological, ideational, security dilemma, and interdependence arguments. Similarly, if economic interdependence arguments provide analytic traction, they should help explain strategies in situations such as Britain faced in postwar Europe when, following a surge in Anglo-American economic relations during World War II, the United States looked to establish an open economic order. Combined, the more evidence that predation theory explains the cases better than alternative explanations, the more confidence we have in the argument.

Third, examining post-1945 cases of decline helps control for the influence of nuclear weapons on international politics. For years, scholars regularly argued that nuclear weapons constrained individual states' foreign policies and international relations writ large. According to this argument, because nuclear weapons can inflict extensive damage on opponents, states possessing them can readily deter external challenges and virtually free themselves from the chance of foreign attack. In turn, this situation is supposed to lower states' incentives to compete and mitigate the risks of international conflict. As Robert Jervis—one of the main proponents of the argument—puts it, the nuclear revolution implies that "there will be peace between the superpowers, crises will be rare, [rivals will not] be eager to press bargaining advantages to the limit, the status quo will be relatively easy to maintain, and political outcomes will not be closely related to either the nuclear or the conventional balance."[122]

Increasingly, however, scholars are challenging key parts of the "nuclear revolution" thesis. Even if nuclear weapons reduce the odds of war and overt aggression, states can still have good reasons to compete for economic and military advantages.[123] Not only can such relative gains be used to shape diplomatic and military outcomes in situations where nuclear weapons are not employed, but nuclear-armed states may adopt more ambitious foreign policies and pursue objectives beyond strict national survival—for instance, extending deterrence over allies; likewise, cumulative economic, military, and technological gains may help states counter others' nuclear arsenals through, for example, counterforce operations.[124] In short, even if nuclear weapons diminish the risk of war, they may not reduce competition in international affairs.[125]

Focusing on the period after 1945—and particularly the Soviet Union's decline late in the Cold War—helps address this debate. The more states adopt predatory or supportive behavior in line with my argument despite the presence of nuclear weapons, the more likely the argument is to accurately describe rising state behavior even when nuclear weapons are absent. By the same token, and although not a direct focus of the book, finding that rising states prey on or support declining states in the nuclear era in line with predation theory provides ancillary evidence in support of claims that international politics in the nuclear era is much the same as international affairs in the prenuclear world.

Finally, the cases offer a worst-case analysis from the perspective of the declining state to show what happens when a rising great power has overtaken a decliner. In both case studies, rising states had already surpassed the declining state in overall capabilities. As a result, these cases should be among the least likely for rising states to focus primarily on power and security concerns vis-à-vis the decliner, as risers' relative strength means that other factors can affect their behavior without compromising their overall growth. The more rising state strategy conforms to predation theory's predictions under extreme conditions, the more confidence we have in the argument's generalizability.[126] Simply put, if rising states are sensitive to power and security concerns even after capabilities have shifted in their favor, they are likely to be similarly concerned before power has decisively moved in their direction.

The case studies themselves perform two functions. First, they show that predation theory provides a powerful account of rising state strategy. Each case shows a correlation between the argument's explanatory variables and rising state behavior. Second, by process tracing sequences of events, leveraging intra-case variation, and reconstructing the arguments used by policymakers, I demonstrate the causal logic and mechanisms in action. In doing so, the research benefits from extensive use of primary sources involving thousands of archival documents collected over the course of several months from the Truman, Reagan, and George H. W. Bush Presidential Libraries; the U.S. National Archives and Records Administration; the personal papers of Secretary of State James A. Baker III at Princeton University; and the National Security Archive at George Washington University, as well as the online records of the British National Archives. Many of these documents, especially for the Soviet case, have only recently been declassified and have never before been used by scholars. To supplement the still-evolving archival record in the Soviet case, I also interviewed fifty mid- and senior-level policymakers in the Ronald Reagan and George H. W. Bush administrations, compiling the most extensive set of interviews with American officials involved in shaping U.S.-Soviet relations during that period available (Appendix 2). Combined with existing primary and secondary sources, this work allows for fine-grained tests of the argument through careful reconstruction of the case histories.

What evidence would confirm my argument? The cases support predation theory if rising states undermine declining states with low strategic value, while preventing declining states with high value from weakening further. Policymakers in rising states should also emphasize the opportunity of gaining power at the expense of a low-value decliner to better position their state for future competition or to improve its relative position, while focusing on avoiding war with the decliner. When a declining state has high value, however, policymakers in rising states should argue for preserving the decliner so it can share the costs of confronting other states, and highlight the risks of losing a valuable proxy.

The case studies also reinforce the argument if a declining state's military posture affects the assertiveness of predation or support. Because declining states with robust postures can harm friend and foe alike, rising states should limit their assertiveness when helping or harming decliners. Indeed, we expect policymakers to talk about the undesirability of committing to fully helping or harming a robust decliner for fear of blowback. Alternatively, a declining state with a weak posture should encourage rising states to use intense means to affect the decliner's position, with policymakers in rising states arguing for intense policies in light of the decliner's reduced threat.

A Formerly Great Britain

Predicting U.S. and Soviet Strategy

The decline of Great Britain is one of the turning points of postwar international relations. Despite Europe's self-immolation during World War II, policymakers and scholars entered the postwar period anticipating that Britain would operate alongside the United States and Soviet Union as one of the "Big Three" powers able to shape postwar European security.[1] After all, the United Kingdom fought against Germany from the opening of hostilities in 1939 to the war's conclusion in 1945—making it difficult, as the scholar William T. R. Fox retrospectively noted, "to assign a lower status to a gallant and fully mobilized Britain than to a Johnny-come-lately United States."[2] Nevertheless, these hopes were soon dashed. By 1946, the British economy was in freefall even as U.S. and Soviet strength surged. By the close of the decade, Britain's time as a great power was quickly drawing to an end: not only had most of its military strength evaporated, but it was increasingly dependent on U.S. assistance to sustain even a truncated role in European security. The Cold War's familiar bipolar structure, in large part the result of Britain's decline and the rise of the United States and Soviet Union, became a reality.

This chapter serves two functions. First, I discuss the changes in the distribution of power in the second half of the 1940s, alongside U.S. and Soviet efforts to monitor these shifts. Policymakers are most likely to enact strategic adjustments when they recognize that a key factor shaping strategy—here, the relative distribution of power—is changing. Thus, showing both that the relative distribution of power shifted and that U.S. and Soviet strategists recognized these changes is a necessary first step in assessing responses to Britain's decline.

Next, I derive predictions for U.S. and Soviet strategy from predation theory and compare these accounts to the alternative arguments. Along the way, I relate these competing predictions to existing historiographic and political science treatments of Britain's decline and the early postwar era. I test these predictions in chapter 3.

The Decline of British Power in the late 1940s

Great Britain tumbled down and then out of the great power ranks in the years immediately after World War II. Of course, Britain had declined relative to its peers by some measures since the 1800s, as states such as Prussia (later Germany), the United States, and the Soviet Union grew economically and developed the military tools to match.[3] Still, the varying fortunes of other states in the wars of the nineteenth and twentieth centuries meant that Britain's place among the great powers remained secure until after World War II. Indeed, although Britain held nearly 20 percent of European great power capabilities—as measured by the Correlates of War Composite Index of Capabilities—immediately before World War II and ended the war nearly on par with the Soviet Union, British strength eroded soon after the conflict (figure 2.1).[4] As Fox, who coined the term "superpower" in 1944 and included the United Kingdom in his original list, later explained, "It became obvious that only two powers were according each other first-ranking status" as "the smoke of battle" from the Second World War cleared away.[5]

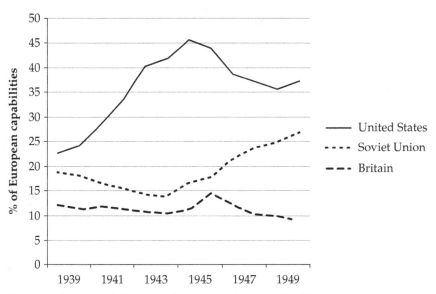

Figure 2.1. Change in the European distribution of power, 1939–50.

Two factors drove Britain's postwar decline. First, the conflict left Britain worse off than before the war in absolute economic terms. German bombing and wartime damage alone cost Britain $5.8 billion.[6] More important, the conflict left Britain heavily in debt:[7] having begun the war a net creditor, Britain ended the war owing other countries approximately $13.5 billion against a gross domestic product (GDP) of approximately $40 billion.[8] Clearly, Britain needed to raise revenue to finance its debt while modernizing, repairing, and transitioning its economy to a peacetime footing.[9] However, there were few options for obtaining the necessary funds. Income from foreign investments was less than half its 1938 level even in 1946–47.[10] Nor could Britain recover through trade. Exports at the end of the war were only one-third their prewar volume and unlikely to recover quickly, as there was no money to pay for raw materials.[11] And even if goods could be produced, selling them was problematic, as wartime losses left few of Britain's traditional trading partners with funds to purchase British goods, while the United States—a huge potential market—was competing with Britain for overseas trade.[12] At a time when British analysts estimated that exports needed to grow by at least 50 percent over their prewar level simply for the country to obtain prewar living standards and income, British prospects were bleak.[13]

In short, having spent one-quarter of its accumulated national wealth prosecuting the war, Britain entered the postwar era virtually bankrupt.[14] Reflecting this situation, British GDP shrank in 1946–47 as the country attempted to get back on its feet, and although growth returned in 1948–50, it was barely sufficient to recover lost ground; even in 1950, real GDP was below its 1941 level.[15] Balance of payments crises in 1947 and 1949 further hindered Britain's recovery, leaving the government struggling to finance short-term spending and long-term investment.[16] Epitomizing Britain's weakness, its leaders had to turn to the United States for economic support in 1945, 1947, and 1949 and to devalue the pound in September 1949 to stave off further economic dislocations.[17]

Second, wartime-driven growth of the United States and the Soviet Union ensured that British absolute losses translated into a relative decline. The United States emerged from World War II in a dominant economic position. Already wealthier than the United Kingdom in 1938–39, U.S. GDP nearly doubled during the war and continued growing afterward.[18] U.S. industrial strength and per capita productivity also surged. Despite not entering the war until 1941, for example, the United States produced more than twice as many tanks and aircraft as Britain during the conflict, while U.S. manufacturing output grew from less than three times that of Britain in 1938 to over five times British output by 1953.[19] The military balance tracked these economic changes. By 1945, the United States had proved itself adept at mobilizing and sustaining forces that totaled over eleven million soldiers and sailors compared to five million for Britain, had far outpaced British naval strength, and ended the war as the only state with nuclear weapons.[20]

The Soviet Union experienced similar growth.[21] To be sure, the war dev-astated much of the country following the June 1941 German invasion. Pre-cise figures are unavailable, but the best estimates suggest the Soviet Union lost between one-fifth and one-third of its prewar wealth, leaving it facing a daunting recovery.[22] Still, aggregate wealth belies the wartime surge in So-viet strength.[23] Despite losing much of its territory in the German attack, for instance, Soviet iron and steel production remained close to prewar levels during the conflict.[24] Equally telling, Soviet industrial potential was double prewar figures by the early 1950s, meaning that the country emerged from the conflict strong enough to recover from wartime damage and still expand. British industrial capacity, in contrast, grew by less than 50 percent over the same period.[25] Armaments production tells a similar story. By the war's end, the Soviet Union had more than twice as many soldiers under arms as Brit-ain, and had produced over three times as many tanks and nearly 20 percent more combat aircraft than the United Kingdom.[26]

U.S. and Soviet Policymakers Monitored British Decline

Policymakers recognized that Britain was losing ground relative to the So-viet Union and United States. Unsurprisingly, British leaders were especially concerned with the postwar situation, wondering—as Prime Minister Win-ston Churchill asked in April 1945—"How could the British Commonwealth, as the third of the three Great Powers, match the power and influence which would be wielded after the war by Russia and the United States?"[27] Britain, the Foreign Office concluded, was "numerically the weakest and geograph-ically the smallest of the three great powers."[28] If it did not increase its strength, the country was destined to become what one senior Foreign Of-fice official termed "Lepidus in the triumvirate with Mark Antony and Augustus."[29]

U.S. and Soviet officials also recognized the change.[30] "The successful ter-mination of the war," the Joint Chiefs of Staff wrote to Secretary of State Cordell Hull in mid-1944, "will find a world profoundly changed in respect of relative national military strength, a change more comparable indeed with that occasioned by the fall of Rome than with any other change occurring during the succeeding fifteen hundred years."[31] The United States and So-viet Union "will be the strongest military powers in the world," with Brit-ain following behind. Scholars consulting for the U.S. government echoed this position, finding that "For fifty years, the British power position has been declining." "On present evidence," they wrote, "this process seems likely to continue" and lead to the emergence of the "Big Two"—the Soviet Union and United States.[32]

Nor were these just the conclusions of low-level officials. Already in May 1944, Chief of Staff Admiral William Leahy advised Hull that "several developments have combined to lessen [Britain's] relative military and economic strength and gravely impair, if not preclude, her ability to offer effective military opposition to Russia on the Continent."[33] Briefings prepared for the 1945 Potsdam Conference likewise informed President Harry Truman that Britain was "the weakest of the three major powers."[34] Intelligence reports amplified these findings. By December 1945, the military's Joint Intelligence Staff found that Britain "will rank behind the United States and the U.S.S.R. among the powers capable of making war on a modern scale"; by January 1947, this view developed to the point where planners concluded that British wartime potential "will diminish proportionately in comparison to that of the Dominions, the U.S., and the Soviet Union."[35] Ultimately, no less an official than State Department Director of Policy Planning George Kennan argued in mid-1947 that "there is a large factor of uncertainty in all calculations about Britain's future." British economic problems were such that it remained unclear whether the United Kingdom could be "placed on her feet" or would end up dismantling its "defense and imperial establishment, in attempting to achieve the status of a greater Denmark or Sweden."[36] And within a few years of Kennan's note, policymakers concluded that Britain was unable to play an independent role in the European distribution of power and began assessing—as a February 1950 report described—the "effects of British decline as a world military power on U.S. security interests."[37]

Although evidence is not as readily available, it appears that Soviet officials reached similar conclusions. Already in January 1944, for example, a report designed to help Soviet General Secretary Joseph Stalin understand postwar politics noted that Great Britain would enter the postwar period "impoverished and weakened."[38] One year later, a similar analysis by former foreign minister Maxim Litvinov reached even blunter conclusions, offering, "The current war will result in a great disturbance of not only the European but the global balance of power, which will especially affect England." Postwar Britain would face mounting pressure to reduce its foreign footprint and seek a "long tranquility in Europe."[39]

As British problems deepened after 1945, Soviet assessments grew starker. Tasked with assessing Western policy in mid-1946, Soviet ambassador to the United States Nikolai Novikov cabled Foreign Minister Vyacheslav Molotov: "The third great power, Great Britain, which had taken heavy blows during the war, now faces enormous economic and political problems." "The political foundations of the British Empire," Novikov added, "were appreciably shaken," and the country faced growing incentives to retrench abroad. In contrast, the United States was experiencing "a serious strengthening of [its] economic position" and increasingly competing with a Soviet Union that was itself "stronger than it was in the prewar period."[40] The United States and Soviet Union, in short, outpaced Britain, as British leaders lacked what Molotov in 1947 called "any serious means of overcoming their economic difficulties."[41] By March 1948, no less an official than Stalin was arguing that the world was divided into two camps headed by the Soviet Union and United States—Britain was of secondary importance.[42]

The U.S. and Soviet Response to British Decline: Existing Arguments

Facing Britain's decline, what policies do we expect the United States and Soviet Union to adopt? For the last seven decades, many discussions of early postwar politics have given a consistent answer: whereas an expansionist Soviet Union preyed upon the United Kingdom in Europe and beyond, the United States readily supported the United Kingdom and protected it against Soviet machinations.[43] This argument is implicit in major studies of early Cold War diplomacy, with scholars such as John Lewis Gaddis describing the quick emergence of an Anglo-American alliance characterized by strategic coordination, significant U.S. economic aid, and security guarantees such as the North Atlantic Treaty Organization.[44] Aptly capturing this perspective, Raymond Dawson and Richard Rosecrance ground their study of Anglo-American relations in the idea that during "the immediate postwar period, the disappearance of the Nazi menace was succeeded by the Russian threat, and very soon again the two nations closed ranks."[45] According to this view, U.S. and Soviet strategies diverged early on, as the United States quickly assisted the United Kingdom while the Soviet Union tried to exploit British problems. "An Anglo-American partnership was a reality" by mid-1946, writes the historian Terry Anderson, as Soviet behavior drove the United States and United Kingdom together.[46]

EXPLAINING DIVERGING U.S. AND SOVIET POLICIES

The basic distinction between U.S. accommodation and Soviet predation matches what we expect from theories emphasizing the role of ideological affinity, economic interests, or the security dilemma. If ideological similarity models apply anywhere, they should explain the early postwar British-Soviet-U.S. triangular relationship.[47] It would be hard to find two states more ideologically similar than the United States and Great Britain, with both sharing an ingrained commitment to liberal values, economic exchange, and democratic governance.[48] In contrast, the Soviet Union—committed to autocratic rule, centralized planning, and a hierarchical state-society relationship—was the antithesis of the Anglo-American liberal model.[49] In fact, the early postwar period saw Stalin turn even further away from liberalism by reimposing controls on political dissent and debate that had been relaxed during the war. By early 1947, as Yoram Gorlizki and Oleg Khlevniuk write, a "full-blown ideological conflict" was underway between the Soviet Union and its former Anglo-American allies.[50] Accordingly, Anglo-American ideological similarity should facilitate rapid and growing U.S. support for the United Kingdom as the United States tries to prevent the loss of an ideological fellow traveler in the face of a growing Soviet ideological challenge,[51] whereas the Anglo-Soviet relationship should be marked by escalating misunderstanding, hostility, and predation.[52]

Interdependence models predict similar behaviors. Here, growing Anglo-American economic integration should cause the United States to support the United Kingdom after World War II to preserve an economic partner.[53] Given extensive Anglo-American economic collaboration during the war—epitomized by combined boards that coordinated the Anglo-American economies and U.S. Lend-Lease economic assistance[54]—plans for sustained postwar exchange via the Bretton Woods system, and the United States' abiding faith in the salutary effects of economic interdependence, the United States enjoyed a growing stake in the United Kingdom's continuation as a capable member of the postwar economic order.[55] American support for the United Kingdom should follow: as Britain becomes economically weaker, U.S. support should increase.[56] Conversely, the Soviet Union not only remained comparatively aloof from wartime economic collaboration but also refused to ratify the Bretton Woods arrangements and was generally ambivalent about economic exchange with the West;[57] furthermore, what exchange there was centered on the United States rather than the United Kingdom and was waning by the end of World War II.[58] With no economic stake in the survival of the declining United Kingdom, the Soviet Union had no reason to pull its punches.

Proponents of the security dilemma, meanwhile, suggest that the divergence of Soviet and U.S. policy resulted from a deepening Soviet-Western insecurity spiral.[59] On the one hand, the United States and Britain effectively saw one another as security-seeking actors helping to maintain, as David Reynolds puts it, "the independence of Western Europe in the face of powers apparently focused on continental domination."[60] Successful Anglo-American reassurance in the early 1900s likely helped this situation: with the United Kingdom signaling its interest in cooperation by settling outstanding territorial disputes with the United States and withdrawing the Royal Navy from North America, both sides overcame past mistrust to establish a foundation for future collaboration.[61] On the other hand, Anglo-Soviet relations remained problematic.[62] Not only had Britain opposed the Soviet Union during much of the interwar period, but postwar Soviet policymakers may have feared confrontation by the capitalist world just as British leaders feared Soviet expansionism.[63] Given, too, the Soviet Union's proximity to the United Kingdom and the advent of long-range airpower that enabled both states to attack one another, the stage was set for Anglo-Soviet insecurity.[64] Thus, growing Soviet mistrust of Britain plausibly led the Soviet Union to weaken Britain, just as mutual interest in maintaining the status quo led the United States to sustain British power.[65]

REVISIONIST ACCOUNTS: U.S. PREDATION, SOVIET SUPPORT

Of course, not all scholars accept this account of Anglo-American cooperation and Anglo-Soviet competition. Since the 1960s, a variety of scholars have argued that the United States initially preyed upon the United Kingdom more than the Soviet Union. By the middle of World War II, Warren Kimball writes, U.S. leaders recognized that the United Kingdom had "neither the leeway nor the desire to act independently" of the United States.[66] Accordingly, the United States pushed the United Kingdom during and after the conflict to accept U.S. visions of postwar order involving decolonization, an open economic system, and a limited U.S. role in European security. Notably, the administrations of Presidents Franklin Roosevelt and Harry Truman adopted this course despite British warnings that U.S. policy harmed British security—or, as one British observer noted, the United States was "straining to put the British Empire into liquidation."[67] Far from supporting Britain, Anglo-American relations were marked by disputes over British colonial policy, military disengagement, and—above all—economic competition at odds with conventional accounts of Anglo-American accord.[68]

Accompanying this image of a predatory United States is a related argument that the Soviet Union sought cooperation with Britain. Soviet leaders, according to Peter Ruggenthaler, desired a quid pro quo with Britain and the United States whereby "the Western powers would refrain from interfering in countries occupied by the Red Army in the same way that the Soviet Union refrained from exerting its influence on the formation of governments in Belgium, France, Greece, etc."[69] Put differently, Stalin sought a Soviet sphere of influence in Eastern Europe but, as Reynolds elaborates, "would not fuss about areas that he acknowledged to be in the Western sphere."[70] In this view, Soviet postwar policy was premised on sustaining good relations among the great powers, reinforced by the Soviet need to recover from wartime losses (and, by extension, the Soviet Union's relative inability to harm the United Kingdom); to this end, Stalin offered concessions to the United States and Britain to make cooperation a reality. Many of these concessions were disproportionately advantageous to the United Kingdom, as it was assumed that Britain would play the leading role in Western Europe. As the British Foreign Office recognized when negotiating the future of Italy, for example, Soviet policy helped to bring Italy "willing and joyfully into the British orbit."[71]

In advancing this story of U.S. predation and Soviet support, scholars often focus on the ideas motivating U.S. and Soviet leaders. On the U.S. side, analysts such as Christopher Layne see U.S strategy as spurred by policymakers whose expansive geopolitical and economic ambitions were informed by an "Open Door" ideology—the belief that the United States must project power to dominate international politics and thus to ensure the spread of liberal governance and economic arrangements perceived as vital to U.S. security. As Layne writes, U.S. leaders driven by Open Door ideas worked to "ensure that Britain was weakened to the point where it could not challenge U.S. power."[72] In this telling, an independent Britain might adopt a closed economic order seen as inimical to U.S. interests while contesting U.S political influence in Western Europe.[73] This risk led the United States to undermine Britain. Indeed, although the United States moderated its efforts somewhat after 1947–48 as U.S. strategists decided to reconstitute European (including British) economic and military strength to balance Soviet power, this was a secondary concern: U.S. policymakers persistently sought dominance in postwar Europe and exploited British problems to this end.

In contrast, Stalin and other Soviet leaders held a firm belief in Marxist-Leninist theory. Among other things, this set of ideas prescribed an eventual fight between capitalist and communist countries for world dominance. Marxism-Leninism, however, was not clear about how this process would occur, leaving postwar Soviet leaders to debate two different interpretations. One approach—what Geoffrey Roberts terms a "radical" Marxist position—predicted a world in which capitalist powers such as the United States and the United Kingdom would collude against the Soviet Union, thereby mandating Soviet efforts to preventively weaken the capitalist bloc. In contrast, a "moderate" position foreshadowed a world in which the capitalist powers would first compete among themselves for dominance. This would create opportunities for the Soviet Union to play capitalist states off each other, incentivizing Soviet support for some foreign powers.[74]

As Roberts and others describe, the moderate position dominated Soviet thinking in 1945–47 as Soviet policymakers expected an Anglo-American dustup that Britain was unlikely to win.[75] In response, the Soviet Union supported Britain by abetting its reconstruction and ensuring stability in Western Europe so as to (1) strengthen Britain's political and economic position, and (2) prevent the United States from quickly overwhelming the United Kingdom and moving against the Soviet Union.[76] By implication, this effort would give the Soviet Union a partner that could both help manage postwar Europe and contain (or oppose) the United States. This policy changed only after mid-1947 when Stalin finally rejected what Vladislav Zubok and Constantine Pleshakov call "the hope that the United States and British empire would be entangled" in a lengthy contest.[77] Afterward, the hard-line interpretation of Marxist theory dominated Soviet politics, and the Soviet Union embraced a Weakening strategy to confront the capitalist world.[78]

Predation Theory and Responses to British Decline

Predation theory, in contrast, suggests that both the United States and Soviet Union should support the United Kingdom in 1945–47, only for the strategies to diverge as the Soviet Union becomes predatory after the second half of 1947. These policies reflect the incentives both states had to retain Britain as a partner against the other in the postwar environment, the U.S. success in this effort, and the eventual loss of the United Kingdom as a potential Soviet partner.

BRITAIN: SHIFTING STRATEGIC VALUE TO THE UNITED STATES AND SOVIET UNION

The dominant factor driving U.S. and Soviet strategy should be the United Kingdom's varying strategic value. In brief, the United Kingdom offered (1) high strategic value to both the United States and Soviet Union in the period immediately after World War II, followed by (2) continued high strategic value to the United States but low strategic value to the Soviet Union from late 1947. Looking back after seven decades, it is easy to forget that postwar Europe was initially a multipolar environment as the United States, Soviet Union, and United Kingdom emerged from the war with the capabilities to affect one another's security.[79] Britain's decline would soon transform this system into the familiar postwar bipolar arrangement, but at first, the country was roughly on par with the United States and Soviet Union.[80] After all, Britain was the only major power to fight against Germany from the beginning of World War II through 1945, and had mobilized an extensive economic-military apparatus to prosecute the war. War helps reveal the comparative strength of different nations, and Britain's performance suggested that it might be the weakest of the great powers yet could still make a good stand.[81] Indeed, British resiliency and economic-military capacity during the war implied that once Britain repaired its wartime damage, it might arrest its relative losses, stabilize its position, and play a significant role in European politics.[82] With Germany occupied by Britain, the United States, and the Soviet Union,[83] and with France a shell of its prewar self, the wartime Big Three looked set to dominate postwar European politics.[84]

Geography reinforced Britain's importance: given its location off Europe's northwestern coast and between the United States and Soviet Union, the country was positioned to assist either state. As World War II experience suggested, Britain could provide the United States a staging area and bases for any effort to deter or defeat Soviet actions in Europe.[85] Equally important, Britain's relative proximity to the Soviet Union meant that the country was well placed to help obstruct any Soviet effort to dominate Europe. Just as U.S. planners in 1939–40 expected Germany to first exhaust itself fighting Britain and France, so U.S. strategists could expect Britain to weaken the Soviet Union prior to U.S. involvement while keeping the Western Hemisphere isolated from a conflict.[86] Similarly for the Soviet Union, Britain guarded the maritime and air approaches to Europe. Hence, it could theoretically help keep the United States at bay and might even act as an independent military force that the United States would have to defeat before attacking the Soviet Union.[87] Both states, meanwhile, could also use Britain as a first line of defense against a possible German resurgence.

Finally, Britain was politically available as a partner for both the United States and the Soviet Union, at least until the second half of 1947. Admittedly, many British policymakers in the governments of Prime Ministers Winston Churchill (1940–45) and Clement Attlee (1945–51) sought deeper Anglo-American ties even at the expense of the Anglo-Soviet relationship. That said, a significant portion of the British public and many members of the Labour Party wanted to keep Britain on friendly terms with both the United States and the Soviet Union, hoping to maneuver between the two without linking Britain too firmly to either.[88] If anything, the victory of the British Labour Party in the 1945 elections and presence of committed leftists among Labour supporters in Parliament augured a leftward tilt in British politics that might rebound to the Soviet Union's advantage.[89] Meanwhile, the United States' initial ambivalence about cooperating with Britain (described in the next chapter) ensured that Anglo-American relations remained distant, creating an opening for a Soviet bid for British partnership.

It was only after the second half of 1947 that Britain's availability as a partner to the United States and Soviet Union diverged. At that time, British efforts to coordinate foreign and military positions with the United States had been increasing for more than a year. Just as important, repeated Soviet attempts to engage Britain in discussing Anglo-Soviet relations and to develop a similarly close association faltered.[90] The success of cold warriors such as Foreign Secretary Ernest Bevin and Attlee in contests with Labour members inclined to a neutral or even a pro-Soviet position also suggested Britain's political unreliability for Soviet purposes.[91] In short, Britain was available as a U.S. partner throughout 1945–49, but was a viable Soviet partner only before the latter part of 1947. As British Defense Minister Albert Alexander commented in 1948, "Up to the period ending December, 1947, there was always a hope that we could come to perhaps a fairly speedy understanding in matters which were outstanding" with the Soviet Union. Afterwards that hope was gone.[92]

Under these conditions, Great Britain presented (1) both the United States and Soviet Union with high strategic value in 1945–47, but (2) diverging strategic value—high for the United States, low for the Soviet Union—from late 1947 onward. With other great powers around and the United Kingdom positioned, potentially capable, and available to help in 1945–47, the United States and Soviet Union alike had incentives to treat Britain with kid gloves and adopt a supportive strategy. In context, support would help the Soviet Union and the United States address three problems. First, it would help each side seek the United Kingdom's assistance against the other while limiting the costs of balancing a peer competitor. Given the postwar situation, this means taking military, economic, and diplomatic steps that work in some fashion to Britain's advantage to sustain Anglo-American or Anglo-Soviet relations. Second, support prevents the other side from unilaterally gaining the United Kingdom as a partner. Policymakers are expected to worry about losing Britain as a counterweight in the distribution of power, while emphasizing the strategic advantages of Anglo-American or Anglo-Soviet cooperation. Finally, support minimizes fruitless security competitions: not only might Britain strike out against the United States or—more likely—Soviet Union, but reckless British actions might provoke a U.S.-Soviet clash that neither the United States nor the Soviet Union sought. Done properly, supporting Britain minimizes the risk of an Anglo-American or Anglo-Soviet competition while providing tools to restrain Britain from pursuing risky behavior.

After 1947, however, Soviet strategy should become predatory while U.S. strategy should stay supportive. Again, this change in Soviet behavior reflects the United Kingdom's growing unavailability as a prospective partner and transition from high to low strategic value to the Soviet Union. Under these circumstances, predation limits Britain's ability to contribute to an Anglo-American front and, by gaining at the United Kingdom's expense, improves the Soviet Union's relative position. To this end, Soviet leaders will reject steps that might make life easier for the United Kingdom, instead adopting policies singularly beneficial for the Soviet Union and harmful to Britain.

BRITISH MILITARY POSTURE SHAPED
U.S. AND SOVIET ASSERTIVENESS

Just because the United Kingdom's varying strategic value incentivizes U.S. and Soviet support or predation, however, does not mean that these strategies will be equally assertive over time. Rather, shifts in British military posture should affect whether the United States and the Soviet Union engage Britain with intense or limited means. Especially important should be the collapse of British military posture in the latter part of 1946 and early 1947. As British posture shifts from robust to weak, we anticipate that the United States and the Soviet Union will more assertively aid the United Kingdom before the Soviet Union attempts to undermine the United Kingdom from late 1947 onward.

The United Kingdom: Robust Military Posture until Late 1946 Despite the widening lead of the Soviet Union and United States in the distribution of power, the United Kingdom maintained a robust military posture in Europe from 1945 through late 1946. This posture consisted of several interlocking elements.[93] First, Great Britain maintained a large and reasonably well-trained military in and around Europe. These forces gave the country a strong peacetime base of operations that provided leverage in diplomatic negotiations with the Soviet Union and United States, protected the sea and air lines of communication around the Continent, and ensured stability within occupied areas of Europe.[94] Tellingly, policymakers such as Bevin fought to sustain British strength in 1945–46 despite pressure to save money by reducing defense spending and calls from within the Labour Party to find resources to construct a British welfare state.[95] As Attlee told the Cabinet in early 1946, "there was no doubt that the nation could not afford either the manpower or the money for forces of the size suggested by the Chiefs of Staff. A cut in the size of the forces was unavoidable. The cut could not be large in June [1946], mainly for reasons of foreign policy . . . but it would have to be drastic after that date."[96] Some military reductions went forward, but the resulting scheme preserved British access to Western Europe, Southeastern Europe, and the Mediterranean/Middle East while maintaining the British occupation zone in Germany, as policymakers saw these areas as vital to British security given their war-making potential and location.[97] To this end, Britain reduced its footprint in Asia and Africa, pouring its remaining resources into maintaining a large force equivalent to several divisions in Germany (a comparable force was maintained in the Middle East).[98] These units were joined by additional troops based in Austria, Italy, and Greece, and supported by airpower from the Continent and around the Mediterranean/Middle East. Although further drawdowns were planned after 1947, Britain's efforts were such that the country had the second-largest military in Europe through 1946 (table 2.1).

Table 2.1 Military forces in Europe, 1946–47

Date	Ground and Air Force Personnel in Europe		
	United Kingdom	United States	Soviet Union
June–July 1946	>342,900	330,000	1,600,000
Winter 1946–47	>252,950	181,000	unknown
July–December 1947	>219,970	117,000	1,655,000

United Kingdom and Soviet military strength does not include forces based in their home territories. U.S. military strength from Walter Elkins, "United States Forces European Theater," accessed June 2016, https://www.usarmygermany.com/Sont.htm?https&&&www.usarmygermany.com/Units/Occupation/USAREUR_HqUSFET.htm. Soviet strength is from Central Intelligence Group, "Effect of Demobilization on Soviet Military Potential," September 20, 1946, in *Assessing the Soviet Threat: The Early Cold War Years*, ed. Woodrow J. Kuhns (Washington, DC: Center for the Study of Intelligence, 2007), 83, and Cristann Gibson, "Patterns of Demobilization: The US and USSR after World War Two" (PhD diss., University of Denver, 1983), 309. British strength is estimated from figures in Chiefs of Staff, "Size of the Armed Forces—30th June, 1946 and 31st December, 1946," Appendix A, February 13, 1946, DO(46) 20, NA; Chiefs of Staff, "Call-Up of the Forces in the Transitional Period," May 10, 1946, DO(46) 66, NA; Secretary of State for War, "Size of the Army at 31st December 1946," Annex, July 15, 1946, DO(46) 91, NA. Figure for July–December 1947 is given by subtracting from the Winter 1946–47 figure the planned army reductions for late 1947, as reported in Minister of Defence, "Strength of the Armed Forces," and Annexes, August 2, 1947, DO(47) 63, NA. Note that British figures do not include British air force personnel, such that total British forces are likely higher than the reported numbers.

Second, British forces were prepared for a variety of missions. Admittedly, the land forces deployed in Europe focused predominantly on occupation duties in Germany, Austria, and Italy.[99] However, British units were still prepared (albeit in limited form) to fight conventional wars, as British leaders worked to sustain unit performance and reliability by improving pay and delaying the release of World War II draftees.[100] Equally important, strategists designed British forces—especially air and naval units—to make a good showing in another great power conflict. No war was expected in the near future, but British planners hedged their bets by preparing air, sea, and land forces to serve as the nucleus for larger forces that would be mobilized if hostilities erupted.[101]

Furthermore, although British leaders debated until mid-1947 whether Britain should commit its forces to a continental defense or adopt a strategy emphasizing long-range air power and maritime dominance, British strategy in practice was a mix of both approaches.[102] Standing forces in Europe would defend as far forward for as long as possible, while airpower staging from Britain and around the Mediterranean/Middle East attrited an opponent's strength and ability to wage war; to this end, planners worked to keep over two dozen heavy bomber squadrons in Europe as a deterrent and striking force.[103] Behind this glacis, Britain would prepare for a drawn-out struggle. In effect, British forces were optimized for deterrence and defense:[104] standing forces would delineate a defensive perimeter extending from the United Kingdom as far to the east as possible to threaten damage against an aggressor's military and/or homeland, while the country mobilized to ensure that an aggressor suffered additional future punishment.[105] There remained no margin for what the undersecretary of state for war termed "unforeseen commitments," but adversaries would need to think twice before challenging British security.[106]

Finally, and as the preceding discussion suggests, British air and sea power ensured that Britain enjoyed reliable lines of communication and could project power when and where challenged. Postwar British policy concentrated the bulk of British air and naval forces in and around Europe.[107] In particular, strategists focused on retaining bases in and around Europe from which British bombers could strike across the Continent, including into the Soviet Union.[108] Similarly, naval planners focused on keeping sufficient forces around home waters and in the Mediterranean to protect trade routes, ensure that British units could be moved and/or resupplied, and prevent prospective opponents from operating freely. Not coincidentally, British forces in Greece and Italy abetted this objective by keeping Greek and Italian territory—which could otherwise be used to disrupt the sea lines of communication—in friendly hands.

British Military Posture Collapsed Starting in Late 1946 to Early 1947 Starting at the turn of 1946–47, however, economic exigencies led to a collapse of British military strength. To be clear, British strategists had understood since at least mid-1946 that economic constraints, reinforced by demands for spending on social welfare programs, would leave the armed forces below the levels necessary for Britain to meet its foreign commitments and protect British security from late 1946 onward.[109] In the winter of 1946–47, however, the widening gap between income and expenditures mandated even more drastic cuts.[110] Chancellor of the Exchequer Hugh Dalton put the point crisply in January 1947, warning that "we cannot afford either the money or the men" to meet Britain's commitments.[111] Although Bevin and Attlee again argued that Britain needed military strength for leverage against the United States and the Soviet Union, economic pressures meant that additional military cuts were unavoidable and, given previous reductions, had to come from Europe.[112] The early months of 1947 thus saw the military accept an additional 15 percent budget reduction;[113] by the middle of the year, economic conditions prompted Attlee to withdraw nearly a third of British forces overseas and call for an accelerated reduction in the total number of British forces.[114] This trend subsequently accelerated, such that defense spending in 1948–49 was less than half that in 1945–46.[115]

Even as growing tensions with the Soviet Union led British strategists to place greater emphasis on defending Western Europe, these cuts weakened British military posture (table 2.2).[116] First, reduced military expenditures required draconian cuts to military forces stationed in and around Europe. Starting in late 1946, policymakers began eliminating Britain's military presence in Greece, Austria, and Italy.[117] As economic pressure mounted, strategists also planned for a serious drawdown of British strength in Germany, and by mid-1947, considered virtually abandoning Britain's presence on the Continent while keeping only token forces in place.[118] Although outright withdrawals were delayed in 1947–48, retrenchment continued as pressure to reduce military expenditures grew.[119] In the middle of 1948, the country barely had the equivalent of two understrength divisions in all of Europe, with additional reductions ongoing (table 2.3).[120]

Table 2.2 Changes in British military posture

Robust Posture, 1945–46	Weak Posture, 1947–49
Forces deployed and sustained in Western Europe	Forces withdrawn from much of Western Europe
Relatively large standing forces slowly being reequipped	Military reductions accelerating
Forces optimized for occupation duties, but able to fight if required	Loss of trained personnel and force multipliers limits operational capacity
Veterans in force aid unit reliability	Units composed largely of short-term conscripts of uncertain reliability
Naval and air forces ensure stable lines of communication and power projection	Lines of communication uncertain owing to air and naval reductions; unclear if reinforcements can deploy to affect crisis or wartime outcomes

Table 2.3 Britain's retrenchment from Europe, 1946–48

	Mid-1946 (Deployed)	Late 1946 Retrenchment Plan	Late 1947 Retrenchment Plan (Projected)	Late 1948 (Deployed)[a]
Germany				
Armored divisions	1	1	0	0
Infantry divisions	2	2	0	0
Occupational divisions	1	0	0	0
Armored brigades	1	1	0	1
Infantry brigades	1	0	1	5[b]
Armored car regiments	5	3	0	4[c]
Southeast Europe (Austria, Italy, Greece)				
Armored divisions	1	0	0	0
Infantry divisions	3[d]	0	0	0
Occupational divisions	2	0	0	0
Armored brigades	0	0	0	0
Infantry brigades	0	0	0	2
Armored regiments	2	0	0	0
EUROPEAN TOTAL	10+ divisions	3+ divisions	1 brigade (plus 2 training divisions and 2 training brigades)	8+ brigades

Data is from Chiefs of Staff, "Call-Up of the Forces in the Transitional Period," May 10, 1946, DO(46) 66, NA; Secretary of State for War, "Size of the Army at 31st December 1946," July 15, 1946, DO(46) 91, NA; Chiefs of Staff, "Strength of the Armed Forces at 31st December, 1946 and 31st March, 1948," November 8, 1946, DO(46) 135, NA; Minister of Defence, "The Defence Position," and Annexes, July 26, 1948, DO(48) 46, NA; L.V. Scott, *Conscription and the Attlee Government* (New York: Clarendon Press, 1993), appendix 5. Precise figures for mid-1946 are difficult to obtain but can be inferred from statements and projected figures for late 1946—given in reference to mid-1946 deployments—in the above documents. Most 1948 deployment figures are from Scott, *Conscription*, though unit readiness and armored car regiments are from Minister of Defence, "Defence Position" and Annexes, July 26, 1948. Scott and the defence minister in July 1948 report different unit formations, but roughly the same deployed forces.

[a]All units in static positions as of July 1948.

[b]4 infantry brigades and 1 parachute brigade.

[c]As of July 1948.

[d]Includes one ad hoc division in Greece.

Air and naval forces suffered similar losses. The Royal Navy warned that the sea lines of communication were imperiled, as dozens of ships were mothballed and remaining vessels staffed at reduced levels.[121] Meanwhile, manpower reductions, equipment losses, and budget cuts left the Royal Air Force below the required levels: where British strategists in 1946 criticized plans to keep 352 long-range bombers in Europe as offering "meagre" strength with which to deter an aggressor, there were only 144 bombers of questionable operational effectiveness in service by mid-1948.[122] Collectively, the British military was simply too small and ill-prepared to present a credible deterrent.[123] Not only was it doubtful that standing forces could give an opponent pause, but it became increasingly uncertain whether the limited reinforcements—roughly two divisions and a small number of airplanes—that could be mobilized in a crisis could be deployed quickly enough to affect a conflict or be numerous enough to matter.[124]

Second, the quality and reliability of remaining forces suffered.[125] Budget cuts, coming on top of previous reductions, led to a large and unexpectedly rapid drawdown of personnel, alongside the loss of skilled World War II veterans. Although the military could have replaced these losses with new recruits, budgetary limits foreclosed this option as military pay stagnated and high-quality, long-service volunteers were difficult to obtain in a tight postwar labor market.[126] Making matters worse, British draftees had their terms of service capped at eighteen months after 1948.[127] This short stint meant that personnel lacked the experience to do their jobs effectively—by the time draftees acquired the needed skills, their commitments would end and they would depart—while limiting the size of the force that British leaders could call upon.[128] Adding to the dilemma, military reductions asymmetrically affected headquarters, maintenance, and logistical support units: money and remaining personnel went to sustaining forces in the field rather than to the force multipliers that ensured staying power and battlefield effectiveness.[129] To top things off, falling military budgets hindered reequipping remaining forces with modern weapons such as jet aircraft and new tanks.[130]

Finally, accompanying falling numbers, reliability, and quality was a concomitant decrease in the military's ability to conduct specified missions. Simply put, carrying out the deterrent strategy laid down after 1945 required the British military to maintain a presence in Western Europe and fight reasonably well—even if it was ultimately defeated—if war erupted. By 1947, the ability to succeed in this latter mission was in doubt, as British leaders opted to focus on what Minister of Defence Alexander termed "visible offensive strength"—the show of strength rather than real capabilities.[131] In practice, British forces were designed to simply conduct occupation duties and allow the United Kingdom to wave the flag when required, while lacking the training to conduct wartime operations.[132] By the middle of 1948, this situation was sufficiently advanced that British military leaders warned that army units in Europe "consist mainly of young soldiers" of uncertain reliability and with an administrative organization "not designed for war," while the Royal Air Force's "fighting efficiency [in wartime] would be low owing to a lack of experienced ground personnel."[133] Although British forces would fight if necessary, it was doubtful that forces which still needed to be "reorganized and trained" as combat units could perform the requisite missions.[134]

Prediction: Shifts in Posture Affected the Assertiveness of U.S. and Soviet Strategies Variation in Britain's military posture should influence U.S. and

Soviet policy toward the United Kingdom. Throughout 1945–46, both Soviet and U.S. policymakers should worry about the strategic challenge posed by the United Kingdom. On one level, a militarily capable Britain might undertake preventive action against either state. Given the Soviet Union's location and U.S. efforts to exit Europe after 1945, this should be a particular concern for Soviet leaders. Although highly unlikely, it was not beyond the realm of possibility that Britain would use its remaining strength to try to set back the Soviet Union as much as possible before British power declined further.[135] At the same time, militarily robust Britain also posed a more general entrapment risk to both states: given that a strong Britain might provoke either the Soviet Union or the United States into rivalry or war, both sides should be fearful of being ensnared by Britain in an unwanted competition.

Starting in late 1946, however, the collapse of British military strength should eliminate the British challenge to U.S. and Soviet security. Instead of seeing Britain as capable enough to cause problems, U.S. and Soviet policymakers are apt to view the United Kingdom as weak and vulnerable. Hence, we expect the anticipated costs of being manipulated, attacked, or trapped by Britain to disappear—even if Britain wanted to, it could not craft an independent foreign policy that challenged other great powers. U.S. and Soviet policymakers are therefore likely to see Britain as needing either to find a foreign patron or to accept further losses—possibly including its independence.

PREDICTIONS: DIFFERENT SUPPORTIVE AND PREDATORY STRATEGIES

In contrast to many competing accounts, the initial combination of Britain's high strategic value to the United States and Soviet Union amid shifting British posture means that the United States and Soviet Union should adopt a Bolstering strategy until the turn of 1946–47 and a Strengthening strategy afterward. This means that U.S. and Soviet policymakers will try to prevent Britain from exiting the great power ranks. Put differently, even if the United States and Soviet Union are more supportive of Britain after late 1946 to early 1947 than before, the United Kingdom's high strategic value means that U.S. and Soviet policymakers will still generally want to prevent Britain from being so weak that it can no longer help against other major threats. Both rising states, in short, should want to retain Britain's strategic assistance.

Still, before the winter of 1946–47, decision makers should recognize that being too supportive carries large risks. In context, this means that U.S. and Soviet policymakers should be leery of committing significant resources or effort to assisting Britain when British strength meant that such actions might embolden Britain; provoke other states by suggesting the formation of a threatening alliance with Britain; or facilitate Britain's arming or launching a preventive war. U.S. and Soviet policymakers should therefore remain attentive to signs that even limited backing is antagonizing the other rising state or facilitating reckless British behavior. Above all, we expect U.S. and Soviet policymakers to advance clear rationales for their policies: they are likely to emphasize the desirability of sustaining and relying on Britain for use against the other great power, while also highlighting the importance of offering only limited aid given Britain's ongoing challenge to U.S and Soviet interests. In internal deliberations, U.S. and Soviet leaders will tend to emphasize the need to play for time vis-à-vis the United Kingdom by limiting U.S. and Soviet support.

These trends should change in the winter of 1946–47. Initially, both the United States and Soviet Union should pursue Strengthening strategies. With British military strength collapsing, policymakers in both the United States and the Soviet Union will no longer be concerned with the dangers of intensely backing the United Kingdom. Instead, they are likely to be galvanized into offering intensive support by worries of both losing the United Kingdom as a partner with which to confront other great powers and of seeing other great powers gain at Britain's expense. To this end, decision makers should recognize that limiting support for Britain is no longer viable if Britain is to be used against either the United States (from the Soviet perspective) or the Soviet Union (from the U.S. perspective). Leaders will thus generally ignore signs of opposition by other great powers and remaining hints of British security challenges, calculating instead that intense backing offers tools to shape British policy in a manner conducive to U.S. or Soviet aims. Finally, the rising states will provide Britain with significant economic, military, and diplomatic backing but—crucially—should calibrate their assistance to ensure that Britain operates as a junior partner in their postwar plans. The result is likely to be parallel U.S. and Soviet efforts to assist Britain, albeit on U.S. and Soviet terms.

However, while the United States will continue its Strengthening strategy until Britain exits the great powers at the end of the 1940s, the Soviet Union will transition to a predatory strategy starting in late 1947 falling between Weakening and Relegation. As noted above, the failure of pro-Soviet voices inside the British government coupled with Britain's growing alignment with the United States undermined Britain's strategic value to the Soviet Union after the second half of 1947. In combination with Britain's weak military posture, this is likely to create an opportunity for the Soviet Union to attempt to knock Britain out of the great power ranks with few concerns surrounding Britain's ability to defend itself. To this end, Soviet leaders should see an opportunity to gain at Britain's expense, to deny Britain as a capable partner to the United States, and to position the Soviet Union to compete with an Anglo-American front. In this situation, the only factor militating against intense Soviet predation is the risk of the United States using force on Brit-

Table 2.4 Summary of competing predictions

Argument	Key Predictions	Mechanisms
Predation Theory	(1) The United States and Soviet Union adopt Bolstering strategies through 1946–47; (2) both adopt Strengthening strategies in early 1947; (3) U.S. and Soviet strategies diverge from late 1947, as the United States continues to use a Strengthening strategy and the Soviet Union pursues predation	Through late 1947, the United States and the Soviet Union both try to gain Britain as a partner, with assertiveness varying due to shifts in British military posture; after Anglo-American alignment tightens in 1947, the Soviet Union tries to weaken the Anglo-American bloc, while the United States rebuilds its British ally
Security Dilemma	The United States supports and the Soviet Union preys upon the United Kingdom from 1945 on	British signals and reassurance convince U.S. policymakers that the United Kingdom seeks to maintain status quo in Europe, leading to cooperation; Anglo-Soviet mistrust, reinforced by geography and the state of military technology, generate insecurity and Soviet predation
Ideological Distance	The United States supports and the Soviet Union preys upon the United Kingdom from 1945 on	Anglo-American ideological similarity ensures smooth U.S.-U.K. relations, abetting U.S. support; Anglo-Soviet ideological distance raises Soviet threat perceptions, encouraging predation
Economic Interdependence	The United States supports and the Soviet Union preys upon the United Kingdom from 1945 on	Anglo-American economic integration gives the United States a stake in Britain's survival as a capable great power; the absence of Anglo-Soviet economic integration does little to inhibit Soviet predation
Ideational Arguments: Open Door Thesis vs. Marxist Theory	The United States intensely preys upon Britain in 1945–47 and engages in limited predation afterward; the Soviet Union supports Britain in 1945–47 and engages in limited predation afterward	U.S. policymakers undermine British strength to prevent British challenges to U.S. extra-regional hegemony, tempered only when the United States begins to reconstruct Europe; Soviet leaders support Britain to reinforce intra-capitalist differences before revised accounts of Marxist-Leninist theory suggest that cooperation with the capitalist world is infeasible

ain's behalf while Britain rebuilds its strength. Given intensifying American efforts to support Britain, Soviet policymakers should therefore prey on Britain while being careful not to push the United States into using force to protect Britain. In turn, Soviet leaders are likely to carefully monitor trends in Anglo-American relations, adopting intensely predatory efforts if the United States appears unlikely to use force, and using more limited means to prey when the risk of conflict is high.

In short, the different arguments evaluated in this volume present distinct predictions regarding the course and rationale for U.S. and Soviet strategy toward the declining United Kingdom (table 2.4). Arguments based on the security dilemma, economic interdependence, and ideological affinity expect a clear divergence in U.S. and Soviet strategies toward the United Kingdom soon after 1945. According to these theories, prior Anglo-American reassurance, economic interdependence, and ideological similarity should lead the United States to quickly and assertively assist the United Kingdom. Conversely, Anglo-Soviet mistrust, the absence of meaningful or expected economic exchange, and divergent domestic orders should push the Soviet Union to exploit British weaknesses. Conversely, theories based on the particular ideas of U.S. and Soviet elites suggest that it was the United States that preyed on the United Kingdom and the Soviet Union that tried to reinforce British power. These theories hold that while U.S. leaders focused on pushing Britain from the great power ranks as part of an effort to establish U.S. hegemony in Western Europe, Soviet leaders sought a capable Britain as a glacis against a capitalist United States seen as hell-bent on destroying Soviet communism.

For predation theory, in contrast, the United Kingdom's shifting strategic value and military posture suggests that (1) both the United States and the Soviet Union will adopt Bolstering strategies in 1945–46; (2) both rising powers will pursue Strengthening strategies in late 1946 and early 1947; and (3) after late 1947, the United States will sustain its Strengthening strategy, while the Soviet Union adopts a predatory strategy between Weakening and Relegation. Here, initial recognition that Britain's decline will deny both the United States and Soviet Union a valuable partner will propel both sides into trying to keep Britain among the great powers so as to gain its help against and share the costs of confronting the other side. Still, British military posture will influence the assertiveness of U.S. and Soviet efforts: only after British military strength collapses will Soviet and U.S. strategists conclude that it is now safe to intensely back Britain. Yet whereas the United States will intensely support Britain from the winter of 1946–47 onward, burgeoning Anglo-American cooperation and the failure of pro-Soviet voices in British policy circles will cause Soviet policymakers to see the futility of seeking British assistance. In response, Soviet policy will transition again as Soviet policymakers conclude that preying on a Britain now offering low strategic value is the best way to advance Soviet security.

The U.S. and Soviet Response to Britain's Decline

Building on the previous chapter, this chapter evaluates the U.S. and Soviet responses to Britain's postwar decline, showing that predation theory better explains U.S. and Soviet strategies than alternate accounts. Other arguments predict a clear and early divergence in Soviet and U.S. policies toward Britain. Instead, I illustrate below that no such split in U.S. and Soviet strategies occurred in the immediate postwar period. In fact, the United States and the Soviet Union *both* supported Britain at this time, with U.S. and Soviet efforts intensifying as British military posture weakened. These parallel U.S. and Soviet policies are uniquely predicted by predation theory. That said, U.S. and Soviet strategies did eventually diverge after late 1947 as the United States increasingly pursued a Strengthening strategy while the Soviet Union preyed on Britain. Even this change, however, is strongly consistent with my argument but largely incompatible with the alternative explanations. After all, not only was there no change in late 1947 in the intensity of security dilemmas, levels of economic interdependence, domestic ideologies, or the motivating ideas of leading statesmen that might cause U.S. and Soviet policy to change, but a careful reconstruction of U.S. and Soviet policy also shows how Britain's diverging strategic value to the U.S. and the Soviet Union (respectively) drove the ultimate departure in U.S. and Soviet approaches.

This does not mean that there is no evidence backing the alternative arguments. In particular, U.S. strategists often emphasized economic concerns when dealing with Britain in a way that resonates with both interdependence and ideational arguments. Likewise, Soviet arguments sometimes suggested that the security dilemma and ideational logics were at play. Overall, however, the other approaches do not fare as well as my argument in explaining the trajectory of Anglo-American and Anglo-Soviet relations in 1945–49. Baldly stated, the course and conduct of U.S. and Soviet strategies with regard to the declining Great Britain are best explained by predation theory.

One clarification is necessary at the start. While this chapter is focused on a period in which the familiar cleavages of Cold War Europe emerged, it is not about the origins of the Cold War.[1] In Raymond Aron's phrase, the United States and Soviet Union were "enemies by position," with competition probable due to their rival ideologies and immense size.[2] Instead, the chapter explains how U.S. and Soviet strategists dealt with the United Kingdom in the context of the emerging Cold War, with events in Europe the backdrop for evolving Anglo-American and Anglo-Soviet relations. Although, U.S.-Soviet rivalry clearly reinforced the incentives both states had to find partners, the rivalry did not dictate U.S. and Soviet behavior vis-à-vis Britain. Instead, and in contrast to what one expects if Cold War competition alone drove U.S. and Soviet policies toward Britain, the evidence shows that policymakers in both states were initially reluctant to intensely assist Britain out of concern that doing so would foster East-West competition. And, just as important, it took Britain's military collapse in 1946–47 to catalyze Soviet and U.S. efforts to improve British fortunes. In short, U.S. and Soviet policies toward Britain were driven by factors related to but separate from Cold War dynamics. By extension, had Britain not fallen from the ranks of the great powers, there might still have been U.S.-Soviet competition, but Britain's role in it—and the accompanying U.S. and Soviet policies—would have looked substantially different.

The Strategic Context of British Decline

World War II altered the strategic map of Europe. With Germany occupied and France devastated, the end of the war left a power vacuum and unsettled conditions on the Continent that could sully great power relations. Entering the postwar era, the United States, United Kingdom, and Soviet Union were determined to prevent a German resurgence that could once again threaten European security.[3] With each state occupying a portion of Germany, however, this also meant that unless the German issue was handled cooperatively, each side could end up threatening and threatened by others. After all, if great power cooperation faltered and any side established sole control of Germany, then that side would be positioned to mobilize German economic and military potential for its own purposes. This would threaten the other great powers, inviting countervailing moves that could result in rivalry or war.[4] In the early postwar world, there was significant room for miscalculation with possibly dire consequences for the United States, United Kingdom, and Soviet Union alike.

Within this environment, British policymakers focused on preventing any one state from dominating Europe. In context, this meant the Soviet Union.[5] Yet because the Soviet Union was stronger than the United Kingdom, the latter would be hard-pressed to offset Soviet capabilities. "Time," wrote Deputy Permanent Under-Secretary of State for Foreign Affairs Sir Orme Sargent in July 1945, "is not necessarily on our side," partly because Britain was "the weakest and geographically smallest of the three Great Powers."[6] Left to its own devices, the country would need to commit a growing share of its scarce resources to blocking Soviet moves. While viable in the short term, this option risked long-term disaster as it promised an Anglo-Soviet rivalry that a waning Britain could neither sustain nor win.[7]

British leaders therefore sought a firm U.S. security commitment and assistance.[8] Prime Minister Winston Churchill focused on this problem even before World War II ended, telling colleagues in 1943 that "Germany is finished, though it may take some time to clean up the mess. The real problem now is Russia. I can't get the Americans to see it."[9] Within a year of the war's end, Churchill—by then out of office—was warning of an "Iron Curtain" dividing Europe into rival blocs.[10] Wartime experience, moreover, provided room for British optimism. After all, Anglo-American leaders had coordinated military strategy during the conflict, and the United States had provided extensive economic aid as the financial affairs of the two states were heavily integrated.[11] Equally significant, potential stumbling blocks in Anglo-American relations were gradually reduced through wartime experience. For instance, where the early stages of the war saw the United States focus on undermining the British Empire by encouraging decolonization and opening British-controlled areas to U.S. economic influence, by the end of the war U.S. policymakers had muted criticism of British colonial rule and agreed to continue Lend-Lease after the conflict to facilitate Britain's economic recovery.[12] Seeking to capitalize on the wartime relationship, British leaders desired a peacetime ally that could share the costs of preventing Soviet aggrandizement, help rebuild Western Europe, and abet British recovery.[13]

Of course, if the United States retrenched, Britain could attempt to take the lead in constructing a Western European grouping by using whatever resources it could to help France, Belgium, the Netherlands, and other states in the area recover. Still, this was a second-best option, since Britain's problems meant the requisite resources were unlikely to be available, while unilaterally building up Western Europe risked antagonizing the United States and aggravating relations with the Soviet Union.[14] Though British leaders occasionally paid lip service to constructing a Western European group able to counterpoise both the United States and Soviet Union, they appear to have understood that U.S. support—or at least acquiescence—was a precondition for the success of any such program.[15] Postwar British security ran through Washington and Moscow.

The U.S. Response to British Decline

Rather than firmly backing the United Kingdom, however, the United States initially tried to limit its diplomatic, military, and economic support. Britain might be declining, but U.S. policymakers assumed that they could, as State

Department official Paul Nitze later recalled, "rely on the British to deal with the wide array of political problems arising out of the chaos of a world destroyed by two wars."[16] This was especially true in Europe: though the British Empire extended to Asia, the Middle East, and beyond, Europe was the center of early postwar strategy debates so far as the Anglo-American relationship was concerned. Relying on Britain to manage Continental politics would allow the United States to distance itself from European security debates, conserving resources, minimizing risks, and limiting the domestic political repercussions of injecting itself into the active management of European affairs.[17] Sustained despite mounting U.S.-Soviet tensions in 1945–46, American policy only transitioned to a Strengthening strategy after British military strength collapsed in the winter of 1946–47. Although still seeking to minimize commitments in Europe, the United States then began intensely supporting Britain.

BOLSTERING IN 1945–46: SEEKING A GOLDILOCKS SOLUTION

As World War II came to an end in Europe, the Roosevelt administration resisted British efforts to commit the United States to an active role in postwar Europe.[18] This was particularly the case in security affairs. In Roosevelt's vision, the "Four Policemen"—meaning the three great powers plus China—would have responsibility for security within their respective areas of operation. Britain would thus have primary responsibility for Western Europe:

> In as much as the United States is approximately 3,500 miles removed from Europe, it is not its natural task to bear the postwar burden of re-constituting France, Italy and the Balkans. This is properly the task of Great Britain which is far more vitally interested than is the United States. The United States will be only too glad to retire all its military forces from Europe as soon as this is feasible.[19]

This did not mean abandoning Europe, as the United States retained a vested interest in ensuring that no single state dominated the Continent, and in guaranteeing that it could influence European diplomatic, economic, and military debates when U.S. concerns dictated. Day-to-day management of European politics, however, would be left to others as the United States capped its commitment and withdrew its forces.[20]

Nor was this just talk. Plans presented before the 1945 Yalta and Potsdam summits envisioned a de facto spheres of influence solution for Europe, whereby Eastern Europe would fall into the Soviet orbit; Western Europe and the Mediterranean would largely be a British domain, with the United States assisting when necessary; and Germany would be effectively divided.[21] Publicly, of course, officials in the Roosevelt and Truman administrations denounced spheres of influence as dangerous vestiges of the realpolitik that had precipitated the world wars. In private, however, U.S. leaders quietly embraced a spheres arrangement as the most efficient path to limit American involvement in European politics while still keeping the Continent's economic and military might from falling under the sway of a single state.[22] This approach also had the added benefit of seeming to help prevent great power conflict. As the Joint Chiefs of Staff and State Department discussed in late 1945, another war was most likely only if there were "a breakdown in peaceful relations among Britain, Russia, and the United States." To avoid this, the United States needed to preserve the existing "relationship in military potential" among the wartime coalition and, since leaders assumed the United States had no hostile designs itself, prevent or moderate competition between the United Kingdom and the Soviet Union.[23]

This desire to pass the buck to Britain while sustaining friendly relations among the great powers provided the initial rationale for the United States to adopt a Bolstering strategy. On one level, keeping Anglo-American relations warm but limited might alleviate Soviet concerns about an Anglo-American front directed against it. "Having regard to the inherent suspicions of the Russians," Chief of Staff William Leahy wrote Secretary of State Cordell Hull in 1944 (advice that was also delivered verbatim to Truman in 1945), "to present Russia with any agreement on [European security] as between the British and ourselves, prior to consultation with Russia, might well result in starting a train of events that would lead eventually to a situation we most wish to avoid"—namely, growing tensions and a war in which the Soviet Union might conquer continental Europe.[24] Hence, avoiding a tight Anglo-American relationship reduced the chance that the process of arranging a European settlement would upset the Soviet Union and imperil European stability.[25]

At the same time, limiting the Anglo-American relationship helped protect the United States from British machinations that could entangle it in undesired competitions. Britain might be declining, but it could still cause problems. Even as Leahy cautioned against arousing Soviet suspicions, he also warned that either the Soviet Union or Britain could provoke war by "seeking to attach to herself parts of Europe to the disadvantage and possible danger of her potential adversary."[26] Nor was Leahy alone in these warnings, as political confidantes advised Truman that British leaders were "basically more concerned over preserving England's position in Europe than in preserving Peace" and sought to use American power for that purpose.[27] Though the United States regarded Britain as its "first line of defense" and assumed that "any threat to their [British] security would most likely cause armed intervention on our part," distancing the United States from Britain could mitigate the risk of conflict in the first place by neither emboldening Britain nor antagonizing the Soviet Union.[28] Limiting the Anglo-American relationship allowed the United States to retain Britain in the wings as an ally without risking its own security.

To this end, the United States moved in 1945 to restrain Anglo-American relations. Before both Yalta and Potsdam, for example, U.S. policymakers refused to formulate joint positions with their British counterparts for use with the Soviets.[29] Similarly, the United States cooperated more with the Soviets more than with the United Kingdom in the negotiations themselves. At Yalta, for instance, the United States went along with Soviet efforts to set a figure on German reparations ($20 billion overall, with $10 billion for the Soviet Union), rather than accept British calls to leave the matter for later negotiations.[30] The Potsdam Conference followed a similar trajectory as the United States and the Soviet Union negotiated reparations arrangements without British officials present before presenting British leaders with faits accomplis.[31]

Reconstructing Britain's Economy on the Cheap Despite cooling its relationship with Britain, however, the United States still sought to prevent additional British losses. First and foremost, U.S. backing for a spheres settlement and desire for a more limited Anglo-American relationship were not viewed as inimical to British security. Indeed, Truman was expressly advised by the State Department that U.S. policy "must be attuned to events in Europe as a whole and to the consequences of general European conditions on the stability of Great Britain. Specifically, it is not in our interest to deny to the United Kingdom protection against possible dangers from the Soviet Union, especially since the Soviets have established domination of Eastern Europe."[32] And at Potsdam, Truman, Secretary of State James Byrnes, and their aides underscored the point, blocking Soviet efforts to play a role in political developments in Western Europe[33] and proposing that all sides have a free hand in their respective areas of influence.[34] The United States, in other words, implied that Soviet efforts that might harm Britain—above all, attempts to gain influence in Western Europe—would be opposed.

This same desire to protect Britain within limits influenced U.S. efforts, starting in the summer of 1945, to help Britain reconstruct its economy. To be certain, this policy developed in fits and starts and was never as robust as British policymakers desired. In fact, U.S. policy immediately after World War II exacerbated British economic problems by cancelling Lend-Lease after Japan's surrender in contravention of wartime pledges.[35] Because Lend-Lease allowed Britain to import more goods than it could afford, canceling the program left Britain's economy in dire straits: without U.S. assistance, Britain would be unable to pay for the materials necessary for its economic recovery.[36]

Still, U.S. policy changed as it became clear that its efforts harmed Britain. Two different rationales were at play. First, U.S. officials in charge of economic policy worried that an economically faltering Britain—particularly at a time when much of Western Europe was in even worse economic shape—would become a "barrier to rapid progress towards free multilateral payments" and trade that had been agreed at the 1944 Bretton Woods accords.[37] Thus, officials pressed for U.S. assistance to help Britain transition to a liberal economic order.[38]

Second, and equally significant, U.S. policymakers understood that aid to Britain was vital to keeping it in the U.S. camp as tensions with the Soviet Union escalated. "Economic arguments in favor of [assistance] are on the whole much less convincing," Representative Christian Herter told Assistant Secretary of State William Clayton in early 1946, than arguments that economic assistance "may serve us in good stead in holding up a hand of a nation whom we may need badly as a friend because of impending Russian troubles."[39] Officials such as then-undersecretary of state Dean Acheson shared this view, arguing that cancellation of Lend-Lease "knocked the financial bottom out of the whole allied military position."[40] This, in turn, required the United States to assist Britain to prevent, as the historian Randall Woods puts it, an "adventurist policy" by Moscow that exploited British problems.[41] Hoping to avoid Britain's potential loss as a partner and Soviet opportunism, the United States agreed to negotiate a one-time aid package for Britain's recovery intended to tide Britain over for "two or three years" as world trade resumed.

To arrange a deal, British officials led by the economist John Maynard Keynes arrived in Washington in September 1945 seeking a $6 billion grant to defray Britain's $14 billion debt and a foreign exchange deficit projected to reach $3.3–$5.3 billion over the next three years.[42] Yet while desiring Britain's economic recovery, U.S. officials believed that Britain was exaggerating the extent of its economic problems and fretted that unqualified assistance would allow Britain to delay making the pound convertible into dollars in violation of the Bretton Woods agreements.[43] Accordingly, U.S. negotiators countered with narrower terms, offering a $3.5 billion loan at the interest rate paid by the U.S. Treasury with the proviso that Britain make its currency convertible by the start of 1947.[44] Nevertheless, when Keynes and his colleagues protested that Britain needed at least $4–$4.5 billion and an escape clause on convertibility in case of a run on the pound, the United States moved toward the British position. Though still insisting on a loan, the revised terms came closer to Britain's initial request: a $3.75 billion loan at 2 percent interest, repayable over fifty years with interest waived when Britain ran a trade deficit.[45] In return, U.S. negotiators insisted that Britain remove financial controls blocking sterling-dollar convertibility by mid-1947 but, in another concession, agreed that convertibility could be suspended in "exceptional" circumstances.[46]

From the U.S. perspective these were reasonably generous terms.[47] Although the amounts involved were "relatively small," Britain received a loan at below-market rates and with mechanisms to limit the damage if convertibility harmed the British economy.[48] Signed in December 1945 and approved by the U.S. Congress in early 1946, the Anglo-American loan thus saw the United States help Britain's economy within narrow and hard-bargained limits.

Fighting for Britain? A similar story played out in military affairs, where the United States sought to reinforce British security at limited cost. Before the war even ended, the United States committed itself to a rapid peacetime military withdrawal from Europe. Asked how long U.S. military forces might stay in Europe, Roosevelt famously told Churchill and Soviet Premier Joseph Stalin that U.S. troops would likely be gone within "two years."[49] In fact, retrenchment in 1945–46 was even faster than anticipated, as U.S. forces fell from over 3.1 million to barely 300,000 troops in a low state of readiness.[50] Moreover, this withdrawal occurred despite British opposition, as Prime Minister Clement Attlee (who succeeded Churchill in July 1945), Foreign Secretary Ernest Bevin, and other officials saw maintenance of a robust U.S. presence as the best way of deterring—and subsidizing Britain's own need to balance—the Soviet Union.[51]

U.S. strategists disagreed with their British counterparts. The United States recognized, as a 1946 State Department report to the State-War-Navy Coordinating Committee (forerunner of the National Security Council) explained, that "if Soviet Russia is to be denied the hegemony of Europe, [then] the United Kingdom must continue in existence as the principal power in Western Europe."[52] To this end, the United States was even willing to accept "political arrangements" for a British-dominated Western European economic and military bloc.[53] Still, an overly strong U.S. commitment to British security seemed dangerous. As former Ambassador to the Soviet Union Joseph Davies explained to Truman in the spring of 1945, not only would a firm commitment scare Soviet leaders into thinking the United States and United Kingdom were "ganging up" against them, but the British themselves had ulterior motives in seeking "American manpower and resources to sustain Britain's 'lead' in Europe."[54] Other advisers—including Secretary of War Henry Stimson and political aide Harry Hopkins—agreed, warning Truman of what Robert Hathaway describes as "British balance-of-power machinations in Europe and of Churchill's obvious desire to enlist American might in the creation of a solid bloc opposing the Russians."[55] Britain, the Joint Intelligence Staff argued, sought "to improve her position in every possible way in order to bring her more nearly to Russia's level," risking a conflict that would "rapidly involve other countries so that global warfare would again result."[56] Under these conditions, intensive U.S. support could both abet British misbehavior and—as Leahy had cautioned in 1944—antagonize the Soviet Union. In short, as Hopkins emphasized to Secretary of the Navy James Forrestal, "It was of vital importance that we not be maneuvered into a position where Great Britain had us lined up with them as a bloc against Russia to implement England's European policy."[57]

Realizing that British opposition to the Soviet Union depended "on the extent to which the British government believed it could count on American *military* support [emphasis in original]," U.S. leaders responded by loosening the Anglo-American military relationship.[58] Within weeks of the war's end, for example, the United States curtailed the activities of the combined boards and Combined Chiefs of Staff that had coordinated the joint war effort. Though British officials tried to sustain joint military planning, U.S. military leaders demurred, arguing "Matters relating to post-war armies are . . . not susceptible to combined military commitments. Any arrangements which the British wish to make on these subjects are beyond the purview of the United States Chiefs of Staff and should be taken up on the governmental level."[59] By the winter of 1945–46, British officers stationed in Washington reported difficulty garnering information on U.S. military policy from their American counterparts.

Military plans further reflected the United States' effort to limit its support for Britain. At the time, strategists assumed that the most likely source of great power conflict would be an Anglo-Soviet clash in Europe or the Middle East that Britain was unlikely to win. As U.S. military analysts concluded, because Britain's defeat would "eliminate from Eurasia the last bulwark of resistance to Russian aggression," the United States had a strong interest in assisting Britain against the Soviet Union.[60] Nevertheless, the scope of this assistance was pointedly limited at first, as military plans left it unclear whether and when the United States would intervene in a military contest on Britain's behalf. In fact, plans in the winter and spring of 1946 raised the possibility that that the United States might first stay away from an Anglo-Soviet fight, withdrawing its remaining forces from Europe and intervening only after several months.[61] In the interim, the Soviets were expected to quickly overrun Western Europe and subject Britain to air and missile attack. This would have a disastrous effect on British security and might force Britain to surrender. Even after intervening, meanwhile, the United States intended to attack the Soviet Union using long-range air power, leaving Western Europe under Soviet control and Britain exposed to ongoing Soviet assault.[62] Nor were these plans just talk, as the United States avoided acquiring bases in or near Europe even while gaining overseas hubs in South America, Asia, and Africa.[63] By virtue of this system, the United States would not find itself automatically committed to a fight in Europe and could decide whether and when to come to Britain's defense.[64]

The U.S. approach left Britain facing a significant dilemma. Absent a clear U.S. military commitment, not only would Britain need to unilaterally take costly steps to deter Soviet aggression but, if war came, the nature of U.S. involvement might not meet British needs.[65] American policy therefore did just enough to offer a Britain some hope for survival to sustain its counter-Soviet efforts, without significantly reducing Britain's military burdens.

Constraining Nuclear Cooperation Truman compounded these military problems by denying Britain access to nuclear weapons, arguably the one tool that might give Britain an edge vis-à-vis the Soviet Union. This move also reneged on wartime promises. In fact, British influence was central to the establishment of the Manhattan Project, U.S. and British scientists collaborated in developing the first nuclear weapons, and the project itself was supported by the combined boards that pooled Anglo-American resources.[66] Mutual investment was such that Churchill and Roosevelt signed a 1943 agreement pledging that "full collaboration between the United States and the British Government in developing [nuclear technology] for military and commercial purposes shall continue after the defeat of Japan unless and until terminated by joint agreement."[67]

Immediately after Japan's surrender, however, Truman imposed a moratorium on sharing nuclear information with foreign countries.[68] Angered by U.S. actions, Attlee demanded a meeting with Truman to press the British case and, following November talks, got Truman to sign a new agreement promising "full and effective cooperation in the field of atomic energy."[69] The November 1945 agreement, however, had little practical effect. Throughout 1946, the British were rebuffed in their efforts to exchange scientific information related to nuclear weapons with American officials, and were not allowed to tour U.S. nuclear production facilities.[70] By April 1946, the problem was so acute that British diplomats "reported difficulties in getting scientific and technical information [related to nuclear weapons] from the Americans."[71] Subsequent passage of the 1946 McMahon Act, which classified all technical nuclear information as a "born secret," punctuated the end of Anglo-American nuclear sharing.[72] Britain was compelled to begin its own nuclear program with what resources could be spared, recognizing that the "task would [be] both much longer and more costly" than if Anglo-American cooperation had continued.[73] Far from providing Britain a tool to offset Soviet strengths, U.S. policy continued to limit Anglo-American relations.

Sustaining Bolstering Amid Rising Tensions The United States' Bolstering strategy continued even in the face of rising U.S.-Soviet tensions over the future of Germany (discussed below) and seeming Soviet challenges in Southeastern Europe and the Middle East.[74] In late 1945 and 1946, American policymakers saw growing Soviet threats to Greece, Turkey, and Iran. The resulting crises helped convince U.S. leaders of Soviet hostility and the need to oppose Soviet machinations.[75] However, putative Soviet actions were even more direct challenges to Britain: Greece and Turkey anchored British sea lines of communication in the Mediterranean, while Iran was Britain's major oil supplier.[76] These facts were appreciated by U.S. strategists, as the Joint Chiefs of Staff warned Truman and Byrnes that Soviet domination of the Mediterranean could lead to the "eventual disintegration of the [British] Empire," denying the United States vital military support and resulting in a situation in which remaining U.S. and allied forces "might be insufficient to match those of an expanded Soviet Union."[77] The implication of this analysis, as the historian Walter Poole observes, was clear: "the United States should buttress the British Empire."[78]

Nevertheless, the United States avoided regular Anglo-American diplomatic and military cooperation. Diplomatic notes and military deployments meant to back Turkey, for example, were sent unilaterally and not coordinated with Britain.[79] Likewise, while the United States and United Kingdom issued a joint demarche demanding that the Soviet Union withdraw from Iran, it took significant British lobbying for the United States to embrace a joint approach.[80] Meanwhile, although British leaders welcomed indications of U.S. support, the United States rejected British attempts to translate episodic backing into regular collaboration. Instead, U.S. leaders wanted Britain to bear the risks of defending these areas. As a 1946 report designed to guide U.S. policy on Turkey explained, it was "preferable for Great Britain to assume the obligation of providing military equipment and munitions whenever necessary."[81]

Similarly, Anglo-American military relations remained supportive within limits. By 1946 American analysts concluded that, as Leahy wrote Byrnes in March, "defeat or disintegration of the British Empire would eliminate from Eurasia the last bulwark of resistance between the United States and Soviet Union," thus requiring U.S. efforts to forestall further British losses.[82] Accordingly, revised war plans acknowledged at mid-1946 that the United States would likely become involved in a European war as soon as hostilities erupted. Still, U.S. policy remained ambiguous and flexible, with the overall war plan simply noting that "the sooner we support Britain" in a war with the Soviet Union, "the more favorable will be our military position."[83] Meanwhile, U.S. forces continued leaving Europe just as planning documents still consigned Western Europe to the Soviet Union in the event of war; this approach guaranteed that Britain would be subject to heavy attack if conflict erupted. Making matters worse, U.S. planners estimated that British forces could defend the British Isles against the Soviet Union and so made protection of the United Kingdom itself a relatively low wartime priority.[84] Above all, the United States' growing willingness to intervene—in some fashion—for Britain was never fully communicated to British officials. In fact, and even after informal Anglo-American military talks in late 1946, the United States refused to pledge action on Britain's behalf.[85] As a result, British leaders remained uncertain, in Elisabeth Barker's description, of the "American commitment to help Britain in any part of the world in a future war."[86]

Equally ad hoc assistance continued in economic affairs. By the spring of 1946, British policymakers wanted to reduce Britain's foreign footprint to save money, and the British zone of occupation in Germany, costing £80 million per year in nonmilitary expenses, presented the most inviting target.[87] British officials therefore decided to seek U.S. backing in fusing the French, British, and American zones into a single unit, hoping that "full and continued financial and military support of the United States" would alleviate British burdens.[88] Nevertheless, the United States initially refused these proposals.[89] At the time, U.S. policy remained fixed on preventing an overt break in East-West relations over Germany, a goal that creation of a single Western zone in Germany would endanger.[90] Only in July 1946—after it seemed that the Soviet Union was setting up a zone against the Western powers—did the United States agree to combine the British and American zones. Even then, it continued to distance itself from Britain by holding to a strict interpretation of joint responsibilities and refusing to assume more than 50 percent of the costs for the Anglo-American zone. Despite Britain's protestations that the occupation ate into its financial reserves, U.S. officials refused to budge.[91]

In the final analysis, U.S. policy in 1945–46 was divided between assisting Britain and hedging U.S. security bets. As the above discussion underscores, U.S. policymakers were clearly focused on sustaining Britain as a counterweight to the Soviet Union and a way of reducing U.S. postwar burdens.[92] "It was a necessity," a classified 1945 study explained, "to support the British position in Europe" since, ultimately, "every accretion in British . . . strength reduces the burden on the United States in the postwar period." Thus, "the continued existence, prosperity, and strength of an independent, democratic, and friendly Great Britain" was rapidly becoming "a vital interest to be defended."[93] Still, this did not mean giving Britain what the State Department termed "a blank check of American support." Rather, backing would occur "only in respect of areas and interests . . . vital to the maintenance of the United Kingdom and the British Commonwealth of nations as a great power," limited to what the United States judged to be "feasible" economic, political, and—"if necessary"—military assistance.[94] After all, as Secretary of Commerce Henry Wallace warned in late 1946, the United States "must not let British balance of power manipulations determine whether and when the United States gets into war."[95] The United States would support the United Kingdom, but only in a prudent and limited fashion that avoided giving a potent Britain too much influence over U.S. policy, wasting resources, or courting antagonism with the Soviet Union.

STRENGTHENING IN 1947 AND BEYOND

By late 1946, the United States had embraced the need to support Britain but remained cautious in the scope and extent of its backing. Despite recognizing Britain's centrality to European security, Anglo-American military cooperation faltered after World War II, while U.S. diplomatic and economic support was circumscribed and inconsistent. Into the winter of 1946–47, it remained unclear how far the United States would go to prop up the United Kingdom.

Backing when Britain Beckons In the middle of February, however, Britain dropped a bombshell.[96] As part of the retrenchment program developed in the second half of 1946 and early 1947, Britain announced the suspension of economic and military aid to Greece and Turkey and the withdrawal of British troops from Greece later in 1947.[97] Though U.S. strategists expected some British retrenchment, the scope of the British collapse was shocking. Policymakers immediately began evaluating the consequences for U.S. national security.[98] The implications were stark.[99] Britain, the State Department noted, was reducing its overseas presence and "seemed to feel itself unable to maintain its imperial structure on the same scale as in the past."[100] If Britain stopped protecting these countries, it could set off a cascade leading to the loss of the Near East and Western Europe to the Soviet Union.[101] Indeed, Britain itself appeared to be tottering, and U.S. officials scrambled to determine "the future policy which might be followed by the British Government."[102] Put simply, as Acheson recalled in his memoirs, the British retrenchment meant that the United States was "met at Armageddon."[103]

U.S. policymakers were jolted into action.[104] The British withdrawal from Greece and Turkey was—as a major interagency report from early 1947 observed—"only part of a much broader problem arising for this country in consequence of Britain's economic and political situation." U.S. leaders thus worried that "if Great Britain finds that the United States is unwilling to finance and otherwise back up the avowed policies of the American government [with respect to British security] it may come to the conclusion that it has no other course open to it than to seek a breathing spell by coming to terms with the Soviet Union," including a possible Anglo-Soviet "arrangement." This would be a disaster for the United States, as "such an arrangement would greatly strengthen the Soviet Union, would weaken the United Kingdom, and would tend to isolate the United States." Above all, it substantially increased the risk of a war that the United States would have to fight "without the effective military support of Great Britain."[105]

Seeking to ensure Britain's "continued loyal cooperation" and avoid a possible "British deal with the Russians," the United States began to intensify its support.[106] Within one week of the British announcement, the Truman administration proposed Anglo-American consultations with the aim of the United States taking responsibility for Greek and Turkish security.[107] Then on March 12, Truman went before Congress to depict a world threatened by Soviet expansionism. Since Britain, "owing to its own difficulties," could not address the threat, the United States needed to step into the breach and provide economic and political support for those actors resisting the Soviet threat (a policy soon known as the Truman Doctrine).[108] Although the United States encouraged Britain to retain a symbolic force in Greece, U.S. assistance began to flow to Greece and Turkey shortly after Truman's speech.[109] Between the extension of U.S. aid to countries central to British security and the promise of open-ended U.S. assistance following Truman's speech, the United States intensified its steps to back Britain.

Reconstructing Britain's Economy The move into Greece and Turkey signaled the start of increasing U.S. efforts to back the United Kingdom as the extent to which Britain was faltering became clear. Already in March 1947, Acheson underscored that the British pullout from Greece and Turkey represented "only part of a much larger problem growing out of the change in Great Britain's strength."[110] Although Britain was rapidly shedding military commitments, the reduction in overseas expenditures did not alleviate the country's guns-versus-butter dilemma: industrial recovery lagged while the British trade deficit, exacerbated by an absence of overseas markets and the need to import raw materials, ate into the 1945–46 Anglo-American loan faster than anticipated. By the middle of 1947, British leaders warned that the country was close to bankruptcy.[111] Once sterling-dollar convertibility began in July, the problem reached crisis proportions, as convertibility led to a run on the pound that British policymakers could address only by using the loaned funds. The result was that by mid-August 1947, the loan was nearly exhausted and the British economy still suffering.[112] Not only was U.S. assistance unable to meet Britain's needs, but its terms harmed Britain's position.

U.S. policymakers now began to address Britain's economic problems. As stopgap measures, the United States assumed responsibility for financing the merged Anglo-American zone in Germany and endorsed Britain's plans to suspend sterling-dollar convertibility.[113] This latter move contravened the terms of the Anglo-American loan and the Bretton Woods accords. Nevertheless, rather than risk further harm to the British economy, U.S. leaders accepted Britain's need to back away from convertibility and defended the move against domestic critics.[114] Seeking a long-term solution to Britain's economic plight, the Truman administration soon thereafter decided to address British problems as part of Europe's broader economic recovery. Believing Britain's problems were due to a lack of markets rather than a lack of resources, policymakers anticipated that a Europe-wide approach would put Britain on a sustainable footing by creating markets for its goods and trading partners from whom it could import, thereby spurring British economic growth.

The solution, presented in a series of reports in the spring and summer of 1947, was what became the European Recovery Program (ERP; informally known as the Marshall Plan after Secretary of State George Marshall). In brief, the ERP called for the United States to transfer large quantities of resources to prime the Western European (including the western zone of Germany) economic pump, while spurring the region's economic and political integration via supranational institutions to include and contain a revived Germany.[115] This program, of course, was not solely focused on Britain or caused uniquely by British problems: as even contemporary analysts acknowledged, the ERP was driven heavily by Western Europe's own political and economic dislocations that seemingly left the region susceptible to

Soviet influence. Still, the plan addressed the need to aid Britain and placed special emphasis on reconstituting British strength. In fact, policymakers expected Britain to take the lead in working out the ERP's political and economic arrangements and to facilitate Western European reconstruction writ large, affording Britain the opportunity to ensure that the program was aligned with its interests.[116]

Accordingly, the United States forewarned the United Kingdom of the ERP, while the State Department's Policy Planning Staff called for "secret discussions" with the British to structure "the general approach" to the program.[117] To make the program viable, the United States also provided Britain with the lion's share of ERP aid as $3.2 billion out of a total $13 billion—nearly a quarter overall—went to Britain. This was 20 percent more than France received, and nearly double the amount given to the future West Germany.[118] Meanwhile, having decided that the United Kingdom was central to U.S. strategy, U.S. policymakers increasingly let Britain shape the terms of U.S. assistance. For example, after British opposition to European integration spiked, the United States backed away from calls for a European federation in favor of British-backed plans for a looser arrangement that involved generalized collaboration among Western European states.[119] Unlike the discord surrounding the Anglo-American loan, the United States thus quickly committed significant resources and political capital to Britain's recovery under terms preferred by the United Kingdom.

Policymakers worried that British economic weakness was uniquely injurious to American interests. As with the Anglo-American loan, two different arguments were at play. First, failure to assist the United Kingdom would risk Britain's movement away from an open economic order—as British leaders themselves warned, they would retreat "further and further from the concept of a multilateral world economy."[120] Second, and equally significant, were the deleterious consequences for U.S. security. Without more generous U.S. aid, Britain might decide that—as the State Department's Policy Planning Staff argued—it had "no choice but to dismantle extensively [its] defense and imperial commitments;" even withdrawal from Germany was possible.[121] This could seriously impair U.S. national security. As a report designed to guide U.S. foreign assistance explained, "two world wars in the past thirty years have demonstrated the interdependence of France, Great Britain, and the United States in case of war with central or eastern European powers." Ensuring that these countries had the "economies able to support the armed forces necessary for the continued maintenance of their independence" was therefore "of first importance"; otherwise, they would remain a burden on the United States and have limited ability to help oppose the Soviet Union. Ultimately, because of both its "importance to United States security" and the "urgency of [its] need," Britain topped the list of countries meriting American assistance.[122] As the State Department bluntly concluded in mid-1948, "The policies and actions of no other country in the world, with the possible exception of the USSR, are of greater importance to us. It is our objective that the United Kingdom shall have a viable economy and adequate standard of living and with sufficient margin to permit her to play her full part in maintaining overseas commitments."[123]

In turn, facilitating Britain's recovery would allow it to take the lead in stabilizing Western Europe and help the United States avoid active management of European security affairs. This could be achieved either by the aforementioned supranational institutions proposed by the United States, or by following British suggestions for a "Western European Union" that would involve regional economic and military cooperation without "any transfer of sovereignty to a supra-national body."[124] At a time of British weakness, though U.S. policymakers preferred the supranational option, the United States proved willing to accommodate Britain. As the State Department observed, the United States did not intend "to exert pressure on the UK to lead the way to a political union" as per U.S. preferences, but rather "to secure the formation of a western alliance and the progressively closer integration of the western European countries" as Britain desired.[125] In this, U.S. officials recognized that Western Europe's recovery would be sustainable only if the western zones of Germany recovered. With memories of the war still fresh, however, a revived Germany was anathema to many Western European states. If the United States retrenched, then only Britain could provide the necessary reassurance to those states and to do so, Britain needed to be strengthened on terms it found acceptable. As State Department Policy Planning Director George Kennan explained, "some form of political, military, and economic union in Western Europe will be necessary" to oppose Moscow, but "it is questionable whether this union could be strong enough to serve its designed purpose unless it had the participation and support of Great Britain"—all of which required addressing "Britain's long term economic problem."[126] Summarizing the issue, State Department analysts emphasized in 1949 that "no effective integration of Europe would be possible without UK participation because of the belief . . . by western continental powers of potential German domination if such UK participation did not take place."[127]

Of course, rebuilding British strength did not mean enabling Britain (or a British-led coalition) to position itself to compete with the United States— but by 1947–48, this was not a serious concern. British policy was now "dependent upon and limited by US defense policy since the British themselves [were] not in position to implement a Western European Union through effective military guarantees."[128] Combined with its economic reliance on the United States, Britain had limited ability to compete with the United States even if it wanted to and even if a Western European Union existed. Nor does it seem that British policymakers entertained ideas to the contrary: as the U.S. ambassador to Britain cabled Secretary of State Marshall in mid-1948, British leaders did not expect "to regain their former relative supremacy" so much as they hoped that "they will again become a power to be reckoned with, which, associated with the US, can maintain the balance of power in the world."[129] Provided that the United States considered "the apprehensions of the USSR" and avoided war by forcing "the USSR into a position from which it cannot retreat," it could thus obtain a junior partner in European security affairs.[130]

Strengthening Britain's Military Hand Having strengthened Britain's economy, U.S. strategists turned to improving the country's military position. Even into late 1947, the Anglo-American military relationship remained distant. Although Britain's survival as a great power was considered a vital U.S. interest, talk of an Anglo-American peacetime alliance was avoided throughout 1945–46, while military coordination declined. This changed after the August 1947 suspension of sterling convertibility.

Even as the Marshall Plan took shape, Bevin warned that further British retrenchment was likely, as "the reduction in British overseas forces had not yet been definitely fixed."[131] In August 1947, Attlee told Parliament that reductions were undergoing an "acceleration," and word soon arrived in Washington that British forces were leaving Italy and Greece.[132] The danger to the United States and Britain loomed large. As the State Department noted, a British pullout exposed the area to Soviet dominance, with potentially dire consequences:

> In the specific case of the United States, this would mean a retreat to the Western Hemisphere and facing the prospect of a war of attrition which would spell the end of the American way of life. In the case of the United Kingdom, the maintenance of a Middle Eastern front would be essential in order that the British "home base" should not be isolated and subjected to the full impact of a Soviet attack directed from Europe.[133]

Seeking "the maintenance of Britain's position to the greatest possible extent," the Truman administration responded by authorizing Anglo-American staff talks to develop joint war plans for the defense of the Mediterranean and Middle East.[134] Begun in October, the talks were the first official high-level Anglo-American strategy discussions since World War II, opening the door—in John Baylis's description—"for a greater degree of strategic planning."[135] Indeed, the two countries were developing coordinated contingency plans for a European war by the spring of 1948.[136]

The plans themselves also underwent important changes. As noted above, U.S. war plans through 1946 emphasized strategic flexibility and the possible withdrawal of U.S. forces from Europe. If war came, the United States would neither commit to coming to Britain's defense nor necessarily fight in a way that aided Britain's security. Now, however, the scope and substance of U.S. efforts intensified. First, instead of withdrawing from

Europe in the event of Anglo-Soviet hostilities, U.S. forces were directed to fight alongside British units to delay a Soviet advance.[137] Strategists also anticipated a troop buildup to aid a European conventional defense as far to the east as possible—in part, it seems, to reduce the military pressure Britain would otherwise face and to address British concerns about the security of Western Europe.[138] Second, preparations were made for the immediate wartime dispatch of nuclear-capable bombers to Britain, from where they would be able attack Soviet industry and try to slow a Soviet offensive.[139] The United States remained unwilling to share nuclear technology with the United Kingdom, but it would at least use its nuclear arsenal in Britain's defense. Planners further decided that U.S. military aid would flow to the United Kingdom as soon as the military situation required, and that Britain would have priority call on U.S. resources.[140] Meanwhile, U.S. policymakers privately informed their British interlocutors that Britain would likely have U.S. wartime backing. Early indications of this shift came in January 1948, when U.S. officials praised British efforts to craft a Western European alliance while underscoring that "if it should be felt in western Europe that the direct participation of the United States in a defense arrangement" was required for its success, then "the United States would no doubt be prepared, very carefully[,] to consider this question."[141] In March, U.S. officials were even clearer, emphasizing to British strategists that "US full [wartime] support should be assumed."[142]

At the time, U.S. policymakers believed these efforts were necessary to ensure "the security of the British Isles" and Britain's ability to remain a partner against the Soviet Union. As the Joint Chiefs of Staff observed, "So long as the U.S. elects to take these steps . . . it may be anticipated that Britain and the remaining western powers will be sufficiently reassured to remain joined with the U.S. in a firm policy counter to that of the Soviets. In this event, the most probable short-term trend in world politics should be one of improving western democratic political and power position."[143] If not, then not only might Western Europe be lost, but Britain might move away from the United States and "consider a variation of [its] traditional 'balance of power' role in Europe, this time as mediators on a global scale between the United States and U.S.S.R"; the probability of a war that the United States might lose would increase accordingly.[144] Nor was this view confined to military circles. Senior State Department officials cautioned that one of the chief dangers in Europe was the risk that "too many people in the remaining free countries will be intimidated by the Soviet colossus and the absence of tangible American support to the point of losing their will to resist."[145] Indeed, Acting Secretary of State Robert Lovett was sufficiently concerned that Britain might bandwagon with the Soviet Union that he dispatched diplomats in mid-1948 to assess British intentions.[146] In effect, only strong American support "would permit Britain to remain resolute in opposition to Soviet pressure."[147]

Formalizing U.S. Security Guarantees The stage was set to formalize an Anglo-American alliance.[148] Already in mid-March 1948, Marshall cabled Bevin that the United States was "prepared at once to proceed in the joint discussion on the establishment of an Atlantic security system."[149] Truman followed suit on March 17, announcing the United States' willingness to "extend to the free nations [of Europe] the support which the situation requires."[150] Within two weeks, talks began between U.S., British, and Canadian officials as the United States sought to backstop British efforts to create a Western European security system.[151]

As in economic affairs, the United States gave Britain pride of place in U.S. policy and modified its positions in response to British concerns. As talks began, American leaders were undecided between offering a simple unilateral pledge that the United States would defend members of the British-backed Brussels Pact—a March 1948 alignment of Britain, France, and the smaller states of Western Europe designed to hedge against both German and Soviet aggression—or crafting a new security arrangement that included the United States from the outset.[152] British influence helped direct the United States toward the latter option.[153] In April, Bevin cabled Lovett, "We feel that American support only in the form of a declaration by the President would be inadequate. It would leave the situation in doubt." Bevin also played to U.S. fears of British surrender, warning:

> One of my great anxieties in this business is whether, if trouble did come, we should be left waiting as in 1940 in a state of uncertainty. In view of our experience then it would be very difficult to be able to stand up to it again unless there was a definite worked out arrangement for the Western area, together with other assistance, on the basis of collective security to resist the aggressor.[154]

Similar warnings followed, and the balance of opinion in the United States government soon moved toward a new security system.[155] Exploratory talks for a new defensive pact involving the United States began in the summer of 1948, with formal negotiations commencing that fall. Even then, U.S. policymakers continued to prioritize British concerns, going so far as to clear proposals in the talks with British diplomats before presenting them to other European states.[156] This process culminated in the signing of the North Atlantic Treaty (NAT), which laid the foundation for the North Atlantic Treaty Organization (NATO), in April 1949.[157] Although American strategists crafted an escape clause in the NAT to hedge against allied misbehavior—pledging only what assistance was "deem[ed] necessary" to meet an attack on a partner—the United States was now formally committed to Britain's protection.[158] Funding for the reconstruction of British and Western European military power followed in October and, in December, plans were laid for an integrated defense of the North Atlantic area.[159]

To be explicit, Britain's decline did not cause the United States to balance the Soviet Union and create NATO. Given tensions with the Soviet Union—punctuated by the 1948–49 Berlin Crisis, during which the United States dispatched bombers to Britain partly to provide reassurance—some kind of an U.S. security commitment to Western Europe was likely.[160] Still, Britain's decline at a time when the United States sought to minimize involvement in European affairs shaped the form of the U.S. response. Into the winter of 1948–49, U.S. strategists argued that plans for a North Atlantic Pact "should be considered a supplement to and in no sense a replacement" for European integration and, for integration to succeed, British strength needed to recover.[161] Britain, after all, was the only country with a serviceable military in Western Europe, the United States saw Britain as its "spokesman" with other states in Western Europe, and the country was needed to contain Germany within an anti-Soviet group.[162] As Acheson, by then secretary of state, commented in late 1949, "There can be no unity of Europe, or among groups of European countries, effective enough to move matters forward without the strong support and, to the greatest extent possible, participation of the UK."[163] Until Britain recovered, the United States would thus strengthen a necessary partner.

Denouement: Additional Economic Support at Britain's Twilight In short, having tried to limit its support in the immediate postwar period, the United States intensely supported the United Kingdom in 1947–49. This revised policy was on display as the British economy, still reeling and with Marshall Plan aid not yet having the desired effect, deteriorated further in the summer and fall of 1949.[164] Britain, U.S. diplomats warned, might shed "more military and political commitments abroad,"[165] or erect further trade and financial barriers.[166] By September, British economic conditions were so bad that Bevin and his advisers visited the United States seeking additional economic assistance.

Acheson and his staff anticipated British requests. Fearing that failure to provide additional aid might lead to "deterioration of military and general cooperation between the United States and Britain, and in our ability to utilize the British to help us protect our world position," U.S. officials were prepared to be accommodating.[167] To this end, the United States agreed to increase its investment in Britain, loosen restrictions placed on what economic transactions Britain could finance with Marshall Plan aid, reduce tariffs on British goods, and simplify customs procedures for British imports.[168] In other words, and in contrast to the situation in 1945–46, the United States rapidly adopted policies that directly worked to Britain's advantage without significant haggling or bargaining.

Nevertheless, these efforts proved insufficient, and Britain's economy continued to lose ground. Highlighting the loss of Britain's great power status, the Attlee government was forced to devalue the pound at the end of 1949. By early 1950, U.S. policymakers were struggling to determine not the prospects for a British recovery, but the depths to which Britain might sink.[169] Britain's fall from the ranks of the great powers, however, was not for want of U.S. support. In the final analysis, the United States committed growing economic and military resources to Britain's survival and recovery once Britain's military position unraveled. Although these efforts failed, Britain would at least decline with U.S. protection and diplomatic backing at hand.

Soviet Strategy and British Decline

If the United States supported the United Kingdom, what policies did the Soviet Union pursue? Prima facie, the fact that British policymakers such as Churchill, Attlee, and Bevin feared Soviet ambitions suggests that the Soviet Union was interested in exploiting Britain's postwar weakness and pursuing predation.[170] Considering that the Cold War eventually resulted in a breakdown of great power relations as the United States and United Kingdom aligned against the Soviet Union, this interpretation certainly seems to capture the flow of history; indeed, a prominent tradition in postwar diplomatic historiography proposes that Soviet ambitions played an outsized role in triggering the Cold War. Nevertheless, this view of a Soviet Union out to prey upon Britain is incomplete. It is true that, after late 1947, the Soviet Union began to arm against the United Kingdom and try to undermine British security in Europe. Strikingly, however, Soviet policy prior to that point broadly paralleled that of the United States. Historians do not quite make the point, but materials that have come to light since the end of the Cold War and several recent monographs on postwar Soviet foreign policy indicate that the Soviet Union bolstered Britain in 1945–46 and, in the first part of 1947, pursued a Strengthening strategy. Only after Britain moved decisively into alignment with the United States and British policymakers expressed no interest in cooperating with the Soviet Union did Soviet support give way to predation.

BOLSTERED BRITAIN IN 1945–46

The thrust of Soviet strategy in 1945–46 was described in a series of studies conducted at Stalin's behest in 1944–45 that were intended to structure Soviet postwar policy. Directed by the diplomats Maxim Litvinov, Andrei Gromyko, and Ivan Maisky, the reports emphasized the singular importance of Britain to Soviet security and the broad possibilities for postwar Anglo-Soviet cooperation.[171] At the root, the two states shared a common interest in preventing Germany's resurgence and would need to find ways of partnering against it if the United States reduced its presence in Europe. In fact, if Germany remained the focus of postwar politics, then the Soviet Union,

United Kingdom, and United States were likely to sustain their wartime collaboration and smoothly manage European security affairs.[172] However, growing U.S. power during the war made stable great power relations unlikely. Instead, as a "stronghold of dynamic imperialism," the United States would likely try to expand its economic, political, and military reach in the postwar world and eventually challenge the Soviet Union.[173]

The Soviet Union would need allies in this situation, and Britain was the obvious candidate. Just as an expansionist United States was liable to target the Soviet Union, so too was it likely to try to "[open] the doors of the British empire" to gain access to British markets and supplant Britain as a leading power.[174] The Soviet Union and the United Kingdom thus had a stake in each other's survival—it was strongly in the former's interest to bid for British friendship and "keep Britain as a strong power."[175] Admittedly, this did not mean helping Britain achieve a position from which it could threaten the Soviet Union, as the Soviets intended to be the dominant European military power.[176] The Soviet task was also complicated by the expectation that Britain would turn to the United States for economic assistance and to hedge against the growth of Soviet power. Furthermore, it was conceivable that Britain, seeking a "balance of power in Europe" and threatened by the Soviet Union's rise, might engage in provocative behavior such as building up Germany against the Soviet Union or supporting anti-Soviet groups in Eastern Europe.[177] Still, the Soviet Union and Britain had successfully put aside past differences when fighting Germany, it seemed that both had similar incentives to offset the United States in the postwar world, and it was strongly in the Soviet interest to prevent what one Soviet diplomat termed "a bloc of Great Britain and the U.S.A. against us."[178] Hence, if Britain was to be kept out of the U.S. orbit without imperiling Soviet security, then Soviet policy needed to avoid deepening British suspicions of the Soviet Union that could either lead Britain away from, or encourage it to lash out against, the Soviet Union.

Soviet Plans for Spheres of Influence To this end, Soviet strategists recommended dividing Europe into Soviet and British spheres of interest. Resembling early U.S. plans, the Soviet Union would control "Finland, Sweden, Poland, Hungary, Czechoslovakia, Romania, the Slav countries of the Balkans, and also Turkey," while Britain dominated "Holland, Belgium, France, Spain, Portugal, and Greece." Germany, Italy, and Denmark would constitute a neutral zone between the two spheres.[179] Except for Sweden and Turkey, where the Soviets allowed that they might have to "compromise," the envisioned Soviet sphere covered only areas that Soviet forces currently occupied. The British sphere, meanwhile, encompassed nearly the whole of Western Europe deemed crucial to British security.[180] What would emerge, as Vladimir Pechatnov concludes, was "an Anglo-Soviet strategic condominium."[181]

Even as Stalin began a broad crackdown against domestic groups calling for liberalization in the Soviet Union and Eastern Europe, Soviet behavior followed these guidelines.[182] Vladislav Zubok and Constantine Pleshakov capture the point, observing that "at no point did Stalin's demands and ambitions in 1945–1946 exceed the maximum zone of responsibility discussed by Litvinov and Maisky . . . in some cases, Stalin's moves in the international arena were more modest in scope."[183] Foreign Minister Vyacheslav Molotov also highlighted the policy, noting in late 1945: "But how governments are being organized in Belgium, France, Greece, etc. we do not know. We do not say that we like one or another of these governments. We have not interfered, because there is the Anglo-American zone of military action."[184] Similarly, Stalin readily agreed to a November 1944 British proposal to divide Southeastern Europe into Soviet and British areas, with Romania, Hungary, and Bulgaria assigned to the Soviet Union, Greece given to the United Kingdom, and Yugoslavia under joint control.[185] Yugoslavia's later liberation by Communist partisans vitiated this part of the deal, but the Soviet Union adhered to the agreement in Greece, where British interests were most affected.[186] In fact, Stalin denied aid to Greek Communists fighting against the British-backed Greek government and criticized Greek Communist efforts, telling one colleague in January 1945: "I advised not starting this fighting in Greece. . . . They were evidently counting on the Red Army's coming down to the Aegean. We cannot do that."[187] Likewise, the Soviet leader pressured Yugoslavia—the main backer of the Greek Communists—to end its assistance, remarking that it was "necessary to be circumspect in relation to foreign policy questions."[188] Indeed, "in relation to bourgeois politicians, you have to be careful. They are . . . touchy and vindictive"—there was no telling how British or U.S. leaders might respond to provocations.[189]

Seeking to strengthen Britain's hand vis-à-vis the United States and generate goodwill with both Western powers, the Soviet Union also tried to reinforce Britain's position in Western Europe.[190] Owing to wartime losses, the Soviet Union could not readily provide Britain with economic assistance akin to the Anglo-American loan. What it could do was discourage local Communist parties from opposing what was expected to be a British-led reconstruction effort and so assist in moving Western European states into the British sphere. Consistent with this objective, Stalin delayed restarting the Communist International (Comintern)—through which Moscow had organized the prewar activities of international Communist parties—even though his advisers planned for its resumption.[191] Along similar lines, the Soviet leader encouraged Communist parties in France and Italy—that is, countries central to British security—to cooperate with other political parties in stabilizing postwar Western European politics.[192] This effort continued throughout 1945–46 as East-West tensions mounted. As part of this policy, Stalin even criticized the French Communist party for having what Eduard Mark describes as "too confrontational an attitude toward potential allies," while also restraining German Communist efforts to quickly construct a social-ist state in the Soviet zone of occupation in Germany.[193] Zubok and Pleshakov conclude that Stalin "did not want to provoke premature confrontation."[194]

Nor did signs of Anglo-American cooperation in 1945–46 discourage So-viet efforts. Soviet leaders were convinced that any Anglo-American collab-oration would be ephemeral and Anglo-American relations would eventually collapse. Ambassador to the United States Nikolai Novikov captured this thinking well in November 1946, cabling Molotov and Stalin that "current relations between England and the United States, despite the temporary attainment of agreements on very important questions, are plagued with great internal contradictions and cannot be lasting." The Soviet Union needed to be ready to exploit Anglo-American differences when they emerged by offering Britain an alternative at a time when the "policy of the American government with regard to the USSR is also directed at limiting or dislodging the influence of the Soviet Union."[195] By sustaining a spheres of influence settlement in Europe and maintaining a cooperative approach toward Britain, the Soviet Union kept this option open.

Limited Cooperation in Germany and Beyond To be clear, Soviet policy was not designed just to reinforce British strength. In addition to strengthen-ing Britain's hand in Western Europe and sustaining Anglo-Soviet bonho-mie, this approach helped ensure that British strength did not grow too much, too fast. Given the postwar context, it seems reasonable to conclude that discouraging Communist parties in Italy, France, and beyond from resisting reconstruction efforts provided the Soviet Union leverage to use in opposing possible British—or U.S.—machinations. Litvinov and other Soviet analysts recognized the long history of Anglo-Russian and Anglo-Soviet discord and, given postwar uncertainty, worried that Britain and the United States might sponsor "anti-Soviet elements" in Eastern Europe against the Soviet Union.[196] Besides limiting the challenge to British inter-ests, encouraging Western European Communists to cooperate thereby gave the Soviets a tool they could turn on or off to punish or reward Brit-ish behavior. This policy may have also been intended to lay the founda-tion for future Communist political success and the long-term growth of Soviet influence by giving Communist parties entrée into Western Euro-pean politics and so (in theory) helping Communists take power through the ballot box.[197] In short, Soviet plans seemingly had both a short- and long-term logic: encouraging Communist cooperation would strengthen Britain in the near term in case of a showdown with the United States, while over time providing levers that could be used to limit British (or U.S.) threats and potentially magnify Soviet influence.

Efforts at mollifying Britain within limits even extended to Soviet policies on Germany. As it became clear that a neutral Germany was not attractive to either the Western powers or the Soviet Union, Stalin shifted course from wartime calls to keep Germany nonaligned. Instead, Soviet decision makers went along with Anglo-American plans in 1945 to divide Germany in order to avoid conflict over that state's future. Of course, these efforts collapsed late in 1945 as the three states failed to agree on German reparations or Germany's economic revival.[198] Even then, however, the Soviets responded to growing East-West tensions largely by consolidating control in their occupation zone and downplaying the significance of great power discord. Missing, in other words, were systematic efforts to spur German opposition in the Western occupation zones that would make Britain's occupation any more expensive, or to challenge the value of a negotiated settlement.[199] Indicative of its overall approach, the Soviet Union responded to deepening East-West fissures over Germany during 1946 by seeking a diplomatic solution: even after successive meetings of U.S., Soviet, and British diplomats failed to reach a negotiated agreement on Germany's future, the Soviet Union tried to keep the talks alive and avoid what would be a major breach in Anglo-Soviet relations over a core issue in European security.[200] Put simply, the Soviets stayed in their zone and tried to resolve problems with the United Kingdom and United States diplomatically.[201]

Reducing the Soviet Military Challenge Although not primarily focused on addressing British security problems, Soviet military policy also provided incidental advantages for Great Britain. The most direct benefit came when, in keeping with its spheres of influence approach, the Soviet Union withdrew forces from areas intended to be under British influence. Less directly, postwar Soviet military reductions circumscribed the threat posed to Western European and British security, thereby mitigating—albeit in circuitous fashion—Britain's need to balance the Soviet Union. Postwar demobilization resulted in large Soviet force withdrawals even from areas allocated to the Soviet sphere, such as Czechoslovakia and Bulgaria.[202] The size of the Red Army fell precipitously: where the Soviet Union had approximately 11.3 million people under arms at the end of World War II, troop levels fell to 3 million in mid-1946 and to 2.8 million in 1948.[203] Moreover, although significant Soviet forces remained in and around Eastern Europe, many of the remaining divisions were maintained at far less than full strength or were converted into garrison units unsuited for combat operations.[204] The release of veterans and the fact that many units were engaged in reconstruction projects or suppressing local anti-Soviet insurgencies further undermined the combat potential of Soviet forces.[205]

Though British leaders feared otherwise, the Soviet Union under these conditions was optimized for what Matthew Evangelista terms "defensive operations" and could not attack westward without substantial reinforcement.[206] In fact, Soviet strategists themselves accepted that the Soviet Union would have been hard-pressed simply to sustain the territorial status quo if war erupted: as Pechatnov and Earl Edmondson write, into late

1946 "Soviet contingency plans did not call for offensive operations in western Europe," focusing instead "on holding the line of defense in Germany."[207] Although operating indirectly, Soviet military choices thereby limited the resources and risks that a declining Britain would need to run to obtain security.

The 1945–46 Turkish and Iranian Crises: Departure from Bolstering? Nonetheless, not all Soviet policies looked benign to Western analysts. Nor have other scholars seen the desire for Anglo-Soviet cooperation as a pervasive theme in Soviet strategy in the immediate postwar years. In particular, apparent Soviet threats to Greece, Turkey, and Iran in 1945–46 are taken as evidence that the Soviet Union wanted—as two leading scholars suggest—to "rub at the edges of the declining British empire."[208] Even in these crises, however, evidence of Soviet aggrandizement at Britain's expense is more mixed than leaders perceived at the time.

For example, as noted above, the Greek crisis witnessed Soviet leaders attempt to restrain Yugoslav and Greek Communist forces from threatening the British-backed Greek government. Instead of operating against Britain, the Soviet Union tried to limit challenges to the status quo. The Soviet role in the Turkish crisis is more ambiguous. Admittedly, the Soviet Union pressured Turkey to allow a Soviet military base on the Turkish Straits and to give it unfettered access to the Mediterranean.[209] These demands were backed by what Western analysts in 1946 reported was a buildup of Soviet forces, as the resulting tensions created severe friction in Soviet relations with the United Kingdom and the United States.[210]

In retrospect, however, it seems that contemporary reports of a Soviet military buildup were at least partly wrong, the result of faulty intelligence.[211] Equally important, the Soviet campaign came after the United States and the United Kingdom had informally agreed to Soviet requests that the Soviet Union be given a greater role in controlling the Turkish Straits.[212] Meanwhile, it remains unclear how damaging a Soviet base on the Turkish Straits would have been.[213] In fact, contemporary assessments concluded that granting the Soviet Union a base on the straits was militarily irrelevant, as modern air and sea power meant that the United Kingdom or the United States could defend the Mediterranean from bases elsewhere—blocking Soviet entry to the Mediterranean via the straits was unimportant.[214] Britain and the United States responded as if the Soviets were predatory, but it appears that Soviet demands were themselves not necessarily problematic. And, in still further evidence that Soviet moves may have been misinterpreted, the Soviet Union de-escalated the crisis once the United States aligned with Britain to oppose Soviet terms.[215]

In contrast, the Iran crisis of 1946 seems closer to a case of Soviet aggrandizement. The trouble began when the Soviet Union violated an agreement whereby British and Soviet forces stationed in the country during World War

II were supposed to withdraw by March 5, 1946.[216] Instead, the Soviet Union kept its forces in the country, fomented unrest among local Azeri and Kurdish populations against the British-backed Iranian government, and demanded oil exploration rights in northern Iran.[217] Besides seeming to presage Soviet moves to dominate Middle Eastern oil and evict Britain from the area, the challenge to Iran threatened British security. After all, British war plans called for a bomber offensive out of Persian Gulf and Middle Eastern bases against Soviet oilfields in the Caucasus, and Soviet control over northern Iran could hinder such an offensive.[218]

Once, however, Soviet violations became clear, the United States again joined the United Kingdom to oppose Soviet moves. As in the Turkish crisis, this resulted in the rapid de-escalation of the crisis as the Soviet Union withdrew its forces, ceased backing local autonomy movements, and signed an Iran-supported agreement allowing for joint Soviet-Iranian oil exploration.[219] These moves resolved the standoff. "Stalin," Geoffrey Roberts notes, "was prepared to push hard for strategic gains but not at the expense of a break in relations with Britain and the United States."[220] As Stalin explained to a fellow Communist official, failure to withdraw troops from Iran would justify the British and Americans in keeping substantial forces overseas and spur Anglo-American cooperation.[221]

STRENGTHENING, THEN PREYING UPON, BRITAIN, 1947–49

Despite rising discord in Anglo-Soviet relations and growing bonhomie between the United States and the United Kingdom, the Soviet Union continued seeking British partnership throughout 1945–46. In the winter of 1946–47, this effort intensified, apparently driven by the Soviets' growing sense of a mounting U.S. threat and their calculation that Britain was just as threatened but waning militarily. By the fall of 1946, Soviet officials noted the shifting military balance. From Washington, Ambassador Novikov warned that the United States sought "world dominance" and was increasingly targeting both the Soviet Union and United Kingdom. Britain, in particular, faced an immediate challenge, as "the American navy occupies first place in the world, leaving England's far behind," while the projection of American naval power into the Eastern Mediterranean (as during the Turkish crisis) "cannot help but be in conflict with the basic interests of the British Empire."[222] Stalin echoed these themes when interviewed by Western journalists in October, drawing an implicit contrast between U.S. and Soviet military policy by observing that Soviet forces in Eastern Europe were demobilizing, while suggesting that Britain's military presence in Greece was "unnecessary."[223] Hinting at Soviet awareness of British guns-versus-butter tradeoffs, Stalin also questioned a Danish trade delegation in June as to Britain's ability to feed and pay for British troops and German prisoners of war stationed in that country.[224]

Shifting toward Strengthening, Early to Mid-1947 The time seemed ripe for a firmer Anglo-Soviet understanding. With Britain economically on the ropes and under military duress, and with Anglo-American relations uncertain, it was not inconceivable that the Soviet Union might pull Britain into its orbit.[225] Needed, of course, would be an understanding to limit Anglo-Soviet competition, settle political disputes (especially related to Germany), reassure Britain about Soviet goodwill, and emphasize the Soviet Union's ability to address British economic and security needs.[226] Starting in late 1946, Stalin and other Soviet policymakers pursued precisely this course.

In August, a delegation from Attlee's Labour Party visited the Soviet Union, emphasizing "the desire of the Labour Movement . . . and the whole of the British people for real and enduring friendship with the people of Russia."[227] At the time, the extent of Anglo-American cooperation remained unclear. Attlee and other British leaders were also facing intensifying pressure from domestic opponents averse to Britain's adopting a firm anti-Soviet position and leery of greater Anglo-American cooperation; by the late fall of 1946, critics of British policy began openly challenging the Attlee government's foreign policy.[228] Seemingly cueing to these trends, Stalin protégé Andrei Zhdanov noted in September 1946 that elements of the British Labour Party "wanted to prepare the ground for the moment when, should they be in a tight spot, they would have some support from the Soviet Union."[229] For his part, Stalin underscored the desirability of Anglo-Soviet cooperation, telling a reporter from the *Sunday Times* that he was "confident in the possibility of friendly relations between the Soviet Union and Great Britain."[230]

To do so, the Soviet Union quickly moved to explore a formal military alliance—more than one year before the United States did the same—with the United Kingdom. The catalyzing event was a January 1947 visit to Moscow by British Field Marshall Bernard Montgomery. At the time, Montgomery was one of the British officers involved in unofficial staff talks with members of the U.S. military; meanwhile, other British officials were exploring options for a Western European alliance.[231] Stalin may have known of both developments and been willing to play along, telling Montgomery that the Soviet Union had no objection to British alliances with the United States or any other country provided they were not directed against the Soviet Union. Then, in an apparent effort to prevent Britain from associating too closely with the United States, Stalin proposed revising the 1942 Anglo-Soviet alliance—designed for cooperation against Nazi Germany—for the postwar era.[232]

Though cautious, British leaders decided to explore the Soviet offer. Bevin's view is instructive, with the foreign secretary concluding in late January that "we should certainly welcome this opportunity of clarifying our relations with the Soviet Union by bringing our Treaty with them up to date."[233] An Anglo-Soviet alliance, Bevin elaborated in a subsequent meeting, could not be rejected out of hand—it required "very careful examination" to assess Soviet intentions and weigh the possible reaction of the United States.[234] Accordingly, British leaders planned to begin negotiations to revise the 1942 Anglo-Soviet arrangement and to explore a postwar Anglo-Soviet alliance at a March–April 1947 meeting of U.S., British, and Soviet diplomats in Moscow. As Bevin prepared to depart for Moscow, the cabinet thus authorized him to "negotiate a Treaty, going as far as . . . the Anglo-French Treaty, giving him full latitude to make variations as he may think necessary."[235] Considering that the Anglo-French treaty pledged both states to help one another to "prevent Germany from becoming a menace again," the implications of a similar Anglo-Soviet treaty were clear: the Soviet Union and Britain would support each other if Germany again threatened Europe's peace.[236]

More broadly, an Anglo-Soviet alliance might lay the foundation for an entente in Europe and beyond.[237] Indeed, the Soviet Union continued pressing Britain to transform Anglo-Soviet cooperation against Germany into a fuller Anglo-Soviet relationship. To this end, the Soviet Union tabled a revised treaty in mid-April promising not only an alliance against Germany, but "military and other aid and co-operation" in a war with any state allied or associated with Germany; the proposal also pledged the two states "not to conclude any alliances and not to take part in any coalitions or actions or measures directly or indirectly directed" against one another.[238] In effect, this arrangement would have kept Britain out of an anti-Soviet coalition, ensured British backing for the Soviet Union (and vice versa) if the United States fashioned an anti-Soviet alliance using Germany, and denied Britain as a partner to the United States. Of course, British policymakers recognized the implications and worried that this arrangement might set Britain against the United States.[239] This did not, however, stop Britain from continuing talks for a revised Anglo-Soviet alliance. In fact, Attlee and Bevin even considered a counteroffer pledging that "support and assistance will be afforded . . . against any other power which may join with Germany in such an attack in Europe." This would go beyond even the terms of the Anglo-French treaty. Although opposition from the military and Foreign Office blocked this particular offer, treaty negotiations proceeded.[240]

Amid discord at the Moscow talks, however, the United Kingdom reversed course.[241] Meeting on April 22, the cabinet "decided, on reflection, that it would be inadvisable to extend the military clauses on the lines discussed." The best Britain was now willing to offer was general cooperation against Germany, with no guarantee of assistance against other states.[242] Rather than a general alliance, this would prevent the intense Anglo-Soviet cooperation sought by the Soviet Union. Negotiations soon petered out.[243] Within a few days of the cabinet's decision, the Moscow talks also ended amid mutual recriminations as the Soviet Union opposed U.S. and British plans to restart the German economy.[244] Already mistrustful of the Soviet Union, Britain sided with the United States against Soviet efforts to exert influence over German industry in the British occupation zone and, despite Soviet opposition, backed a U.S. plan to keep Germany disarmed for twenty-five years.[245]

Nevertheless, Soviet leaders continued to leave the door open to greater Anglo-Soviet cooperation. Even after the Moscow meeting ended, for example, Stalin extended an olive branch to both the United States and United Kingdom, remarking that "compromises were possible on all main questions."[246] Other Soviet policymakers and media outlets repeated this theme in April and May.[247] Likewise, Soviet leaders reacted positively when first presented with the Marshall Plan in June 1947. Indeed, Stalin accepted an Anglo-French invitation to discuss the parameters of U.S. assistance, dispatching Molotov and nearly one hundred advisers to meet with British and French officials, and authorizing its East European client states to do the same. In embracing the Anglo-French offer, Soviet leaders thereby raised the possibility of acquiring U.S. economic assistance and avoided an immediate break in Anglo-Soviet relations.[248]

Instead, Soviet interest in cooperation collapsed only after it became clear that the Anglo-French offer would challenge the Soviet Union's own position. Meeting with Molotov, Bevin and French Foreign Minister Georges Bidault emphasized that U.S. assistance would require the Soviet Union and its Eastern European proxies to coordinate their economic policies with Western Europe and the United States.[249] This could imperil Soviet influence in Eastern Europe.[250] Meanwhile, reports before and during the talks warned that the Marshall Plan was designed to foster what Novikov termed a "West European bloc" directed against the Soviet Union, to facilitate German recovery, and to pull Eastern Europe out of the Soviet orbit.[251] Significantly, reports also indicated that the United States was not acting alone in this initiative, as intelligence analyses and diplomatic cables indicated (correctly) that Bevin and Assistant Secretary of State Clayton met in London before the negotiations to fashion the ERP's anti-Soviet hook.[252]

In response, the Soviet Union backed away from the nascent ERP. Stalin ordered Eastern European governments to end ERP discussions with Britain and France, while Molotov openly denounced the ERP itself on July 2 to the assembled French and British diplomats, remarking that U.S. aid "served as a pretext for the British and French governments to insist on the creation of a new organization, standing above the European countries and intervening in the internal affairs of the countries of Europe." If enacted, the ERP would "lead to Britain, France and the group of countries that follow them separating from the rest of Europe, which will split Europe into two groups of states."[253] The Soviet foreign minister repeated these themes in private, advising Stalin that an agreement with Britain and France over the ERP was unlikely given the "collusion of the USA and Great Britain."[254] Significantly, this was not simply a matter of the United States manipulating the United Kingdom for its own purposes. Instead, Britain *wanted* to collaborate with the United States, seeing the ERP as a way out of its own economic difficulties and hoping, as Molotov explained, to use U.S. assistance "to promote their own interests."[255] The United States and United Kingdom, in other words, were doing more than colluding—they had made common cause.

Turning to Predation, Late 1947 through 1949 By the second half of 1947, the Soviet Union thus faced growing evidence that Britain was no longer available as a partner. Not only had the United Kingdom benefited from U.S. support throughout 1945–46, but as the Marshall Plan negotiations illustrated, British policymakers desired U.S. backing for Britain's own purposes. In contrast to Soviet expectations that Anglo-American differences would proliferate in the postwar world, U.S. and British interests overlapped. Nor, given the state of British domestic politics, was it conceivable that British policy would soon change: in May and June 1947, Attlee and Bevin silenced opponents within the Labour Party calling for a softer stance towards the Soviet Union, receiving overwhelming support at the annual Labour Party conference.[256] Given that the opposition Conservative Party sought an equally hard line against the Soviet Union, with many Conservative Party members calling for the creation of an anti-Soviet bloc, both past experience and domestic conditions meant that Britain was effectively opposed to the Soviet Union.[257]

The Soviet Union noted the change. Even at the start of the summer, Soviet analysts preparing for a fall conference of European Communist parties optimistically concluded that the United States was as focused on "the need to stop Britain from escaping from the dependent position established during the war" and reducing Britain "to the status of a vassal-power" as it was on isolating the Soviet Union[258]—an Anglo-American falling-out remained plausible. By August, however, policymakers revised their assessments. In charge of the conference, Zhdanov edited reports to remove references to "Anglo-American friction" that would pit the United States against Britain and drive Britain into the Soviet camp.[259] Instead, Britain and the United States were now portrayed as firmly aligned against the Soviet Union, as Britain's transformation into an American "vassal" was complete.[260] As Anna Di Biagio notes, "The possibility of exploiting Anglo-American friction to avoid consolidation of the Western bloc was no longer an option."[261]

In response, the Soviet Union embraced a predatory strategy designed to challenge the United Kingdom—and the United States. In September, the changing nature of the Anglo-American threat led the Soviets to finally establish the Communist Information Bureau (Cominform) as a successor to the Comintern. Plans for a pan-Communist organization had been under discussion since 1946, concurrent with the conservative turn in Soviet ideology, but it took until late 1947 for the Soviet Union to announce the creation of a new forum to direct European Communist activities.[262] The nature of Soviet instructions to European Communist parties also changed: instead of pushing Western European parties to cooperate with U.S.- and British-led reconstruction efforts in Western Europe, the Soviet Union now urged confrontation with non-Communist groups. The result was a wave of strikes and political maneuvers that convulsed Western Europe[263] and accompanied a political crackdown throughout Eastern Europe as the Soviet Union also solidified its control of the Eastern bloc.[264] As Zhdanov explained at the September conference, these steps were necessary since "the Anglo-American imperialists have shown their unwillingness to take into account the legitimate interests of the Soviet Union" and were working to "create a jumping-off place for attacking Soviet Russia."[265] Politburo member Georgii Malenkov employed similar logic, arguing that "the game of the U.S.A. and Great Britain [is] fraught with great danger to repudiate obligations taken in World War II" by building up an anti-Soviet bloc.[266] If the United Kingdom was going to work with the United States against the Soviet Union, then the Soviet Union would treat Britain as an opponent.

Alongside mounting Cold War tensions, deepening Anglo-American cooperation in 1947–49 paralleled further Soviet opposition. By early 1948, the Soviet Union devolved increased authority to Communist officials in the Soviet occupation zone in Germany and began creating institutions that could serve as the nucleus of a separate state under Communist control. It also pushed German communists to actively campaign for influence in the Western zones of Germany, promoting the idea of an independent, unified, and neutral Germany that would presumably fall under Soviet influence.[267] These steps would help keep the area out of Western control and limit its contribution to British-led and U.S.-backed plans for Western European recovery. In June 1948, Soviet efforts accelerated again, as the Soviet Union suspended rail and vehicle traffic to Berlin in an effort to pressure the Western powers to end plans for the military and economic rehabilitation of their occupation zones, and to help the Soviet Union consolidate control over the eastern part of Germany.[268] The West responded with the Berlin Airlift and defeated the Soviet ploy, but the effort reflected a Soviet attempt at preventing steps that would, in part, strengthen Britain's hand in the nascent Cold War.

Concurrently, the Soviets inaugurated a propaganda campaign against the West and expanded their influence in Eastern Europe.[269] In February 1948, the Soviet Union facilitated a Communist coup in Czechoslovakia that displaced a government seeking to remain neutral in the onrushing Cold War.[270] Soon afterward, the Soviet Union accelerated its efforts to consolidate Eastern Europe's war-making potential by concluding alliances with Romania, Bulgaria, and Hungary. These complemented earlier agreements with Poland, Yugoslavia, and Czechoslovakia.[271]

Of course, Soviet efforts to challenge the Anglo-American bloc had limits, as Stalin sought to avoid triggering a war before the Soviet Union was prepared.[272] For example, the Soviet leader told Bulgarian and Yugoslav officials in February 1948 that the Greek insurgency should be "terminated" since Britain and the United States would never allow Greece to go Communist.[273] He was even clearer with the Italian Communist Party, warning that a plan for a Communist seizure of power must not be pursued "for any reason"—as Italian Communist leaders themselves recognized, armed insurrection could "lead to a big war."[274] That said, the Soviet Union also began trying to shift the distribution of economic and military power in its favor and against the United States now that Britain was firmly in the U.S. camp. As Stalin explained to the Soviet senior leadership in March 1948, Britain and other European states "follow America out of necessity, and yield to her through fear cast to them by adroit propaganda." In this situation, the Soviet Union needed to develop its economic base and acquire military capabilities to offset those of the United States and United Kingdom. Particularly important was "the development of the Soviet Army and Navy," as the country was behind the United States and the United Kingdom in terms of its "surface water fleet, whilst in all other respects, we are far superior."[275] Thereafter, Soviet military budgets increased and the Soviet military began rearming, incidentally increasing the threat to Britain.[276]

The denouement came in 1949 as Soviet leaders, while recognizing that their actions reinforced Anglo-American solidarity, continued attacking the Anglo-American partnership. Even during the Berlin Blockade, Molotov decried the Anglo-American alignment, noting that Soviet actions were driven partly by "the fact that the ruling circles of the United States and Great Britain have gone over to a frankly aggressive political course."[277] With ERP assistance forthcoming and the North Atlantic Treaty signed in the spring of 1949, these denunciations continued as Soviet leaders, in Roberts's words, "linking the proposed North Atlantic Pact with the Marshall Plan and with Anglo-American plans to establish their domination not only of Europe but of the whole world."[278] Seeking to keep pace, the Soviet Union established the Council for Mutual Economic Assistance in October 1949.[279] Meanwhile, Stalin urged German Communists to prepare for the creation of an independent state in Eastern Germany that would be announced if the United States established an independent Western Germany that, per U.S. plans, would work with Britain against the Soviet Union.[280] Having thus initially sought to keep the United Kingdom a potential ally, the Soviet Union was resigned to Britain's loss as a partner as Britain exited the great power ranks.

In sum, evidence from an array of primary and secondary sources illustrates that both the United States and Soviet Union supported the United Kingdom in much of the early postwar period. In 1945–47, the two states took limited steps to sustain British strength, seeking to keep Britain available as a partner in a fluid postwar world yet also fearing that intensely backing the United Kingdom could lead to entrapment or precipitate a conflict with the other side. Furthermore, the Soviet Union—though not the United States—

appeared concerned that a declining Britain might directly threaten its security. The collapse of British military strength in 1946–47, however, forced reevaluation of these plans. Worried that Britain might defect and join an opposing coalition, both the United States and the Soviet Union upped the ante by increasing assistance to a vulnerable Britain. By mid-1947, the United States had won the race for Britain's hand, as Anglo-American cooperation deepened and British leaders turned uniformly against the Soviet Union. Only then did the latter try to undercut British strength.

This case offered an easy test of alternative accounts of rising state strategy. In particular, arguments rooted in differing ideologies, the intensity of the security dilemma, and economic interdependence all predicted U.S. support for Britain would quickly emerge and deepen, while Soviet strategy moved in the opposite direction. This did not happen. Put simply, U.S. and Soviet strategy moved along parallel tracks from 1945 through mid-1947, while the substance of and rationales for U.S. and Soviet policies belie the predictions of many of these accounts. The United States remained skeptical of intensely supporting Britain despite recognizing the two countries' shared ideologies, compatible security interests, and—notwithstanding occasional concerns during the negotiations for the 1945–46 loan and the ERP—growing economic interdependence. Conversely, the Soviet Union supported Britain despite their disparate worldviews and lack of significant economic exchange. Just as important, the case shows that the United States and Soviet Union both used military policy, economic exchange, and ideological competition instrumentally to support or eventually (in the Soviet case) weaken the United Kingdom. The balance of evidence suggests that, rather than causing U.S. or Soviet strategy, these factors were by-products of policies pursued for other reasons.

Arguments focused on the views held by U.S. and Soviet leaders perform somewhat better but also face limits. Accounts stressing the Open Door beliefs of U.S. leaders capture the United States' ambivalence about fully backing a militarily capable Britain. However, the accompanying hypothesis that U.S. strategists pushed American dominance in Europe to the point of weakening the United Kingdom does not fare well. Not only were U.S. leaders wedded to preserving Britain as a counterweight to the Soviet Union, but policymakers such as Marshall, Acheson, and Kennan sought to sustain British strength and were willing to accommodate British preferences—even accepting British schemes for intra-Western European cooperation rather than the European integration preferred by the United States—to use Britain against the Soviet Union. Soviet strategy, meanwhile, was initially informed by ideas that capitalist contradictions would lead to an Anglo-American fight and drive the United Kingdom toward the Soviet Union: in fact, Soviet leaders from Stalin on down justified Soviet policies in these terms. Conversely, the growing sense that intracapitalist contradictions were not as powerful as expected and that the Soviet Union faced a stable Anglo-American bloc accompanied the Soviet turn to predation. That said, these ideas did not develop or gain traction in a vacuum. At a minimum, as the mid-1947 ideational shift suggests, the changing content of Soviet ideas followed international developments that affected Soviet security; at maximum, the ideas were the outgrowth of a strategy developed for other reasons.

In contrast, the results offer significant backing to three core predictions from predation theory, namely that (1) rising states support declining great powers that offer them high strategic value, (2) shifts in the declining state's military posture in these circumstances affect the assertiveness of support, and (3) alterations in a declining state's strategic value affect a rising state's fundamental choice of supporting or preying upon a decliner. Of course, events in postwar Europe and the escalating U.S.-Soviet rivalry reinforced these dynamics by boosting the two rising states' incentives to find partners. Nevertheless, a Cold War–centric account does not adequately capture the specific policies directed at Britain—instead, the variables central to predation theory are needed to explain the course of Anglo-American and Anglo-Soviet relations.

Indeed, and as predicted by my argument, the Soviet Union and United States supported Britain when it had high strategic value. Furthermore, these efforts transitioned from Bolstering to Strengthening strategies as British military posture changed. When it appeared in 1945–46 that Britain could handle threats to its security on its own, both rising states refrained from offering intense backing. This behavior is especially striking in the case of the United States, given the strong signals that Britain would have welcomed a closer Anglo-American relationship. As British military options collapsed in 1946–47, however, both the United States and the Soviet Union increased their assistance to Britain by offering it security guarantees and, in the case of the United States, significant economic aid. Such escalating support is particularly notable in the Soviet case given signs throughout 1945–46 that British policymakers feared Soviet power and sought to hedge against the Soviet Union. Above all, only after Britain firmly aligned itself with the United States and so offered the Soviet Union low strategic value did Soviet and U.S. strategies diverge: as expected by my argument, the United States continued its Strengthening course, while the Soviet Union tried to prey upon the United Kingdom to deny it as a prop to the United States.

Internal deliberations provide additional evidence, as policymakers debated and discussed strategic options in terms consonant with predation theory. Through late 1947, strategists in both the Soviet Union and the United States recognized that supporting Britain could improve their states' relative position. U.S. policymakers emphasized that cooperation would transfer some of the security costs of confronting the Soviet Union to Britain and abet U.S. retrenchment schemes. Soviet leaders saw supporting Britain as a way to provide the Soviet Union to obtain a partner against what was expected to be an aggressive United States. To these ends, Soviet policymakers affirmed the need to reinforce Britain's hand in Europe and shaped policies to accommodate British interests.

That said, both rising powers also emphasized the desirability of supporting Britain in a way that minimized the risks of entrapment, averted conflict with other great powers, and—for the Soviet Union—avoided making British perfidy more likely. These concerns only dissipated in the winter of 1946–47, when U.S. and Soviet strategists realized that changes to British military capabilities left Britain so weak that only concerted efforts to restore its strength would allow it to play a meaningful role in European politics and prevent it from aligning itself with the other side. Although these calculations continued for the United States through 1949, Soviet policymakers recognized by mid-1947 that their efforts to secure British friendship had failed. In response, Soviet leaders moved to weaken the United Kingdom and undercut the Anglo-American alignment.

In sum, the process of establishing the familiar blocs of Cold War Europe saw the United States and Soviet Union monitor the distribution of power, assess the dangers and opportunities created by Britain's decline, and adopt policies calibrated to Britain's strategic value and military posture. To a greater extent than has been widely appreciated, the incentive to maximize power by finding partners with which to confront other great powers led both the United States and Soviet Union to support a declining Britain after World War II. This strategy was not sacrosanct, as the emergence of the familiar Anglo-American alignment led the Soviet Union to try to weaken the United Kingdom, but even this shift is understandable given the need for a rising state to focus on ensuring its own security and protect its relative position. Baldly stated, the Soviet and U.S. responses to Britain's decline were driven by predictable concerns about maximizing Soviet and U.S. relative strength and security in the postwar world, the results of which shaped European politics within the onrushing Cold War.

Watching the Soviet Union Decline

Assessing Change and Predicting U.S. Strategy

The preceding chapters showed that the rising United States and Soviet Union adopted similarly supportive strategies toward the declining United Kingdom in much of the early postwar period, only for these efforts to later diverge. These strategies emerged in response to Britain's shifting strategic value and military posture, and shaped the familiar battle lines of Cold War Europe. Here, I fast-forward to examine the U.S. response to the Soviet Union's decline at Cold War's end.

Like Britain's fall from the great powers, the Soviet Union's decline represents one of the seminal events of modern international history. No serious U.S. policymaker in the early 1980s would have predicted that the Cold War would be a thing of the past within a decade.[1] The Reagan administration—hardly dovish when it came to U.S.-Soviet relations—expressly called for preparations for an ongoing U.S.-Soviet rivalry that might last into the twenty-first century.[2] Nevertheless, a shift in the international distribution of power to the Soviet Union's detriment, carrying with it wide international implications, occurred during the 1980s and early 1990s. By 1991, the strategic map of Europe had fundamentally changed: Soviet military power was within its pre-1941 borders; the Soviet-led Warsaw Pact was defunct; Germany—the great strategic prize in Cold War Europe—had reunified on Western terms; and the Soviet Union itself was nearing economic and political collapse. American primacy was on.[3]

This chapter serves two purposes. First, I discuss the power shift that occurred in the 1980s and early 1990s, alongside U.S. efforts to monitor this change. Second, I use predation theory and the alternative arguments to develop predictions for U.S. strategy as power shifts in favor of the United States and against the Soviet Union. In the process, I also situate these competing predictions in current scholarship on U.S.-Soviet relations in the late Cold War, showing that predation theory offers a unique account of the U.S.-Soviet relationship. I then evaluate the competing predictions in chapter 5.

The Decline of the Soviet Union: Shifting Power at the Cold War's End

Few analysts would dispute that the Soviet Union declined relative to the United States during the 1980s. This change is ironic: not only had U.S. officials throughout the Cold War feared that the United States was soon to wane relative to the Soviet Union, but the start of the 1980s saw particularly pronounced concerns of American decline owing to U.S. economic and military weaknesses.[4] Starting around 1982–84, however, two trends spurred the relative ascendance of the United States and the relative decline of the Soviet Union. First, the revival of U.S. economic power from its nadir in the late 1970s and early 1980s, coupled with a defense buildup under Presidents Jimmy Carter and Reagan, helped arrest the United States' ostensible decline.[5] Second, Soviet economic and social problems began to exact a toll.[6] Although Soviet economic growth slowed and social problems mounted beginning in the 1970s (if not earlier), these trends became increasingly intractable and, as the United States recovered, affected the Soviet Union's relative position.[7] By the middle of the 1980s, Soviet gross domestic product (GDP) fell below 40 percent of U.S. GDP for the first time since the early Cold War and continued falling thereafter, ending the decade barely one-third that of the United States (figure 4.1). As discussed below, these changes led U.S. policymakers to conclude the United States was recovering ground and rising relative to the Soviet Union.[8]

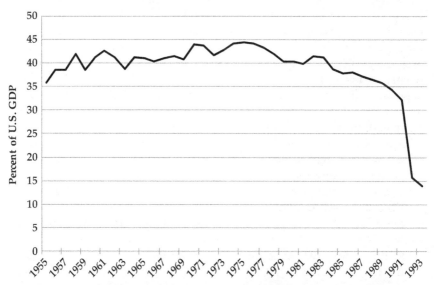

Figure 4.1. Soviet GDP as a percentage of U.S. GDP, 1955–93. Author calculations based on Angus Maddison, *Statistics on World Population, GDP, and Per Capita GDP, 1–2008 A.D.* (Groningen, the Netherlands: University of Groningen, 2008).

Table 4.1 CIA estimates of the Soviet lag in critical technologies

Technology	U.S. Lead, 1985	U.S. Lead, 1988–89
Microprocessors/Microcircuits	4–6 years	8–10 years
Minicomputers	4–6 years	4–10 years
Mainframes	6–8 years	9–15 years
Computer-operated Machine Tools	3–4 years	5–9 years
Flexible Manufacturing Systems	5–6 years	7–10 years

Data is from Central Intelligence Agency, *A Comparison of the US and Soviet Economies: Evaluating the Performance of the Soviet System*, October 1985, 15, https://www.cia.gov/library/readingroom/docs/DOC_0000497165.pdf; Joint Economic Committee, Congress of the United States, Subcommittee on National Security Economics, *Allocation of Resources in the Soviet Union and China, April 14, 1989* (Washington, DC: Government Printing Office, 1990), 47.

Still, the overall distribution of power does not fully capture the qualitative change in strength. Even as U.S. growth surged, for example, Soviet economic efficiency—the rate at which economic inputs are converted into goods and services—collapsed; in fact, Soviet factor productivity growth was negative over the course of the 1980s.[9] The Soviet Union also fell further behind the West technologically (table 4.1), with intelligence analysts concluding in 1989 that the Soviet Union was unable "to compete in high-technology fields and to efficiently integrate technological advances in the production process."[10] These trends promised to further hinder Soviet economic strength.

For their part, Soviet leaders proved unable to address these problems. At the start of the 1980s, a succession of geriatric leaders—Leonid Brezhnev through 1982, Yuri Andropov in 1982–84, and Konstantin Chernenko in 1984–85—left a power vacuum at the highest Soviet levels that ensured problems went unaddressed. Even when leaders focused on the Soviet Union's ills, as Andropov attempted during his brief rule, their solutions were constrained by a system favoring stability over radical reform.[11] And while Mikhail Gorbachev's 1985 selection as Chernenko's successor promised a change in the status quo, Gorbachev's subsequent reforms only worsened Soviet problems.[12] Gorbachev initially looked to boost economic performance through managerial accountability and efforts to improve worker productivity by, for instance, reducing workers' alcohol use.[13] When these efforts failed, he enacted more extensive reforms starting in 1986 with the goal of emulating Western economic systems while liberalizing Soviet politics to give Soviet citizens a stake in the efforts' success. These steps culminated in 1987–88 with laws that liberalized the Soviet economy by reducing the state's role in economic planning and permitting ownership of private property, and opening the political system by calling for competitive elections and protecting civil liberties.[14] At the close of 1988, Gorbachev went still further, announcing cuts to the Soviet defense budget, changes to Soviet military doctrine, and the withdrawal of certain military forces from Central-Eastern Europe.[15] Shortly afterward, his government tolerated and, in some cases, even encouraged reforms in Warsaw Pact member states as opposition movements challenged and then swept away Communist rule throughout Eastern Europe in the Revolutions of 1989–90.[16]

No matter what Gorbachev tried, however, Soviet efforts proved futile. By 1989, the Soviet economy was in crisis. Instead of spurring growth, reforms led to uncertainty and confusion that worsened economic performance. The loss of Eastern Europe following the Revolutions of 1989–90 exacerbated this problem by upsetting Soviet trade and foreign economic arrangements.[17] The military balance was similarly in flux as the Soviet Union reduced foreign commitments, cut spending, and pared back forces.[18] Political liberalization added to these dilemmas by sowing disagreement among Soviet leaders over whether and how reforms should continue.[19] These disputes became so acrimonious and Soviet problems so daunting that the integrity of the Soviet Union was increasingly in question. By early 1991, with economic problems worsening and Soviet political authority challenged by secessionist movements, the country was on the verge of collapse. Indeed, the state slipped into history with the final lowering of the Soviet flag over the Kremlin on Christmas Day 1991.

U.S. Policymakers: Monitoring the Changing Distribution of Power

On their end, U.S. policymakers carefully monitored and recognized the shifting distribution of power. Intelligence and diplomatic reports from the early 1980s alerted policymakers to the slowdown in Soviet economic growth as well as the mounting structural and political problems that militated against a Soviet recovery. Even in 1980, Central Intelligence Agency (hereafter CIA) briefings to President-elect Ronald Reagan emphasized that Soviet "industrial growth has slowed to its lowest level since WW II; growth in GNP [Gross National Product] has averaged only 1% in each of the last 2 years."[20] One year later, National Security Advisor Richard Allen sent Reagan a similar assessment arguing that, "Soviet economic performance has deteriorated to the point that, if military expenditures continue to expand as in the past, there will be few if any resources left with which to raise living standards."[21] This followed other "diplomatic and intelligence reporting providing startling evidence of real economic distress" in the Soviet Union and Eastern Europe.[22] By mid-1982, Reagan himself argued that "the Soviet Union is economically on the ropes," just as "the Soviets do not believe that they can keep up" if the U.S. engaged in an all-out competition.[23]

Still, whether Soviet problems would translate into relative American gains remained questionable owing to the poor performance of the U.S. economy in the late 1970s and early 1980s.[24] Notably, while Soviet growth

Table 4.2   U.S. and Soviet average percent annual economic growth, 1971–82

Period	United States (Gross National Income)	Soviet Union (Gross National Product)
1971–75	2.8	3.7
1976–80	3.7	2.7
1981–82	1	2.1

Soviet data is from CIA, Office of Soviet Analysis, "USSR: Economic Trends and Policy Developments: Joint Economic Committee Briefing Paper," September 14, 1983, table 14, CIA Records Search Tool, National Archives and Records Administration, College Park, Maryland. U.S. data is from the World Bank, DataBank, accessed March 2013, http://databank.worldbank.org/.

fell compared to its postwar highs, it remained comparable to that of the United States in the 1970s and higher than the U.S. at the turn of the 1980s (table 4.2). Concern was such that a November 1981 National Security Council (NSC) report summarizing U.S. foreign policy in the Reagan administration's first year emphasized that "our primary foreign policy objective has been to restore the domestic capabilities (economic and military) and credibility . . . of America's foreign policy leadership."[25] This concern continued into 1982–83, as policymakers continued to emphasize the United States' economic recovery.[26] Put simply, although the United States had the potential to recover ground against the Soviet Union, it was uncertain in the early 1980s whether the desired power shift would occur.[27]

The U.S. economic recovery that started in 1981–82, however, soon began to tell. By 1983–84, U.S. policymakers noticed the distribution of power shifting against the Soviet Union. National Security Advisor William Clark, for instance, observed at the start of 1983 that although "the Soviets may well have considered us a nation in decline" in the late 1970s, now "there is a very solid basis for concluding that the Soviets may be reconciled to the fact that by the end of the decade we will have passed them again."[28] Other senior advisors, such as Secretary of State George Shultz, shared this view, writing Reagan that the United States was in a strong bargaining position given the "economic recovery now under way," and would grow stronger as military recovery followed.[29] Meanwhile, intelligence analysts led by CIA director William Casey and diplomats fed senior policymakers a steady stream of information that the Soviet Union remained in economic and military arrears.[30] In short order, a core contingent of U.S. decision makers came to conclude—as an interagency memorandum put it in early 1984—that "we have arrested U.S. decline and are in [a] strong negotiating position," whereas the "Soviets are on [the] diplomatic defensive and have growing problems at home."[31]

This vision of a surging United States and a declining Soviet Union soon became the received wisdom. At mid-1986, NSC staffer Jack Matlock could offer Reagan talking points on U.S.-Soviet relations based on the premise that "the U.S. position is strong, and the momentum in the balance of power is with us."[32] Even clearer was Frank Carlucci—another of Reagan's national security advisors—who reminded Reagan in late 1987 that "The Soviet empire is in deep trouble at home, in East Europe, and around the world. It can only get out of that trouble with far-reaching reforms and, even then, only with Western help."[33] And by the time George H.W. Bush became president in 1989, the notion of a relatively declining Soviet Union was an article of faith. A critical mass of policymakers in the Bush administration—including Secretary of State James Baker, National Security Advisor Brent Scowcroft, Deputy National Security Advisor Robert Gates, Chairman of the Joint Chiefs of Staff Colin Powell, and Bush himself—had either served in the Reagan administration or were privy to Reagan-era assessments of the U.S.-Soviet competition, and generally agreed with the conclusions. Around the time Carlucci described Gorbachev's need for Western help, for example, Gates—then the Deputy Director of the CIA—offered that "The Soviets' need to relax tensions is critical because only thus can massive new expenditures for defense be avoided and Western help in economic development be obtained."[34] In early February 1989, newly confirmed secretary of state Baker similarly argued that Gorbachev needed to cope with an "era of stagnation" that constrained Soviet foreign policy options.[35] Soon thereafter, Bush and Scowcroft launched a review of U.S.-Soviet relations premised on the idea that "the pressures of a failing system at home and frustrated policies abroad" meant that the Soviet Union was focused on domestic developments; this created "trends in US-Soviet relations [that] are, in large part, favorable to us."[36] As long as the United States maintained its economic health and a strong military, the Soviet Union would continue to fall behind.[37]

The U.S. Response to Soviet Decline: Competing Perspectives

As power moves in the United States' favor and against the Soviet Union, how do we expect the United States to respond? For most of the past three decades, many political science and historiographic treatments of the U.S.-Soviet relationship have given a clear and consistent answer: from the mid-1980s through early 1990s, a surging United States and waning Soviet Union cooperated in reducing Cold War tensions and improving superpower relations.[38] Indeed, the case is often treated as a leading example of states supporting and cooperating with one another amid a shifting distribution of power.[39] One prominent scholar captures this theme well, arguing that the puzzle of the Cold War's end hinges largely on why "the Western powers . . . never attempted to exploit the situation, thereby accelerating their opponent's collapse."[40] There are several different accounts of this process, and not all are mutually compatible. Still, a conventional analysis would go something like the following.

After a period of intense rivalry in the early 1980s, both the United States and Soviet Union altered course to ensure a more peaceful relationship.[41] For the Reagan administration, the emergence of comparatively moderate poli-cymakers such as Shultz over hard-liners such as Secretary of Defense Caspar Weinberger, coupled with the realization that intense U.S.-Soviet competition was roiling international politics, led to diplomatic overtures aimed at stabi-lizing superpower relations. The timing of the U.S. turn was fortuitous, as it corresponded with Gorbachev's ascendance and his growing focus on revi-talizing Soviet strength by opening up Soviet political and economic life while seeking a cooperative relationship with the West.[42] Combined, these trends spurred a U.S.-Soviet rapprochement as the superpowers came to trust one another and dampen their rivalry through diplomatic accommoda-tion and arms control.[43]

This bonhomie subsequently proved important as the Soviet Union's sphere of influence in Eastern Europe crumbled during the Revolutions of 1989–90. Initially skeptical of Gorbachev's intentions,[44] the Bush administra-tion nevertheless reassured Soviet leaders that Soviet problems would not be exploited as the Soviet Union left the area.[45] In doing so, the United States engaged the Soviets in discussions to resolve the future of Eastern Europe; offered the Soviet Union diplomatic and economic concessions to compen-sate it for its losses; and limited the threat posed by the United States to the much-weakened Soviet Union after the Cold War by capping the size of NATO military forces and limiting the alliance's geopolitical reach. Although the Soviet Union collapsed in 1991, this was not for want of U.S. kindness—the United States accommodated the Soviet Union during its decline.[46]

ACCOUNTING FOR SUPPORT

Significantly, the putative emergence of a supportive U.S. strategy toward the declining Soviet Union makes sense in light of several competing ac-counts of rising state behavior. Proponents of the security dilemma, for ex-ample, see the U.S. turn toward cooperation as part of a successful Soviet campaign to reassure the United States. By conciliating the United States and offering increasingly costly signals of its benign intentions—culminating in a December 1988 announcement that the Soviet Union would adopt a de-fensive military doctrine and remove large numbers of troops from Eastern Europe—Gorbachev eventually convinced U.S. leaders that the Soviet Union sought cooperation rather than competition.[47] This effort was aided by the fact that both states had diversified and secure nuclear arsenals (defensive weapons par excellence) that guaranteed their survival.[48] As benign Soviet intentions became clear and credible around 1987–88, the United States matched cooperative Soviet gestures.[49]

For scholars emphasizing the role of ideology, on the other hand, the So-viet Union's liberalization under Gorbachev diminished the ideological distance between it and the United States. By increasing individual liberties, reducing centralized economic planning, and allowing for competitive elections after 1987–88, Gorbachev's reforms moved the Soviet Union closer to U.S. political values and effectively called off the ideological rivalry between the two states.[50] With the Soviets no longer pushing an alternative worldview that challenged core U.S. precepts, the United States no longer needed to push back and compete as intensely with a weakening and ideologically compatible Soviet Union. This lowered U.S. threat perceptions, created conditions for the United States to explore ways of engaging the Soviet Union, and spurred cooperation.[51]

From an interdependence perspective, meanwhile, the economic opening of the Soviet Union starting in 1986 gave the United States incentives to pursue a supportive strategy. The United States had long been committed to an open international economic order. With the Soviet Union seeking economic integration with the Western world, the United States therefore had a golden opportunity to find new markets and enhance East-West economic transactions by responding to Soviet overtures.[52] Moreover, since Gorbachev and a small group of Soviet policymakers led the Soviet economic opening, cooperation would have the advantage of reinforcing the influence of Soviet reformers.[53] Indeed, as it became clear by late 1989 that Gorbachev was sincerely interested in East-West economic exchanges, the Bush administration—as Dale Copeland writes—"made a definitive decision that Gorbachev's reforms must be supported" through Western economic and diplomatic backing.[54]

THE COMPETITION NARRATIVE AND IDEATIONAL ARGUMENTS

Not all analysts, however, accept this cooperative account of U.S. policy. A second school of thought proposes that, far from conciliating the Soviet Union, the United States used economic and ideological subversion and military competition to pressure the Soviet Union during its decline.[55] Although scholars differ on the scope and consistency of U.S. efforts, this alternative account stresses the predatory elements of U.S. policy, especially during the Reagan administration: the Soviet Union may have tried to cooperate to decrease U.S. pressure, but U.S. competition played a major role in facilitating the decline of the Soviet Union and spurring it to sue for peace.[56] Thus, Francis Marlo argues that the Reagan administration worked to "undermine the cohesion of the Soviet Union and ultimately destroy the Soviet state."[57] Steven Hayward sees the Reagan administration pursuing an integrated plan to compete with the Soviet Union and force it to end the Cold War on U.S. terms,[58] while John Prados suggests that U.S. predation reached its apogee in the 1990s as the Bush administration embraced "a policy of seeking U.S. advantage through a process of diplomatic engagement with Moscow."[59] Aptly summarizing the competition narrative, John Lewis Gaddis proposes that the United States employed a range of economic, political, and military tools to exhaust and challenge the declining Soviet Union, thereby creating incentives for Soviet leaders to end the Cold War on U.S. terms.[60]

This description of U.S. policy meshes with theories stressing the ideas held by U.S. leaders. Two interpretations of these views during the 1980s and 1990s dominate the literature. First, some scholars emphasize the importance of a crusading and hawkish form of conservatism prevalent among U.S. policymakers in the Reagan years. In this view, a particular aversion to Communism and belief in the moral and material power of conservative principles spurred U.S. policymakers to increase pressure on the Soviet Union starting in the early 1980s. Colin Dueck captures the argument well, noting that "Reagan looked to use every available foreign policy instrument to pressure the Soviet Union, with the long-term goal of weakening the USSR and reducing cold war tensions on American terms."[61] Consequently, the United States engaged in a sustained arms buildup, pushed economic and ideological subversion of the Soviet Union, and undermined the cohesion of Soviet alliances.[62] Conversely, Bush is seen as less ideologically conservative than Reagan and predisposed to a moderate brand of pragmatic conservatism—in George Will's quip, "Bushism is Reaganism minus the passion for freedom."[63] Bush thus moved away from Reagan's confrontational stance vis-à-vis the Soviet Union and embraced a supportive policy calling for diplomatic and economic backing for Soviet domestic reforms, cooperatively reunifying Germany, and opposing the breakup of the Soviet Union.[64] In short, hard-line conservative views among U.S. leaders in the Reagan years led to a Weakening strategy, before the more pragmatic Bush administration adopted a Bolstering strategy.

Alternatively, treatments emphasizing the importance of liberal values in U.S. strategy debates suggest that that it was Bush more than Reagan who pursued a predatory policy against the Soviet Union. In this view, the United States' pursuit of outcomes informed by Open Door ideas pushed the Bush administration to exploit Soviet weakness following the 1989–90 Revolutions. As Christopher Layne, the leading proponent of this approach, explains, "The United States was determined to take advantage of a weakened Soviet Union to marginalize Russia as a future player in European security and ensure that it could not challenge America's global dominance."[65] Prior to 1989–90, however, the Open Door thesis also suggests that the United States focused on pursuing a status quo strategy and doing little to weaken the Soviet Union. After all, at the heart of the Open Door argument is the notion that the United States seeks extra-regional hegemony to ensure a liberal order, yet also needs to be invited in and to have a reason to stay engaged abroad. Otherwise, states targeted by the United States' hegemonic ambitions are liable to resist and question the need for a U.S. overseas presence. As such, the Open Door thesis suggests that the United States should try to avoid weakening the Soviet Union before 1989, as doing so would eliminate the rationale for the U.S. presence in Europe in the first place. Overall, this approach sees U.S. strategy moving from a broadly cooperative and supportive course to a Relegation strategy.[66]

Predation Theory and U.S. Strategy

In contrast to the preceding accounts, predation theory uniquely predicts the United States should prey on the Soviet Union from 1983 through 1991, and do so intensely when Soviet military options collapse. These predictions reflect the incentives facing the United States to eliminate its only great power rival, alongside the shifting constraints imposed by the Soviet Union's military posture. In short, and similar to recent historical interpretations advanced by scholars such as Melvyn Leffler, the desire to prey upon the Soviet Union is expected to be a common theme shared by policymakers across the Reagan and Bush administrations.[67]

THE SOVIET UNION: LOW STRATEGIC VALUE
TO THE UNITED STATES

The first and overriding factor driving U.S. strategy is the Soviet Union's low strategic value stemming from the Cold War's bipolar structure. Few would dispute that the Cold War was, at root, a contest between the United States and Soviet Union for dominance in Europe. Economically, the two states were the largest on the Continent, with even the declining Soviet economy approximately twice the size of the next strongest state (figure 4.2). The military balance reflected this situation, as the Soviet Union and United States spent nearly six times as much as even the next-wealthiest European states and retained the largest militaries, armed with a diverse array of conventional and nuclear assets (table 4.3).[68] Europe's political geography further mirrored and reinforced this situation, as both the United States and Soviet Union established highly integrated alliance networks—NATO for the United States and the Warsaw Pact for the Soviet Union. These alliances allowed the two superpowers to project power into the heart of Europe, organize the resources of Europe's smaller states to suit their ends, and exert oversight of their clients.[69]

In this environment, the declining Soviet Union held low strategic value for the United States. With no other great powers around, the United States lacked reason or opportunity to use the Soviet Union to keep other great powers in check. Admittedly, far-sighted strategists may have expected the future European Union (then the European Community, or EC) to challenge the United States. However, with European integration still uncertain, it would require a planner with a particularly long time horizon making best-case assumptions about the European project to consider the EC a future

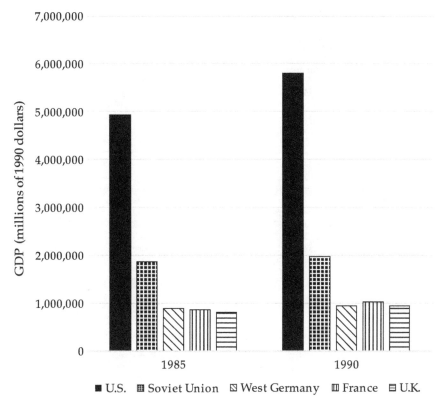

Figure 4.2. Comparative economic strength, major European states.

GDP for the United States, Soviet Union, France, and the United Kingdom from Maddison, *Statistics on World Population*. GDP for West Germany estimated as 75 percent of the combined East and West German total in ibid., which is generally consistent with data in Central Intelligence Agency (CIA), *The World Factbook: 1987* (Washington, DC: CIA, 1987).

competitor. Instead, a more realistic assessment would conclude that the United States and Soviet Union were each other's only peer competitor in the 1980s and early 1990s.

As a result, we expect the United States to pursue a predatory strategy. Predation helps the United States address two dilemmas. First, it improves U.S. security vis-à-vis the system's only other great power by ensuring that, even if the Soviet Union eventually recovers from its decline, it starts from a weaker position than would otherwise be the case—predation primes the United States to better compete with the Soviet Union. Second, predation facilitates U.S. hegemony. As Soviet decline continues, abetting Soviet problems is a way of moving the United States toward a world without great power threats. Policymakers should thus see Soviet decline as presenting an opportunity to move toward American dominance in Europe by undercutting

Table 4.3 Comparing military assets

State	Ground Forces (Active and Reserve)	Tanks	Artillery Tubes	Tactical Aircraft (Fighters and Attack)	Strategic Nuclear Warheads
United States	1,850,000	15,992	5,397	3,205	13,967
Soviet Union	4,600,000	53,350	31,500	4,595	12,117
United Kingdom	410,700	1,290	550	570	128 (estimated)
France	559,500	1,340	764	598	294–314 (estimated)
West Germany	1,057,000	5,005	1,272	507	0
East Germany	370,000	3,140	1,260	335	0

Data on conventional forces is from International Institute for Strategic Studies, *The Military Balance,* *1989* (London: International Institute for Strategic Studies, 1990). Data on U.S. and Soviet nuclear forces is from National Resource Defense Council, "Archive of Nuclear Data," accessed January 2018, http://web.archive.org/web/20060209030802/http://www.nrdc.org/nuclear/nudb/datainx.asp. Data on British and French forces is estimated based on United Nations Department for Disarmament Affairs, *Nuclear Weapons: A Comprehensive Study* (New York: United Nations, 1991), 17–18.

Soviet power and unifying what George Kennan called one of the major centers of "industrial and military power" under the United States' aegis.[70] U.S. diplomatic, military, and economic policies should therefore focus on initiatives that are uniquely beneficial to the United States and injurious to the Soviet Union.

SHIFTS IN SOVIET MILITARY POSTURE SHAPED
U.S. ASSERTIVENESS

Simply because the Soviet Union's low strategic value incentivizes U.S. predation does not mean, however, that the United States should mount an all-out campaign to destroy the Soviet Union from the start of Soviet decline. Instead, Soviet military posture should mediate American assertiveness. In particular, there should be a shift in American strategy in 1989–90 as Soviet military posture moves from robust to weak. The period around the Soviet Union's 1991 collapse presents another inflection point, an issue that I address below.

The Robust Soviet Posture through Early 1990 Prior to the winter of 1989–90, the Soviet Union had a robust military posture (table 4.4). First, the Soviet Union retained a large and well-trained conventional military, much of which was deployed in the East European member states of the Warsaw Pact.[71] The Group of Soviet Forces Germany alone numbered more than 380,000 soldiers and 6,200 tanks, while an additional 185,000 soldiers and 3,200 tanks were stationed elsewhere in Warsaw Pact territory; still other units were in the Soviet Union itself.[72] These forces provided the Soviet Union

Table 4.4 Changes in Soviet military posture

Robust Posture, 1983–89	*Weak Posture (Eastern Europe), 1990*
Soviet forces could deploy to and from the Soviet Union and throughout Eastern Europe	Soviet forces could no longer reliably deploy to or from Eastern Europe
Large standing forces forward-deployed in Eastern Europe	Soviet territory secure due to nuclear arsenal, but forces in Eastern Europe being expelled from region
Units capable of defense, offense, and maintaining regional or internal stability	Political and economic conditions in Eastern Europe limit Soviet military missions
Units willing to fight	Units' reliability uncertain
Reliable allies in Warsaw Pact supported Soviet lines of communication into Eastern Europe	Allies of questionable loyalty leave Soviet lines of communication in doubt
Soviet homeland protected by extensive nuclear forces and additional military units	Soviet homeland protected by extensive nuclear forces and additional military units

with a potent instrument to advance its objectives: Soviet units could attack Western Europe or defend Soviet positions if attacked themselves, or intervene in members of the Warsaw Pact to maintain regional stability and Soviet dominance in the area.

Second, because states in the Pact were led by Communist regimes closely aligned with the Soviet Union, Soviet forces enjoyed significant operational freedom. Guaranteed local backing, the Soviet Union could redeploy, reinforce, and sustain its forces in either peace or war.[73] It could also stage its forces from Eastern European bases instead of operating from Soviet home territory, and could likely call upon Eastern European forces to operate alongside Soviet units when necessary.[74] Simply put, friendly regimes sustained Soviet lines of communication in peace and war.

Finally, the Soviet Union had a large nuclear arsenal that minimally precluded attacks on the Soviet homeland. Scholars still debate when the Soviet Union reached nuclear parity with the United States, but most agree that the U.S. and Soviet nuclear arsenals were broadly secure from a disarming first strike by the late 1960s.[75] At minimum, this meant that if the survival of the Soviet Union were at risk, missiles might fly and any attacker suffer massive damage. At maximum, the coupling of Soviet conventional and nuclear forces meant that the Soviet Union could extend deterrence over its Eastern European sphere of influence to keep other states at bay—the United States could not challenge the Soviet Union in Central-Eastern Europe without risking an eventual nuclear exchange.

Soviet Military Posture Changed in the Winter of 1989–1990 In the winter of 1989–90, however, Soviet posture abruptly collapsed (table 4.4). Although the Soviet homeland remained protected by Soviet nuclear forces, the Soviet Union became unable to wage a conventional war against the United States and NATO in Central-Eastern Europe; Soviet extended deterrence unraveled as well.[76] This situation reduced the risks for U.S. involvement in the Soviet Union's Eastern European sphere of influence.

The strategic fallout from the Revolutions of 1989–90 was the primary cause of this shift. Initially a series of domestic political transformations in states across Central and Eastern Europe, the changes attendant to the 1989–90 upheavals carried major consequences for European security. At the most general level, the political changes in Eastern Europe raised the bar for Soviet military intervention. Although the documentary record is sparse, Soviet forces attempting to sustain control over the area after 1989 would have needed to suppress highly mobilized populations. Local citizens would likely rally to the defense of their newly non-Communist governments, while the forces required for a crackdown would be scarce as Soviet assets would be tied down throughout the region.[77] Similarly, and unlike previous crackdowns in Hungary (1956) and Czechoslovakia (1968), the Soviet Union could no longer rely on local forces to help it retain control in Eastern Europe if it decided to intervene.[78] Indeed, by the start of 1990, non-Communist governments in Eastern Europe were consolidating their authority by limiting Communist and Soviet influence while reforming their security services.[79] Morale in local military and security services also waned as economic problems worsened and political change accelerated.[80] Hence, whereas the Soviet Union led successful crackdowns against unrest in 1956 and 1968—mobilizing members of the Warsaw Pact in the latter case—doing so across the region after the 1989–90 Revolutions would have been significantly more difficult.[81] Collectively, the Revolutions of 1989–90 altered Moscow's strategic landscape by undermining the Soviet Union's ability to maintain order in its sphere of influence.[82]

The collapse of Eastern European Communism further threatened the Soviet Union's military position.[83] With political changes underway in Eastern Europe, the Soviet Union could no longer count on other members of the Warsaw Pact to fight against the United States and NATO.[84] At the start of 1990, in fact, former Soviet clients demanded and received autonomy over their defense policies.[85] Given, too, that a Pact-NATO confrontation might involve serious risks to Eastern Europe, Moscow could not rely on Eastern European states to allow Soviet forces wartime transit, leaving Soviet lines of communication in doubt.[86] Alongside Soviet military reductions announced in December 1988, these changes nearly eliminated the threat of a Soviet conventional attack against Western Europe while bringing the Soviet Union's ability to defend Eastern Europe into question.[87]

In addition, the Soviet Union's faltering position hindered its ability to extend its nuclear umbrella across Eastern Europe. As analysts learned during the Cold War, credible extended deterrence in the nuclear age required a range of options below a strategic nuclear exchange. Otherwise, because a strategic nuclear exchange threatened both sides with destruction, opponents might question the Soviet Union's promise to commit suicide for its allies. By simultaneously removing Soviet conventional options and signaling that nominal allies did not want Soviet protection, the 1989–90 Revolutions decoupled the Soviet Union from Eastern Europe. Reinforcing the trend, the Soviet Union removed its nonstrategic nuclear weapons from Poland, Hungary, and Czechoslovakia in early 1990, and from the German Democratic Republic (GDR, or East Germany) later that year.[88]

Finally, key members of the Warsaw Pact demanded the withdrawal of Soviet troops from their territory.[89] This process started in the late fall of 1989 before accelerating in December 1989–January 1990 after the Soviets announced their intention to withdraw troops from the region by 2000.[90] Sensing an opportunity, Hungarian and Czechoslovak leaders instead pushed for the removal of Soviet forces by the end of 1990 and the Pact's transformation into a purely "political" organization.[91] Surprisingly—although previous moves by Soviet allies to withdraw from the Pact's military arrangements resulted in Soviet intervention, and membership in the Pact was seen as the minimum Soviet demand for states in Eastern Europe—the Soviets agreed to negotiate on these terms.[92] Poland soon followed suit as Polish policymakers sought to remove their forces from Soviet military command and signaled their desire for an eventual Soviet withdrawal, despite the fact that withdrawal would separate the Soviet Union from East Germany, strand the main body of Soviet forces in Eastern Europe in the GDR, and require any Soviet campaign against the West to begin from Soviet territory. These efforts culminated in mid-March 1990 when the Soviet Union agreed to withdraw forces from Hungary and Czechoslovakia by the end of 1991; unofficial talks and diplomatic maneuvering between Poland and the Soviet Union began at the same time, with official Polish-Soviet negotiations starting in the fall.[93]

Combined, these changes undermined the Soviet Union's strategic position in Eastern Europe, moving Soviet posture from robust to weak.[94] By March 1990, Soviet officials concluded that Eastern European changes had "shifted the military balance on the European continent in favor of the West."[95] Simply put, the Revolutions of 1989–90 upended the military and security picture throughout Europe.

Prediction: Shifts in Posture Affected the Risks of Challenging the Soviet Union
This change in Soviet posture should affect U.S. assessments of the Soviet threat. From around 1983–84 through 1989–90, U.S. policymakers should be leery of trying to immediately shift the distribution of power in the United States' favor, worrying that doing so might push the Soviet Union to lash out. Not only might the Soviet Union attack NATO, but if U.S. policy were to foment unrest in Eastern Europe or the Soviet Union, then the same Soviet

forces available for war could also be used to repress domestic turmoil and maintain the status quo. As events in Hungary in 1956 and Czechoslovakia in 1968 illustrated, crackdowns risked increasing strains in U.S.-Soviet relations; crises, miscalculation, and war were not impossible.[96]

From the start of 1990, however, the Soviet Union's weak posture should reduce the risks where U.S. options in Eastern Europe are concerned. It was not the Soviet decision to forgo the use of force in the 1989–90 Revolutions so much as its inability to employ force afterward that matters.[97] On one level, the absence of Soviet control over East European states virtually proscribed a Soviet conventional attack. With Soviet forces withdrawing and lacking secure lines of communication, the Soviet Union would find it difficult to launch or sustain an attack on Western Europe. The threat of a crisis or war emerging from Soviet intervention fell for the same reasons: as Supreme Allied Commander General John Galvin noted at the time, "the Warsaw Pact is not only in transition, but . . . there is great doubt that the Soviet Union could pull it together to do anything militarily that the Soviets wanted to do."[98] If the Soviet Union was unable to secure its position in Eastern Europe, then the risks to the United States of attempting to move states in the area out of the Soviet orbit did not carry the same dangers as before.

PREDICTIONS: MOVING FROM A WEAKENING TO A RELEGATION STRATEGY

In contrast to competing accounts, the combination of bipolarity and Soviet military posture means that the United States should adopt a Weakening strategy before 1990, but a Relegation strategy—so far as the Soviet Union's Eastern European sphere of influence is concerned—afterward. Several implications follow. First, U.S. policymakers should avoid steps throughout the period that aid the Soviet Union, and instead craft policies expected to weaken the United States' rival. This is common sense: even if American policy were to become more predatory after 1990, we still expect it to be predatory before and to avoid efforts that rebound to the Soviet Union's advantage. Nevertheless, before the posture shift of 1990, U.S. policymakers should be acutely aware of the risks of harming Soviet interests and testing Soviet resolve. In practice, this means policymakers should attempt to identify the limits of Soviet tolerance and avoid going beyond this threshold. Signs that U.S. policy is antagonizing the Soviet Union should also prompt the United States to scale back its efforts. Still, U.S. policy is likely to focus on gradually gaining military advantages over the Soviet Union while crafting diplomatic and economic arrangements to limit Soviet opportunities to recover—all without posing an immediate and obvious threat to the Soviet Union.

Above all, we expect policymakers to offer two explanations for these policies. First, U.S. strategists should discuss the security benefits—primarily, fewer threats to the United States—resulting from a weakened Soviet Union. Second, strategists should anticipate that being too assertive toward the Soviet Union is dangerous. In private analyses, policymakers ought to justify limited predation out of concern of triggering a hostile Soviet response and the desirability of maintaining a positive trend in U.S.-Soviet relations that allows the United States' position to gradually improve.

These trends should change in the winter of 1989–90. With Soviet military options significantly reduced, U.S. policymakers will see no need to limit the extent of U.S. predation. Thus, Soviet concessions and signs of weakness should be met with additional U.S. demands and efforts to further harm the Soviet Union: U.S. policymakers will not only look to exploit Soviet weaknesses but try to create new opportunities to gain at the Soviet Union's expense. Concurrently, policymakers are likely to ignore signs of Soviet opposition, with even threats of force (including the use of nuclear weapons) discounted as not credible. Finally, U.S. leaders should recognize the advantages of pushing the Soviet Union out of Eastern Europe by treating it as a way of helping the United States better compete against the Soviet Union and establishing U.S. dominance in Europe, all while underscoring the Soviet Union's limited options for opposing U.S. ambitions.

DENOUEMENT: PREDICTING U.S. STRATEGY IN 1991

What about U.S. strategy in 1991? This episode offers a particular test of my argument, since the Soviet Union was not just a declining great power but also a collapsing state. Since state failure can be an extreme manifestation and particular type of decline, assessing U.S. strategy in 1991 helps check that predation theory explains situations in which states are both waning as great powers and imploding as sovereign political actors.

The intermingling of Soviet decline and collapse is clear when one looks beyond macro measures of Soviet power such as GDP, which almost certainly overstate contemporary Soviet strength. Although the Soviet Union retained large economic, population, and technological bases, its economy was in free fall by 1991 as Gorbachev's reforms led to rampant inflation, economic bottlenecks, and shrinking government revenue. At the close of 1990, U.S. intelligence agencies warned of possible "economic breakdown," just as policymakers monitoring Soviet developments saw the economic situation as "hopeless."[99] The Soviet political scene was equally fraught as secessionist movements multiplied and Soviet elites divided over the future of the country.[100] The political situation was sufficiently dire that U.S. planners in late 1990 began considering the scenarios that might lead to a Soviet political collapse or revolution.[101] These planning efforts came none too soon, as Soviet problems culminated in a failed coup by hard-liners against Gorbachev in August 1991, the disintegration of Soviet central authority that fall, and the official end of the Soviet Union on Christmas Day of the same year. Collectively, these changes meant that the Soviet Union remained a great power in terms of latent potential but was quickly falling from the great power ranks—and, as we know in retrospect, would soon exit world affairs entirely.[102]

In theory, if ever an opportunity for the United States to make dramatic gains at the Soviet Union's expense existed, one might expect this to be it and for the United States to exploit Soviet internal fissures for rapid U.S. gains. In practice, however, predation theory predicts that U.S. strategy should move back from 1990's Relegation toward Weakening. In the absence of other great power threats, the Soviet Union still offered low strategic value. Unlike the situation in 1990, however, the Soviet Union enjoyed a robust posture for the mission at hand: having lost Eastern Europe, the question became what the Soviet Union could do to protect its own territorial, political, and economic integrity. And here, the Soviet Union retained significant strengths. Although Soviet forces were leaving Central and Eastern Europe, the Soviet Union retained a large conventional military backed by over 350,000 internal security troops.[103] Political and economic unrest brought the reliability of these forces into question, but they were still large, numerous, reasonably well-trained, and could move at will around the Soviet Union.[104] Thus, even if the Soviet military could no longer attack Western Europe,[105] it could still make an attack against the Soviet homeland difficult, intervene in support of Soviet central authorities, or suppress unrest within the Soviet Union itself.[106]

These actions, moreover, might roil U.S.-Soviet relations and precipitate a crisis with a Soviet Union which still commanded a large nuclear arsenal.[107] Nuclear weapons, in turn, raised the stakes for the United States when contemplating a challenge to Soviet integrity: since the Soviet Union could threaten nuclear use to defend itself, opponents would have to weigh the prospective risks of a nuclear crisis against the prospective gains of challenging the Soviet Union. This would be an uncertain calculation at best, as the chance of a nuclear exchange with the survival of the Soviet Union itself at stake makes external actors run scared. In short, not only did the Soviet Union retain military tools to defend its homeland, but it was not hard to imagine how such forces could be used to harm the United States. Hence, where the collapse of Soviet military strength in Eastern Europe left that area vulnerable to U.S. machinations in 1990, the Soviets retained the ability to defend their homeland and gave the United States reasons to act judiciously in 1991.

Under these circumstances, U.S. policymakers are liable to adopt a Weakening strategy to foster the Soviet Union's continued decline without antagonizing what was, for the issues at hand, a state that could lash out if pressed. In fact, U.S. policy in 1991 should be similar to that in 1983–89: U.S. strategists should attempt to create conditions that facilitate gradual Soviet losses, slowly undermine Soviet political stability, continue shifting the military balance in favor of the United States, and prevent the Soviet Union from recovering. Conversely, efforts to expedite the collapse of Soviet political authority, exacerbate crises in the Soviet economy, or encourage challenges to Soviet control over Soviet territory should be ignored; at minimum, U.S. strategists should be leery of triggering a situation that could provoke either large-scale violence in the Soviet Union or a nuclear crisis. Thus, if forced to choose between rapidly shifting the distribution of power against the Soviet Union or settling for slower change, U.S. policymakers are expected to err on the side of caution, calculating that slowly but steadily increasing U.S. advantages will strengthen the United States' position in European affairs.

To summarize, each of the arguments tested in this book offers a distinct set of predictions regarding the course and rationale for U.S. strategy toward the declining Soviet Union (table 4.5). Arguments based on the security

Table 4.5 Summary of competing predictions

Argument	Key Prediction	Mechanisms
Predation Theory	The United States pursues a Weakening strategy in 1983–89, a Relegation strategy in 1990, and shifts back to Weakening in 1991	The United States seeks to reduce the Soviet threat and become a hegemon, with the varying Soviet threat of force shaping the assertiveness of these efforts
Security Dilemma	The United States pursues a predatory strategy before 1987–88 and a supportive strategy afterward	Soviet costly signals and reassurance convince U.S. policymakers that the Soviet Union can be trusted, resulting in an end to U.S.-Soviet competition
Ideological Distance	The United States pursues a predatory strategy before 1987–88 and a supportive strategy afterward	Liberalizing reforms in the Soviet Union lower U.S. perceptions of the Soviet threat, leading to U.S. support for the Soviet Union
Economic Interdependence	The United States pursues a strategy of limited support beginning in 1986, and an intensely supportive strategy after 1987	Soviet reformers seek economic integration with the West, and the United States responds
Ideational Argument 1: Crusading Conservatism	The United States preys upon the Soviet Union during the Reagan administration, but supports the Soviet Union during the Bush administration	Crusading conservative beliefs held by Reagan administration officials encourage the United States to maximize power, before more pragmatic conservative views in the Bush administration lead to a supportive strategy
Ideational Argument 2: Liberal Values/the Open Door Thesis	The United States maintains the Cold War status quo before 1989–90 but pursues a Relegation strategy afterward	U.S. officials seek a rationale for U.S. dominance in Western Europe until 1989–90, before trying to extend U.S. hegemony once Soviet power in Eastern Europe collapses

dilemma, economic interdependence, and the similarity or divergence of states' ideologies suggests the United States should become increasingly supportive of the Soviet Union over time. Here, Soviet efforts to (1) reassure the United States about Soviet intentions and reduce the military threat to the West, (2) develop economic ties with the United States, and (3) liberalize the Soviet system, each created reasons for U.S. policymakers to ratchet down the Cold War rivalry. By the mid- to late-1980s, we therefore expect to see U.S. policymakers seeking to support the Soviet Union while justifying their policies by citing Soviet reassurance efforts, the benefits of economic exchange, or the waning ideological rivalry.

Arguments based on the ideas held by U.S. leaders predict one of two different outcomes. First, arguments emphasizing the importance of crusading conservative ideas predict that a period of predation under Reagan should give way to support under Bush, stemming from the latter's less doctrinaire conservatism. Second, the Open Door thesis suggests that the United States will attempt to sustain Europe's status quo before 1990 to facilitate the U.S. presence in Western Europe, only to pursue a Relegation strategy after 1990 due to the collapse of Soviet power attendant to the Revolutions of 1989–90 and the opportunities this created for the United States to extend its influence.

In contrast, my argument predicts that the United States will adopt a Weakening strategy before 1989, a Relegation strategy in 1990, and a Weakening strategy again in 1991. By this logic, recognition that the Soviet decline will simultaneously reduce the only great power threat to the United States and potentially allow the United States to become a hegemon should induce efforts at maximizing power from the early 1980s onward. However, Soviet military posture should shape the assertiveness of U.S. efforts: only when the Soviet Union looks unable to secure its own interests will the United States pursue Relegation. Otherwise, the United States will pursue a Weakening strategy and focus its efforts on creating long-term conditions that facilitate the United States' relative rise without risking war with the Soviet Union.

U.S. Strategy and the Decline of the Soviet Union

This chapter evaluates U.S. policy during the Soviet Union's decline, showing that predation theory better explains the course and conduct of U.S. strategy than alternative accounts. As with Anglo-Soviet relations after 1947, I demonstrate that rising states tend to prey upon declining states with low strategic value, and that shifts in the declining state's posture affect the assertiveness of predation.

More precisely, because the United States faced no other great power competitors at the time, it preyed upon the Soviet Union as relative power shifted in favor of the United States starting around 1983. Initially, Soviet military strength led U.S. policymakers in the administrations of Presidents Ronald Reagan and George H. W. Bush to adopt a Weakening strategy to gradually undercut Soviet military options, constrain Soviet economic growth, and pressure the Soviet political system. Spurred, however, by the collapse of Soviet military power in Central-Eastern Europe after the Revolutions of 1989–90, the U.S. transitioned to a Relegation strategy and took the lead in rapidly reunifying Germany in the United States' camp. Not only did German reunification "rip the heart"—in National Security Advisor Brent Scowcroft's evocative phrase—out of the Soviet alliance network, but the terms of reunification were designed to maximize U.S. dominance in European security affairs while minimizing Soviet influence.[1] Yet faced in 1991 with the collapse of the Soviet Union itself, concerns with Soviet nuclear options and a domestic crackdown with uncertain consequences pushed U.S. strategy back toward Weakening, this time facilitating the gradual break-up of the Soviet state. Collectively, not only are these outcomes uniquely predicted by predation theory, but the deliberations of and calculations motivating U.S. strategists are strongly consistent with predation theory's causal logic.

Dealing with a Sick Bear: U.S. Predation and Soviet Decline, 1983–88

Evidence in this case strongly supports predation theory: U.S. strategy exacerbated and exploited Soviet problems as Soviet decline occurred. Given the strength of Soviet military forces, however, U.S. policymakers proceeded carefully. Rather than making an all-out effort to roll back Soviet power, U.S. strategists first embraced a Weakening strategy. At the center of this effort were initiatives designed to foster asymmetric Soviet military reductions and hinder Soviet economic growth, move the military balance of power in the United States' favor, subtly challenge the political status quo in Eastern Europe and Soviet Union, and gradually improve the United States' leverage over the Soviet Union.

STARTING FROM WEAKNESS

The Reagan administration arrived in office in 1981 worried about what it perceived as growing Soviet military power and the problems this posed for U.S. security.[2] Particularly worrisome was the Soviet Union's force of highly accurate land-based intercontinental ballistic missiles (ICBMs) targeting the United States, and intermediate-range nuclear forces aimed at the European members of NATO. In the U.S. estimation, it was possible that the Soviet Union would use these capabilities in a crisis to intimidate and coerce U.S. allies, or eliminate the U.S. ICBM force and leave the United States with the choice of either surrendering or escalating to attacks on Soviet and U.S. cities.[3] Alongside U.S. economic problems in the 1970s and early 1980s, these changes augured a shift in the distribution of power at the United States' expense. As Reagan—overstating the problem—put it 1976, "The evidence mounts that we are Number Two in a world where it is dangerous, if not fatal, to be second best."[4]

To rectify this imbalance, the Reagan administration adopted a policy to simultaneously confront the Soviet Union and rebuild U.S. power.[5] To signal the increasingly tough line emanating from Washington, diplomats led by Secretary of State Alexander Haig reduced contacts with their Soviet counterparts, while senior U.S. officials denounced the Soviet political system and its policies.[6] Reagan, for example, used his first presidential press conference to charge that Soviet leaders "reserve unto themselves the right to commit any crime, to lie, to cheat, in order to attain" their political objectives.[7] Nor were these just rhetorical flourishes. Beginning in 1981–82, the United States challenged the integrity of the Warsaw Pact by pressuring the Soviet Union to allow the non-Communist trade union Solidarity to operate freely in Poland.[8] A similar effort occurred in Central Asia, where Reagan administration officials—continuing a program begun late in the Carter administration—funded groups resisting the Soviet invasion of Afghanistan to help bleed the Soviets militarily.[9] Economic efforts complemented these steps as the United States unilaterally adopted export controls designed to sharply limit the flow of goods and services to the Soviet Union.[10] Although these steps toward economic warfare were opposed by U.S. allies, policymakers believed them to be necessary to prevent the West's technological advantages from aiding Soviet economic and military power.

Above all, the United States began a wide-ranging arms buildup to restore U.S. military options and reestablish the perception that the United States would match the Soviet Union when challenged. Military budgets swelled. By 1984, U.S. defense spending was 20 percent higher in real terms than in 1982 and, though the rate of increase soon leveled off, up nearly 60 percent by 1988.[11] As National Security Council (NSC) member Thomas Reed described, these steps were taken to "counter Soviet expansionism, to encourage liberalizing tendencies in the Soviet bloc, and to force the Soviet Union to bear the brunt of its economic mismanagement," premised on the idea that—as Reagan elaborated—"the Soviets do not believe that they can keep up with us."[12]

TRANSLATING SOVIET LOSSES INTO U.S. GAINS

As Soviet decline and the United States' relative rise began, however, the link between U.S. ends and means came into question.[13] On one level, initiatives designed to confront and challenge the Soviet Union led to superpower tensions. Although Reagan calculated that the Soviet Union would, as he put it in 1982, simply "not engage us if they feel threatened," the U.S. public, allies, and key policymakers increasingly feared that war might erupt.[14] Reagan himself recognized the danger, telling his deputy national security advisor in December 1982, "This inexorable building of nuclear weapons on our side and the Russians' side can only lead to Armageddon."[15] Indeed, by June 1982, Soviet diplomats were directly asking whether the United States was moving "toward war or preparation for war."[16] By mid- to late-1983, signs of a crisis reached an acute level, punctuated by the Soviet shoot-down of a Korean airliner in September 1983 and indications that the Soviet Union may have interpreted NATO war games as the prelude to a nuclear attack.[17] As predicted by predation theory, signs of a crisis generated pressure for reduced U.S.-Soviet hostility, and U.S. leaders, realizing that Soviet officials "feared us not only as potential adversaries but as potential aggressors," began to respond.[18]

Equally important, the question emerged of how to translate growing U.S. power into tangible gains.[19] Although the United States sought—as a December 1982 report emphasized—"to compete effectively on a sustained basis" with the Soviet Union by undertaking "a coordinated, long-term effort" to reduce the Soviet threat, U.S. leaders were divided on how to achieve these ends;[20] after all, as another contemporary analysis underlined, the United States could not "force broad Soviet retreat."[21] Led by Secretary of Defense Caspar Weinberger, hard-liners saw the pre-1983 approach as a winning gambit. If overt confrontation contributed to a shift in the distribution of power, then this approach should continue. Eventually, Soviet leaders would realize that their country could no longer compete with the United States and would have no choice but to accept whatever terms the United States offered.[22]

In contrast, comparative moderates believed the United States' rise gave it leverage to seek concessions from the Soviet Union through limited diplomatic engagement. The logic was that the Soviet Union might be declining, but it could still resist American pressure; the United States should therefore try to get the Soviet Union to make concessions, pocket the results, and compete with it in the future from a reinforced position.[23] As George Shultz (who replaced Haig as secretary of state in June 1982) argued in early 1983, "We have in place a sound policy, which gives us the foundation for an intensified dialogue with Moscow. . . . Such a dialogue would protect our security interests while giving the Soviets incentives to address our concerns—as long as we do not waver on the essentials of the policy approach we have established over the last two years."[24] The United States, in other words, would negotiate to push the weakening Soviet Union to meet its demands.

Led by Shultz, Vice President George Bush, and NSC Senior Director for European and Soviet Affairs Jack Matlock, the comparatively moderate approach won out over the course of 1983–88.[25] As predation theory predicts, the necessity of avoiding conflict, especially during heightened tension, played a prominent role in this approach. As Shultz and the State Department explained, isolating the Soviet Union as hard-liners proposed

> overlooks the fact the fact that we are in a dynamic situation, dealing with volatile problems which could lead to dangerous instabilities we may not be able to control. . . . Simply put, while we may be able to damage Soviet interests through uncontrolled competition, we cannot be confident of safeguarding our own. Thus, we want to contain and reduce conflict, even as we force the Soviets to pay a high price for their misdeeds.[26]

Changing tactics, this revised effort called for the United States to continue competing with the Soviet Union while moving to negotiate on four themes: regional conflicts in the Third World, human rights issues in the Soviet Union, "bilateral issues" (a catchall category for economic and technical matters), and arms control. In fact, Reagan seems to have always intended to negotiate with the Soviet Union once U.S. strength recovered.[27] Now, Shultz, Matlock, and others cued to these instincts to push what the historian Hal Brands describes as "coercive diplomacy"—the United States would engage the Soviet Union on matters of interest by bringing U.S. power to bear.[28]

As Shultz explained, this dual approach would ideally contribute to "progress toward a more stable and constructive US-Soviet relationship" by spurring the Soviet Union to "deal with the Administration on the basis of the comprehensive agenda we have established." Even if the best-case scenario failed to materialize, the United States would have still signaled that it saw "the US-Soviet relationship as fundamentally adversarial" by indicating that the United States was "fully prepared to compete effectively and vigorously."[29] Negotiations would therefore be a win-win situation for the United States: either it could cheaply buy the shop from the Soviet Union, or shifting power would pressure the Soviet Union to make these concessions regardless.

However, the United States needed to proceed deliberately given concerns about Soviet military power. As Shultz also underscored, the Soviet Union remained ready and able to "use its growing military power in ways that threaten our security."[30] National Security Advisor William Clark took the logic a step further, noting that the Soviet Union was now at its "position of maximum relative strength." "In this respect," Clark elaborated, the Soviets were "not unlike the Japanese in 1941" and could either "attempt to inflict a devastating military defeat upon us, or they can seek to restrain our military buildup through negotiation." Conflict was not necessarily likely, but the United States needed to act with that possibility in mind.[31]

Accordingly, not all parts of the U.S. approach were created equal, with arms control afforded singular importance.[32] Although both Intermediate Nuclear Forces (INF) and Strategic Arms Reductions Talks (START) with the Soviet Union began in 1981–82, initial negotiations broke down as the United States adopted bargaining stances tantamount to demanding immediate Soviet surrender. In INF talks, for example, the United States pursued the so-called zero option—meaning neither side would retain any intermediate-range missiles—at a time when the Soviet Union deployed hundreds of such weapons and the United States none.[33] Similarly, START saw the United States focus on eliminating "heavy" ballistic missiles—weapons only the Soviet Union possessed—and pushing the Soviets to restructure their nuclear arsenal.[34] Both options served an instrumental purpose: by adopting positions likely to be rejected by the Soviet Union, the United States facilitated domestic and allied support for the U.S. arms buildup.[35] Now the United States changed tactics by simultaneously trying to encourage and coerce Soviet concessions.[36] The objective remained having the Soviet Union make disproportionate cuts in intermediate and heavy missiles,[37] but U.S. negotiators by 1983–84 were willing to sweeten the pot by talking about sequential steps leading to asymmetric Soviet reductions over time rather than an all-out dismantlement effort.[38]

To maintain pressure on the Soviet Union, however, the United States continued building up forces intended to winnow down Soviet military advantages.[39] By the mid-1980s, U.S. military planners contemplated both conventional attacks into Eastern Europe and hunting Soviet nuclear forces in the event of hostilities.[40] Concurrently, Reagan announced the Strategic

Defense Initiative (SDI), a research program notionally designed to defend the United States against ballistic missiles. SDI was motivated by many factors but was partly designed to (1) suggest that the United States would have a way to defend itself against a Soviet nuclear attack, and (2) scare the Soviets by threatening to move the U.S.-Soviet military competition into a high-technology, capital-intensive domain in which the declining Soviet Union could not easily compete.[41] SDI succeeded admirably in the latter goal, prompting Soviet concerns that the U.S. gambit might work and require another round of military competition at a time when the Soviet economy and technological base was unlikely to be up to the task.[42] Thus, if the Soviet Union did not reach a deal, then the United States would use its technological and economic advantages to back the Soviet Union into a corner.

Revised economic and diplomatic tools were also used to pressure the Soviet Union and challenge the Cold War status quo.[43] Notably, the United States reversed its earlier efforts at economic warfare, instead working with its allies to harmonize efforts designed to economically undermine the Soviet Union.[44] For example, in exchange for the U.S. reducing controls on low-end technologies, Western Europe and Japan agreed to add a range of high-technology items to export control lists to retard Soviet economic and military growth, accepted a U.S. advisory program to monitor export controls, and promised to improve compliance with export regulations.[45] Lobbied by the United States, meanwhile, members of the Organization for Economic Cooperation and Development ceased offering the Soviet Union financial credits at below-market rates after mid-1983, thereby inhibiting trade and raising the financial costs to the Soviet Union of importing Western goods.[46] The objective, as an interagency report described in late 1982, was "to reduce Western contributions to Soviet power" and "avoid subsidizing the Soviet economy or unduly easing the burden of Soviet resource allocation decisions"—in other words, helping the Soviet Union exhaust itself.[47]

Given the asymmetric demands, policymakers did not expect U.S. initiatives to yield quick results.[48] This was especially true for arms control, where proposals were again designed to create a win-win scenario for the United States: either the Soviet Union would accept U.S. demands, or U.S. capabilities would increase while the Soviet Union was blamed for the failure of the negotiations.[49] The latter was indeed the case through 1984, as the still-nascent relative rise of U.S. power and the political vacuum in the Soviet Union caused by the successive deaths of General Secretaries Yuri Andropov and Konstantin Chernenko precluded substantive negotiations. Talks began on the whole of the U.S.-defined agenda, but that was the extent of progress.[50] Epitomizing the trend, U.S. insistence on an INF zero option led to a Soviet walk out of arms control talks once the United States began deploying intermediate-range missiles to Europe in late 1983.[51] Progress was difficult as the United States sought major reductions in the Soviets' heavy ICBMs, pushed for elimination of Soviet intermediate-range missiles, and was unwilling to negotiate on SDI.[52] With time on the United States' side, however, policymakers were willing to let pressure increase while avoiding steps that, as a senior intelligence official offered, would either "prop up" or "try to bring down" the Soviet Union.[53]

Two developments after 1985 modified U.S. plans. First, Soviet officials agreed to what were termed "umbrella talks" in which the Soviet Union would negotiate on START and INF provided the United States discussed SDI. The United States agreed to this idea after initial deliberation and, in a nominal concession, put SDI on the table. In practice, agreeing to discuss SDI was not intended as a real concession since U.S. strategists expected they could "propose language which protects . . . internal U.S. objectives" on both SDI and the nuclear balance.[54] In fact, Shultz and others saw a possible advantage in working in umbrella talks since Soviet concerns with SDI meant that the United States could "use the leverage of SDI to press them to reduce sharply their offensive weapons."[55]

Second, Mikhail Gorbachev's accession as Soviet leader altered Soviet strategy. Gorbachev arrived in office intent on reforming the Soviet Union and arresting its economic and political stagnation. As a result, the Soviets began to move toward U.S. positions across the U.S.-Soviet agenda with the intention of reducing U.S.-Soviet competition in order to obtain U.S. support for Soviet reforms, reduce the Soviet Union's military burden, and free up resources for domestic recovery. Given their importance to the United States and potential to liberate resources, arms control talks set the tone of the U.S.-Soviet relationship as Gorbachev authorized Soviet diplomats to negotiate on the basis of U.S. proposals.[56]

As predation theory expects, however, U.S. negotiators refused to take Soviet concessions at face value. U.S. policymakers opposed the type of "decentralized, modern, and efficient" Soviet Union desired by Gorbachev— Matlock, in an internal assessment asking "Would this USSR be good for the US?," bluntly concluded, "Absolutely not."[57] Seeking to weaken the Soviet Union while still putting U.S.-Soviet relations on a "less dangerous footing," U.S. leaders instead used Soviet conciliation to press for additional gains.[58] In the process, the United States reduced what it was willing to offer in return while maintaining economic and political pressure on the Soviet Union.

Already in May 1985, Shultz saw the Soviet Union's preoccupation with its internal problems as creating incentives for it to accommodate U.S. ambitions.[59] With the Geneva Summit between Reagan and Gorbachev scheduled for November 1985, the Soviet Union soon adopted arms control positions close to the United States' own: Soviet leaders proposed cutting up to 50 percent of strategic forces, separating INF discussions from the umbrella talks, and implied they might accept the United States' right to conduct SDI research provided the U.S. did not actually deploy the system.[60] In response, however, the United States pocketed Soviet offers and sought more. Although happy to separate INF discussions and make progress on START, U.S. strategists refused to compromise on SDI, reasoning that Soviet concern with the program gave the United States leverage.[61] In fact, Gorbachev's evident worry over SDI at Geneva led U.S. officials to see the program as a bargaining chip par excellence. Since the technology behind SDI would not be ready for years, policymakers concluded that by refusing to compromise on the program now while raising the prospect of future negotiations, they would enjoy the best of both worlds: Gorbachev's desire to lower tensions with the United States would compel the Soviet Union to sweeten arms control deals to get at SDI, while the United States would not be surrendering real capabilities.[62]

This realization influenced U.S. strategy. Seizing an idea floated at Geneva, the Soviets launched an arms control initiative early in 1986 aimed at a quid pro quo, whereby the United States and the Soviet Union would eliminate all nuclear weapons by the year 2000 and, because there would be nothing to defend against, abandon SDI. Since SDI remained a research program, and eliminating all nuclear weapons met U.S. calls to eliminate intermediate-range missiles, the Soviet proposal seemingly aligned with U.S. demands.[63] Nevertheless, the United States pushed to "lock Soviets into some agreements which protect U.S. interests."[64] In the short term, the United States countered by proposing to separate the INF talks and eliminate all intermediate-range nuclear forces without addressing strategic weapons or SDI.[65] A few months later, it responded with a proposal to keep SDI as a research program for five years while both the United States and the Soviet Union reduced their strategic nuclear arsenals—particularly ballistic missiles (i.e., ICBMs and submarine-launched ballistic missiles, or SLBMs)—by 50 percent. As the Soviet Union depended on ballistic missiles to deliver nuclear weapons far more heavily than the United States, the U.S. proposal was weighted against the Soviet Union.[66] The proposal also kept the SDI threat alive, since the United States could either move ahead with the system after five years or seek new Soviet concessions for continuing to limit SDI research and/or deployment.[67] In fact, SDI became the core point of contention at the October 1986 Reykjavik Summit, as negotiations to eliminate all ballistic missiles (and potentially all nuclear weapons) foundered on the U.S. desire to preserve SDI as a spur to further Soviet concessions.[68]

Outside arms control, meanwhile, the United States continued pressuring the Soviet economic and political system.[69] Sustained efforts ensured that the United States and its allies limited the flow of credits and technology to the Soviet Union.[70] Concurrently, U.S. strategists regularized limited challenges to the political status quo in the Soviet Union, members of the Warsaw Pact, and beyond. For example, despite the Polish government's move to ban Solidarity, the Central Intelligence Agency (CIA) and government-funded National Endowment for Democracy provided sufficient backing to keep the Polish movement on life-support. The sums involved were never large—CIA support totaled roughly $2 million per year from 1983 onward—but helped Solidarity leaders coordinate the movement's activities and sustained it as a challenge to Communist authority.[71] Meanwhile, officials such as U.S. chargé d'affaires to Poland John Davis and Deputy Secretary of State John Whitehead kept the issue alive in East-West diplomatic discussions, applying tacit coercion by tying U.S.-Polish relations to the Polish government's willingness to liberalize domestic politics.[72] As Whitehead explained in early 1987, these efforts were built on the idea that the United States "should be alert to every chance to influence these countries when and where we can . . . the situation in these countries in relation to the Soviet Union is not hopeless."[73] The conflict in Afghanistan witnessed an analogous dynamic: as the Soviet Union escalated its military campaign, the United States responded by increasing funding to Afghan militants in an ongoing effort to make the Soviets hurt and deny them a victory.[74]

The United States also gently challenged the political order in the Soviet Union. Premised partly on the idea that there was "a link between Soviet efforts to tyrannize at home and abroad," Reagan, Shultz, and other leaders tied the importance of Soviet respect for human rights to improvements in U.S.-Soviet relations.[75] Shultz, for example, at one point told Soviet Foreign Minister Eduard Shevardnadze that "it was critical for Shevardnadze to understand the central role of human rights for Americans and for our relationship."[76] Likewise, U.S. policymakers underscored that economic growth in an increasingly globalized world required a liberal and open society. "The gap," Shultz explained to Shevardnadze, "will widen between nations that adapt to the information age and those that do not."[77] Although not a delegitimation campaign akin to that of 1981–82, the emphasis on "US scientific and technological preeminence" provided what a 1985 briefing paper termed "a source of psychological advantage/political leverage."[78]

WAITING FOR SOVIET PROBLEMS TO MOUNT

U.S efforts to "pocket" Soviet concessions and seek more culminated after the Reykjavik Summit.[79] Despite Soviet reforms and movement toward U.S. positions, U.S. strategy remained driven by concerns that the Soviet Union simply sought "breathing space" to overcome stagnation while enhancing "its ability to project power (including military power) in the long run" and preserving "past Soviet gains as a superpower."[80] In response, as Shultz described in a candid assessment of U.S. policy, the United States aimed "to keep the Russians well behind us," yet "not so far behind that they become desperate and dangerous." Accordingly, U.S. policy needed to focus on "managing change" in U.S.-Soviet relations "through a balance of toughness and inducement" that exploited Soviet problems as they appeared and sought Soviet concessions "on American terms."[81]

This approach colored the post-Reykjavik U.S. arms control agenda. Early in 1987, Soviet negotiators agreed to separate INF talks, eliminate all INF missiles in Europe, and limit INF missiles in Asia to only one hundred warheads.[82] The United States accepted the proposal, yet in subsequent talks insisted on the 1981 zero option and pressed the Soviet Union to eliminate intermediate-range missiles in both Europe and Asia. This not only meant that the Soviets would have to eliminate significantly more missiles than the Americans, but further ensured that the Soviets could not move missiles into Europe during a crisis. Meanwhile, the United States continued pushing the Soviet Union to limit its heavy missiles while refusing to compromise on SDI. At one point, Gorbachev expressly challenged U.S. efforts, telling Shultz that "U.S. policy is one of extorting more and more concessions." Shultz replied, "I'm weeping for you."[83]

Increasingly, the United States not only sought to limit Soviet heavy ICBMs but pressed to limit or ban the mobile missiles that would replace them if heavy ICBMs were withdrawn. This seemingly reinforced efforts to find and attack Soviet retaliatory forces—if mobile missiles were constrained, then the U.S. military mission would be simpler.[84] Coupled with plans to attack Soviet nuclear missile submarines,[85] reducing Soviet heavies and banning or limiting mobile missiles meant that the United States was positioning itself to exert leverage over Soviet military options. It would do this by either threatening Soviet forces with destruction, or compelling a restructuring in Soviet nuclear assets that worked to the the United States' advantage.[86] Reagan himself captured this coercive logic in early 1988, arguing that the Soviets "have an innate eye to protect the homeland at all cost, and it may be that they recognized . . . that facing the nuclear forces they face, they can't do this."[87] U.S. pressure therefore continued. Although INF talks concluded in late 1987 with the INF Treaty eliminating all intermediate nuclear missiles, the U.S. refusal to negotiate SDI and efforts to constrain the Soviet nuclear arsenal while protecting areas of U.S. superiority left a START agreement beyond reach.[88]

Nor was U.S. coercion limited to the nuclear race. By 1988, Soviet leaders were actively exploring ways to trade Soviet military concessions for Western economic and diplomatic support.[89] This would require the United States to cease pursuing gains at the Soviet Union's expense. The United States, however, maintained its Weakening strategy. U.S. diplomats, for instance, continued to call on Poland to allow non-Communist political groups to operate; similarly, the United States refused to renounce support for Afghan militants even after Soviet forces began leaving Afghanistan in May 1988, seeking to deny local Soviet clients a political victory.[90] If anything, Reagan, Shultz, and other policymakers used Gorbachev's desire for U.S. backing as leverage. A State Department report on U.S.-Soviet economic relations, for example, argued that U.S.-Soviet economic cooperation would depend "on progress in other areas of the [U.S.-Soviet] political relationship."[91] Similarly, Reagan told Gorbachev that lingering mistrust of the Soviet Union represented "a great obstacle which would affect economic relations and even negotiations on disarmament."[92] These steps sustained pressure for the Soviet Union to accept U.S. demands as the price for ending Cold War tensions.

Ultimately, the Reagan administration left office in January 1989 having tried to weaken the Soviet Union. U.S. policy had challenged the political status quo inside the Soviet Union and among Soviet allies while bringing economic pressure to bear to hinder Soviet growth. In the military realm, a combination of arms racing and asymmetric arms control reduced Soviet military capabilities. Soviet and U.S. leaders never reached a deal settling the Cold War—or even ending the arms race—but U.S. leaders were pleased with these developments. As National Security Advisor Frank Carlucci observed before the December 1987 Washington Summit, time and the distribution of power were on the United States' side: "Despite its formidable military power and resourceful political leadership, the Soviet empire is in deep trouble . . . it can only get out of that trouble with far reaching reforms and, even then, only with Western help."[93] The implication, as it had been for the preceding half-decade, was clear:

> In historic and strategic terms, the Soviets need more from us than we need from them. We can afford to set high conditions for agreement, and to hold to them patiently. We can afford to be sure that the agreements we reach push future events in our direction. If they don't promise to do that, we can afford to forego agreement. We want accommodation on our terms, but don't need it. They want accommodation on their terms, but need it on almost any terms they can get.[94]

Baldly stated, the United States would wait for weakness to bring the Soviet Union around to accommodate the United States, on whatever terms the United States offered.

Walking Back the Bear: U.S. Strategy and the Soviet Denouement, 1989

Although the specific issues on which the United States challenged the Soviet Union shifted, the United States' Weakening strategy remained steady through the first year of the George H. W. Bush administration. The Bush administration came into office believing that the Soviet Union was making a virtue out of its growing relative weakness. By trading military reductions for Western economic, military, and political concessions, U.S. policymakers feared that Gorbachev would undermine Western efforts to contain the

Soviet Union.[95] This was dangerous. In the U.S. assessment, the Soviet Union remained the principal threat to Western Europe and "an adversary with awesome military power."[96] Moreover, it was unclear whether Gorbachev sincerely sought to end the Cold War, or simply an opportunity to revitalize Soviet fortunes.[97] And even if Gorbachev sought cooperation, there was no guarantee that his successors would be so benign.[98] Summarizing the prevailing attitude, Scowcroft told the NSC in early 1989 that although the Soviet Union was no longer an "ideological and economic challenge," it remained "a considerable military threat."[99]

Policymakers therefore sought to maintain pressure on the Soviet Union.[100] Breaking from Reagan's focus on the nuclear balance and economic competition, however, the focus under Bush became conventional arms control and, as the 1989–90 Revolutions challenged the stability of Warsaw Pact member states, undermining the Soviet Union's Eastern European sphere of influence. Short of a domestic revolution, the only way the Soviet Union could revitalize its fortunes was to trade arms reductions and diplomatic concessions for Western assistance.[101] Because Soviet weakness and conciliation were largely "a response to Western, especially U.S., policies," the United States wanted to deny the Soviet Union this option.[102] Instead, the United States would remain in Europe in case the Soviet threat spiked, while positioning itself "to capitalize on the changes underway in Eastern Europe and the Soviet Union."[103] As before, leaders pursued gradual gains to strengthen the U.S. position at the Soviet Union's expense, while avoiding the dangers of pressing too hard while the Soviets could push back.

REDUCING SOVIET MILITARY ADVANTAGES CONTINUED IN EARLY 1989

This Janus-faced interpretation of the Soviet Union colored the Bush administration's approach to U.S.-Soviet military competition. As noted above, the Bush administration changed focus to prioritize conventional arms reductions over nuclear negotiations. Politics played some role in this, as a Soviet plan announced on December 7, 1988, to remove 50,000 troops and 5000 tanks from Eastern Europe generated pressure for the United States to respond in kind.[104] More important, however, was the strategic dimension. Policymakers saw the recently ratified INF treaty as removing one rung on the nuclear escalation ladder and reducing U.S. military options. Facing mounting calls in West Germany (the Federal Republic of Germany, or FRG) to also cut short-range nuclear forces, strategists worried that the United States would need to both deploy additional conventional assets to maintain a credible deterrent and find some way to avoid further handicapping NATO's nuclear options.[105] The focus thus turned to conventional force reductions. If Soviet conventional forces were reduced, then the United States would not need additional assets to reinforce deterrence as the Soviet military threat declined; by linking conventional reductions to future nuclear force cuts, pressure to eliminate short-range forces would also diminish.[106] In fact, if the Soviet Union were pressed hard enough on conventional reductions, the United States might acquire conventional military advantages.

As preparatory talks for a Conventional Forces in Europe (CFE) treaty began, however, a further Soviet proposal to reduce NATO and Warsaw Pact forces 10–15 percent below the lowest levels held by either alliance disrupted U.S. plans.[107] Although the Soviet proposal meant that the Pact would reduce more than NATO, inclusion of aircraft, helicopters, naval forces, and short-range nuclear forces—alongside calls for a demilitarized zone in Central Europe—in the proposal seemed geared toward undermining NATO's military advantages and political solidarity.[108] It also left the United States in a bind: since the United States intended to propose a 5 percent reduction, the Soviet plan meant that the United States would be advocating for higher numbers of stationed forces than the Soviet Union.[109]

To counter, the United States decided to probe the Soviet Union's willingness to make military concessions to the U.S. advantage, proposing to leave nuclear and naval assets off the table but cap U.S. and Soviet forces at 275,000 troops each. As Bush explained, although a 275,000 limit represented a 20 percent cut in U.S. combat power in Europe, it would disproportionately hamstring the Soviets by requiring them "to reduce their forces in Eastern Europe by 325,000"—more than half of Soviet forces in Central-Eastern Europe.[110] Significantly, this counteroffer represented a compromise between a cautious Defense Department proposal that called for ignoring the Soviet offer entirely, and a more aggressive approach that would have withdrawn all Soviet and U.S. forces from Central Europe, premised on the idea that Warsaw Pact members would defect if Soviet units were removed. The plan was a moderate course given the options at hand.

Cautiously predatory logic drove this policy. Since the United States structured its forces for qualitative superiority versus the Pact's quantitative superiority, numerical parity would leave the United States in a stronger conventional position.[111] Equally important, the proposal helped test Soviet intentions. As Scowcroft noted in May, the U.S. plan sought "cuts in Soviet forces stationed in Eastern Europe beyond the level Gorbachev is currently willing to accept." If the Soviets accepted the plan, U.S. military gains would be locked in and members of the Warsaw Pact potentially encouraged to challenge Soviet dominance. Conversely, if the Soviets rejected the proposal, then the United States would have signaled its interest in a "less militarized" Europe, reinforced NATO unity by suggesting the Soviet Union still presented a military threat, and created pressure on the the Soviets for future reductions.[112] Summarizing this logic, Baker later recalled that U.S. policy sought "the kind of political effect we were looking for, while not endangering us militarily."[113]

RUMBLINGS IN EASTERN EUROPE, PART I: POLAND,
HUNGARY, AND THE U.S. RESPONSE

American Opportunism and Caution The U.S. proposal became the corner-stone of NATO's CFE position as talks began that summer. Increasingly, however, events in Eastern Europe rendered CFE negotiations obsolete. Conventional reductions were important because policymakers hoped to shift the military balance in favor of the United States and produce political dividends in Eastern Europe. By May, though, growing unrest in Poland and Hungary, followed shortly thereafter in the rest of Eastern Europe, imperiled the Soviet Union's influence over Warsaw Pact members. By autumn 1989, non-Communist governments were consolidating power in Poland and Hungary while the East German government was tottering. Although Soviet allies had yet to defect from the Warsaw Pact or overtly challenge Soviet dominance, instability throughout Eastern Europe created new opportunities for the United States to undermine Soviet power.

Prima facie, Eastern European developments were advantageous to the United States. After all, the United States retained what Bush and Scowcroft termed a "long-term goal of freeing the region" from Soviet control and seeing "Soviet troops reduced or removed."[114] The division of Europe might then end as "the Soviet army of occupation" went home, and the process created pressure inside the Soviet Union for further reforms.[115] Not for nothing did NSC Director for European Affairs Robert Hutchings conclude that "The Cold War began . . . in Eastern Europe, and it was there that it had to end."[116]

Rather than jumping into the breach, however, the United States continued its Weakening strategy by pursuing slow, steady gains—or, as Scowcroft described in a March 1989 memo, "Eastern Europe is a weak link in Gorbachev's strategy. We should exploit this but must do so in a prudent way."[117] In fact, the United States was attuned to possible change in Eastern Europe beginning in early 1989, as the collapsing Polish and Hungarian economies forced ruling Communist regimes to consider liberalizing domestic reforms. Problems in East Germany (the German Democratic Republic, or GDR) were a second but potentially more important issue, raising the possibility that the GDR and FRG might seek to reunify Germany and, in doing so, upset the U.S. and Soviet alliance networks. Yet although U.S. policymakers welcomed Eastern European developments, they worried—as Bush put it—that attempting to influence the situation might cause events to "turn violent and get out of hand" by generating "an internal crackdown" or "a Soviet backlash."[118] It was impossible, as Scowcroft observed, to know where Soviet red lines fell, such that U.S. aggrandizement risked provoking Soviet military intervention and a U.S.-Soviet crisis.[119]

The Kissinger Plan and Early Caution To mitigate this risk, Bush authorized former Secretary of State Henry Kissinger to explore a U.S.-Soviet modus vivendi at the start of 1989.[120] In return for a Soviet promise to forswear intervention in Eastern Europe, the United States pledged not to lure states in the area out of the Warsaw Pact. Gorbachev was receptive to the idea, and despite later disavowals, so were senior U.S. officials. Baker, for example, publicly praised the plan as "worthy of consideration," reasoning that the approach would be especially attractive "if there was a reversal, or if you had anarchy and a reaction by the Soviets."[121] However, public backlash and bureaucratic opposition led to the plan's collapse that spring.[122]

Despite the Kissinger Plan's failure, gradualism continued even as Polish and Hungarian developments accelerated. In April, what were termed the "Roundtable Talks" between the Polish government and its Solidarity opponents culminated in an agreement liberalizing the political system; by the summer, the Hungarian government had inaugurated domestic reforms and begun removing the Hungarian Communist Party (the Hungarian Socialist Workers' Party) from positions of authority.[123] With the pace of change quickening, the United States again signaled the Soviet Union that it was not interested in exacerbating Eastern European tensions. Bush, for instance, ignored pressure from political advisers to use the conclusion of the Roundtable Talks to call for sweeping change throughout Eastern Europe.[124] Instead, officials were careful to treat Poland as a unique case and not a harbinger of what the United States necessarily wanted for Eastern Europe overall, with Bush announcing that "No two Eastern European countries are the same."[125] The point was to avoid antagonizing the Soviet Union by steering events in, as Scowcroft put it, "productive directions, but at a speed Moscow could accept."[126] As Deputy Assistant Secretary of State for European Affairs Tom Simons explained to allied leaders, the United States recognized "the risks of instability" and had "no interest in encouraging it."[127]

Nor was this simply rhetoric, as the United States limited its involvement in Polish and Hungarian affairs. At a time when Poland needed extensive help to service its debt obligations, and Polish and Hungarian leaders sought billions more to reform their systems, the United States refused to provide this aid.[128] There would not be, as Bush told Canadian Prime Minister Brian Mulroney, "a new Marshall Plan" for Eastern Europe.[129] Instead, assistance to Poland was confined to $100 million in direct U.S. aid and World Bank loans of $325 million; Hungary received a $25 million grant. Moreover, these funds were intended to foster the long-term foundations for free-market economies rather than to provide the near-term financial relief that might give the United States political leverage.[130] Even in retrospect, Scowcroft labeled these measures "embarrassingly meager,"[131] given what ambassador to Poland John Davis called an opportunity "to lead with concrete steps to reinforce our values and our interests."[132]

Keeping Communists in Office and the Soviet Union Secure The United States' Weakening strategy reached its apogee in the summer and fall of 1989. In

June, Polish elections handed the Community Party an overwhelming defeat, as Solidarity won all but one of the available seats in the Polish legislature.[133] The results discredited the party and made it doubtful that Communist leader Wojtech Jaruzelski could garner sufficient support to be elected president by the legislature. This threatened Poland's reforms, as participants in the Roundtable Talks assumed Jaruzelski would serve as Poland's president under the new system, broker the political deals necessary to ensure the country's stability, and reassure the Soviet Union that change in Eastern Europe was not inimical to Soviet security.[134]

If ever there was an opportunity to roll back Communist influence and Soviet dominance in Poland, this was it. To challenge a major Soviet ally, all the United States had to do was call for both sides to acknowledge the results of Poland's elections, support a diminished role for the Communist Party, and encourage Jaruzelski to retire.[135] Instead, the United States did the opposite. As Bush prepared to visit the region in July, Ambassador Davis explained to Solidarity members how they could—and, implicitly, should—ensure Jaruzelski's election without actually voting for him simply by being absent on the day of the vote.[136] Not only is this counterintuitive, considering what the United States might have done if it wanted to directly challenge the Soviet Union, but the fact that the United States was Solidarity's primary backer throughout the 1980s makes its action even more remarkable: the United States effectively told a democratic movement it had nurtured to elect its autocratic opponents!

This policy continued during and after Bush's visit. Meeting with Jaruzelski, for example, Bush urged him to run for president, noting that "his refusal to run might inadvertently lead to serious instability";[137] vowed that the United States would not complicate Polish reforms; and pledged not to "place strains on [Poland's] Soviet alliance."[138] The United States soon made good on this promise: with Poland's Communist Party unable to create a governing coalition that August, Baker cabled Davis to push Solidarity to cooperate with its Communist opponents.[139] This helped resolve the standoff.[140] Again, the United States chose gradualism.

Even at this late date, concern with Soviet opposition constrained U.S. strategy.[141] Not only did Gorbachev caution that efforts to overthrow Communist regimes would be "a course toward confrontation, if not worse," but U.S. policymakers could not determine where Soviet forbearance ended and intervention might begin.[142] Though the Soviet Union had tolerated Eastern European developments so far, U.S. analysts assumed that minimum Soviet goals involved regional stability, a leading role for the Communist Party in each country, and continued fidelity to the Warsaw Pact—and it was unclear what Moscow would interpret as imperiling these objectives.[143] A senior NSC official captured these concerns well, writing that "For all the ferment we see in Eastern Europe, I simply do not believe that the *Soviet Union* has yet evolved to the point where it will permit the disintegration of its security buffer which has depended for four decades on Communist Party control."[144] Scowcroft shared this worry later, explaining:

> Let's take a particular case, like Poland. . . . I remember when Nixon went there and there were almost riots. That's the last thing we wanted, because what we didn't want was either Gorbachev to have to turn hard, or the . . . hard-liners in the Kremlin kicking out Gorbachev. So we wanted the pace of events to be underneath their radar screen. And don't accelerate. Keep them at a pace that will not force a reaction by the Soviets. Of course, we didn't know what that pace was. But that was our goal.[145]

As such, the United States sought to reassure the Soviet Union by downplaying U.S. interest in Eastern Europe. Speaking to reporters before his July visit, for example, Bush emphasized that "the last thing we ought to do is appear to be dictating and fine-tuning the political processes in these countries."[146] Bush's meetings with his foreign counterparts reinforced the point. Told by Jaruzelski that Gorbachev worried the United States was trying to evict the Soviet Union from Poland and Hungary, Bush emphasized that he had no desire to " 'stick a finger' in Gorbachev's eye."[147] Shortly afterward, he told French President François Mitterrand that Jaruzelski was "probably the best candidate" to lead Poland, since he could broker deals to avert violence, whereas other solutions risked a "crackdown . . . which would lead to intervention."[148] And during the August standoff over configuring Poland's government, U.S. policy was again driven by consideration of the Soviet reaction, with Scowcroft concluding, "Moscow still had large forces in Eastern Europe and we did not want to embarrass the Soviet Union with Polish freedom at stake. Our public posture was therefore very restrained."[149]

RUMBLINGS IN EASTERN EUROPE, PART II: THE GERMAN QUESTION RETURNS

By September, the situation in Poland and Hungary had stabilized. Now, however, the stability of East Germany came into question, raising fundamental questions about the future of European security affairs writ large. Not only was the GDR the Soviet Union's largest trading partner and widely seen as the most economically advanced member of the Soviet sphere, but it represented what the State Department called the "jewel in [the Soviet] imperial crown" and the "cornerstone" of the Soviet alliance network.[150] Just as the FRG anchored the U.S. presence in Western Europe via NATO, so the GDR anchored the Soviet presence in Central-Eastern Europe via the Warsaw Pact; moreover, the desire to keep Germany divided so as to prevent a unified Germany from aligning with either the United States or the Soviet Union helped justify the existence of the two alliances in the first place. Unless the GDR's problems were contained, its instability would raise questions regarding whether the time was right for Germany to reunify and, critically, whether the reunified state would be a Soviet ally, U.S. ally, or neutral. Considering that Soviet and U.S. wrangling over Germany's future alignment had nearly led to war earlier in the Cold War, and that reunification would call into question the need for a Soviet presence in Eastern Europe, the return of "the German question" was at the fore of policy discussions in the second half of 1989.[151]

U.S. analysts had recognized the possibility of a move toward reunification since early in 1989. Even in March, the NSC argued that "the top priority for American foreign policy in Europe should be the fate of the Federal Republic of Germany";[152] by May, State Department Counselor Robert Zoellick saw reunification as a "real opportunity to get ahead of the curve."[153] Nevertheless, initial U.S. objectives were essentially defensive, aimed at establishing a "Western anchor" for any reunification discussions and preventing Gorbachev from using the prospect of reunification against NATO.[154]

Events that autumn made this approach untenable. Amid the changes in Poland and Hungary, GDR leader Erich Honecker's government faced similar pressures to reform as economic and political problems mounted. Unable to address the issues, Honecker was replaced in October by Egon Krenz.[155] Krenz, however, barely had time to assess the situation before a GDR spokesman's confusion over new travel regulations led to the opening of the Berlin Wall on November 9, 1989.[156] Immediately, the question became whether the opening presaged moves toward German reunification, and if so, on what terms.

Backing Self-Determination, Downplaying Change Policymakers constantly assessed U.S. options as the GDR's problems mounted. Though seeking to "maximize our leverage" over events,[157] Bush and his advisers preferred stability over rapid change to "avoid the turmoil" that would accompany an immediate reunification push.[158] A major State Department report from mid-October underscored the policy, arguing "We should continue to express our support for reunification . . . without getting out in front of mainstream West German leaders."[159] Bush's public statements before November 9 followed this advice.[160] Regardless, U.S. options were limited by the Soviet military presence and the reality that, as the State Department and CIA acknowledged, Soviet leaders appeared willing to "use force to prevent the collapse of a Communist East German State."[161]

After November 9, meanwhile, the United States moved cautiously toward embracing change in the Soviet Union's keystone ally. Of course, policymakers recognized that the United States "had much to gain from the prospect of a strong, democratic, and united Germany" allied with the United States.[162] Nonetheless, strategists advised Bush to pursue a cautious policy that would (1) avoid upsetting a fraught environment, but without (2) helping the Soviet Union "regulate" change in East Germany.[163] A high-level study later in November elaborated on this approach: though the United States desired change in the GDR, the United States' primary focus was ensuring the FRG's continued fidelity to NATO while guaranteeing that GDR developments "not weaken these links" and avoiding steps that might antagonize the Soviet Union.[164]

With these objectives in mind, the United States could accept outcomes ranging from the maintenance of two German states to reunification—it was too early to endorse a particular result. Still, the United States needed to decide how to proceed. Three options were available: letting the Germans set the pace of reunification, supporting a Four Power (United States, Soviet Union, United Kingdom, France)[165] initiative to control events, or generically emphasizing the Germans' right to what U.S. officials termed "self-determination."[166] The first option would be most problematic for the Soviets by excluding them from the decision-making process. The second would be most conducive to Soviet interests but could "legitimize a Soviet role and veto" over German developments—in fact, the United States had already rejected a Soviet call on November 10 to use Four Power talks to influence East German events.[167] The United States chose the third option.

A stark security rationale drove U.S. policy. With the fate of the GDR the central Soviet security concern in Europe, policymakers feared a Soviet backlash if the United States pushed for reunification. This concern did not exist in a vacuum, as Gorbachev wrote Bush shortly after the Berlin Wall fell that events in the GDR risked creating "a chaotic situation" with "unforeseeable consequences."[168] This veiled threat dovetailed with preexisting American worries. Two days before the Wall fell, for example, Scowcroft received a study on "GDR Crisis Contingencies" that bluntly warned: "In the event of severe internal unrest in the GDR, our overriding objective should be to prevent a Soviet military intervention, which . . . would raise the risk of U.S.-Soviet military confrontation;" indeed, Soviet intervention in the GDR was "among the World War III scenarios for which U.S. and NATO planners have been preparing for decades."[169] Accordingly, Bush was reluctant to accelerate events, reasoning that "this was not the time to gloat about what many in the West would interpret as a defeat for Gorbachev" as his "mind kept racing over a possible Soviet crackdown."[170] As Scowcroft concluded, it remained debatable whether the Soviet Union "would or could sustain the loss of East Germany."[171] Thus, as an interagency report emphasized, the United States needed to "continually to reassure [the Soviet Union] that we are not seeking to destabilize the situation in the GDR or the Warsaw Pact."[172]

Slouching Toward Reunification: The Reassurance Game Events before and after the December 2–3 Malta Summit between Bush, Gorbachev, and their advisers further demonstrated that the United States sought slow gains at the Soviet Union's expense. Only five days before Bush and Gorbachev met, FRG Chancellor Helmut Kohl announced his Ten Point Plan for reunification, marking the first official plan to unify Germany put forward since

November 9.[173] U.S. strategists, however, were far from enthusiastic with Kohl's proposal. Not only had Kohl failed to brief U.S. policymakers before the speech, but the West German leader made no mention of the FRG's future relationship with NATO. Combined, Kohl's moves suggested that the FRG might ignore U.S. concerns and accommodate the Soviet Union.[174] Moreover, it was difficult to know how the Soviets would react to reunification formally appearing on the policy agenda given Gorbachev's "unequivocal" stance endorsing "the existence of two German states."[175] Kohl's initiative presented a dilemma: should the United States endorse its ally's proposal and take a more assertive stance on reunification, or distance itself from Kohl's bid?

Again, U.S. policymakers erred on the side of caution, refusing to back Kohl's plan until they could assess the Soviet reaction at Malta.[176] In the interim, Bush and his team soft-pedaled German developments, recognizing that reunification would "rip the heart out of the Soviet security system" and worrying that the Soviet Union could "still use force" and diplomatic pressure "to stop unwelcomed events."[177] Before the United States agreed to seek German reunification at this time, it needed to assess the Soviet position, remind the Soviet Union that a crackdown "would inevitably harm our relations," and reassure Soviet leaders of "our interest in reform through a peaceful, democratic process."[178]

Nevertheless, U.S. concerns proved unfounded once the Malta Summit began. Instead of threatening, Gorbachev used the Malta meeting to underline his intent to let events continue unfolding, announcing "Peaceful change is the way. Our position is non-interference."[179] These assurances immediately affected U.S. policy. Before Malta, policymakers feared—as one of Scowcroft's memoranda described—that "the instrument of last resort is still available to the Soviet Union and there are no guarantees that the Soviet empire will go quietly into the night."[180] Afterward, however, U.S. policymakers took a more sanguine view of likely Soviet actions, with Bush telling Kohl on December 3, "Gorbachev's chief problem is uncertainty. I don't want to say he went 'ballistic' about [reunification]—he was just uneasy."[181]

In response, Bush now endorsed Kohl's Ten Point Plan, agreeing on December 3 to work with the FRG in reunifying Germany provided that the result kept Germany's relationship with NATO intact.[182] The timing of the U.S. shift was critical.[183] By early December, France and Britain were echoing Soviet calls to slow the pace of events and maintain two German states. In backing Kohl, Bush thereby challenged both the Soviet Union and U.S. allies; even allied opposition at a meeting of NATO heads of state after Malta did not change the U.S. position.[184] This underlines the importance of events in late November and December. Given widespread opposition to reunification, the United States could have rejected Kohl's plan, arguing that the international consensus mandated two German states. That U.S. policymakers rejected this approach without jumping to exploit Soviet problems illustrates the Weakening strategy at work.

Last Grasps of Soviet Military Power: Problems and Prospects in Late 1989 Almost immediately after the United States endorsed German reunification, however, Soviet opposition spiked. Despite the assurances at Malta, Soviet officials railed against calls for reunification, emphasizing the need to preserve Germany's two-state solution.[185] More worrisome, Soviet forces in East Germany went on alert on December 7–8, and U.S. officials "could not exclude the possibility that [this move] might be preparatory to a Soviet-led effort to impose martial law and restore communist [*sic*] rule."[186] The next day, the Soviet government proposed Four Power talks, and although the United States had previously tried to avoid Four Power involvement, concerns that the Soviet Union might use force led the United States to accept Soviet demands.[187] Still, Bush and his advisers would not allow the Soviet Union to block reunification in this fashion. Policymakers had previously recognized that Soviet diplomatic efforts were the most likely way to "blunt the impact of change in the GDR" short of military intervention.[188] To prevent this, Baker lobbied British and French officials to limit the scope of the talks.[189] When the Four Powers met in mid-December, therefore, Soviet efforts to stymie reunification failed.[190]

Nevertheless, the Four Power talks revealed an underlying tension in U.S. strategy. Having begun 1989 trying to prevent the Soviets from seizing the initiative on the German question, the United States ended the year seeking to cautiously reunify Germany and "rip the heart out of the Soviet security system." Predation was alive and well. However, the United States could not help but limit predation to what the Soviets would tolerate: as the Four Powers episode shows, suggestions that the Soviet Union might use force required the United States to moderate its efforts. U.S. ambitions were thus constrained.

Scowcroft recognized this paradox, writing Bush in late December that "Increasingly because of the German problem, the Soviets are pushing—successfully—for the widest possible diplomatic engagement in Europe."[191] Although the United States wanted to move the GDR and Eastern Europe away from the Soviet Union, the desire to avoid provoking the Soviets risked "shoring up [Gorbachev's] long term objectives in Europe" and giving the Soviets sufficient leverage that the United States would end up sustaining Soviet influence in Eastern Europe.[192] This was highly undesirable. As Principal Deputy Assistant Secretary of State for European Affairs James Dobbins later argued, the United States had the opportunity to make "fundamental geopolitical changes" in its favor."[193] Still, because ignoring Soviet interests might lead to threats of "Soviet military intervention in the GDR to reimpose firm control, with all that meant for the future of Germany and East-West relations," the United States had few options for gaining this objective.[194]

Breaking the Soviet Empire, 1990: Relegation and U.S. Policy

As 1990 began, U.S. policy toward the Soviet Union was defined by debates over German reunification.[195] It also left the United States in a bind. Though the United States had slowly come to back reunification, Soviet opposition remained intense, and as post-Malta events showed, policymakers would not risk Soviet backlash by exploiting the GDR's collapse. Exacerbating the problem, Britain and France had supported the Soviet Four Power proposal in December, and it was possible that a tacit Franco-British-Soviet coalition would try to sustain GDR independence.[196] Pushing in the opposite direction, however, West German leaders were increasingly eager to accelerate reunification, spurred by nationalism and the GDR's continued political and economic collapse.[197]

With allies and adversaries divided, U.S. policymakers were compelled to reassess the Weakening strategy.[198] Three options were on the table. First, the United States could sustain the gradual march to reunification envisioned in 1989. Second, it could recognize international opposition to reunification and, shifting course, agree to Franco-British-Soviet demands that reunification slow or stop. Finally, the United States could align with the FRG, speed up reunification, and accelerate the destruction of Soviet empire by stealing the "jewel" of the Soviet alliance network.

The U.S. track record strongly suggests that, even late in 1989, the United States would have endorsed the first or second option to avoid antagonizing the Soviet Union. At the start of 1990, however, the United States moved to intensely prey on the Soviet Union by embracing the third path and accelerating reunification.[199] The point, as NSC staffers argued, was to back and protect the FRG to ensure that reunification "happen fast, not slowly, and around an increasingly detailed blueprint."[200] Doing so would help achieve "a fundamental shift in the strategic balance" by facilitating "the continued and graduated withdrawal of the Soviet Union from Eastern Europe."[201] Changing gears, U.S. policymakers decided to work with the FRG, ignore Soviet opposition, and destroy the Soviet alliance network by expediting the GDR's elimination.

Driving this shift, as predation theory predicts, was what Secretary of Defense Richard Cheney called the "collapsing" Soviet military position as the changes in Eastern Europe following the Revolutions of 1989–90 began to tell.[202] Policymakers were clear in their new assessment. At the start of the year, NSC analysts concluded that the "unraveling of communist power in Eastern Europe . . . has changed the strategic environment," and "if Moscow maintains its present course, it will be impossible within a few years for the Soviet Union to do anything about the changes . . . short of all out invasion."[203] Even this timeline proved too long. Charged near the end of January with assessing what the Soviet Union would do if the United States accelerated reunification, Condoleezza Rice—then a member of the NSC staff—concluded that "that the Soviets would not even threaten the Germans. Within six months, if events continue as they are going, no one would believe them anyway."[204] And when reports arrived in early February that Gorbachev might be replaced by a more conservative Soviet leader, Rice concluded, "The Soviet Union is probably unable to reextend its tentacles into Eastern Europe."[205]

Although some policymakers remained concerned that the Soviet Union might threaten intervention, a general consensus thus emerged by late January to early February 1990 that the Soviets could not forcibly block change as their forces were "being fast pushed out of the region."[206] Accordingly, strategists concluded that they faced "a rare period in which we can seek to achieve a fundamental shift in the strategic balance," a fact that "argues powerfully for moving forward quickly on resolving the German question and concluding CFE [negotiations]." After all, "the quicker the new European order is in place, the more effective will be the quarantine of Eastern Europe from the probable collapse of perestroika."[207]

From late January 1990 on, then, U.S. policymakers enacted a Relegation strategy. The desired end-state was clear: "the liberation of Eastern Europe and the consolidation of pluralistic rule throughout the region; and a dramatic reduction in the Soviet military threat."[208] To attain these outcomes, U.S. strategists began to intensely prey on Soviet vulnerabilities by (1) seeking to quickly reunify Germany, (2) disregarding Soviet and other European opposition to this objective, and (3) ensuring that the reunified state remained in NATO so as to guarantee the alliance's survival as a vehicle for U.S. power projection.[209] On the diplomatic front, U.S. policymakers worked to isolate the Soviet Union and neuter diplomatic negotiations on German reunification to block Soviet opportunism. In security affairs, meanwhile, the United States opposed Soviet plans for European security arrangements that might salvage Soviet influence in Europe and, expanding its ambitions, began consolidating Europe's economic and military potential under the U.S. aegis. I treat each of these efforts in turn.

THE DIPLOMACY OF RELEGATION

The diplomatic implications of Relegation became clear as the United States began structuring a process to reunify Germany. With Soviet forces retreating from Eastern Europe, Soviet leaders no longer opposed reunification per se. Instead, they desired the greatest possible oversight over the reunification process, seeking to sustain the Soviet Union's political influence, limit U.S. dominance, and perhaps keep a residual Soviet military presence in the area.[210] To achieve these objectives, U.S. analysts concluded that the Soviets might demand Four Power talks to settle reunification, seek bilateral negotiations with the FRG, or call a pan-European peace conference under the auspices of the Conference on Security and Cooperation in Europe (CSCE).[211] Each option had pitfalls: Four Power talks could give the Soviets a veto over reunification, a CSCE meeting would dilute U.S. influence, and bilateral talks risked the FRG's trading its relationship with NATO for Soviet backing on reunification.

Facing analogous choices in 1989 between isolating or reassuring the Soviet Union, the United States had erred on the side of gradualism and tried to avoid directly threatening the Soviet position in East Germany. In early 1990, however, the United States rejected each of these options as overly conducive to Soviet interests and injurious to U.S. opportunism. Breaking with efforts to temper predation, U.S. policymakers now led the push for speedy reunification by isolating the Soviet Union from the negotiation process and organizing an anti-Soviet coalition.

This developed in late January and early February as the United States sought Western European and Soviet acceptance of what became known as the Two Plus Four talks. Nominally, the Two Plus Four were designed so the two German states could negotiate bilaterally on the terms of German reunification, while the four allied powers with formal oversight of Germany monitored and certified the result. In theory, this arrangement allowed the Soviet Union to oversee the process and ensure that the results aligned with its interests.

In practice, however, the United States used the Two Plus Four talks to insulate reunification from Soviet influence. For example, although Baker assured Soviet leaders in February that the talks would "take into account Germany's neighbors" and limit "unilateral [U.S.] advantage[s],"[212] Bush and Kohl privately agreed that talks could not begin until after GDR elections returned a pro-reunification government. Otherwise, talks "would open the way for any of the Four to cause mischief" by allowing the Soviet Union to work with the GDR against the United States.[213] The NSC elaborated on the point, proposing that the United States "should try to delay any real discussion of security arrangements . . . until the GDR is so weak that the Six, in fact, dissolves into Five as Germany unites." Meanwhile, and since the goal was to limit "the degree to which [the process] threatens our interests," the United States would "keep the focus of the Six Power talks as limited as possible" and resist Soviet pressure to widen the talks to cover "Germany's membership in NATO" or other security arrangements.[214]

In sum, the very issues that the Soviet Union sought to address—the future of European security arrangements and Germany's role therein—were precisely those that the United States intended to avoid. Thus, although the State Department allowed that issues such as NATO membership might be raised in the talks, underlying this discussion would be recognition "that the ultimate authority to make decisions rests with the sovereign German state" and whatever deals the United States reached bilaterally with the FRG; the Two Plus Four talks themselves were immaterial. As Zoellick explained to Baker in late February 1990, "because Two Plus Four is a discussion, *not a negotiation*, the others can raise what they want to raise. We are not committed to responding at all if we don't want to." The Two Plus Four's advantage, in short, was that it gave Gorbachev "little real control" over events despite appearing otherwise.[215]

Once the Two Plus Four was established in mid-February, the United States then proceeded to block any FRG concessions to the Soviet Union that might imperil U.S. interests, while moving Britain and France away from the Soviet Union. These steps foreclosed Soviet options for salvaging its fortunes at the bargaining table. Britain and France were easy to maneuver. With Germany reunifying and the Soviet Union declining, British Prime Minister Margaret Thatcher and Mitterrand were gently reminded that only the United States could provide Britain and France with the backing needed to deal with Germany's prospective political, economic, and military influence. The implication was clear: if Britain and France opposed U.S. efforts in the short term, then the United States might be less supportive of French and British interests after reunification. Thatcher and Mitterrand quickly came around.[216]

The FRG was more difficult, as Kohl appeared willing to consider loosening Germany's relationship with NATO in exchange for Soviet backing in the reunification talks. Indeed, into late February, Kohl had not explicitly endorsed keeping a united Germany "fully in NATO," even though this constituted the United States' "principal objective."[217] To address the ambiguity, Bush sought what Scowcroft called a "historic bargain" during talks with Kohl on February 24–25, 1990: in exchange for "Kohl's pledge not to alter the form and substance of Germany's security commitments to NATO," the United States promised "that the Two Plus Four process will not interfere with German unity."[218] Absent such agreement—Bush explained during the meeting—Western disunity might "stimulate the Soviets to interfere" and allow the USSR to use the Two Plus Four "to force you to create the Germany they might want."[219] The American offer thus involved carrots and sticks. If the United States and FRG made common cause, then speedy reunification on Western terms was likely; however, if the FRG ignored U.S. demands, then the United States might be less inclined to back the FRG and leave it exposed to anti-reunification forces. The FRG leadership accepted the deal.

Collectively, emerging by late February was a coordinated Western approach toward rapid German reunification within NATO that isolated the Soviet Union. U.S. efforts guaranteed that Soviet attempts to influence reunification would be met by a solid Western front, ensuring that Soviet demands would be either ignored or overtaken by events.[220] This became clear once preliminary Two Plus Four discussions began that winter: Western unity allowed the United States to block Soviet efforts to start high-level negotiations on the terms of reunification, while coordinating with the FRG, France, and Britain to ensure that lower-level discussions focused on procedural rather than substantive matters.[221] Moreover, once substantive discussions began that spring—several weeks after East German elections produced a pro-reunification government—the United States led efforts to present the Soviet Union with a united Western position to convince Soviet policymakers that opposition to reunification within NATO would lead to "a deterioration in the smooth, stable relations" that they desired.[222]

Besides crafting an anti-Soviet Western consensus, the United States continued to severely circumscribe the mandate for Two Plus Four negotiations. Even in mid-February, the United States sought to limit the Two Plus Four's scope to simply "work[ing] out the details of giving up Four Power rights and responsibilities for Berlin and Germany as a whole, not the issue of Germany's full membership in NATO."[223] Despite Soviet pressure—including challenges from Shevardnadze and other Soviet diplomats that Two Plus Four needed to "resolve or at least address" the security issues stemming from reunification—the U.S. position did not change.[224] By March, policymakers resolved that the Two Plus Four mandate should be extremely narrow. As U.S. planning documents (table 5.1) emphasized, the "Four" aspect of the talks would simply involve devolving Four Power rights and shaping German borders, but the security issues central to Soviet security would be decided elsewhere.[225] Indeed, U.S. policymakers even sought to prevent discussion of the FRG-NATO relationship—one of the ostensible focal points of the negotiations! Bush himself captured the point, telling Thatcher in mid-April, "We need to be as clear as we can about the things the Two Plus Four should not decide," including "Germany's membership in NATO."[226] Ultimately, as one State Department official quipped, it was better to call the talks "the 'two by four'" because they actually represented "a lever to insert a united Germany in NATO whether the Soviets like it or not."[227]

Table 5.1 The Two Plus Four mandate: February–March 1990

Issue	Role of Two Plus Four Talks
Four Power rights, including Berlin	Could decide issue
Borders	Could decide issue
NATO relationship to GDR territory	Could not address issue
Soviet troops in GDR	Could discuss issue
Nuclear weapons in FRG	Could not address issue
Germany Alliance Membership	Could not address issue
Prohibition on German nuclear, chemical, or biological (NBC) weapons	Could discuss issue
Size of German army	Could not address issue
German forces in GDR territory	Could discuss issue

Reproduced from Philip Zelikow, "The Two Plus Four Agenda," March 12, 1990, Doc. No. 9001938, NSC PA Files, GBPL.

RELEGATION AND U.S. MILITARY DOMINANCE

On the security front, meanwhile, the United States ensured that the terms of German reunification offered the Soviet Union no opportunity to maintain its military presence in Central-Eastern Europe. This helped establish U.S. military dominance. By reunifying Germany and placing the entire state in NATO, the United States not only extended its hold over Europe's center for war-making potential, but undermined the Soviet Union's ability to project power by tearing the heart out of the Warsaw Pact. In doing so, it also created propitious conditions for the United States to expand NATO into Eastern Europe at a future date.

As noted, U.S. leaders came into the discussions over German reunification with one paramount goal: keeping the FRG in NATO. Whether that meant a reunified Germany in NATO or Germany's continued division, the "overriding" U.S. objective—as the State Department explained in October—was "the maintenance of a democratic FRG, firmly tied to the West."[228] Reflecting the fluidity of European developments, however, Scowcroft had the NSC detail possible outcomes from German reunification. As ranked on February 5, 1990, these varied from a "neutral/nonaligned/demilitarized Germany" that was out of both NATO and the European Commission (the least preferred outcome) to "Germany in NATO," where NATO "forward defense extends to the Oder-Neisse [the German-Polish border]" and with U.S. nuclear weapons remaining (table 5.2). During February 1990, the United States walked its demands up this list while blocking Soviet countermoves as U.S. assertiveness intensified absent a credible Soviet threat.

As before, both opportunism and fear drove U.S policy. Bush and his advisers worried that the diplomacy surrounding reunification might allow the Soviet Union to pull the FRG out of NATO or, less dramatically, establish "some weaker form of association for Germany with NATO."[229] As NSC staff member Robert Blackwill explained, it might then "not be long before pressures from the Germans and within the U.S. Congress would force the size of the American presence down and eventually out as well." The result would forfeit "the prime assets that have made the United States a postwar power and thus have a devastating effect on the U.S. ability to influence Europe in ways that protect our political, commercial, and strategic interests."[230] It also presented a long-term military risk: as Bush, Baker, and others repeatedly explained in late January and early February, "there could be a reversal in the Soviet Union,"[231] and even if the Soviet Union withdrew from Eastern Europe, it would "remain far and away the most powerful single military power on the continent."[232] U.S. efforts thus aimed to preserve "the security of the West" by blocking Soviet moves, walking the Soviet Union out of the GDR, and moving reunified Germany into NATO.[233]

Protecting NATO's post–Cold War role would further allow the United States to dominate European security. In fact, Bush had already used his 1990

Table 5.2 Rank-ordered possible German outcomes, February 5, 1990

Option	Details
1) Germany in NATO	Forward defense and nuclear weapons remain
2) Germany in NATO with GDR territory demilitarized	Otherwise as above
3) Germany in NATO but outside military command (like France). "Beginning with this scenario, the current structure of transatlantic security begins to change fundamentally."	Otherwise as above
4) Germany in NATO but no U.S. nuclear weapons a) Current GDR territory militarized b) Current GDR territory demilitarized	
5) Germany in NATO, GDR territory demilitarized, no U.S. forces	Allied conventional forces remain, U.S. nuclear guarantee continues
6) German-U.S. bilateral security arrangements a) U.S. and allied conventional forces remain b) Allied but no U.S. conventional forces remain c) No stationed forces	Germany out of NATO, no U.S. nuclear weapons, GDR territory demilitarized. Western European Union (WEU) remains
7) German-French and -British bilateral security arrangements a) Stationed French and British conventional forces b) No stationed forces	No U.S.-German security relationship. WEU remains
8) WEU a) Stationed French and British conventional forces b) No stationed forces	
9) European Defense Force a) All CSCE b) European CSCE (no U.S., USSR, or Canada)	No WEU
10) Neutral/aligned Germany	Aligned politically but not militarily with West. EC. No WEU. German forces severely constrained
11) Neutral/nonaligned Germany	German forces severely constrained. EC. No WEU
12) Neutral/nonaligned/demilitarized Germany	No military forces

Adapted from Robert Blackwill, "German Unity: Variations on the Theme," February 5, 1990, CF00716, Rice Files, GBPL.

State of the Union address to propose CFE limits of 195,000 troops each for the United States and Soviet Union that would lock in the Soviet troop withdrawals from Eastern Europe.[234] Since the U.S. proposal excluded the 30,000 U.S. troops in Britain, the new deal would give the United States quantitative as well as qualitative superiority in Europe.[235] By March, State Department analysts concluded that it was strongly in the United States' interest to push reunification within NATO as it would offer "a drastically reduced military problem," "a revived 'active buffer' between the Germans and the Russians," and help move the states of Eastern Europe out of the Soviet orbit.[236] By implication, U.S. military dominance would then be assured, as placing the Soviet Union's keystone ally in NATO would guarantee that the Soviet Union and Warsaw Pact were neutralized, while the United States remained in Europe with NATO intact and U.S. forces forward deployed.[237]

Defending or Expanding NATO: Expansion Wins Out The process of dominating European security began in February 1990. At the time, Soviet leaders demanded that the FRG leave NATO as a precondition for reunification, and West German leaders eager to reunify their country appeared willing to meet this demand.[238] U.S. officials sought to stop this slide, and in early February, Baker met with West German Foreign Minister Hans-Dietrich Genscher to reach a compromise. The result was U.S.-FRG agreement on a modified version of a plan initially proposed by Genscher: in return for an FRG pledge that Germany would remain in NATO, U.S. policymakers agreed that NATO would not expand into the former GDR or points beyond. All parties might have benefited from this arrangement: Germany could have reunified, NATO would have remained a vehicle for U.S. power projection, and the Soviets would have been reassured by a de facto guarantee that their former ally would remain outside of NATO. In a further sop to the Soviets, the United States and FRG even pledged to forswear NATO expansion beyond Germany into Eastern Europe.[239] Unsurprisingly, Gorbachev and other Soviet leaders were enthusiastic when Baker presented the offer on February 8–9 as part of his pitch to sell the Soviets on Two Plus Four talks. Within days, the Soviet leaders implicitly accepted the deal by agreeing to the proposed negotiations.[240] A path to reunification was within reach.

Almost as soon as the quid pro quo appeared, however, the deal came undone. In Washington, NSC officials balked at the idea of the former GDR existing within Germany but remaining outside NATO. In response, Bush and Baker backtracked on the arrangement and were now only willing to offer "special arrangements" regarding the extension of NATO forces "eastward"[241]—what Bush and others soon started referring to as "special military status" for former East German territory.[242] This represented the first escalation of U.S. policy: in U.S. eyes, the new deal would not halt NATO at the inner-German border but extend it to the Oder-Neisse line inside the former Pact. NATO guarantees would thus cover all of reunified Germany, while guarantees against further NATO expansion fell by the wayside.

However, the United States had not coordinated its revised offer with the FRG. Subsequently, a gap opened between the U.S. and West German positions, as the United States pressed ahead with the special military status offer while the FRG continued advocating for the non-expansion deal. Bush administration officials worried that this divergence would provide the Soviets an opportunity to entice the FRG to break with the United States; Baker was sufficiently concerned that he proposed allowing Soviet forces to remain in the former GDR to address Soviet security concerns and avoid a separate FRG-Soviet deal.[243] Confronting similar choices in 1989, between taking a more assertive stance against the Soviet Union and moving ahead of German and Soviet leaders, or avoiding positions that might antagonize the Soviets, American policymakers had limited U.S. assertiveness. Illustrating the Relegation strategy at work, the United States now did the opposite and, during the aforementioned February 24–25 talks with Kohl, pressured him into seeking terms that went even beyond the "special military status" offer. Instead of keeping the former GDR outside of NATO, the United States and West Germany now agreed to seek (1) full membership of a unified Germany in NATO, including NATO guarantees over the former GDR; (2) the continued deployment of U.S. conventional and nuclear forces in Germany; (3) allowance for the FRG to deploy its forces in the GDR; and (4) a rapid withdrawal of remaining Soviet forces from East German territory.[244] In doing so, policymakers explicitly noted the Soviet inability to oppose U.S. ambitions, with Scowcroft arguing:

> Soviet leverage to influence the fate of Germany is marginal, however much Moscow complains. Stalin and his successors set as their principal goal for European security in the postwar era the fractioning of the FRG's ties to NATO. Adenauer said no. The West did not give in to Moscow's demands when the Soviets were strong; hopefully Kohl will agree . . . that we should certainly not do so now when the Soviet Union is weak.[245]

In taking these steps, U.S. policymakers ensured that the non-expansion plan fell by the wayside so far as U.S. planning was concerned, and killed any notions that Soviet forces might remain in the former East Germany.[246] Tellingly, by March 1990 U.S. strategists began exploring ways of expanding NATO further into Eastern Europe and gaining influence over members of the rapidly dissolving Warsaw Pact; within months, policymakers were debating whether and when to signal that Eastern European states could join the alliance.[247] Dominance was the name of the game as the United States and FRG agreed to expand NATO while ignoring Soviet concerns and eliminating the Soviet Union's ability to negotiate alternative arrangements. As

Bush explained to Kohl on February 24, the United States would not let the Soviets "clutch victory from the jaws of defeat."[248]

Indeed, once U.S. policymakers settled on this approach, Soviet opposition proved unable to alter the thrust of U.S. strategy. By March and April, Gorbachev, Shevardnadze, and other Soviet policymakers moved against German reunification and NATO expansion plans as U.S.-FRG efforts became clear. Soviet officials regularly denounced the idea of a reunified Germany in NATO, seeking instead the creation of new, pan-European security institutions to replace both NATO and the Warsaw Pact. In the U.S. analysis, the Soviets sought to circumscribe U.S. dominance in post-Cold War Europe by creating room for the Soviet Union to influence European security affairs.[249] As Soviet opposition mounted, U.S. officials also increasingly recognized that Western positions caused political problems for Gorbachev and other Soviet reformers, as conservatives charged the Soviet leaders with surrendering vital Soviet interests. In fact, Shevardnadze complained about this issue directly to Baker, warning that "if others attempt to put us into a restricted condition in matters of our security, then this will lead to a situation . . . where the degree of our political flexibility is severely limited."[250] Yet where in 1989 similar indications that U.S. policy was driving the Soviets into a corner led the United States to restrain its ambitions, now the United States maintained maximalist positions. Accordingly, Soviet calls for continued Four Power oversight of Germany, a pan-European peace conference, and Germany's admission to both NATO and the Warsaw Pact elicited no change in U.S. policy.[251] After one such exchange in April, Baker recorded his sense of the difficulties created by Soviet domestic politics, noting that "progress was harder to come by than at previous ministerials"—but, reflecting U.S. equanimity, went on to remark, "We've had better [talks]! We'll probably have worse."[252] Similar Soviet pushback in May prompted an equally ambivalent U.S. response.[253]

Adding Insult to Injury: No Guarantees and No Economic Assistance Having blocked Soviet initiatives, the U.S. sustained pressure for speedy reunification and for the Soviet Union to acquiesce to Western terms.[254] Along the way, it continued to deny concessions to a Soviet Union whose position in Europe was in tatters.

The endgame began in mid-May. To catalyze Soviet movement, Baker used a visit to Moscow to offer the Soviets "nine assurances" on the future of a reunified Germany in NATO (table 5.3, left column), including pledges to transform NATO into a political alliance and cap the size of the German military. Much has been made of this offer, with proponents of the cooperation narrative seeing it as a sincere effort emerging out of the Two Plus Four to address Soviet security concerns.[255] New evidence, however, challenges this interpretation. In fact, the United States had decided upon all of these terms

Table 5.3 Comparing the nine assurances to pre–Two Plus Four plans

Nine Assurances, May 1990[a]	State Department Plan, Mid-February[b]
1) Capping German army size	"Bundeswehr reductions"
2) Accelerating SNF [short-range nuclear forces] negotiations	[Not included in the plan but raised during the Bush-Kohl meeting in February][c]
3) German renunciation of NBC weapons	"No German possession or production" of NBC weapons[d]
4) No NATO forces in the GDR for transition period	"No NATO forces in the GDR"; "special provisions for German troops in the GDR"
5) Transition period for Soviet withdrawal from the GDR	"Delayed Soviet troop withdrawals from the GDR"
6) Transforming NATO politically	[Not included in the plan but raised by Baker in December and proposed by the NSC in January; interagency plans began in March][e]
7) Settling German borders	"Legally binding commitments on borders"
8) Developing the CSCE	[Not included in the plan but raised by Baker in December and January; interagency discussions were held in March][f]
9) Developing German-Soviet economic relations	"German economic benefits for the Soviets"

[a]Summarized from Baker, *The Politics of Diplomacy*, 250–51.

[b]All quoted material is from Robert Zoellick, "Two Plus Four: Advantages, Possible Concerns, and Rebuttal Points," February 21, 1990, box 38, Soviet Flashpoints, NSA.

[c]Memcon, "Meeting with Helmut Kohl, Chancellor of the Federal Republic of Germany," February 24, 1990, https://bush41library.tamu.edu/files/memcons-telcons/1990-02-24—Kohl.pdf.

[d]Baker also pitched this point to Gorbachev on February 7–9.

[e]Baker raised the political transformation of NATO in a December 1989 speech; see Zelikow and Rice, *Germany Unified and Europe Transformed*, 142–43. For subsequent discussions, see Robert Blackwill, "1990," January 19, 1990, CF00182, Blackwill Files, GBPL; Reg Bartholomew, "Memorandum for the Thursday Group," and enclosures, March 12, 1990, CF00293, Wilson Files, GBPL.

[f]James Baker, "Proposed Agenda for Meeting with the President," January 24, 1990, box 115, BP; Bartholomew, "Memorandum for the Thursday Group" and enclosures.

before Two Plus Four deliberations began: Baker and the State Department settled on six of these nine assurances in February 1990, while the other three points came from internal deliberations during that winter (table 5.3, right column). More importantly, the United States saw these pledges not as substantive concessions so much as fig leaves to placate Soviet domestic audiences—as a State Department briefing paper described, the assurances were meant to help the Soviets "say their interests and 'sacred rights' were respected," even though "from the Soviet perspective, the 'nine assurances' do not give sufficient guarantees that their concerns will be met."[256] In short, the assurances were a pittance compared to what the United States would gain from German reunification within NATO and the accompanying changes to Europe's strategic map.[257] Baker captured this dynamic well, writing that when the proposed terms were weighed against what the United States stood to gain, "you haven't seen a leveraged buy-out until you've seen this one!"[258] Unsurprisingly, Gorbachev was dismissive of U.S. efforts: when pressed by Baker as to whether a settlement would "have to say that Germany would not have the right to remain in NATO," Gorbachev insisted, "Yes."[259]

During the May–June 1990 Washington Summit, however, Gorbachev reversed course. Facing sustained U.S. opposition to Soviet demands, the Soviet leader used a meeting with Bush to concede Germany's right to choose its alliances. This meant that Germany could remain in NATO after reunification if it so wanted.[260] Still, the Soviet move was not just capitulation, coming as part of a Soviet campaign to trade security concessions for Western economic assistance to stabilize a Soviet economy in free fall.[261] Two weeks before the Washington Summit, in fact, Gorbachev alerted Bush that the Soviet Union sought a $15–$20 billion loan to "tide [the Soviet Union] over" during its transition to a market economy.[262] If security issues topped the Soviet agenda in mid-1990, then economic concerns were not far behind.[263]

Nevertheless, the United States refused to trade U.S. butter for Soviet guns. Although Bush and Gorbachev signed a trade treaty at the Washington Summit, Bush refused to submit the agreement for Congressional ratification or grant the Soviet Union waivers to allow it access to U.S. financial credits.[264] Adding insult to injury, the United States then took the lead in blocking other assistance to the Soviet Union. Already in May, for example, Bush told Kohl that the prospect of a large-scale aid package was unacceptable due to a Soviet crackdown in the Baltics; in the run-up to the July 1990 Houston Economic Summit, he similarly argued that Soviet aid to Cuba made U.S. assistance impossible.[265] More directly, the United States opposed French and West German efforts to provide assistance to the Soviet Union, instead looking to utilize Western economic aid as a lever to further undermine Soviet strength. As Bush offered during the Houston meeting, decisions on aid to the Soviet Union would be influenced by "Soviet steps to reduce the proportion of their economic output devoted to the military" and "Soviet decisions to provide foreign aid to regimes that consistently act contrary to the objectives of the international community of states." Moreover, if other countries went ahead with their plans, then the United States was "prepared to stand alone . . . on the issue of aid to the USSR."[266] By mid-July, U.S. opposition thereby ensured that the aid sought by the Soviet Union was not forthcoming—instead, all the Soviets obtained were offers of "observer" status in international economic organizations, "technical assistance," and a joint International Monetary Fund–World Bank study on the Soviet economy.[267]

Endgame: Extending U.S. Forces Eastward Having agreed that reunified Germany had the right to join NATO and with hopes of Western economic assistance dashed, Gorbachev moved to settle. During an FRG-USSR meeting in mid-July, the Soviet leader and Kohl agreed that Germany could reunify in the immediate future, that Soviet forces would withdraw from the GDR by 1994, and that the entire reunified country could enter NATO. Following the Soviet withdrawal, NATO guarantees would officially extend to the GDR, and German military forces allocated to NATO could move into former GDR territory.[268] A September date was set for members of the Two Plus Four to sign a treaty codifying the terms and conditions of German reunification.[269]

Still, the United States was not done preying. Although Gorbachev had agreed that FRG forces allocated to NATO could move into the GDR after Soviet troops withdrew, the United States now sought to ensure that forces from any NATO member—including units with "dual use" systems able to deliver either conventional or nuclear weapons—could enter former GDR territory.[270] With the date for signing the Two Plus Four Agreement (formally the Treaty on the Final Settlement with Respect to Germany) approaching, Soviet officials agreed. Not only was all of Germany to be in NATO, but U.S. military forces could now begin move into territory that had previously been part of the Warsaw Pact.[271] The eviction of Soviet power from Central-Eastern Europe was complete.

DENOUEMENT: WEAKENING IN 1991

For all the drama surrounding the Soviet expulsion from Central-Eastern Europe, Germany's formal reunification in October received scant notice. Less than one month after the July meeting between Gorbachev and Kohl, Iraq invaded Kuwait and touched off the 1990–91 Gulf War. As American attention turned to the Middle East, events in Europe moved to the back burner. Only toward the start of 1991 did the United States reengage in Europe, by which time the Soviet Union was beginning to collapse.

Accordingly, U.S. policy centered on whether the United States would side with a growing number of independence and secessionist movements in the Soviet Union to encourage the breakup of the Soviet state, or play for time and let Soviet decline continue without intense involvement by working with Soviet central authorities under Gorbachev. Prima facie, one might have expected U.S. strategists to expedite the Soviet Union's collapse. After all, the United States had been happy to hobble the Soviet Union in 1989–90 by destroying its alliance network; presumably, it would be as (if not more) interested in encouraging the breakup of the Soviet Union itself. Indeed, key U.S. policymakers—including Cheney and Deputy National Security Advisor

Robert Gates—advocated precisely this approach, reasoning that doing so "significantly reduc[ed] the chance [that the Soviet Union] could ever threaten our security again."[272]

Yet while U.S. leaders sought the continued decline of the Soviet Union, the United States again embraced a Weakening strategy, using limited means to challenge the Soviet Union and doing little to accelerate its collapse. In fact, initial U.S. efforts at the turn of 1990–91 contradict what predation theory predicts, as Bush authorized limited steps to bolster the Soviet state by waiving certain export restrictions and sending the Soviet Union emergency food aid.[273] By spring 1991, however, U.S. policy increasingly centered on facilitating the gradual and peaceful demise of the Soviet Union rather than an all-out surge to break the state or—alternatively—reinforce Soviet central authorities.[274]

This approach encompassed three interrelated elements. First, the United States refrained from backing secessionist or independence movements within the Soviet Union. President of the Russian Soviet Republic Boris Yeltsin was the leading proponent of U.S. involvement, but pressure to intervene also came from the Baltic republics, Ukraine, Georgia, and groups in Central Asia.[275] However, U.S. policymakers preferred to simply let Soviet central authority gradually weaken without expediting the process. By March 1991, Bush was describing his basic approach in blunt terms, writing in his diary, "My view is, you dance with who is on the dance floor—you don't try to influence this success [in the Soviet Union], and you especially don't do something that would [give the] blatant appearance [of encouraging] destabilization."[276] Members of the NSC offered similar input, calling for the United States to have "minimal involvement" in Soviet internal affairs and "avoiding entanglement in the morass of Soviet domestic politics."[277] As Rice explained, doing otherwise would harm "our ability to work with the [Soviet] central government on key foreign policy issues" and "contribute to a sharpening of the Soviet Union's domestic conflict."[278]

Nor did U.S. policy change appreciably after a failed conservative coup in August 1991 weakened Gorbachev politically and strengthened Yeltsin and other nationalist leaders. As an interagency group charged with shaping U.S. policy toward the disintegrating Soviet Union emphasized that fall, the United States would "continue to deal with central government institutions on some issues—nuclear/military issues and some portions of foreign policy—at the same time building new and more vigorous relationships with the republics."[279] And as it became clear that the Soviet Union would soon break apart, Bush and Baker set preconditions that Soviet republics would have to meet—focusing heavily on nuclear command and control arrangements—to obtain U.S. recognition of their independence.[280] As Baker explained when opposing Cheney's call for a speedy Soviet dissolution, the United States "should not establish a policy of supporting the breakup of the Soviet Union" so much as allow centrifugal tendencies to continue "subject to our principles."[281] As Gates—now siding with Baker—later elaborated, he, Baker, Bush, and others were heavily influenced by the question of "who would control the nuclear arsenal" and direct the Soviet military amid a collapse.[282]

Still—second—except for the humanitarian assistance supplied in early 1991, neither did the the United States help Soviet central authorities. If the United States was unwilling to quickly exploit Soviet weaknesses, it also avoided steps to reinforce Soviet power. This was particularly an issue in mid-1991 as Soviet leaders again sought Western economic assistance.[283] This time, the approach was pitched as part of a "Grand Bargain" whereby the Soviets would further liberalize their economic and political systems, and the West would respond with billions in economic aid.[284] As before, policymakers worried that the United States would end up supporting the Soviet Union and abet its continuation as a competitor.

The solution, laid out in a June 1991 Cabinet meeting, was to muddy the issue and block Soviet efforts. In the U.S. assessment, the Soviet initiative looked to trade Soviet reforms that did not affect the U.S.-Soviet competition for substantive concessions by the United States—or, as Baker put it, "how do you beat something for nothing?" To deflect Soviet requests, Baker, Scowcroft, Cheney, and other senior leaders decided instead to "come up with a package that does not cost" the United States. At the end of the day—as Scowcroft put it—the United States needed to "set conditions they [the Soviets] would find it hard to meet" so as to be seen as cooperating with the Soviet Union, without truly providing assistance.[285] Thus, when Soviet attempts to win U.S. backing resumed in the summer and fall, U.S. policymakers referred to a policy that demanded additional Soviet concessions without a U.S. response in kind.[286]

Finally, paralleling cautious efforts to facilitate the Soviet Union's political dissolution were continuing steps to reinforce U.S. military advantages. With Soviet forces withdrawing from Central-Eastern Europe and the Warsaw Pact effectively defunct, Bush pushed Congress to ratify the CFE treaty and codify an American military edge in Europe.[287] Concurrently, he endorsed initiatives designed to retain a significant U.S. military presence in Europe.[288] Although the United States planned to reduce its stationed forces, the collapse of the Soviet military threat meant that it enjoyed a significant net military advantage over potential challengers; by keeping significant assets in the region, the United States thereby ensured both its current preeminence and hedged against a possible future Soviet challenge.[289] After the August 1991 coup, meanwhile, the Bush administration proposed removing U.S. and Soviet tactical nuclear weapons from Europe, taking U.S. nuclear bombers off alert while requesting the Soviets reciprocate by confining their mobile ICBMs to garrisons, and reducing U.S. ICBM modernization programs while calling on the Soviets to do the same.[290] Though these efforts were heavily motivated by the desire to avoid nuclear anarchy in the fragmenting Soviet Union, this final U.S nuclear initiative seems not to have been wholly altruistic, as it left the area of greatest U.S. nuclear advantage—the submarine-launched ballistic missile force—untouched. The result would foster an improved U.S. military position, especially as the prospective breakup of the Soviet Union promised "to dilute" what Scowcroft called "the size of an [nuclear] attack we might have to face."[291]

Policymakers were explicit in both the predatory logic driving U.S. policy and the limits to U.S. efforts. As Scowcroft wrote Bush in March 1991, U.S. leaders sought "to consolidate our gains" vis-à-vis the Soviet Union.[292] This meant, Baker explained, "trying to get as much as we could out of the Soviets before there was an even greater turn to the right or shift into disintegration."[293] Baker, Scowcroft, and other senior officials were even more direct in June, agreeing that the United States wanted "to see the Soviet military radically reduced" while recognizing that "a real reform program would turn [the Soviet Union] into a third-rate power."[294] Hence, while the United States maneuvered to address Soviet unrest, it needed to keep its eyes on the prize of a much weaker Soviet Union. An NSC report submitted to Bush in mid-June elaborated on this point, concluding:

> Our priority now should be to lock in moderate Soviet international behavior and limits on their ability to threaten us or their neighbors. We want to create barriers against any resumption of past misconduct. . . . We also want to see the Soviet defense sector—and the conventional and military capabilities it sustains—drastically reduced . . . this is among the most vital interests we have both in arms control and in engaging the Soviets on the reform of their system.[295]

Meanwhile, when it became clear later in 1991 that centrifugal pressures imperiled the Soviet Union's continuation as a sovereign actor, Bush embraced the possibility of a world in which Soviet capabilities would diffuse across "many different states, none of which would have the awesome power of the Soviet Union."[296] Put simply, U.S. strategists sought to let the Soviet Union weaken and to incorporate a world in which the United States constituted what the Defense Department termed "the world's sole superpower."[297] As Acting Secretary of State Lawrence Eagleburger wrote Bush in July 1991, it was in the interest of the United States "to see the peaceful end of the Soviet empire as we have known it since 1917—a strong, totalitarian central government able to mobilize the vast human and material resources at its control in the service of global confrontation."[298]

Nevertheless, and as Eagleburger's reference to the Soviet Union's "peaceful end" implies, U.S. efforts were constrained by the danger of antagonizing a Soviet Union which remained—for now—militarily potent. Particularly worrisome was the possibility that accelerating the Soviet breakup would lead to Gorbachev's eviction by conservatives wedded to salvaging what they could of Soviet fortunes, a military coup, or a Faustian bargain between Gorbachev and Soviet hard-liners. Though the outcome from the Soviet Union's internal turmoil was seemingly a matter of Soviet domestic politics, U.S. policymakers understood the potentialities in strategic terms.[299] After all, and as Gates recalled in his memoirs, a hard-line turn could "erase many, if not most, of the internal and external changes" witnessed in the Soviet Union.[300] Although hard-liners—as analyses from early 1991 onward underscored—were unlikely to overcome the Soviet Union's problems, they could attempt to undo Gorbachev's reforms to slow Soviet losses, prevent the wholesale dissolution of the state, and pursue what an NSC-commissioned CIA report called "targets of opportunity to reassert Soviet influence abroad."[301] As problematic would be further competition between hard-liners and reformers: not only could this precipitate "civil war and dangerous instability in a country with tens of thousands of nuclear warheads" but—since hard-liners were likely to triumph in an internal conflict—it might result in what Baker termed "fascism with nuclear weapons" and a crisis in U.S.-Soviet relations.[302] The August 1991 coup attempt brought these concerns into relief as U.S. leaders initially refrained from condemning the coup, reasoning that "there was no point in needlessly antagonizing a new and potentially unstable government with tens of thousands of nuclear warheads."[303] Nor did the coup's failure eliminate the danger: into the fall, U.S. policymakers were unenthusiastic about the Soviet Union's collapse, partly driven by worries over "who would control the nuclear arsenal."[304]

Independent of U.S. actions, however, the Soviet Union's collapse accelerated in the final months of 1991.[305] Following an early December referendum on Ukrainian independence, Russia, Ukraine, and Belarus—representing three of the four largest economies inside the Soviet Union, accounting for over 80 percent of Soviet gross national product—declared their independence.[306] These steps effectively ended the Soviet Union's existence as a sovereign actor, as local authorities assumed its governance functions. Watching events unfold, U.S. policymakers remained uneasy, preferring more time to ensure the Soviet Union's peaceful breakup, prevent ethnic unrest, secure its nuclear assets, and limit arms races between (former) Soviet republics.[307] Nevertheless, with Gorbachev's announcement on Christmas Day 1991 that the Soviet Union was dissolved and with the final lowering of the Soviet flag above the Kremlin that evening, the Soviet Union was finished as a sovereign actor. As Baker was already explaining to his foreign counterparts, the United States was now the world's "sole superpower."[308]

To summarize, evidence from primary and secondary sources shows how U.S. strategists preyed with varying assertiveness on the declining Soviet Union from the mid-1980s onward. Prior to the turn of 1989–90, U.S. policymakers cautiously exploited Soviet problems, reasoning that the United States would benefit from a weaker Soviet Union while worrying about pressing the Soviet Union too hard and too soon. Faced with the collapse of Soviet military power in Central-Eastern Europe following the Revolutions of 1989–90, however, U.S. policymakers hit the accelerator to permanently roll back Soviet power in Europe by—above all—reunifying Germany within NATO. Still, U.S. strategy again turned cautious in 1991: confronting the collapse of the Soviet Union itself, U.S policymakers pursued limited gains at its expense rather than undertaking an all-out effort to break up the United States' only peer competitor.

This case should have provided an easy success for competing accounts of the rising United States' strategy. Accounts rooted in security dilemma, economic interdependence, and ideational logics, for example, strongly predicted burgeoning U.S. support for the Soviet Union from the mid-1980s onward, due to a combination of Soviet domestic reforms, arms reductions, diplomatic outreach, and efforts toward economic integration with the West. Yet while U.S. policymakers recognized that Soviet policymakers adopted such steps partly to win U.S. cooperation, U.S. strategists refused to bite. As internal deliberations show, U.S. policymakers opposed any policy that might help the Soviet Union recover from its problems. In fact, U.S. leaders sought to translate Soviet problems into U.S. strengths by maintaining a supportive façade while pocketing Soviet concessions and seeking additional gains. This is not to deny that U.S. policymakers often spoke of possible U.S.-Soviet cooperation, praised Soviet efforts to end Cold War competition, and appreciated the increasingly accommodating Soviet stance. Nevertheless, repeatedly faced with the choice between reciprocating Soviet moves or pursuing further gains, U.S. policymakers opted for the latter, reasoning that doing so maximized the United States' power and better positioned it to influence world politics. In short, these policies are the opposite of accounts that stress the supportive nature of U.S. strategy.

Theories predicting that the particular ideas held by U.S. leaders drove the United States toward predation fare better, but also face important limitations. Arguments stressing the militantly conservative beliefs of the Reagan administration correctly predicted the predatory nature of U.S. strategy in 1983–89. However, this approach has difficulty explaining why the United States became more predatory in 1990 under the comparatively moderate Bush administration—Bush's pragmatic conservatism should have contributed to a lessening of U.S. predation. The Open Door thesis, meanwhile, has trouble accounting for the U.S. Weakening strategy before 1989 and the turn back toward Weakening in 1991. Furthermore, although U.S. policymakers often emphasized the benefits the United States would reap in expanding liberal democracy and free trade in Europe—seeking, for instance, to ensure the "process of reform" in Eastern Europe and the Soviet Union—these concerns were largely rhetorical window dressing and a by-product of growing

U.S. hard power advantages. Not only were U.S. policymakers willing to ignore opposition movements such as Solidarity and reformist groups in the Soviet Union itself when U.S. security dictated, but policymakers in both the Reagan and Bush administrations privately emphasized the material and strategic benefits of maximizing U.S. power. Capturing U.S. tendencies to think beyond ideational dictates, Baker aptly noted in June 1991 that "It's not what happens internally in the USSR that is important; it's what happens externally."[309]

In contrast, the results provide strong support for predation theory. As expected at a time when the Soviet Union offered low strategic value, the United States systematically preyed on Soviet weaknesses. Moreover, when Soviet military options were robust, the United States limited the assertiveness of its predation compared to the options it could have pursued, adopting a Weakening strategy. Conversely, when Soviet military options collapsed—as in 1990—the United States pursued an intensely predatory Relegation strategy by regularly choosing among the most assertive means on the policy menu to challenge the Soviet Union. Equally striking, the predatory thrust of U.S. strategy persisted despite growing signs that the Soviet Union sought to reduce U.S.-Soviet competition: Reagan, Bush, and their advisers recognized the changes in the Soviet Union and the Soviet desire for rapprochement yet sustained U.S. predation.

In internal deliberations, meanwhile, policymakers spoke and argued in terms consistent with what predation theory predicts. First, leaders recognized that preying on the Soviet Union improved the relative power of the United States, affording it advantages in peacetime negotiations and improving the odds of wartime victory. By the late 1980s and early 1990s, the evidence shows that U.S. leaders looked towards establishing a hegemonic position in Europe and operating free of superpower constraints. This parallels a core prediction of the theory—namely, that rising states prey on declining states having low strategic value, as doing so helps risers seek hegemony. Second, members of the Bush and Reagan administrations consciously referred to the need to shape U.S. policy (1) to operate below a level estimated to trigger Soviet retaliation, or (2) to press the Soviet Union only when Soviet military options were significantly reduced. In doing so, they carefully monitored the state of Soviet military posture and discussed the implications of shifts in Soviet military options for U.S. predation. In other words, policymakers tracked and responded to shifts in Soviet military posture to pick the optimal times to intensely harm the Soviet Union.

Ultimately, en route to establishing U.S. dominance in post–Cold War Europe, the United States systematically maximized power at the Soviet Union's expense. Acting strategically, U.S. leaders carefully assessed the distribution of power and the risks and opportunities afforded by Soviet decline, and calibrated U.S. efforts to likely Soviet countermoves in order to eliminate the Soviet Union as a great power. Of course, U.S. policy was not pitched this way to all audiences. Although policymakers privately emphasized the desirability of ensuring that the declining Soviet Union never recovered, public rhetoric was framed in cooperative overtones. Overall, however, U.S. strategists across the Reagan and Bush years enacted a predatory strategy at the Cold War's end and, when the Soviet threat of force was off the table, expedited the rollback of Soviet power. Faced with good strategic reasons to weaken its Cold War opponent, the United States exploited its growing opportunities to improve its security by cutting down its only peer competitor.

Conclusion

Rising Powers, the Fate of Declining States, and the Future of Great Power Politics

Rising states vary widely in their approaches toward declining great powers. As one might expect from states living in a competitive world, some rising states, at some times, use their growing power to intensely compete with and prey upon their declining peers. Just as a rising United States went after the Soviet Union and ancient Athens sought to dominate Sparta, these states aim to knock decliners out of the ranks of the great powers, pushing them toward the dustbin of history. At other times and places, however, rising states are not nearly as predatory. Even if they seek to weaken great powers, risers can adopt less-assertive policies that only gradually shift the distribution of power in their favor. And in other cases, rising states try to support declining states and prevent them from slipping further down the ranks—they do not prey upon decliners at all. Before World War I, for example, a rising Germany protected a declining Austria-Hungary; likewise, the United States—at the height of its postwar power—gave a faltering Britain economic assistance through the Marshall Plan and military protection via NATO. Simply stated, rising states sometimes prey upon decliners, sometimes support them, and can do so more or less assertively.

The central purpose of this volume has been to develop an argument that explains variation in rising state strategy and to test it using detailed case studies of great power rise and decline in postwar Europe. Together, the theory and evidence illustrate that rising state behavior emerges and changes in predictable ways, depending on a declining state's ability (1) to help rising states offset other great powers, and (2) to deter or defend against challengers. In brief, rising states tend to prey upon decliners that offer little assistance against other great powers, seeing predation as an effective way of eliminating potential competitors. Declining states that can do little to protect themselves under such circumstances present especially inviting targets, as rising states can use any and all means at their disposal to undermine decliners without fearing significant backlash. Conversely, rising states generally support decliners that can help oppose or weaken other competitors. Here, declining states function as useful partners that can share the burden of confronting other great powers. Counterintuitively, a declining state's inability to defend itself under these conditions is a blessing in disguise, as rising states tend to offer substantial aid to forestall a decliner's loss as a partner.

Ultimately, this argument provides an original explanation for rising states' behavior toward declining states, but it is born of familiar realist roots. At base, the theory proposes that decision makers are attuned to changes in the distribution of power and privilege the resulting concerns and opportunities when shaping strategy. This is not to suggest that other factors such ideology, economic interdependence, security dilemma dynamics, and leadership beliefs are unimportant so much as it argues that predation theory provides the most powerful and consistent account of rising state behavior. Accordingly, this final chapter reviews the evidence supporting the argument, offers brief additional tests of the theory in two further cases of great power decline, describes its scholarly implications, and highlights ramifications for policy.

Empirical Results

Prior chapters presented detailed case studies on the U.S. and Soviet responses to Britain's decline in the mid- to late 1940s, and on U.S. strategy toward the declining Soviet Union in the late 1980s and early 1990s, as tests of the theoretical argument. These episodes represent the universe of post-1945 interactions between rising and declining great powers in Europe. Although the population is small, a combination of process tracing and congruence tests provided many points of observation with which to evaluate the argument. Equally important, the case studies offered a series of strong tests for predation theory against existing accounts of rising state strategy. Put simply, the causal factors emphasized by alternative arguments—drawing on the logic of the security dilemma, theories of economic interdependence, ideological compatibility between rising and declining states, and the particular ideas held by rising states' leaders—were all present in the cases. Furthermore, many alternative approaches were previously used to explain these episodes. Based on extensive archival research and primary documents, interviews, and secondary sources, the results instead show that declining states' varying ability to help or hinder rising states, and the different military threats posed in the process, produced different rising state responses. These outcomes are precisely what one expects if predation theory were correct, illustrating that alternative arguments tell only part of the story.

SUMMARIZING THE EVIDENCE

More specifically, chapters 2 and 3 examined the responses by the relatively rising United States and Soviet Union to the United Kingdom's postwar decline. In chapter 2, I reviewed existing studies of U.S. and Soviet strategy toward the United Kingdom, related these studies to alternative arguments addressing rising state strategy, and contrasted these arguments with what predation theory expects in the case. In brief, many treatments propose that U.S. and Soviet strategy toward Great Britain sharply diverged after World War II as the United States broadly supported the United Kingdom and the Soviet Union preyed on British weakness. These outcomes make sense given variation in the security dilemma, economic independence, and ideological affinities among the three states. In contrast, studies arguing that the United States preyed upon Britain while the Soviets supported the United Kingdom attribute these policies to the particular ideas held by contemporaneous U.S. and Soviet leaders. Conversely, predation theory highlighted the reasons that both the United States and Soviet Union enjoyed to support Britain in the immediate postwar world: facing an uncertain international environment and with other great powers looming, the United Kingdom could be a useful pawn in Soviet and U.S. plans against the other side. Only after Britain was firmly aligned with the United States from late 1947 onward did one expect these calculations to shift as, absent the possibility of Anglo-Soviet alignment, Soviet leaders confronted incentives to undercut Britain's position. In short, and distinct from prevailing treatments of U.S. and Soviet strategy, chapter 2 proposed that U.S. and Soviet policy would move along parallel tracks immediately after 1945 and diverge only once Britain was securely in the U.S. camp.

The case bore out these expectations. As shown in chapter 3, Britain initially occupied a central role in U.S. and Soviet postwar plans. The United States hoped to use Britain to offset the Soviets and to facilitate the United States' withdrawal from European politics; similarly, the Soviet Union expected Britain to be a keystone ally against a hostile United States. While Britain retained a robust posture in 1945–46, U.S. and Soviet strategists concluded that limited support for Britain—a Bolstering strategy— could keep it functioning as a junior partner without requiring greater assistance. Once British military posture collapsed, however, the United States and Soviet Union upped the ante. Starting in late 1946, the two sides separately intensified their efforts to win Britain's friendship, adopting Strengthening strategies by offering Britain security guarantees and, in the U.S. case, extensive economic aid. Only after this point, as it became clear that the United States was winning the competition for Britain as the Anglo-American relationship matured, did the Soviet Union change gears. Starting in mid- to late 1947, Soviet policy became predatory by challenging plans for British-led Western European reconstruction, engaging in an arms buildup, and diplomatically opposing the state. In this, Soviet policymakers increasingly saw themselves confronting a united Anglo-American front and so tried to limit the dangers to their country.

Whereas chapters 2 and 3 generally showcased supportive strategies in action, chapters 4 and 5 illustrated the logic of rising state predation by examining the relatively rising United States' response to the decline of the Soviet Union. Chapter 4 explained why the United States had strong incentives to prey: given the Soviet Union's low strategic value, U.S. strategists were likely to try to exacerbate and exploit Soviet problems as a way of eliminating the United States' only great power competitor. Moreover, I expected U.S. predation to begin in limited form, intensify after Soviet military posture in Eastern Europe collapsed following the Revolutions of 1989–90, yet moderate again when the breakup of the nuclear-armed Soviet Union loomed in 1991. In short, U.S. strategy was predicted to shift from Weakening to Relegation, and back to Weakening. Notably, the expectation of persistent U.S. predation differs markedly from existing research proposing that U.S. strategy oscillated between support for and predation of the waning Soviet Union.

Chapter 5 then showed the Weakening and Relegation strategies in action. Once Soviet relative decline began, U.S. policymakers set out to undermine their Cold War opponent. Owing to the possible Soviet use of force, however, leaders initially circumscribed the extent of U.S. predation: trying to operate below a level that could trigger conflict, U.S. policies focused on gradually weakening the Soviet Union by shifting the distribution of economic and military power in favor of the United States, delegitimating the Soviet political system, and exacerbating the Soviet Union's economic problems. This trend reached its apogee early in the Revolutions of 1989–90 as the George H. W. Bush administration opted for middle-of-the-road policies intended to avoid a direct challenge to Soviet dominance in Eastern Europe. Once Soviet military posture outside the Soviet homeland weakened in late 1989, however, the United States hit the accelerator. Within a few months, Germany—the great prize of Cold War Europe—reunified on U.S. terms and the United States began preparing to expand its footprint into Eastern Europe. Still, once it became clear in 1991 that the Soviet Union itself might collapse, the United States again limited predation by seeking a soft landing for the fragmenting Soviet Union and reducing the speed of the Soviet dissolution. Fearful that assertive efforts might trigger a backlash and a military crisis with a nuclear-armed adversary, the United States again preyed within limits.

WEIGHING THE RESULTS

Overall, the case studies offer strong evidence for predation theory. First, the outcomes matched hypotheses derived from the theory. Rising powers generally supported declining states with high strategic value, preyed upon decliners with low strategic value, and modulated the assertiveness of support or predation depending on the declining state's military posture. Furthermore, many of the theory's predictions were unique, as competing accounts either predicted different outcomes or expected strategies to change at different points than they actually did. Overall, shifts in a declining state's value and/or its military posture corresponded closely with shifts in rising state behavior—there was a strong correlation between variation in the independent variables central to predation theory and changes in rising state strategy.

Second, process tracing provides strong support for the theory's causal mechanisms. Across and within cases, policymakers thought about strategy in terms consistent with predation theory. More than that, leaders monitored the variables at the heart of the argument and referred to these factors when justifying their policies or debating the merits of alternatives. In fact, not only did policymakers often reject strategies that were inconsistent with my argument, but they did so by noting that other strategies were unattractive or infeasible given the declining state's military options and/or utility as a partner. Of course, this does not mean that strategists always chose policies consistent with the theory. As Soviet behavior in the Iran crisis shows, rising states sometimes opted for overly aggressive or supportive strategies. Even then, however, strategists tended to monitor feedback from the international system, adjusting course by becoming more or less predatory (or supportive) as appropriate. In sum, process tracing provides evidence that the causal mechanisms at the heart of predation theory operated and powerfully influenced rising state strategy.

Finally, the argument developed here outperformed competing accounts of rising state policy. Baldly stated, there is limited evidence that policymakers were driven by the insecurity spirals central to the security dilemma, felt constrained by economic exchange, or were especially generous toward ideological fellow travelers (or antagonistic toward ideological rivals). Not only did rising states often hang back from supporting states with which they were ideological brethren or economically interdependent—as the United States did with Britain in the early postwar period—but they were also willing to ignore past rivalries with decliners when doing so was in their interest. The Soviet Union's willingness to set aside past competition with Britain in 1945–47 exemplifies this latter trend. Meanwhile, changes in security dilemma, interdependence, and ideological variables often did not produce a discernible strategic shift in the manner expected. The United States, for instance, became more predatory as Soviet power waned late in the Cold War even though the Soviet Union ended its ideological rivalry with the United States and sought integration into the global economy; if economic interdependence or ideological distance arguments were correct, the United States should instead have become less predatory in this period.

If anything, as growing Anglo-Soviet animosity and deepening Anglo-American cooperation from 1947 onward imply, it appears that insecurity, economic exchange, and ideological rivalries were by-products of strategies arrived at for other reasons, rather than causal factors themselves.

Arguments rooted in the particular ideas held by leaders performed better but are still wanting. The strongest evidence for these arguments is the fact that policymakers occasionally used ideational language when rationalizing and explaining strategy. This was especially notable in (1) the Anglo-Soviet case, where Communism-inspired expectations of a contest between the United States and United Kingdom loomed large in Soviet strategy, and (2) in American discussions of crafting an open economic order during the negotiations surrounding the Anglo-American loan and the Marshall Plan. Still, the evidence is far from dispositive. Other ideas such as the U.S. commitment to what Christopher Layne terms the Open Door thesis, or the hawkish anti-Communist views of the Reagan administration, failed to capture the strategies that rising states actually pursued.[1] Similarly, for all of the evidence that policymakers sometimes subscribed to particular ideas, strategies shifted and policymakers adjusted their arguments when the variables emphasized by predation theory also changed. Thus, Soviet leaders highlighted Anglo-American infighting only when other factors made it plausible that Britain might be a Soviet ally; when these conditions changed, so did Soviet beliefs.

Two Additional Assessments

Beyond the evidence marshaled in the case studies, however, it is worth considering how the theory fares in explaining other instances of rising state strategy. After all, the post-1945 era represents a particular moment in diplomatic history that may be uniquely explicable by predation theory. Accordingly, this section briefly examines the responses of Germany, Russia, and Great Britain to the declines of Austria-Hungary[2] and France from the 1860s through the outbreak of World War I. Europe at this time was the archetype of a multipolar system, replete with waxing and waning rivalries and alignments among the great powers. Austria and France, moreover, were the biggest and most persistent losers in this period (see Appendix 1 and below): although neither state declined monotonically, both went from rough parity with the other great powers in the mid-nineteenth century to spots significantly behind their nominal peers by 1914. Hence, an overview of rising state behavior in these cases—recognizing, of course, that much of the data needed to fully evaluate the argument remains practically unavailable in European archives, while space limitations constrain the analysis—provides numerous opportunities with which to further explore predation theory and assess its external validity.

To be clear, the fact that Europe was a multipolar and highly competitive arena in the 1860–1914 period means that predation theory is unlikely to single-handedly account as fully for the dynamics of rise and decline as it did the cases in chapters 2–5. Put simply, the fact that several powers operated against one another means that the odds of insecurity spirals and misperception, competing ideologies, economic factors, and leadership beliefs—to say nothing of other factors—affecting states' specific decisions is greater in this period. Moreover, as other scholars rightly note, much of great power politics at this time was dominated by three interrelated trends in the distribution of power, namely: Germany's unification in the 1860s–1870s and its rise as an economic and military giant; Britain's decline vis-à-vis Germany and the subsequent emergence of an Anglo-Germany rivalry; and Russia's military and economic growth around the start of the twentieth century.[3] Although these events were related to the Austrian and French declines, they also mean that rising state strategies did not emerge in a vacuum.

That said, I show below that predation theory helps us understand how Germany, Russia, and Britain managed relations with Austria and France as the former three states' relative advantages over the latter two countries grew. In the process, I also demonstrate that examining these cases in light of predation theory can help scholars understand three of the core strategic developments in the decades before World War I. First, the argument helps to explain why Prussia, en route to unifying Germany, chose to prey on Austria-Hungary and France and was able to do so without precipitating Russian or British intervention.[4] Second, predation theory helps account for the durability of peace among the great powers amid fluid European alliances and alignments in the 1870s through the 1890s.[5] Finally, the theory helps analysts understand the growing tightness of European alliances in the run-up to World War I. Although these trends have been analyzed in the history and political science literatures, predation theory provides insight into specific puzzles connected to each, including Anglo-Russian apathy during Germany's unification, Germany's subsequent decision to support a declining Austria rather than a waning France, and the eventual hardening of political-military arrangements that left little room for strategic maneuver.

AUSTRIA, FRANCE, AND THE POLITICS OF GERMAN UNIFICATION

Germany's unification was accomplished in under one decade. Under the leadership of Chancellor Otto von Bismarck, Prussia speedily defeated Denmark (1864), Austria (1866), and France (1870–71) in a series of wars and united the states of the German Confederation into a single nation. It did so, moreover, without intervention by Britain or Russia—notable omissions in the Austrian and French episodes, given that Prussia's successes moved it significantly closer to dominating Central Europe and overturning Europe's distribution of power. Indeed, the combination of Prussian aggression and Anglo-Russian ambivalence as Austria and France went down to defeat has led many scholars to see Bismarck as a strategic genius, able to manipulate the other great powers to create opportunities for Prussian aggrandizement.[6]

Predation theory, on the other hand, argues that putting too much emphasis on Prussian agency understates the structural logic of the episode. Viewed in light of the argument developed in this volume, both Prussian predation and Anglo-Russian apathy were likely to emerge in this period due to systemic forces. From Prussia's perspective, a relatively declining Austria and France offered low strategic value: Austria's long-standing rivalry with Prussia for dominance in the German Confederation left it politically unavailable,[7] while France's geographic isolation—located due west of Prussia, it was poorly positioned to help against other potential threats—precluded its utility as a Prussian partner. As a result, Prussia had strong incentives to undercut Austrian and French power—predation made sense. That said, Austria and France also held robust military postures at this time, with both sides deploying reasonably well-equipped and trained armies that had performed adequately in recent conflicts.[8] Combined, low value and robust military postures meant that Prussia was likely to try to prey upon France and Austria but generally do so in limited fashion, with low cost and risk to itself.

The wars themselves aside, limited predation was indeed the overriding theme of Prussian strategy. In the early to mid-1860s, for example, Prussia worked to undercut Austrian strength in central Europe, economically and diplomatically hindering Austria by drawing the small states of the German Confederation into its own orbit.[9] As Prussia's Kaiser Wilhelm I declared, competition would continue "until Austria has convinced herself that Prussia is her equal as a European Power and her superior as a German one."[10] Only as these efforts faltered and it became clear that Austria's defeat was needed for Prussia to dominate the German Confederation did Prussia—pushed by Bismarck—turn to a military solution. And although Prussia's inauguration of the 1866 war is closer to a Relegation than a Weakening strategy, Prussian actions during and after the conflict suggest that the structural factors described by my argument shaped Prussian policy. Tellingly, once Prussian forces proved victorious, Prussian leaders specifically decided against overthrowing the Austrian monarchy and made peace, reasoning that eliminating Austria as a great power would invite intervention by the other great powers to preserve an Austrian counterweight to Prussia in Central Europe, and would needlessly increase future Austro-Prussian tensions.[11]

A similar trend obtained in Franco-German relations. As Prussia grew and France declined in the 1860s (especially after Prussia's victory over Austria), Prussia's leaders adopted a Weakening strategy toward France. This gradualist approach emphasized undercutting French credibility by making France appear to be both party to Prussian expansionism and wedded to its own growth at others' expense.[12] As the historian Otto Pflanze notes, this approach was necessitated by French strength and potential for aggression if Prussia grew too far, too fast.[13] Of course, Prussia's decision to inaugurate a war with France in 1870, which culminated in the victorious Prussia's seizing portions of French territory and imposing a large financial indemnity to damage the French economy, contradicts the argument.[14] Still, after 1871 Prussia—now Germany—returned to a strategy of limited predation: the new state focused principally on developing its economy, and its leaders were content simply to forestall French revisionism. As Bismarck observed in the mid-1870s, "We wish to keep the peace, but if the French so order their preparations that in five years they will be ready and determined to strike, then in three years we shall begin the war."[15]

What of Britain and Russia? Unlike the situation vis-à-vis Prussia, Austria and France offered Britain and Russia high strategic value: located near Germany, with meaningful latent power, and seeking help against Prussia (and desiring independent foreign policies more generally), both Austria and France could plausibly be of assistance to Britain and Russia in capping Prussian growth.[16] Here, however, Austrian and French military strength was a double-edged sword. Since both states looked capable of taking care of themselves, Britain and Russia could each use limited means to aid Austria and France, using a Bolstering strategy to preserve the states at limited cost and risk to themselves.

In fact, British and Russian strategies during the period of German unification were defined by warm but limited efforts to help Austria and France. In the run-up to both the Austro-Prussian and the Franco-Prussian Wars, British and Russian strategists opposed Prussia's push for a military showdown—they wished to avoid upsetting the European distribution of power. Nonetheless, neither state was willing to intervene in the conflicts, limiting their assistance to calls for a diplomatic settlement before and during the wars. In a telling statement before the 1866 contest, for instance, Britain's foreign minister wrote Bismarck "that we purposely abstain from making any official communication upon the present state of affairs, but that we earnestly beg of him to pause before he embarks in a war of which no man can foresee the results of the termination."[17] Similarly, Russian leaders during the 1870–71 conflict sought what the British ambassador to Russia characterized as "the early convocation in concert with England of a Congress with a view to the restoration of peace . . . and the maintenance of the Balance of Power in Europe."[18] In this, neither Russia nor Britain heeded Austrian or French calls for military action. In fact, just as the British foreign minister wrote in 1866 that "We are willing to do anything for the maintenance of peace except committing ourselves to policy of action," so too did a senior member of Britain's ruling Liberal Party explain to Queen Victoria that "if an opportunity should offer itself, of successfully mediating with a view to the restoration of peace, it was essential to preserve the most impartial neutrality [i.e., nonintervention] between the contending parties."[19] This approach made sense. After all, British strategists during and after the Austro-Prussian conflict argued that it was reasonable to expect that a militarily potent France would not allow Prussia to dominate Germany and— as one British policymaker concluded—the two states "pose a check to each other."[20]

After the conflicts, meanwhile, Britain and Russia continued trying to bolster Austria and France. This was particularly clear in the French case, where both Russia and Britain pledged diplomatic backing to France during the 1875 "War in Sight" crisis in a bid to prevent further German aggression. Again, the two states acted at limited risk to themselves. Stopping short of pledging military intervention, British leaders sought to construct "some concerted movement to preserve the peace in Europe" by undertaking coordinated diplomatic moves with Russia.[21] For their part, Russian leaders promised to warn France of German aggression if war appeared probable.[22] In other words, the aforementioned British and Russian ambivalence in reacting to the rise of Prussia and Prussian predation vis-à-vis France and Austria makes sense in light of predation theory: it corresponds to what one expects if Austria and France offered high strategic value while holding robust military postures.

AUSTRIA, FRANCE, AND EUROPEAN ALIGNMENTS, 1875–1900

Whereas the period around German unification saw Prussian aggression abetted by the Anglo-Russian failure to firmly back France and Austria, the period following unification witnessed proliferating alliances and alignments and a lengthy period of great power peace. Artful diplomacy, ideological affinity—particularly among conservative states such as Austria, Germany, and Russia—and economic ties likely facilitated these outcomes. Still, the politics surrounding the Austrian and French declines were critical: variation in Austrian and French strategic value and posture helps explain why different powers aligned or competed with Austria and France in this era, and why they did so with varying degrees of assertiveness.

The Austrian and French defeats in 1866 and 1870–71 confirmed that these states had fallen behind at least some of their nominal peers. These trends continued afterward (see Appendix 1), as Austria and France lost ground to Britain, Russia, and especially Germany. By the 1880s–90s, both were noticeably weaker than the other great powers and seemed poised to decline further as they faced difficulties in adapting to the Second Industrial Revolution then gathering steam.[23] Austria also suffered from mounting internal dissent as it failed to craft a unified nation-state from its disparate nationalities, thereby threatening its political stability.[24]

Against this backdrop, Austrian and French strategic value and posture exhibited signs of both change and continuity, creating conditions for flux in great power politics. The biggest shift occurred with Austria. With competition for leadership in Germany resolved in Prussia's favor, Austria turned its foreign ambitions toward Southeastern Europe (i.e., the Balkans). These changes revived Austria's political availability to Germany and, when combined with Austria's still-meaningful resources and a geographic position which could help Germany offset Russia, raised Austrian strategic value. By the same token, Austria continued offering high value to Britain and Russia as the state retained its utility in confronting Germany (and, for Britain, Russia) while remaining politically available.[25] That said, Austria had a robust military posture at this time. After its 1866 defeat, Austria reformed its military by enacting conscription, acquiring new weapons, adopting a general staff system to coordinate military activities, and developing new tactics. Combined, these changes enabled Austria-Hungary to dispatch forces to address any likely contingency in Southern or Central Europe.[26] In tandem, and unlike the situation before 1866, Austria's high value and robust posture meant that each of Europe's rising states had reasons to engage in limited support and pursue a Bolstering strategy toward Austria.

France underwent less dramatic changes. The country retained the high strategic value it had for Russia and Britain before 1870, while its value to Germany was, if anything, even lower than before: not only did France remain geographically isolated, but its evident desire for revenge against Germany meant that the state remained politically unavailable.[27] Meanwhile, French military posture remained robust. Indeed, although the 1870–71 defeat revealed deficiencies in French equipment, training, leadership, and logistics, France worked for the next twenty years to correct these problems. In short order, training and tactics improved, new equipment was procured, and new logistical arrangements designed to facilitate mobilization developed, as French military strength recovered from the lows of 1870–71.[28] Combined, the country's high value to Britain and Russia, low value to Germany, and robust military predict broad similarities in rising state policy toward France to those during the unification period: Britain and Russia should adopt Bolstering strategies to back France with limited assertiveness, while Germany should pursue a Weakening strategy.

These predictions are generally borne out in the historical record, with the evidence particularly strong for German and Russian policy. As predicted, Germany pursued a Bolstering strategy toward Austria. Indeed, following its victory in the 1870–71 Franco-Prussian War, Germany aligned itself with Austria and Russia in the Three Emperors' League and, at the decade's end, offered Austria a defensive alliance against possible Russian aggression.[29] At the time, this alliance was largely a paper tiger: the two states engaged in little military planning, neither necessarily intended to fight Russia on behalf of the other,[30] and the arrangement was soon overshadowed by a revived Three Emperors' League.[31] Still, in bidding to retain Austria as a partner and block its collusion with other powers, a foundation for German support was laid. As George Kennan later observed, it was a "basic requirement of Germany's security" into the late 1800s that "the Austro-Hungarian Empire not be broken up or destroyed and that Austria retain its status as one of the Great Powers of Europe."[32]

Bolstering also characterized Russian and British relations with Austria. Austria's interest in the Balkans created potential points of friction with Russia, which traditionally had its own designs on the area. Nevertheless, Russian leaders agreed to cooperate with Austria in the Three Emperors' Leagues of the 1870s and 1880s, giving each side influence over the other's policy and minimizing possible problems in Russo-Austrian relations. And although formal Austro-Russian cooperation ceased following the Three Emperors' League's final collapse in 1887, ad hoc cooperation in the Balkans continued. Following an informal arrangement to consult one another if Ottoman authority in the Balkans collapsed, the two states struck a deal in the 1890s to cooperatively manage changes in the Balkans and preserve the local status quo, reducing the risk of a serious diplomatic dispute between them.[33] In effect, Russia neutralized the Balkans as a flash point in Russo-Austrian diplomacy, leaving Austria in a less-fraught strategic situation.

Britain also supported Austria. As Austrian attention shifted toward Southeastern Europe, for instance, British strategists initially resisted Austrian efforts to secure British backing in maintaining the Balkan status quo. Instead, British backing was limited to periodic Anglo-Austrian coordination to manage the breakup of Ottoman holdings in the area and avoid overly close Austrian collaboration with Russia and Germany.[34] Distinct from what predation theory predicts, however, British policy soon intensified. Worried that Russia might endanger Austria's existence as a Great Power" and threaten Britain's lines of communication with its overseas colonies, British leaders tendered a limited alliance in the 1887 Mediterranean Agreements, pledging to work with Austria to defend the Balkans from external machinations.[35] This arrangement raised the possibility that Britain would fight on behalf of Austria if a threat materialized.[36] Nevertheless, British strategists accepted the risk and, by the late 1890s, were describing Austria as "England's natural ally."[37] Indeed, although the Mediterranean Agreements lapsed in 1897, British and Austrian diplomats continued exploring ways to enhance bilateral cooperation into the 1900s.[38]

Likewise, France's high value to Russia and Britain and low value to Germany helps explain key features of European politics in this era—namely, France's lack of firm allies for the two decades after 1870 and the eventual emergence of a Franco-Russian axis. German policy through the 1890s focused on fostering France's diplomatic containment. Rather than risking another war and inviting British or Russian action, German officials worked to ensure that the other great powers enjoyed better relations with Germany than they did with France. Otherwise, France might become the centerpiece of what Bismarck termed the "nightmare of coalition": an Austro-Russian-French alignment, potentially backed by Britain, that could isolate Germany.[39] German leaders thus encouraged French colonial adventures to foment Anglo-French strife and crafted a series of alliances and alignments—particularly the Three Emperors' League and the 1887 German-Russian Reinsurance Treaty—to keep France from finding military partners.[40] And while containment faltered with the 1891–94 formation of a Franco-Russian alliance, Germany responded by trying to minimize the new alliance's impact on European politics through stronger engagement with Britain and Russia.[41]

Similarly consistent with predation theory, Franco-Russian relations were warm but limited. To be sure, Russian policymakers occasionally signaled to French leaders that a closer Franco-Russian alignment might be attractive. Still, Russian policy into the late 1880s remained anchored by the Three Emperors' League.[42] Thus, when pressed by the French ambassador in 1887 to clarify what Russia would do if Germany attacked France, Russian leaders emphasized that aid would consist of moral support—not necessarily intervention.[43] As a French diplomatic report concluded, Russia "needed France, as a force capable of offering to Russia the support necessary" to hedge against a possible German-Austrian threat—meaning, as George Kennan described, "a France that was strong and stable"—but this did not translate into regular and sustained Russian backing for France.[44] Meanwhile, although Germany's failure to renew the 1887 German-Russian Reinsurance Treaty prompted Russia to ally with France in the course of 1891–94, even this alliance was constrained by Russia's continued interest in good relations with Germany and the absence of sustained Franco-Russian military planning.[45] In short, Russia engaged in a range of behaviors to support France but was generally unwilling to sacrifice much for the privilege.

Contradicting predation theory, however, British policymakers were generally unsupportive of France in the period following German unification. Of course, and as noted above, Britain in the 1870s did not want France further weakened and so backed France diplomatically in the 1875 War in Sight crisis. That said, British policy moved toward Weakening in the 1880s and 1890s as French colonization—encouraged by Germany—in Africa and Asia threatened Britain's imperial holdings and naval dominance. British leaders were unnerved by French moves and, desiring Anglo-French cooperation in Europe, frustrated by what they saw as distracting colonial discord. Still, Britain responded by undermining France's North African empire and engaging France in a naval arms race to sustain British naval superiority.[46] Furthermore, the ad hoc support Britain gave France in the 1860s and 1870s vanished. When, for instance, a war scare between France and Germany erupted in 1886–87, Britain hinted strongly that it would stand aside if Germany attacked France.[47]

Collectively, focusing on Austrian and French strategic value to the relatively rising Germany, Russia, and Britain and on Austrian and French military postures helps explain the fluid alliances and peaceful great power relations in the period after German unification. Ultimately, with Germany, Russia, and France each facing incentives to support at least one of the declining states and the declining states able to create security for themselves, opportunities for aggression were limited, and all states could adjust their foreign policies in response to changing strategic conditions.

THE TIGHTENING OF ALLIANCES, 1900–1914

Above all, analyzing declining states' strategic values and military postures helps account for a final trend in European relations—namely, the tightening of European alliances and hardening of alliances in the roughly fifteen years before World War I. This development, as other scholars have pointed out, was central to the outbreak of violence in 1914 and the conflict's subsequent spread.[48] Without claiming to explain the entirety of this trend, focusing on Austrian and French strategic value and posture helps account for why Europe's two foremost decliners garnered significant backing from their relatively rising peers—a key feature of the tightening alliances—at this time by highlighting the incentives rising states had to either prevent decliners' fall from the great powers, or to expedite the trend.

Central to this phenomenon were changes in Austrian and French value and posture. At the time, the states' continued economic and political problems were compounded by growing Russian and German strength.[49] Unlike the situation in preceding periods, however, Austrian strategic value to Britain and Russia collapsed after the early 1900s as Austrian leaders threw Austria's lot in with Germany.[50] This effectively denied Austria as a partner to Britain and Russia while maintaining Austria's value to Germany. By the same token, France opted to settle its colonial disputes with Britain shortly after the beginning of the twentieth century.[51] This move revised France's political availability and ensured that it offered high value to Great Britain; meanwhile, France's high value to Russia and low value for Germany remained unchanged from before.

Austrian and French military postures also shifted. After the 1890s, Austrian military strength faltered as military spending languished and the rate of conscription declined.[52] Training suffered, and the Austrian military found itself unable to exploit the post-1890s revolution in military technology. Notably, where Germany fielded one artillery piece per 195 troops, Austria deployed only one obsolescent gun per 338 troops![53] The result was an increasingly weak military posture: as its peers armed at a faster rate, Austria's ability to secure itself against challengers grew doubtful.[54] By 1914, Austrian leaders and foreign observers alike were questioning whether its forces would even fight for the country.[55] As Geoffrey Wawro concludes, "The once vaunted Austrian army faded away after 1900."[56]

This change paralleled the situation in France. Starting in the mid-1890s, French military posture collapsed: military budgets stagnated,[57] the military failed to procure new equipment to replace older weapons (culminating by 1905 in a 2:1 German artillery advantage),[58] tactical innovation and training declined,[59] and military professionalism was undermined by civil-military disputes.[60] Concurrently, the army faced problems obtaining enough troops from France's slow-growing population, while budgetary and political pressure in 1905–13 limited draftees to a two-year term of service that reduced troop quality.[61] These processes left France's military options vis-à-vis its peers uncertain at best, so much so that German strategists on the outbreak of World War I counted on (and British and Russian leaders feared) a rapid defeat of the French military.[62]

Under these conditions, predation theory predicts (1) that Germany should intensely support Austria after the 1900s, while Britain and Russia engage in intensive predation, and (2) that Britain and Russia should intensely back, while Germany intensely preys upon, France after the mid-1890s. This is almost exactly what occurred. Whereas, for instance, Germany was reluctant through the 1890s to antagonize other powers on Austria's behalf—seeking good relations with both Russia and Austria—it backed Austria's annexation of Bosnia-Herzegovina in 1908–9 despite substantial British and Russian opposition,[63] and protected Austria during the territorial disputes accompanying the breakup of the Ottoman Empire's European holdings.[64] Germany also signaled that it would assist Austria if Austria were attacked and, as the German chancellor emphasized in 1912, "her existence were thus threatened."[65] This trend was likely reinforced by German concerns surrounding Russia's growing strength beginning in the early 1900s and the challenge this posed to both Germany and Austria.[66] Accordingly, German military support intensified as the Austro-German alliance solidified. Formal military staff talks began in 1909 and soon produced a war plan designed partly to help Austria deal with the mounting Russian military challenge.[67]

Russia and Britain, on the other hand, moved decisively against Austria. With Austria lost as a partner and militarily weak, Russia backed the different states that had emerged in the Balkans since 1880, encouraged their irredentist claims, and helped organize them into an anti-Austrian coalition.[68] In doing so, Russia not only threatened Austria's own Balkan sphere of influence but also, since many of the peoples and territories targeted by Balkan irredentism were part of Austria itself, directly challenged Austria-Hungary's internal cohesion.[69] Reinforcing the trend, Russian diplomats began overtly threatening war, with no less an official than Russia's foreign minister warning in 1909 that Austro-Russian competition in Southeastern Europe "cannot be resolved except by conflict."[70] Meanwhile, Russia began expanding its military and preparing to contest Austrian influence in the Balkans by force.[71] In short, as Paul Schroeder observes, Russia sought to isolate and coerce Austria en route to removing it from European balance-of-power politics.[72] Of course, Russia did not seek conflict while Austria-Hungary was firmly backed by a powerful Germany and while the Russian military was recovering from losses in the 1904–5 Russo-Japanese War.[73] Hence, when Germany periodically threatened military action on Austria's behalf, Russia temporarily pulled in its claws by—for instance—reining in Balkan irredentism.[74] Still, Russia increasingly challenged Austria's position.

Britain pursued a similar course. By 1908–9, British leaders opposed Austria's annexation of Bosnia-Herzegovina, going so far as to coordinate efforts to block Austria's moves and demanding compensation for Russia's Balkan clients.[75] Thereafter, Britain backed Russia's challenge to Austria's Balkan sphere of influence and supported Russia in crafting an anti-Austrian coalition among the Balkan states. Furthermore, when Austro-Russian tensions escalated during the Balkan Wars (1911–13), Britain undermined efforts to resolve the disputes on Austrian terms. As Schroeder emphasizes, British policymakers pursuing this policy expressly sought to isolate Austria and revise the local status quo in ways inimical to Austrian security: in effect, Britain aimed to remove a strategically important area from Austrian control while hindering Austria's ability to resist. Exemplifying the trend, when it appeared on the eve of World War I that Austria might collapse, British strategists reinforced Anglo-Russian ties so that Britain could influence the division of the spoils.[76] Thus, despite having supported Austria in the late 1800s, Britain soon directly challenged Austrian strength.[77]

The opposite trends obtained with France. Germany was constrained in immediately undermining French power given increasingly strong French ties with Britain and Russia; miscalculation could provoke a conflict that Germany might not win.[78] Still, driven partly by the assessment that the "French army is by no means poor, but ours is considerably better,"[79] German policy became markedly more assertive. War plans from the 1890s onward called for an all-out offensive to knock France out of a conflict en route to a dictated peace; conversely, previous plans had envisioned a limited attack and negotiated settlement.[80] Military aggrandizement complemented diplomatic efforts at isolating and coercing France. Improvements in France's relationships with Britain and Russia, for example, led Germany to inaugurate diplomatic disputes (such as the First Moroccan Crisis) intended to disrupt France's burgeoning alliances.[81] Meanwhile, German diplomacy became more aggressive as German leaders threatened war to compel France into accepting German terms in these disputes.[82] Simply stated, German predation intensified as France's military posture collapsed.

Conversely, Russian support for France intensified as French posture weakened. By the mid-1900s, the two states were regularly engaging in joint military planning. At France's behest, by 1912–13 Russia had agreed to attack

Germany upon the outbreak of hostilities to relieve expected German military pressure on France at a time when France seemed ill-prepared to defend itself.[83] A similar trend occurred in diplomatic affairs, as Russia generally backed France in standoffs with Germany and assured French leaders that the Franco-Russian alliance was the centerpiece of Russian diplomacy.[84] This trend was especially notable in the early 1910s when, amid rumors that Russia might abandon France for Germany, Russian leaders hastened to affirm Russia's fidelity.[85]

As for Great Britain, France's high strategic value and waning military strength led Britain to discontinue earlier efforts to undercut France and instead come to France's aid. In fact, British leaders embraced French proposals to settle colonial disputes and soon resolved tensions with the 1904 formation of the Entente Cordiale.[86] Although officially focused on colonial matters, the Entente soon became a de facto Anglo-French alliance, driven by the recognition that, as one British diplomat put it in 1903, "For us France is more important than Germany or Russia. . . . If we are certain of France, no one can have designs upon us."[87] Accordingly, Anglo-French military talks began in 1905, resulting by 1911 in plans for the British Army's wartime deployment to France to help offset German strength.[88] These military provisions paralleled growing British diplomatic support. Where Britain's foreign secretary demurred when pressed in 1906 as to whether Britain would intervene on France's behalf in wartime, British diplomats were soon assuring French strategists of Britain's reliability in the face of German pressure.[89] Failure to do so, as the diplomat Sir Arthur Nicolson warned, might cause France "to make terms with Germany" and isolate Britain.[90] At a time when, in the words of one British planner, "France would in all human probability be defeated" by Germany should war erupt, Britain prepared to come to France's assistance.[91]

In sum, an overview of relatively rising states' responses to the declines of Austria-Hungary and France at the height of European multipolarity provides additional evidence that predation theory provides purchase in explaining rising state strategy. As predicted, rising states generally supported declining states with high strategic value, preyed upon decliners with low strategic value, and modulated their assertiveness depending on the declining state's military posture. To be clear, the evidence in these cases is not as rich as that in chapters 2–5, and more needs to be done to assess alternative explanations. In addition, the theory did not perform flawlessly, as rising states occasionally adopted strategies at odds with the argument. Still, on balance, the dynamics of rise and decline in late nineteenth- and early twentieth-century Europe reinforce the basic argument that rising states shape their strategies toward declining states based on whether and how risers can use decliners to compete with other great powers. The results therefore help demonstrate that predation theory's logic and mechanisms extend beyond the post-1945 world while helping scholars understand three of the macro-strategic developments of the pre-1914 era.

Implications: Scholarly Contributions of the Argument

Taken as a whole, the results presented in this book carry implications for both international relations theory and history. First, the case studies in chapters 2–5 contribute to the historiography of postwar great power relations. Collectively, the historical material shows how great power behavior in the periods around the start and end of the Cold War was heavily influenced by great power rise and decline. Other scholars have noted that power shifts influenced the start and end of the Cold War, but this book is the first to systematically trace the ways in which great power decline affected rising state strategies at those moments.[92] Along similar lines, it uncovers novel features of postwar politics that showcase significant variation, contingency, and contestation in great power relations. Especially notable is evidence that the Soviet Union was more conciliatory toward a principal member of the future Western bloc in the mid-1940s than has widely been portrayed—so much so that the United States and Soviet Union pursued nearly symmetrical strategies toward Britain in 1945–47—and that the United States was not nearly as cooperative toward the Soviet Union at the Cold War's end as often presented in existing research. Although perhaps less surprising, the book also underscores Britain's unique importance in the United States' early postwar plans for Europe and the problems British decline posed for U.S. foreign policy. Considering the prominence of these cases in diplomatic history and international relations theory, this revised and refined history calls for a reevaluation of previous findings.

Just as important, this book has implications for international relations theory. As noted early in the volume, a veritable cottage industry seeks to understand the dynamics of great power rise and decline. Important studies examine why changes in the distribution of power occur, whether and when conflict erupts during power shifts, and the efforts by declining great powers to manage their waning fortunes and the rise of other great powers. Missing from this literature, however, is explicit analysis of rising state interests, preferences, and strategy. The result, as Aaron Friedberg notes when discussing the rise of China, is that "scholars and analysts lack the kinds of powerful predictive tools that would allow them to say with any degree of assurance what the state of relations between the United States and China will be in five years time, to say nothing of ten or twenty."[93]

This book addresses this gap and offers an initial treatment. Not only do rising state strategies vary, but rising states themselves consistently try to shape the behavior of their relatively declining peers. Analysts seeking to understand the potential for conflict or cooperation during periods of rise and decline therefore need to pay as much attention to a rising state's interests and concerns as rising states themselves define them, as they do to a declining state's decision to compete or cooperate with a rising peer. Put simply, predation theory calls for bringing rising states back in to studies of rise and decline.

Above all, this book speaks to debates within realist approaches international politics. Realist theories have long been critiqued for seeming to underpredict great power cooperation. Even as this issue remains unresolved, realist approaches have themselves divided over the question of whether states seek to maximize power in world politics. Offensive realists answer this question strongly in the affirmative, suggesting that cooperation is indeed scarce and any great power conciliation a by-product of exceptional strategic circumstances. Defensive realists, on the other hand, answer this question in the negative, proposing that states are usually content to remain power satisficers that sometimes forgo increasing their power and cooperate; instead, it takes bad domestic politics, misperception, or exceptional military advantages to spur aggression.[94]

The argument and evidence in this book suggest that these divisions within the realist camp may be surmountable. Predation theory uses assumptions rooted in offensive realism—in particular, that states seek power—to show that even rising states that want to maximize power will sometimes cooperate with declining states—behavior more consistent with defensive realist expectations. It does this by highlighting that power-maximizing states sometimes act as if they were power satisficers out of concern with the distribution of power. After all, the game of power politics played hard and fast means that states must minimally sustain their relative position, and can do so either by expanding themselves or preventing others from doing the same; at times, this process can generate support for and cooperation with other states. Predation theory thus suggests that previous offensive realist treatments have tended to underappreciate the systemic reasons states have to limit their aggressiveness, just as advocates of defensive realism have tended to assume too quickly that power maximization is generally at odds with systemic imperatives. Instead, a more fully developed argument grounded in the idea of states as power maximizers may help overcome intra-realist debates. Ultimately, power maximization and cooperation can both result from the same basic set of calculations that emerge when power-seeking states interact in a competitive world.

Extensions: Areas for Further Research

As with all research, the findings reported in this book have limits, some of which might be usefully subjected to additional analysis. First, and with the exception of some of the brief discussions of rise and decline before 1914, this book does not systematically examine cases where one state overtakes another in overall capabilities. The U.S. rise at the end of the Cold War arguably comes closest, as the United States evicted the Soviet Union from Central-Eastern Europe and projected power into areas where it had not previously been active. Still, the United States was demonstrably more materially powerful than the Soviet Union and had been throughout the Cold War. Considering that scholars often equate great power rise and decline with power transitions, the framework developed in this project could thus be extended to directly examine situations in which one state surpasses another.[95]

Here, as in the cases analyzed in this book, we expect a rising state's need for assistance against other great powers and a declining state's military posture to shape rising state strategy. Just because one state surpasses another does not mean that the rising state stops worrying about the challenge posed by the decliner or other great powers. In fact, it is plausible that a rising state that surpasses a declining state will be especially focused on the decliner's military threat, given the decliner's incentive to wage a preventive war before power shifts further, and the possibility that the military balance will still be weighted in the declining state's favor for a period of time if the decliner pumps resources into maintaining a robust military. Contingent on the declining state's strategic value, we would then expect an overtaking state to either engage in limited predation (a Weakening strategy) or limited support (Bolstering). Significantly, these dynamics might explain why rising states, as work by David Edelstein and Michael Glosny indicates, often refrain from either making excessive demands on declining states or offering extensive help even after a power transition.[96]

Second, it is also worth examining whether predation theory's causal logic extends beyond cases of great power rise and decline to explain state behavior in the regular course of world politics. Because periods around power shifts raise questions about states' relative strength, arguments rooted in power, self-interest, and security may be particularly well suited to explaining state behavior at such moments. Nevertheless, the objectives and calculations of rising states highlighted in this volume—their desire to expand when feasible, secure partners against other threats, avoid entrapment or betrayal by partners, and limit antagonism with prospective challengers—influence many actors in international affairs, including at times when the distribution of power is stable. For instance, even comparatively weak states often use predatory or supportive strategies toward one another. Thus, Israel maximized power at the expense of its neighbors during much of its early history, only to subsequently back Jordan and Egypt in their disputes with their own rivals;[97] likewise, South American states have cooperated and competed to varying degrees over time.[98] Future work might therefore explore the broader applicability of predation theory's causal mechanisms by examining situations in which the distribution of power is not in flux and looking at relations among states besides the great powers.

Relatedly, as U.S. policy toward the Soviet Union in 1991 suggests, concerns about blocking other states' expansion or expanding oneself might play a role in shaping responses to a special kind of decline: state failure. Clearly, states witnessing another's political collapse sometimes try to arrest the trend—Iran's effort to support the Syrian government during the Syrian civil war is a prominent recent example—and sometimes try to expedite the fall—as, for instance, Germany did with the fragmenting Yugoslavia.[99] This variation may make sense in light of predation theory: since another state's collapse can create opportunities for a state to expand but risks antagonizing a still-potent collapsing state and/or enabling other states to make disproportionate gains of their own, states may respond to another's failure based on how abetting its collapse is likely to affect their relative position. The fact that the United States slowed the Soviet Union's fragmentation for fear of the resulting blowback provides some evidence of this dynamic, but further work is needed to see if predation theory can systematically explain external responses to state failure as a phenomenon in itself.

Applications: Contributions to Policy

Above all, this book can inform real-world policy issues. Foremost among these are assessing the behavior of current or future rising states, and helping declining states effectively respond to changes to their own relative power.

ASSESSING AND INFLUENCING RISING STATE STRATEGY

This volume's focus on a rising state's need to offset other great powers and on the challenge (or lack thereof) posed to a rising state by a decliner suggests a more nuanced way of assessing rising state strategies toward their declining peers than is often present in policy debates. As noted in the introduction, declining states tend to worry that rising states will eventually pursue predation as shifting power gives risers the wherewithal to push declining states from the great power ranks. These concerns are understandable, and explain why declining states often seek to influence rising state behavior. Still, this approach misses an important point: if rising states are so power hungry that they want to continue expanding, then they are also likely to be concerned about protecting the power they already enjoy. They are thus prone to be as fearful of fruitless competitions with other great powers as they are desirous of continued growth. The real question for policymakers is therefore not "What options does a declining state have to forestall challenges from a rising state?" but "Why would a rising state target a declining state at all, given the risks involved and the opportunities to collaborate?"

The findings in this book help answer the latter question, highlighting the self-interested reasons rising states often have to limit or avoid predation. When great powers decline, it is important not to assume that their lives will be nasty, brutish, and short: rising great powers such as Wilhelmine Germany, the Soviet Union, and the United States all enjoyed reasons to support at least some of their declining peers. Moreover, even when predation emerges, the intensely predatory strategies that declining states most fear have been relatively rare: only when a rising state cannot use a declining state for its own ends and the declining state can no longer defend itself does Relegation occur. Policymakers in declining states are thus advised to more carefully and objectively assess the strategic map and trends in the distribution of power.[100] Though perilous, decline is rarely as unequivocally harmful as one might expect.

The results of this research also direct attention to the tools available to decliners to influence rising state behavior. Of course, studies emphasizing the influence of economic interdependence, strategic reassurance, ideological distance, and leadership beliefs identify analogous options, but the policy levers involved are notoriously slow in producing results. To take a contemporary example, U.S. leaders sought for decades to engage their counterparts in the People's Republic of China (PRC) in bilateral dialogues to shape Chinese views of the U.S.-China relationship while expanding U.S.-Chinese economic ties—hoping to reduce mistrust and moderate potential Chinese hostility. As of this writing, the jury is still out on the efficacy of these efforts.[101] In contrast, predation theory suggests different steps that declining states may be able to take to affect rising state behavior even in the near term.

Most obviously, declining states can try to adjust their military posture to shape the assertiveness of rising state predation or support. Here, decliners face two possibilities. A declining state that concludes it has low value to a rising state such that the riser is out for blood would be well advised to devote whatever resources it can to sustaining a robust posture. For instance, had the Soviet Union somehow suppressed the Revolutions of 1989–90 and sustained its position in Eastern Europe, the intensive U.S. predation witnessed in 1990 would almost certainly not have occurred. Alternatively, a declining state that has high strategic value to rising states should—counterintuitively—consider making itself militarily weaker than might seem optimal in order to give rising states an incentive to extend significant support. In effect, declining states are encouraged to engage in a game of chicken, calculating that rising states need decliners as much as the reverse; by appearing vulnerable, decliners may successfully catalyze significant rising state cooperation. For example, had Britain reduced its military and adopted a weak posture in 1945–46—as some British officials initially suggested—the United States and the Soviet Union would likely have provided intensive support earlier than they actually did.

A declining state can also try to make itself more or less strategically valuable by manipulating its political availability to rising states. Admittedly, the ability to use this tool can be limited. Given that political availability is only one component of a state's strategic value, adjusting availability alone may be insufficient to affect rising state strategy. However, in situations in which rising states might want to support a decliner except for its relationships with other great powers, adjusting political availability can pay. To achieve this result, declining states must be willing to reorient their foreign policies to suit a rising state's needs. This may not be an easy task, requiring overcoming domestic opposition or even abandoning long-standing allies if they are the rising state's opponents. Nevertheless, the benefit can be large: after all, the waning Britain enjoyed a warmer relationship with the Soviet Union when it was not firmly aligned with the United States and its policymakers were open to Anglo-Soviet collaboration than after the Anglo-American special relationship had consolidated. Had, therefore, Britain remained out of the U.S. orbit, it is plausible that the Soviet Union would have continued its efforts to support the United Kingdom.

MANAGING SHIFTING POWER IN EAST ASIA

What does this mean for policymakers seeking to understand and adapt to shifting power in East Asia today? For the last quarter-century, East Asia has been experiencing a double shift in the distribution of power. One shift has been ongoing since the 1990s, when the bursting of Japan's economic bubble undercut its economic growth and contributed to more than two decades of decline relative to the United States and China.[102] The second shift—prominent since the early 2000s—involves China's own stunning economic growth and the resulting rise in that state's political, economic, and military influence. Tellingly, whereas China's gross domestic product (GDP) was barely one-fifth as large as Japan's and not even one-eighth that of the United States in 1992, its economy was one and a half times the size of Japan's and over half that of the United States by 2016.[103] With China growing relative to the United States and Japan, and Japan losing ground to the United States and China, the situation seems ripe for miscalculation.

This research can help analysts understand the strategies today's rising states have pursued and may adopt vis-à-vis their declining peers, while identifying options for declining states to use in adapting to their changing fortunes. Consider, first, the rise of China relative to the United States. Since the early 2000s, China's growth has triggered increasingly pronounced worries that it may prey upon a declining United States and eventually attempt to evict the United States from Asia en route to establishing Chinese regional hegemony.[104] Since the 2010s, comparisons between the dangers posed by a rising China to those ostensibly presented by a surging Germany a century ago have been commonplace; simultaneously, a growing chorus of analysts suggest that war between a rising China and a declining United States is in the offing.[105]

In contrast, predation theory proposes that although concerns with Chinese predation are well-founded, visions of a China wedded to pushing the United States into the dustbin of history are not—Chinese predation should remain limited for a long time. First and foremost, the United States is structurally predisposed to have low strategic value for the PRC. Not only is the United States comparatively isolated from other major states such as India and Japan that might imperil Chinese security, but its own regional preeminence is likely to encourage China to see the United States as an impediment to China's long-term expansion; meanwhile, the United States' growing willingness to oppose China's rise effectively precludes the United States' availability as China's partner. Collectively, these factors make a predatory Chinese strategy more likely than not.

Still, there is room for cautious optimism that the United States can at least prevent China from pursuing Relegation. Even if China seeks gains at the expense of the United States, the surest way for the United States to cap Chinese predation is to maintain as robust a military posture as possible. And here, the assets most useful for deterring or defeating the PRC—a strong nuclear arsenal and long-range air and naval platforms—are the military areas where the United States excels and is likely to do so for some time.[106] China, in contrast, is only slowly developing the high-end military capabilities needed to compete with the United States in those domains.[107] Provided it maintains this military lead, the United States should be able to keep Chinese predation limited. Weakening, not Relegation, is China's most likely course so far as the United States is concerned.

What, however, about U.S. and Chinese strategy toward a declining Japan? In many ways, Japan has been the great loser of the post–Cold War era. Where observers debated into the 1990s whether Japanese power might equal that of the United States, two decades of stagnation have left Japan markedly behind both the United States and China.[108] Notably, although in 1992 Japan had the world's second-largest economy and a GDP that was more than half that of the United States, by 2016 it had fallen to third place, with a GDP barely one-third that of the United States and two-thirds that of China.[109]

Unsurprisingly, the United States and China have pursued divergent strategies toward Japan in light of the country's increasing relative weakness, Since the 1990s, the United States has generally pursued a Bolstering strategy. Of course, the U.S.-Japan alliance helps protect Japan from attack. Still, the United States has often proved reluctant to bear significant risks (particularly in antagonizing China, though this situation may be changing) in backing Japan in its maritime and political disputes with other East Asian states, consistently tried to have Japan do and pay more for its own defense, and done little to actively assist Japan's economic recovery.[110] This approach makes sense in light of predation theory: Japan retains a robust military—involving large, technologically advanced, and well-trained air and maritime forces[111]—and has high strategic value given its location off China's coast, its large economy, and the interest of many Japanese leaders in sustaining U.S.-Japanese cooperation.[112] Providing limited assistance to keep Japan as a partner without risking entrapment or entanglement is eminently rational.

Conversely, China has pursued a Weakening strategy. The PRC is adopting an increasingly confrontational stance as it vies with Japan for influence and the two advance competing maritime claims in East Asia. Just as important, the PRC has shown itself willing to use economic leverage to pressure Japan to accede to Chinese demands in their diplomatic disputes, while engaging in a military buildup designed partly to limit Japan's military options. This strategy also makes sense. Seeking to avoid conflict with militarily potent Japan—or its U.S. backer—China likely sees Japan as offering little strategic value: despite Japan's latent potential and a geographic position that could help limit the United State' reach in East Asia, Japan's apparent interest in balancing China and cooperating with the United States likely hinders its political availability.[113] Steady pressure short of overtly and directly challenging Japan is thus a sensible route toward undercutting Japanese power over time without risking a short-term conflict that could impede China's rise.

Current trends suggest that Japan is therefore likely to continue facing problems with China and receiving support from the United States. This is hardly a counterintuitive finding. That said, predation theory's logic highlights three scenarios in which Chinese and/or American strategies could change. Moreover, depending on Japan's military posture and future political developments, Japan might even be poised to gain from U.S. and Chinese efforts to seek Japanese friendship against the other.

In the first scenario, Japan would continue to have high value for the United States and low value for China, but see Japan's military posture collapse. This might result from Japan's failure to increase military spending in the face of U.S. and Chinese military growth, and/or further economic losses that leave Japan unable to provide adequate military forces. In response, China—seeing an opportunity to exploit Japan's military weakness—would face strong incentives to pursue Relegation by, inter alia, pressing maritime claims so as to dominate East Asia's maritime space or crafting exclusionary economic or political arrangements to Japan's detriment; a Japanese-Chinese war resulting from Chinese aggrandizement is also possible. In fact, the only limit on Chinese predation in this scenario would come from the United States' own threat to use force on Japan's behalf.

Thankfully (from Japan's perspective), however, under these conditions the United States would have strong incentives to adopt a Strengthening strategy to protect Japan and forestall Chinese gains. Here it would not be surprising to see the United States reinforce its alliance with Japan, forward deploy additional military units, or offer Japan firmer diplomatic backing in its maritime disputes. Japanese security would then hinge on whether the United States intensified its assistance quickly enough to arrest China's own intensified predation.

In the second scenario, both the United States and China might share an interest in supporting Japan. This could happen only if current trends changed and Japan offered high strategic value to both states, which in turn requires Japan to be politically available for China. Although such a Japanese political shift is unlikely today, it is possible that Chinese-American tensions in East Asia—such as a clash between the two states in the South China Sea, tensions over North Korea, or a fight over Taiwan—could prompt Japan to reevaluate its strategic options. Forced to choose between continued cooperation with the United States that risked war with China, or distancing Japan from the United States and seeking rapprochement with the PRC, Japan's leaders—many of whom are already reluctant to adopt an overly confrontational stance toward China—might pursue the latter course.[114] China would then have incentives to reinforce the trend by adopting a supportive strategy to seek Japan's cooperation against the United States, while the United States faced similar incentives to retain Japan as a partner against China. Still, the resulting strategies would likely look more like Bolstering and remain relatively limited as long as Japan retains a robust military. The United States might continue its current low-risk and cost course approach toward Japan, while China might open negotiations to settle some of its diplomatic disputes with Japan or reduce its arms buildup.

Finally, in the third scenario, Japan might have high value for both the United States and China but also see its military posture weaken. Counterintuitively, this might be an advantageous situation for Japan. Facing a valuable but militarily weak Japan, it would not be surprising to see the United States reinforce the U.S.-Japanese alliance or offer Japan regular diplomatic support in its East Asian disputes. More dramatically, China might offer to settle its own territorial disputes with Japan on Japanese terms, provide economic aid to spur growth, or even propose an alliance with Japan. In short, the United States and China might both end up seeking Japanese friendship if Japan's high value for both states were combined with a weak military posture, offering Japan generous terms along the way and allowing the country to capitalize on its relative weaknesses.

There is clearly no way to know whether strategists grappling with East Asia's shifting distribution of power assess the situation in this manner. Furthermore, even if they do, domestic politics or poor decision making may lead relatively rising states to act in ways contrary to the logic of predation theory. The real question, however, is not whether relatively rising states act differently toward declining states than my argument proposes, but rather how cost-insensitive and risk-acceptant they need to be to continue along that path. At the end of the day, predation theory emphasizes the cumulative impact of security costs, military risks, and forfeited opportunities on rising state strategy. Regardless of how policymakers perceive the world or act, only leaders very insensitive to external costs and risks can long ignore the downsides of preying upon or supporting declining states under inopportune conditions. Otherwise, as Soviet and U.S. behavior after World War II illustrates, policymakers in rising states are apt to update their previous assessments and adjust strategy accordingly.

Final Words

The rise and fall of great powers is among the most fundamental changes in international politics. By altering which states can bring what resources to bear against other capable actors, major shifts in the distribution of power invite miscalculation, war, and contestation. This is understandably worrisome to declining states, which seem to be left in an increasingly vulnerable position and facing intractable problems as they try to obtain security for themselves in a world of power-hungry rivals. As this book emphasizes, however, the fate of declining great powers is not uniformly injurious. Rising states, facing their own need to create security for themselves, often extend economic, political, and military assistance to declining states. In other cases, and even if risers seek to expand at a decliner's expense, they often limit the extent of their predation. The net result is that states can decline for an extended period while facing limited rising state challenges, and can sometimes even benefit from rising states' largesse. In short, rising states can pose problems for declining states, but this is far from always the case. To a greater extent than often appreciated, the fate of declining states ultimately depends on what fundamental changes in the distribution of capabilities mean for rising states' own power and security.

Declining Great Powers, 1860–1913

As noted in chapter 1, I adopt a two-step process to identifying declining great powers in postwar Europe. First, I define great powers by whether they held at least 10 percent of the capabilities—particularly economic capabilities—of all states in a region, and at least 25 percent of the capabilities of the strongest state in that area. Second, I capture periods of decline by determining whether great powers lost at least 5 percent of their share of material capabilities within a ten-year window compared to the average over the preceding ten years, after at least 5 years of losses, and continuing the analysis until the states either began sustained growth or exited the great powers.

To extend this approach to capture other instances of decline while checking the general method, I also generated a list of declining great powers from the mid-nineteenth century through World War I and compared the results with existing lists of rising and falling great powers provided by Paul Kennedy, Paul MacDonald, and Joseph Parent.[1] I selected the mid-nineteenth century as a starting point since, as Kennedy notes, it was around then that industrialization began to cause significant shifts in the European distribution of power.[2]

Due to territorial changes throughout the nineteenth and twentieth centuries, neither the Correlates of War National Material Capabilities index nor Angus Maddison's gross domestic product (GDP) data provide the requisite information on economic capabilities. Instead, I used Paul Bairoch's data on gross national product (GNP) in pre–World War I Europe. Since Bairoch's data is reported on a ten-year basis through 1913, I also made three limited changes to measuring and describing decline. First, since Bairoch's data is reported every decade rather than continuously, I relaxed the requirement that power wane for at least five years in favor of assessing power shifts on a decade-by-decade basis; I also compared the 1913 to 1910 figures.[3] Second, I evaluated decline based on both state shares of overall great power capabilities and dyadic changes in great power strength (for example, French capabilities as a percentage of Austrian capabilities). Finally, although I maintained a 5 percent loss as the threshold for decline, I took note of periods in which a state's power waned less than that amount to better capture a complex strategic environment. The point of these changes was not to bias the results, but rather to arrive at holistic assessments of when, why, and in what ways the different great powers in Europe's classical multipolar period declined relative to each other.

The results for the period 1860–1913 show that Austria-Hungary, France, Prussia (Germany after 1870–71), Russia, and the United Kingdom were the leading states of pre-1913 Europe. Furthermore, each of these states declined at some point during the period.

Austria-Hungary declined relative to every great power in the 1860s, measured both by shares of great power capabilities and in dyadic terms. This change likely reflected its failure to prevent Prussia from unifying Germany. Furthermore, although Austria-Hungary's losses tapered off, it continued to decline against Germany through 1900 (and lost further ground through 1913), against Britain in the 1870s, and against Russia after the 1890s. Just as significantly, the Austrian problems described in the conclusion contributed to the state's persistently waning—albeit below the level qualifying as decline—as measured by shares of great power capabilities through 1913.

Overall, France was the biggest loser in this period. Measured as a share of great power capabilities, France declined in the 1870s and again in the period 1890–1910. In fact, even in periods when France is not coded as declining—since its losses did not rise above 5 percent per decade—it still lost ground relative to the other great powers. Dyadic measures make France's problems equally clear: France declined relative to Germany after the 1870s, relative to the United Kingdom in the 1870s–1880s and after 1910, relative to Austria-Hungary in the 1880s and after 1910, and relative to Russia in the 1860s and again after the 1890s. The consequences were stark: where France's economy in 1860 was slightly larger than Germany's and over 80 percent of Britain's, in 1910 it was barely half of Germany's and only two-thirds of Britain's.

Russia declined in the 1870s and 1880s, losing over 25 percent of its relative capabilities. This was the sharpest decline during the period. Every state grew relative to Russia, with Germany and the United Kingdom the biggest winners. Thereafter, however, Russia recovered and, on the eve of World War I, it was growing relative to every other state.

British strength was secure until around the beginning of the twentieth century, after which it declined. By 1910, overall British capabilities were down nearly 9 percent relative to their 1900 level. The dyadic distribution of power shows even more variation, as Britain lost ground to Germany in the 1860s and again from the 1880s through 1910, to Russia in the 1860s and after the 1890s, and—although this was likely an aberration—to Austria-Hungary in the early 1900s.

Finally, Germany did not decline in general terms in the period 1860–1910. Rather, the country was the great success story of the era before World War I,

Table A.1 Percentage of total great power GNP by state, 1860–1913

	State				
Year	Austria-Hungary	France	Germany (Prussia before 1870)	Russia	United Kingdom
1860	15.02	20.02	19.19	21.63	24.14
1870	13.02	19.22	19.10	26.22	22.45
1880	12.75	18.02	20.72	24.10	24.41
1890	13.71	17.61	23.57	18.87	26.24
1900	13.20	15.99	24.36	21.77	24.68
1910	13.26	14.86	25.18	24.24	22.47
1913	13.04	13.72	24.92	26.25	22.07

increasing its overall share of capabilities by nearly one-third (from 19 percent to 25 percent). However, it did lose some ground to Russia in the 1860s and, more importantly, from the 1890s onward. Whereas the German economy was nearly 25 percent larger than Russia's in 1890s, Russia's was slightly larger by 1910–1913.

These findings are broadly consistent with the results from Kennedy, Parent, and MacDonald. For instance, Kennedy identifies Russia, France, Britain, Germany, Austria-Hungary, and Italy as Europe's great powers from the mid-1800s onward. Although my list does not include Italy, this is the exception that proves the rule, as Kennedy acknowledges that Italy was only a marginal great power owing to its pervasive economic limitations.[4] Of the other states on Kennedy's list, France and Austria-Hungary persistently declined in the 1800s, Britain declined around the beginning of the twentieth century, and Russia declined in the late 1800s and early 1900s before recovering ground.[5] These results approximate those here. Meanwhile, Parent and MacDonald include Austria, France, Germany, Italy, Russia, and the United Kingdom among the European great powers. By their measures, France declined in the 1870s and 1880s; Russia in the 1870s, 1880s, and 1900s; and Britain in the 1870s and early 1900s. These results differ in part from my own, but the differences are largely attributable to MacDonald and Parent's focus on change in the ordinal rankings of the different great powers rather than the more general power shifts investigated here.[6]

Table A.1 shows the percentages of total great power GNP held by Europe's leading states in 1860–1913.

Interviews Conducted with Former U.S. Government Officials

I conducted all interviews either by phone or in person over the course of 2011–12. Where possible, I recorded with the interviewee's permission. In some cases, follow-up conversations occurred by phone and/or email. In addition to the individuals listed below, two interviewees—one member of the Bush administration's NSC and a senior member of the intelligence community during the Reagan administration—wished to remain anonymous. I also thank Robert Zoellick, counselor to Secretary of State James Baker, for his willingness to correspond via email on the Bush administration's foreign policy.

Interviewees are listed alphabetically by last name.

Norman Bailey, senior director for international economics, National Security Council (NSC), 1981–83

Dennis Blair, director for Western European affairs, NSC, 1981–83

Nicholas Burns, director for Soviet affairs, NSC, 1990–95

Richard Burt, director of political-military affairs, State Department 1981–83; assistant secretary of state for European and Canadian affairs, 1983–85; ambassador to Germany, 1985–89; chief negotiator, Strategic Arms Reduction Talks, 1989–91

Lee Butler, vice director and director of strategic plans, Joint Chiefs of Staff, 1987–91; commander in chief, Strategic Air Command (SAC), 1991–92

Jack Chain, commander in chief, SAC, 1985–89

Kenneth Dam, deputy secretary of state, 1982–85

Edward Djerejian, head of the political section, Moscow embassy, 1979–82

James Dobbins, principal deputy assistant secretary of state for European affairs, 1989–91

Paula Dobriansky, director for European and Soviet affairs, NSC, 1981–87

Eric Edelman, special assistant to the undersecretary of state for political affairs, 1989–90; assistant deputy undersecretary of defense for Soviet and East European affairs, 1990–93

Fritz Ermarth, senior director for Soviet affairs, NSC, 1987–88

John Galvin, supreme allied commander Europe, 1987–92

Sherwood Goldberg, executive assistant to the secretary of state, 1981–82

David Gompert, senior director for Soviet and European affairs, NSC, 1990–93

Donald Gregg, national security advisor to the vice president, 1982–88

Jonathan Howe, assistant to the chairman of the Joint Chiefs of Staff, 1987–89; deputy national security advisor, 1991–93

Charles Hill, executive assistant to the secretary of state, 1985–89

Robert Hutchings, director for European affairs, NSC, 1989–93

Bobby Ray Inman, deputy director of the Central Intelligence Agency (CIA), 1981–82

Richard Kerr, deputy director of the CIA, 1989–92; acting director of the CIA, 1991

Zalmay Khalilzad, deputy undersecretary of defense for policy planning, 1991–92

Robert Kimmitt, undersecretary of state for political affairs, 1989–91

John Lehman, secretary of the Navy, 1981–87

Jack Matlock, senior director for Soviet affairs, NSC, 1983–87; ambassador to the Soviet Union, 1987–91

Robert McFarlane, deputy national security advisor, 1982–83; national security advisor, 1983–85

Edwin Meese, counselor to the president, 1981–85

Herbert Meyer, special assistant to the director of the CIA, 1982–83; vice chairman of the National Intelligence Council, 1983–85

Larry Napper, director of the Office of Soviet Union affairs, State Department, 1991–94

Henry Nau, director for international economics, NSC, 1981–83

Mark Palmer, deputy assistant secretary of state for European affairs, 1982–86

Richard Pipes, senior director for Soviet affairs, NSC, 1981–83

John Poindexter, military assistant to the president, 1981–83; deputy national security advisor, 1983–85; national security advisor, 1985–86

Colin Powell, deputy national security advisor, 1987; national security advisor, 1988–89; chairman of the Joint Chiefs of Staff, 1989–93

Dan Quayle, vice president, 1989–93

Thomas C. Reed, member at large, NSC, 1982–83

Rozanne Ridgway, assistant secretary of state for European and Canadian affairs, 1985–89

Roger W. Robinson, senior director for international economic affairs, NSC, 1982–85

Henry Rowen, chairman, National Intelligence Council, 1981–83

Brent Scowcroft, national security advisor, 1989–93

Raymond Seitz, assistant secretary of state for Europe and Canada, 1989–91

Stephen Sestanovich, director for Soviet affairs, NSC, 1984–86

George Shultz, secretary of state, 1982–89

Thomas W. Simons, director of the Office of Soviet Union Affairs, State Department, 1981–85; deputy assistant secretary of state, 1985–89; ambassador to Poland, 1990–93

Richard Solomon, director of policy planning, State Department, 1986–89

William Taft IV, deputy secretary of defense, 1985–89; ambassador to the North Atlantic Treaty Organization, 1989–93

John C. Whitehead, deputy secretary of state, 1985–89

Lawrence Wilkerson, chief of staff to the chairman of the Joint Chiefs of Staff, 1989–93

Philip Zelikow, director for European affairs, NSC, 1989–91

Notes

Introduction

1. Orme Sargent, "Stocktaking after VE-Day," July 11, 1945, in *The Foreign Office and the Kremlin: British Documents on Anglo-Soviet Relations, 1941–1945*, ed. Graham Ross (New York: Cambridge University Press, 1984), 211.

2. Robert M. Hathaway, *Ambiguous Partnership: Britain and America, 1944–1947* (New York: Columbia University Press, 1981).

3. Vladimir O. Pechatnov and C. Earl Edmonsdon, "The Russian Perspective," in *Debating the Origins of the Cold War: American and Russian Perspectives*, ed. Ralph D. Levering, Vladimir O. Pechatnov, Verena Botzenhart-Viehe, and C. Earl Edmondson (Lanham, MD: Rowman and Littlefield, 2001), 85–151.

4. Dale C. Copeland, *The Origins of Major War* (Ithaca, NY: Cornell University Press, 2000), 4.

5. Kenneth N. Waltz, *Theory of International Politics* (Boston: McGraw-Hill, 1979), 113–14, 118; John J. Mearsheimer, *The Tragedy of Great Power Politics* (New York: Norton, 2001), 37; Robert Gilpin, *War and Change in World Politics* (Cambridge: Cambridge University Press, 1981).

6. Thucydides, *History of the Peloponnesian War*, trans. Rex Warner and ed. M. I. Finley (Harmondsworth, UK: Penguin Books, 1972), book 1, paragraph 23.

7. Quoted in William C. Wohlforth, "The Perception of Power: Russia in the Pre-1914 Balance," *World Politics* 39, no. 3 (April 1987): 362; Jonathan Haslam, *Russia's Cold War* (New Haven, CT: Yale University Press, 2011), 353.

8. Mary Sarotte, *1989: The Struggle to Create Post-Cold War* (Princeton, NJ: Princeton University Press, 2009); Joshua R. Itzkowitz Shifrinson, "Deal or No Deal? The End of the Cold War and the U.S. Offer to Limit NATO Expansion," *International Security* 40, no. 4 (Spring 2016): 7–44.

9. Ludwig Dehio, *Germany and World Politics in the Twentieth Century* (New York: Knopf, 1959), 14–15; Gordon Craig, *Germany, 1866–1945* (New York: Oxford University Press, 1978), 310–14.

10. Otto Pflanze, *Bismarck and the Development of Germany: The Period of Unification, 1815–1871*, 2nd ed. (Princeton, NJ: Princeton University Press, 1990), 292–317, 446–506.

11. Mearsheimer, *Tragedy of Great Power Politics*, 238–52; John A. Thompson, *A Sense of Power: The Roots of America's Global Role* (Ithaca, NY: Cornell University Press, 2015), 25–34.

12. William L. Langer, "The Franco-Russian Alliance (1890–1894)," *Slavonic Review* 3, no. 9 (March 1925): 554–75.

13. Imanuel Geiss, *German Foreign Policy, 1871–1914* (London: Routledge, 1976), especially 29–71, 110–18, 149–57.

14. Vladislav Zubok, "The Soviet Union and Détente of the 1970s," *Cold War History* 8, no. 4 (November 2008): 427–47; Jeremi Suri, "The Promise and Failure of 'Developed Socialism': The Soviet 'Thaw' and the Crucible of the Prague Spring, 1964–1972," *Contemporary European History* 15, no. 2 (May 2006): 133–58.

15. Samuel P. Huntington, "The U.S.: Decline or Renewal?," *Foreign Affairs* 67, no. 2 (December 1988): 94–95.

16. National Intelligence Council, *Global Trends 2030: Alternative Worlds* (Washington, DC: National Intelligence Council, December 2012), https://www.dni.gov/files/documents/GlobalTrends_2030.pdf; Barack Obama, "Remarks by President Obama at the University of Queensland," November 15, 2014, https://www.whitehouse.gov/the-press-office/2014/11/15/remarks-president-obama-university-queensland.

17. Fareed Zakaria, *From Wealth to Power: The Unusual Origins of America's World Role* (Princeton, NJ: Princeton University Press, 1998), 3. See also Jack Levy, "Declining Power and the Preventive Motivation for War," *World Politics* 40, no. 1 (October 1987): 87.

18. Copeland, *Origins of Major War*, 4.

19. Gilpin, *War and Change*, chap. 5; A. F. K. Organski and Jacek Kugler, *The War Ledger* (Chicago: University of Chicago Press, 1980); Douglas Lemke and Suzanne Werner, "Power Parity, Commitment to Change, and War," *International Studies Quarterly* 40, no. 2 (June 1996): 235–60. See also Geoffrey Blainey, *The Causes of War*, 3rd ed. (Basingstoke, UK: Macmillan, 1988).

20. Copeland, *Origins of Major War*, chap. 2; Evan Braden Montgomery, *In the Hegemon's Shadow: Leading States and the Rise of Regional Powers* (Ithaca, NY: Cornell University Press, 2016); Paul MacDonald and Joseph Parent, *Twilight of the Titans: Great Power Decline and Retrenchment* (Ithaca, NY: Cornell University Press, 2018).

21. See, for example, Daniel S. Geller, "Power Differentials and War in Rival Dyads," *International Studies Quarterly* 37, no. 2 (June 1993): 176–77; Randall L. Schweller, "Domestic Structure and Preventive War: Are Democracies More Pacific?," *World Politics* 44, no. 2 (January 1992): 235–69; Jonathan DiCicco and Jack S. Levy, "Power Shifts and Problem Shifts: The Evolution of the Power Transition Research Program," *Journal of Conflict Resolution* 43, no. 6 (December 1999): 688n36.

22. For overviews of the debate, see Robert Jervis, "Realism, Neoliberalism, and Cooperation: Understanding the Debate," *International Security* 24, no. 1 (Summer 1999): 42–63.

23. Mearsheimer, *Tragedy of Great Power Politics*, 37. Put differently, international politics creates "incentives to think and *sometimes* behave aggressively"; see John J. Mearsheimer, "The False Promise of International Institutions," *International Security* 19, no. 3 (Winter 1994–95): 11, emphasis added.

24. Sebastian Rosato, "Europe's Troubles: Power Politics and the State of the European Project," *International Security* 35, no. 4 (Spring 2011): 48–52.

25. For more on the hole in the literature, see Aaron Friedberg, "The Future of U.S.-China Relations: Is Conflict Inevitable?," *International Security* 30, no. 2 (Fall 2005): 8–10; Jack Levy, "Preventive War: Concept and Propositions," *International Interactions* 37, no. 1 (January–March 2011): 94–95; Jeffrey Legro, "What China Will Want: The Future Intentions of a Rising Power," *Perspectives on Politics* 5, no. 3 (September 2007): 515–34.

26. Paul Kennedy, *The Rise and Fall of the Great Powers: Economic Change and Military Conflict from 1500 to 2000* (New York: Random House, 1987); Mancur Olson, *The Rise and Decline of Nations: Economic Growth, Stagflation, and Social Rigidities* (New Haven, CT: Yale University Press, 1982); Gilpin, *War and Change*, chap. 4.

27. Aaron L. Friedberg, *The Weary Titan: Britain and the Experience of Relative Decline, 1895–1905* (Princeton, NJ: Princeton University Press, 1988); Charles A. Kupchan, *The Vulnerability of Empire* (Ithaca, NY: Cornell University Press, 1996); Paul MacDonald and Joseph M. Parent,

"Graceful Decline? The Surprising Success of Great Power Retrenchment," *International Security* 35, no. 4 (Spring 2011): 7–44.

28. Randall L. Schweller, "Managing the Rise of Great Powers: History and Theory," in *Engaging China: The Management of an Emerging Power,* ed. Alastair Iain Johnston and Robert Ross (New York: Routledge, 1999), 1–31.

29. Gilpin comes closest when arguing that rising states nearly automatically seek revision to an existing international order as their power increases. Most work, however, accepts that rising states vary in their status quo or revisionist orientations without explaining why. See Gilpin, *War and Change,* 106–7, 193–94; Organski and Kugler, *The War Ledger;* Douglas Lemke and William Reed, "Power Is Not Satisfaction: A Comment on De Soysa, Oneal, and Park," *Journal of Conflict Resolution* 42, no. 4 (August 1998): 511–16. See also DiCicco and Levy, "Power Shifts and Problem Shifts," 690.

30. For partial exceptions, see Woosang Kim, "Power, Alliance, and Major Wars, 1816–1975," *Journal of Conflict Resolution* 33, no. 2 (June 1989): 255–73; Lemke and Werner, "Power Parity," 237–39.

31. Robert Jervis, "Cooperation under the Security Dilemma," *World Politics* 30, no. 2 (January 1978): 167–214; Charles L. Glaser, *Rational Theory of International Politics: The Logic of Competition and Cooperation* (Princeton, NJ: Princeton University Press, 2010), 272–81; Friedberg, ""The Future of U.S.-China Relations," 22–23, 27–28.

32. Glenn H. Snyder, "Mearsheimer's World: Offensive Realism and the Struggle for Security," *International Security* 27, no. 1 (Summer 2002): 149–73.

33. Andrew Kydd, "Trust, Reassurance, and Cooperation," *International Organization* 54, no. 2 (Spring 2000): 326–27; Evan Braden Montgomery, "Breaking out of the Security Dilemma: Realism, Reassurance, and the Problem of Uncertainty," *International Security* 31, no. 2 (Fall 2006): 158–67; Schweller, "Managing the Rise of Great Powers," 14–16.

34. Kevin Narizny, *The Political Economy of Grand Strategy* (Ithaca, NY: Cornell University Press, 2007); Steven E. Lobell, *The Challenge of Hegemony: Grand Strategy, Trade, and Domestic Politics* (Ann Arbor: University of Michigan Press, 2003); Erik Gartzke, "The Capitalist Peace," *American Journal of Political Science* 15, no. 1 (January 2007): 172–73. For policy applications, see William J. Clinton, "Remarks at the Paul H. Nitze School of Advanced International Studies," March 8, 2000, http://www.presidency.ucsb.edu/ws/index.php?pid=87714&st=china&st1=wto.

35. Dale C. Copeland, *Economic Interdependence and War* (Princeton, NJ: Princeton University Press, 2015).

36. Mark L. Haas, *The Ideological Origins of Great Power Politics, 1789–1989* (Ithaca, NY: Cornell University Press, 2005), 1. See also Henry R. Nau, *At Home Abroad: Identity and Power in American Foreign Policy* (Ithaca, NY: Cornell University Press, 2002), 9; Jarrod Hayes, *Constructing National Security: U.S. Relations with India and China* (New York: Cambridge University Press, 2013). For application to policy, see George W. Bush, *The National Security Strategy of the United States of America,* September 2002, http://nssarchive.us/NSSR/2002.pdf, 26–27.

37. Colin Dueck, *Reluctant Crusaders: Power, Culture, and Change in American Grand Strategy* (Princeton, NJ: Princeton University Press, 2006), 33–42.

38. Christopher Layne, *The Peace of Illusions: American Grand Strategy from 1940 to the Present* (Ithaca, NY: Cornell University Press, 2006), 8.

39. Nathan Leites, *The Operational Code of the Politburo* (New York: McGraw-Hill, 1951), 66.

40. Dingding Chen, Xiaoyu Pu, and Alastair Iain Johnston, "Debating China's Assertiveness," *International Security* 38, no. 3 (Winter 2013–14): 179.

41. Of course, leaders' ideas may be related to the distribution of power, with expansionist beliefs in particular becoming more prevalent as state power grows. I do not directly evaluate this possibility, but the case studies help control for the issue by evaluating whether power shifts are directly correlated with rising state predation and assessing the justifications policymakers use to explain their policies.

42. Alexander L. George and Andrew Bennett, *Case Studies and Theory Development in the Social Sciences* (Cambridge, MA: MIT Press, 2005).

43. Stephen Van Evera, *Guide to Methods for Students of Political Science* (Ithaca, NY: Cornell University Press, 1997), 31, 79–83.

44. William T. R. Fox, *The Super-Powers: The United States, Britain, and the Soviet Union* (New York: Harcourt, 1944).

1. Predation Theory

1. Robert Gilpin, "The Theory of Hegemonic War," *Journal of Interdisciplinary History* 18, no. 4 (Spring 1988): 602–3.

2. John J. Mearsheimer, *The Tragedy of Great Power Politics* (New York: Norton, 2001), 5.

3. Kenneth N. Waltz, *Theory of International Politics* (Boston: McGraw-Hill, 1979), 131.

4. Joseph M. Parent and Sebastian Rosato, "Balancing in Neorealism," *International Security* 40, no. 2 (Fall 2015): 56; Charles L. Glaser, *Rational Theory of International Politics: The Logic of Competition and Cooperation* (Princeton, NJ: Princeton University Press, 2010), 42.

5. For distinctions among different kinds of power shifts, see Dale C. Copeland, *The Origins of Major War* (Ithaca, NY: Cornell University Press, 2000), 5–6.

6. Robert Gilpin, *War and Change in World Politics* (Cambridge: Cambridge University Press, 1981), 158.

7. Paul MacDonald and Joseph M. Parent, "Graceful Decline? The Surprising Success of Great Power Retrenchment," *International Security* 35, no. 4 (Spring 2011): 22–24; A. F. K. Organski and Jacek Kugler, *The War Ledger* (Chicago: University of Chicago Press, 1980); Paul Kennedy, *The Rise and Fall of the Great Powers: Economic Change and Military Conflict from 1500 to 2000* (New York: Random House, 1987).

8. Robert Powell, *In the Shadow of Power: States and Strategies in International Politics* (Princeton, NJ: Princeton University Press, 1999), 21.

9. Kennedy, *Rise and Fall*, 215–19; Abraham C. Becker, "Intelligence Fiasco or Reasoned Accounting? CIA Estimates of Soviet GNP," *Post-Soviet Affairs* 10, no. 4 (October 1994): 291–329.

10. Quoted in Geoffrey Wawro, *The Franco-Prussian War: The German Conquest of France in 1870–1871* (New York: Cambridge University Press, 2003), 17.

11. Brock Tessman, "Critical Periods and Regime Type: Integrating Power Cycle Theory with the Democratic Peace Hypothesis," *International Interactions* 31, no. 3 (July 2005): 227–28. Likewise, weak states that grow relatively stronger or powerful states that grow stronger still also experience a rise.

12. Robert J. Lieber, *Power and Willpower in the American Future: Why the United States Is Not Destined to Decline* (New York: Cambridge University Press, 2012), 9–12.

13. Arthur A. Stein, "The Hegemon's Dilemma: Great Britain, the United States, and the International Economic Order," *International Organization* 38, no. 2 (Spring 1984): 355; Christopher Layne, "The Unipolar Illusion: Why New Great Powers Will Rise," *International Security* 17, no. 4 (April 1993): 10–11; William R. Thompson and Karen A. Rasler, *The Great Powers and Global Struggle, 1490–1990* (Lexington: University Press of Kentucky, 1994), 81.

14. Vladislav Zubok, *A Failed Empire: The Soviet Union in the Cold War from Stalin to Gorbachev* (Chapel Hill: University of North Carolina Press, 2007), 278–87; Michael Beckley, *Unrivaled: Why America Will Remain the World's Sole Superpower* (Ithaca, NY: Cornell University Press, forthcoming).

15. Robert Gilpin, "The Cycle of Great Powers: Has It Finally Been Broken?," in *The Fall of Great Powers: Peace, Stability, and Legitimacy*, ed. Geir Lundestad (New York: Oxford University Press, 1994), 313.

16. Reflecting its engagement in European politics after 1945, I included the United States as a European power in this analysis. For a related discussion of certain states' ability to influence politics in multiple regions of the world, see the discussion of "polarity" below.

17. This approach builds on the work of MacDonald and Parent, which also adopts a 10 percent threshold; see McDonald and Parent, "Graceful Decline," 23. However, drawing on the idea that great powers are those able to make a strong showing against other powerful states, I also include a comparison relative to the strongest state in the system.

18. Angus Maddison, *Statistics on World Population, GDP, and Per Capita GDP, 1–2008 A.D.* (Groningen, the Netherlands: University of Groningen, 2008), http://www.ggdc.net/maddison /oriindex.htm; Correlates of War Project, National Material Capabilities, v3.02, accessed October 2012, http://www.correlatesofwar.org/data-sets/national-material-capabilities. Data limitations regarding Soviet GDP during and immediately after World War II prevented my using Maddison's data for my entire study period. Note that I also modified NMC scores for 1945–55, artificially assigning Germany 0 percent of European capabilities to reflect its postwar occupation and efforts to remove it from the distribution of power pending the 1955 decision to rearm the country.

19. This approach reflects the fact that there is no standard timeframe in which to determine whether a power shift is occurring or to assess state responses to shifting power. For other approaches, see McDonald and Parent, "Graceful Decline," 22–25; John A. Vasquez, "When Are Power Transitions Dangerous?," in *Parity and War: Evaluations and Extensions of The War Ledger*, ed. Jacek Kugler and Douglas Lemke (Ann Arbor: University of Michigan Press, 1996), 37–38; Sheena Chestnut and Alastair Iain Johnston, "Is China Rising?," in *Global Giant: Is China Changing the Rules of the Game?*, ed. Eva Paus, Penelope Prime, and Jon Western (New York: Palgrave MacMillan, 2009), 237–59.

20. This matches scholarly discussion of the early Cold War, whereby analysts "largely agree that there were four or more states that qualified as poles before 1945; by 1950 or so only two measured up"; see G. John Ikenberry, Michael Mastanduono, and William C. Wohlforth, "Introduction: Unipolarity, State Behavior, and Systemic Consequences," *World Politics* 61, no. 1 (January 2009): 6.

21. Charles Krauthammer, "The Unipolar Moment," *Foreign Affairs* 70, no. 1 (January 1990): 23–33.

22. To further check this conceptualization and general measurement scheme, I also identified declining great powers in Europe during the nineteenth and early twentieth centuries. The results are broadly consistent with standard accounts of great powers in the period: Austria-Hungary, France, Great Britain, Prussia (which became Germany), and Russia all qualified as great powers in the period 1860–1913, and most declined relative to at least one other state. See Appendix 1.

23. Stephen Walt, "Why Alliances Endure or Collapse," *Survival* 39, no. 1 (Spring 1997): 158–59.

24. Jack Levy, "Declining Power and the Preventive Motivation for War," *World Politics* 40, no. 1 (October 1987): 82–107; Geoffrey Blainey, *The Causes of War*, 3rd ed. (Basingstoke, UK: Macmillan, 1988).

25. Quoted in Wawro, *The Franco-Prussian War*, 19.

26. Thus Thucydides's observation that the Peloponnesian War resulted from the growth of Athenian power and "the fear which this caused in Sparta;" see Thucydides, *History of the Peloponnesian War*, trans. Rex Warner and ed. M. I. Finley (Harmondsworth, UK: Penguin Books, 1972), book 1, paragraph 23.

27. For a rising state's overall strategy, see Randall L. Schweller, "Managing the Rise of Great Powers: History and Theory," in *Engaging China: The Management of an Emerging Power*, ed. Alastair Iain Johnston and Robert Ross (New York: Routledge, 1999), 1–31.

28. Colin Dueck, *Reluctant Crusaders: Power, Culture, and Change in American Grand Strategy* (Princeton, NJ: Princeton University Press, 2006), 11.

29. Schweller, "Managing the Rise of Great Powers," 18–23; Jeffrey Legro, "What China Will Want: The Future Intentions of a Rising Power," *Perspectives on Politics*, 5, no 3 (January 2007): 516–18.

30. Gilpin, *War and Change in World Politics*, 187.

31. Robert Jervis, "Unipolarity: A Structural Perspective," *World Politics* 61, no. 1 (January 2009): 190.

32. Kevin Narizny, *The Political Economy of Grand Strategy* (Ithaca, NY: Cornell University Press, 2007), 11.

33. Randall Schweller, "Domestic Structure and Preventive War: Are Democracies More Pacific?," *World Politics* 44, no. 2 (January 1992): 235–69; Daniel Kliman, *Fateful Transitions: How*

Democracies Manage Rising Powers, from the Eve of World War I to China's Ascendance (Philadelphia: University of Pennsylvania Press, 2014).

34. Richard Millman, *British Foreign Policy and the Coming of the Franco-Prussian War* (Oxford: Oxford University Press, 1965), 9; see also 7–8.

35. For related research on weakening states, see Kai He, "Undermining Adversaries: Unipolarity, Threat Perception, and Negative Balancing Strategies after the Cold War," *Security Studies* 21, no. 2 (April 2012): 154–91; Hans Morgenthau, *Politics among Nations: The Struggle for Power and Peace*, 3rd ed. (New York: Knopf, 1963), 178–79.

36. Miranda Priebe, "Fear and Frustration: Rising State Perceptions of Threats and Opportunities" (PhD diss., Massachusetts Institute of Technology, 2014); Julius W. Pratt, *The Expansionists of 1812* (New York: Macmillan, 1925).

37. See the conclusion.

38. Brett Leeds, "Do Alliances Deter Aggression? The Influence of Military Alliances on the Initiation of Militarized Interstate Disputes," *American Journal of Political Science* 47, no. 3 (July 2003): 427–39.

39. Glenn Snyder, *Alliance Politics* (Ithaca: Cornell University Press, 1997), esp. 225–247.

40. For a related discussion, see Randall L. Schweller, "The Future Is Uncertain and the End Is Always Near," *Cambridge Review of International Affairs* 24, no. 2 (June 2011): 179–83.

41. See chapter 5.

42. Analysis of the rise of China and its implications for U.S. strategy in East Asia can be found in Robert J. Art, "The United States and China: Implications for the Long Haul," *Political Science Quarterly* 125, no. 3 (Fall 2010): 359–91.

43. Waltz, *Theory of International Politics*, 113; Mearsheimer, *Tragedy of Great Power Politics*, 30–33.

44. Blainey, *Causes of War*; James D. Fearon, "Rationalist Explanations for War," *International Organization* 49, no. 3 (Summer 1995): 379–414.

45. Mearsheimer, *Tragedy of Great Power Politics*, 138–39; Jack L. Snyder, *Myths of Empire: Domestic Politics and International Ambition* (Ithaca, NY: Cornell University Press, 1991), 6.

46. Mearsheimer, *Tragedy of Great Power Politics*, 37. See also Dueck, *Reluctant Crusaders*, 17.

47. This logic is implicit in theories of alliance politics: by allying with one another, states aggregate resources so that no one state bears all burdens of confronting a challenger. See Stephen Walt, *Origins of Alliances* (Ithaca, NY: Cornell University Press, 1986), 17–18.

48. As Thomas Christensen and Jack Snyder observe, "Some states try to free ride on other states' balancing efforts . . . to avoid bearing unnecessary costs or because they expect their relative position to be strengthened by standing aloof from the mutual bloodletting"; see Thomas J. Christensen and Jack Snyder, "Chain Gangs and Passed Bucks: Predicting Alliance Patterns in Multipolarity," *International Organization* 44, no. 2 (Spring 1990): 141.

49. For example, a great power may be growing but still lack the military ability to defeat competitors if war erupts. See Copeland, *Origins of Major War*, 16–20.

50. Following Mearsheimer, I adopt a geopolitical approach to polarity, examining it at the regional level. Some states—the superpowers—can play roles in multiple regions, and I include them in assessing polarity when appropriate. Although there is an ongoing debate in international relations theory about the utility and measurement of polarity as an organizing principle, the basic idea—that certain states are much more capable than others and are therefore at the center of much of international politics—is generally accepted and is at the crux of what I emphasize here. For overviews of polarity, see Mearsheimer, *Tragedy of Great Power Politics*, esp. 42–46; Nuno Monteiro, *Theory of Unipolar Politics* (New York: Cambridge University Press, 2014); Stephen G. Brooks and William C. Wohlforth, "The Rise and Fall of the Great Powers in the Twenty-First Century," *International Security* 40, no. 3 (Winter 2015–16): 7–53.

51. Waltz, *Theory of International Politics*, 165–70; Mearsheimer, *Tragedy of Great Power Politics* 153–62.

52. Waltz, *Theory of International Politics*, 166. See also Stephen M. Walt, "Alliance Formation and the Balance of World Power," *International Security* 9, no. 4 (1995): 8–10.

53. Norman Stone, "Moltke and Conrad: Relations between the Austro-Hungarian and German General Staffs, 1909–1914," *Historical Journal* 9, no. 2 (January 1966): 201–28.

54. Dale C. Copeland, "Neorealism and the Myth of Bipolar Stability: Toward a New Dynamic Realist Theory of Major War," *Security Studies* 5, no. 3 (March 1996): 50–51.

55. On "structural modifiers" and geography, see Jeffrey Taliaferro, "Security Seeking under Anarchy: Defensive Realism Reconsidered," *International Security* 25, no. 3 (2000–2001): 137–38. See also Barry Posen, "The Best Defense," *National Interest*, March 2002, 122.

56. Walt, "Alliance Formation," 10–11; Stephen Van Evera, *Causes of War: Power and the Roots of Conflict* (Ithaca, NY: Cornell University Press, 1999), 163.

57. Mearsheimer, *Tragedy of Great Power Politics*, 83–84.

58. Jack S. Levy and William R. Thompson, "Balancing on Land and at Sea: Do States Ally against the Leading Global Power?," *International Security* 35, no. 1 (Spring 2012): 7–43; John Schuessler and Joshua Shifrinson, "The Shadow of Exit: Insularity and American Preponderance (unpublished manuscript, January 2018).

59. The argument closest to my own is that of Christopher Layne, who notes that "geographic proximity to rival powers and military capabilities are the key determinants of great power security or insecurity;" see Christopher Layne, *The Peace of Illusions: American Grand Strategy from 1940 to the Present* (Ithaca, NY: Cornell University Press, 2006), 20.

60. Of course, it is hard for rising states to work with or against a declining state that is far away from all great powers (including risers). Still, especially as the distribution of power shifts in rising states' favor, isolation alone is unlikely to be dispositive in a world of power seekers. Instead, once rising states have grown very strong, they are likely to ask even a distant decliner what exactly it can do for them and assess its usefulness accordingly.

61. Mearsheimer, *Tragedy of Great Power Politics*, 60–67; Jeffrey Taliaferro, "State-Building for Future Wars: Neoclassical Realism and the Resource-Extractive State," *Security Studies* 15, no. 3 (July–September 2006): 464–95.

62. Director of the Policy Planning Staff to the Under Secretary of State, May 23, 1947, Department of State, *Foreign Relations of the United States 1947, Volume 3: The British Commonwealth* (Washington, DC: Government Printing Office, 1972), 227.

63. On tight and loose alignments, see Snyder, *Alliance Politics*, 180–92, 352–55. For the influence of domestic politics on alignment, see Randall L. Schweller, *Unanswered Threats: Political Constraints on the Balance of Power* (Princeton, NJ: Princeton University, 2006).

64. That is, states balance other centers of power, and powerful states provoke stronger reactions than weaker ones do. See Davide Fiammenghi, "The Security Curve and the Structure of International Politics: A Neorealist Synthesis," *International Security* 35, no. 4 (Spring 2011): 133.

65. Similarly, Timothy Crawford aptly shows that states often employ accommodating strategies to limit the size of opposing coalitions, thereby limiting the strength of their adversaries; see Timothy Crawford, "Preventing Enemy Coalitions: How Wedge Strategies Shape Power Politics," *International Security* 35, no. 4 (Spring 2011): 160–66.

66. Edward Gulick, *Europe's Classical Balance of Power* (Ithaca, NY: Cornell University Press, 1955), 76–77.

67. Paul Schroeder, "Alliances, 1815–1945: Weapons of Power and Tools of Management," in *Historical Dimensions of National Security Problems*, ed. Klaus Knorr (Lawrence: University Press of Kansas, 1976), 241–42.

68. Jack Levy, "Preventive War: Concept and Propositions," *International Interactions* 37, no. 1 (March 2011): 87–96; Copeland, *Origins of Major War*, 37–46.

69. Jonathan D. Pollack, *China and the Global Strategic Balance* (Santa Monica, CA: RAND Corporation, 1984), 8–10.

70. Schroeder, "Alliances."

71. Jeremy Pressman, *Warring Friends: Alliance Restraint in International Politics* (Ithaca, NY: Cornell University Press, 2008); also Lowell Dittmer, "The Strategic Triangle: An Elementary Game-Theoretical Analysis," *World Politics* 33, no. 4 (July 1981): 490.

72. Josef Becker, "The Franco-Prussian Conflict of 1870 and Bismarck's Concept of a 'Provoked Defensive War': A Reply to David Wetzel," *Central European History* 41, no. 1

(January 2008): 93–109; Imanuel Geiss, *German Foreign Policy, 1871–1914* (London: Routledge, 1976), 18.

73. Mearsheimer, *Tragedy of Great Power Politics*, 238–52; Charles N. Edel, *Nation Builder: John Quincy Adams and the Grand Strategy of the Republic* (Cambridge, MA: Harvard University Press, 2014).

74. Thomas G. Mahnken, "Thinking about Competitive Strategy," in *Competitive Strategies for the 21st Century: Theory, History, and Practice*, ed. Thomas G. Mahnken (Stanford, CA: Stanford University Press, 2012), 3.

75. Samuel R. Williamson, *The Politics of Grand Strategy; Britain and France Prepare for War, 1904–1914* (Cambridge, MA: Harvard University Press, 1969); Robert M. Hathaway, *Ambiguous Partnership: Britain and America, 1944–1947* (New York: Columbia University Press, 1981).

76. Norrin Ripsman and Jack Levy make the same point, observing that preventive wars are most likely if a riser is "rapidly rising, hostile, and likely to surpass [decliners] in military strength and then resort to military force"; see Norrin M. Ripsman and Jack Levy, "British Grand Strategy and the Rise of Germany," in *The Challenge of Grand Strategy: The Great Powers and the Broken Balance between the World Wars*, ed. Jeffrey W. Taliaferro, Norrin M. Ripsman, and Steven E. Lobell (New York: Cambridge University Press, 2012), 174.

77. The historian Norman Stone makes the same point, observing that German chancellor Otto von Bismarck "was careful not to encourage Austro-Hungarian ambitions by granting them military sanction"; see Stone, "Moltke and Conrad," 202.

78. For similar treatments, see John J. Mearsheimer, *Conventional Deterrence* (Ithaca, NY: Cornell University Press, 1983); Barry Posen, *The Sources of Military Doctrine: France, Britain, and Germany between the World Wars* (Ithaca, NY: Cornell University Press, 1984).

79. In theory, military posture could also include allied forces that a declining state can call on. However, since allies can defect and/or face problems aggregating capabilities, allied forces are likely to only loosely determine a state's military posture. For the sake of parsimony, I do not offer a full treatment of alliance politics and decline. That said, I return to the practical effect of allied forces on rising state strategy in the case studies below.

80. Similar treatment of military capabilities can be found in Keren Yarhi-Milo, Alexander Lanoszka, and Zack Cooper, "To Arm or Ally? The Patron's Dilemma and the Strategic Logic of Arms Transfers and Alliances," *International Security* 41, no. 2 (Fall 2016): 99. For contextual and unit-specific factors that can affect military balance, see Glaser, *Rational Theory of International Politics*, 44, 110–11.

81. Because military posture captures whether a state has the forces to perform the military missions in the scenario on hand, two states could have identical militaries but different postures. This may occur, for example, if the states confront different adversaries of varying strength or undertake different foreign commitments.

82. Good discussion of state military capabilities can be found in Posen, *Sources of Military Doctrine*, 14–18; Caitlin Talmadge, *The Dictator's Army: Battlefield Effectiveness in Authoritarian Regimes* (Ithaca, NY: Cornell University Press, 2015); Jasen J. Castillo, *Endurance and War: The National Sources of Military Cohesion* (Stanford, CA: Stanford University Press, 2014).

83. Analysis of the interplay of capabilities, deterrence, and warfighting is in Daryl Press, *Calculating Credibility: How Leaders Assess Military Threats* (Ithaca, NY: Cornell University Press, 2005), 24–25; Michael A. Hunzeker and Alexander Lanoszka, "Landpower and American Credibility," *Parameters* 45, no. 4 (2015–16): 22–23; Alexander Lanoszka, *Atomic Assurance: The Politics of Extended Deterrence* (Ithaca, NY: Cornell University Press, forthcoming), chap. 1.

84. Joshua Rovner, "Sea Power versus Land Power: Cross-Domain Deterrence in the Peloponnesian War," in *Cross-Domain Deterrence: Theory, Concepts, and History*, ed. Erik Gartzke and Jon Lindsay (Oxford: Oxford University Press, forthcoming).

85. See chapter 5.

86. Todd S. Sescher and Matthew Fuhrmann, "Crisis Bargaining and Nuclear Blackmail," *International Organization* 67, no. 1 (Winter 2013): 173–95; Barry R. Posen, *Inadvertent Escalation: Conventional War and Military Risks* (Ithaca, NY: Cornell University Press, 1991).

87. Geoffrey Wawro, *A Mad Catastrophe: The Outbreak of World War I and the Collapse of the Habsburg Empire* (New York: Basic Books, 2014), 29–72.

88. Dean Acheson, *Present at the Creation: My Years in the State Department* (New York: Norton, 1987), 219.

89. Williamson, *Politics of Grand Strategy*; Michael Howard, *The Continental Commitment: The Dilemma of British Defence Policy in the Era of the Two World Wars* (London: Maurice Temple Smith, 1972).

90. Noel E. Firth and James H. Noren, *Soviet Defense Spending: A History of CIA Estimates, 1950–1990* (College Station: Texas A&M University Press, 1998), 129–30, table 5.10. On Germany, see Tom Dyson, *The Politics of German Defence and Security* (New York: Berghahn, 2008).

91. Samuel P. Huntington, "Coping with the Lippmann Gap," *Foreign Affairs* 66, no. 3 (January 1987): 453–77.

92. On military decisions as a choice, see Glaser, *Rational Theory of International Politics*, 41–43.

93. Copeland, *Origins of Major War*, 16–17; Brock F. Tessman and Steve Chan, "Power Cycles, Risk Propensity, and Great-Power Deterrence," *Journal of Conflict Resolution* 48, no. 2 (April 2004): 138–41.

94. Glenn H. Snyder, "The Security Dilemma in Alliance Politics," *World Politics* 36, no. 4 (July 1984): 467–71; also Christensen and Snyder, "Chain Gangs and Passed Bucks," 144–45.

95. Likewise, research on preventive wars and power transitions suggests that rising states tend to wait until they have a meaningful power advantage over potential targets before initiating conflict; Levy, "Declining Power and the Preventive Motivation for War," 84; Organski and Kugler, *The War Ledger*, 58–60.

96. On outbidding dynamics, see Yasuhiro Izumikawa, "To Coerce or Reward? Theorizing Wedge Strategies in Alliance Politics," *Security Studies* 22, no. 4 (July 2013): 505.

97. Fiammenghi, "Security Curve and the Structure of International Politics," 136.

98. Similarly, Gilpin notes that rising states tend to seek more extensive changes to an existing international order over time as shifting power reduces the costs that rising states pay for "forcing changes in the nature of the system." See Gilpin, *War and Change in World Politics*, 187.

99. Van Evera, *Causes of War*, 81–83.

100. Gilpin, "Theory of Hegemonic War," 602.

101. Put differently, if interests expand as relative power grows, then there ought to be a period in which rising state ambitions are limited; see Woosang Kim and James Morrow, "When Do Power Shifts Lead to War?," *American Journal of Political Science* 36, no. 4 (November 1992): 905–7.

102. Sebastian Rosato relatedly argues that states engage in lesser forms of cooperation against a challenger when one state can independently manage the threat; see Sebastian Rosato, "Europe's Troubles: Power Politics and the State of the European Project," *International Security* 35, no. 4 (Spring 2011): 49–50.

103. For related work on "hedging" strategies in alliances, see Patricia A. Weitsman, *Dangerous Alliances: Proponents of Peace, Weapons of War* (Stanford, CA: Stanford University Press, 2004), 20–21.

104. Related work on intra-alliance bargaining is found in Izumikawa, "To Coerce or Reward?," 506–9.

105. For great power recovery, see Parent and MacDonald, "Graceful Decline?," 10, 19, 29.

106. On influence over allies due to security assistance, see Schroeder, "Alliances," 230–31; Jeremy Pressman, *Warring Friends: Alliance Restraint in International Politics* (Ithaca, NY: Cornell University Press, 2008); Michael Mastanduono, "System Maker and Privilege Taker: U.S. Power and the International Political Economy," *World Politics* 61, no. 1 (January 2009): 122–23.

107. That said, a lively debate surrounds whether states can mitigate entrapment by their partners. For the debate, see Michael Beckley, "The Myth of Entangling Alliances: Reassessing the Security Risks of U.S. Defense Pacts," *International Security* 39, no. 4 (Spring 2015): 7–48; David Edelstein and Joshua R. Itzkowitz Shifrinson, "It's a Trap! Allies, Power Shifts, and Entrapment," in *U.S. Grand Strategy in the 21st Century: The Case for Restraint in U.S. Foreign Policy*, ed. Ben Friedman and Trevor Thrall (New York: Routledge, 2018).

108. Indeed, states may be on the lookout for partners to tip the distribution of power in their favor or prevent others from similarly benefiting. See Timothy Crawford, "The Alliance Politics

of Concerted Accommodation: Entente Bargaining and Italian and Ottoman Interventions in the First World War," *Security Studies* 23, no. 1 (January 2014): 119–20.

109. For changes in state strategies in response to external conditions, see T. V. Paul, "Introduction: The Enduring Axioms of Balance of Power Theory and Their Contemporary Relevance," in *Balance of Power: Theory and Practice in the 21st Century*, ed. T. V. Paul, James Wirtz, and Michel Fortmann (Stanford, CA: Stanford University Press, 2004), 5–6; Jack Levy, "What Do Great Powers Balance Against and When?," in *Balance of Power*, 32–34.

110. John A. Thompson, *A Sense of Power: The Roots of America's Global Role* (Ithaca, NY: Cornell University Press, 2015), 186–88, 249–50.

111. Snyder, *Alliance Politics*, 278–99. See also the conclusion.

112. See the conclusion.

113. Raymond L. Garthoff, "CIA Estimates of Soviet Defense Spending: A Review," *Post-Soviet Geography and Economics* 39, no. 9 (November 1998): 552; Simon Miles, "Engaging the 'Evil Empire': East-West Relations in the Second Cold War" (PhD diss., University of Texas, 2017), chap. 5. See also Melvyn P. Leffler, *For the Soul of Mankind: The United States, the Soviet Union, and the Cold War*, Kindle ed. (New York: Hill and Wang, 2008), loc. 6960–67.

114. See the conclusion.

115. For discussion of this issue, see Joseph Parent and Sebastian Rosato, "Balancing in Neorealism," *International Security* 40, no. 2 (Fall 2015): 59.

116. Gideon Rose, "Neoclassical Realism and Theories of Foreign Policy," *World Politics* 51, no. 1 (October 1998): 147.

117. Parent and Rosato, "Balancing in Neorealism," 55–85. On the dangers of miscalculation, see Stephen M. Walt, *Revolution and War* (Ithaca, NY: Cornell University Press, 1996), 30–45.

118. Mearsheimer, *Tragedy of Great Power Politics*, 11–12.

119. Snyder, *Myths of Empire*, 66–111, 212–54.

120. Alexander George and Andrew Bennett, *Case Studies and Theory Development in the Social Sciences* (Cambridge, MA: MIT Press, 2005), 117–24; Stephen Van Evera, *Guide to Methods for Students of Political Science* (Ithaca, NY: Cornell University Press, 1997), 79–83.

121. Put differently, the cases should be difficult for my theory to explain as they are most-likely cases for alternative accounts. See George and Bennett, *Case Studies*, 120–22.

122. Robert Jervis, *The Meaning of the Nuclear Revolution: Statecraft and the Prospect of Armageddon* (Ithaca, NY: Cornell University Press, 1989), 45. See also Kenneth N. Waltz, "Nuclear Myths and Political Realities," *American Political Science Review* 84, no. 3 (September 1990): 731–45.

123. Key works in this literature include Keir A. Lieber and Daryl G. Press, "The New Era of Counterforce: Technological Change and the Future of Nuclear Deterrence," *International Security* 41, no. 4 (Spring 2017): 9–49; Mark Bell, "Beyond Emboldenment: How Acquiring Nuclear Weapons Can Change Foreign Policy," *International Security* 40, no. 1 (Summer 2015): 87–119; Brendan Rittenhouse Green and Austin Long, "The MAD Who Wasn't There: Soviet Reactions to the Late Cold War Nuclear Balance," *Security Studies* 26, no. 4 (July 2017): 606–41.

124. For additional work on relative gains, nuclear weapons, and extended deterrence, see Jasen Castillo, "Deliberate Escalation: Nuclear Strategies to Deter or to Stop Conventional Attacks," in *Coercion: The Power to Hurt in International Politics*, ed. Kelly M. Greenhill and Peter Krause (New York: Oxford University Press, 2018), 291–311.

125. For similar discussion, see Stephen M. Walt, "Rethinking the 'Nuclear Revolution,'" *Foreign Policy*, August 3, 2010, http://foreignpolicy.com/2010/08/03/rethinking-the-nuclear-revolution/.

126. Van Evera, *Guide to Methods*, 59–61.

2. A Formerly Great Britain

1. Ray Merrick, "The Russia Committee of the British Foreign Office and the Cold War, 1946–1947," *Journal of Contemporary History* 20, no. 3 (July 1985): 453.

2. William T. R. Fox, "The Superpowers Then and Now," *International Journal* 35, no. 3 (Summer 1980): 421.

3. Kyle Haynes, "Decline and Devolution: The Sources of Strategic Military Retrenchment," *International Studies Quarterly* 59, no. 3 (September 2015): 495–99.

4. By "great power capabilities," I mean the capabilities held by those states qualifying as great powers at this time. As explained in chapter 1, this group consisted of the United States, the Soviet Union, and Great Britain.

5. Fox, "Superpowers Then and Now," 417. See also David Reynolds, "The 'Big Three' and the Division of Europe, 1945–48: An Overview," *Diplomacy and Statecraft* 1, no. 2 (July 1990): 121–22.

6. Unless otherwise noted, all figures are reported in 1945 dollars, using the official exchange rate of $4.03 dollars per pound sterling.

7. Wartime losses are from *Statistical Material Presented during the Washington Negotiations* (Washington, DC: British Information Services, 1945), 4–13.

8. *Statistical Material*, 11, table 6; Robert M. Hathaway, *Ambiguous Partnership: Britain and America, 1944–1947* (New York: Columbia University Press, 1981), 25. British GDP is calculated from Bank of England, "A Millennium of Macroeconomic Data," table A9, accessed December 2017, https://www.bankofengland.co.uk/statistics/research-datasets.

9. Alec Cairncross, *Years of Recovery: British Economic Policy 1945–51* (London: Methuen, 1985), 6–8.

10. Income on foreign investments comes from Richard N. Gardner, *Sterling-Dollar Diplomacy: Anglo-American Collaboration in the Reconstruction of Multinational Trade* (Oxford: Oxford University Press, 1956), 307, table 3.

11. Hathaway, *Ambiguous Partnership*, 25–27.

12. Ritchie Ovendale, *The English-Speaking Alliance* (London: George Allen and Unwin, 1985), 18.

13. Lord Keynes, "Our Overseas Financial Prospects," August 13, 1945, in *Documents on British Policy Overseas, Series 1, Volume 3: Britain and America: Negotiation of the United States Loan*, ed. R. Bullen and M. E. Pelly (London: Stationery Office, 1986), 27–37.

14. Ovendale, *English-Speaking Alliance*, 18; Gardner, *Sterling-Dollar Diplomacy*, 178–79.

15. Bank of England, "Millennium of Macroeconomic Data."

16. Elisabeth Barker, *The British between the Superpowers, 1945–1950* (London: Macmillan, 1983), 98–102; State Department Policy Planning Staff Paper 61, "Policy Relating to the Financial Crisis of the United Kingdom and the Sterling Area," August 31, 1949, in *The State Department Policy Planning Staff Papers, Volume 3: 1949*, ed. Anna Kasten Nelson (New York: Garland, 1983), 150–56. Subsequent references to Policy Planning Staff papers will be given as PPS followed by the appropriate number.

17. Gardner, *Sterling-Dollar Diplomacy*, 188–206, 306–25; Scott Newton, "The 1949 Sterling Crisis and British Policy towards European Integration," *Review of International Studies* 11, no. 3 (July 1985): 169–82.

18. Mark Harrison, "The Economics of World War II: An Overview," in *The Economics of World War II: Six Great Powers in International Comparison*, ed. Mark Harrison (Cambridge: Cambridge University Press, 1998), 10, table 1.3; Angus Maddison, *Statistics on World Population, GDP, and Per Capita GDP, 1–2008 A.D.* (Groningen, The Netherlands: University of Groningen, 2008), http://www.ggdc.net/maddison/oriindex.htm.

19. Paul Bairoch, "International Industrialization Levels from 1750 to 1980," *Journal of European Economic History* 11 (Fall 1982): 299, table 11.

20. Harrison, "Economics," 14. Before World War II, the Royal Navy had 286 major naval combatants (fleet carriers, battleships, cruisers, destroyers, and submarines), compared to 388 for the U.S. Navy; by 1945, the numbers were 348 and 694, respectively. Numbers are from M. Epstein, ed., *The Statesman's Yearbook, 1939* (London: Macmillan, 1939), 46–50, 502, 1291, and *The Statesman's Yearbook, 1946* (London: Macmillan, 1946), 52–55, 512, 1222.

21. A good overview of Soviet military and economic mobilization during World War II can be found in Mark Harrison, "Resource Mobilization for World War II: The U.S.A., U.K., U.S.S.R., and Germany, 1938–1945," *Economic History Review* 41, no. 2 (May 1988): 177–86.

22. Philip Hanson, *The Rise and Fall of the Soviet Economy: An Economic History of the USSR from 1945* (London: Longman, 2003), 21–25.

23. For a more mixed evaluation of Soviet growth during and after World War II, see Paul M. Kennedy, *The Rise and Fall of the Great Powers: Economic Change and Military Conflict from 1500 to 2000* (New York: Random House, 1987), 362–63.

24. The comparison of Soviet iron and steel production in 1940 to production in 1944 (the last full year of the war) comes from Correlates of War National Material Capabilities Database; see Correlates of War Project, National Material Capabilities, v3.02, accessed October 2012, http://www.correlatesofwar.org/data-sets/national-material-capabilities.

25. Bairoch, "International Industrialization Levels," 299, table 11.

26. Harrison, "Economics," 14–15, tables 1.5 and 1.6.

27. Quoted in Cabinet Office, "Review of the World Situation," April 3, 1945, WM(45) 39th Conclusions, Minute 1, Confidential Annex, National Archives, Kew (hereafter NA).

28. Orme Sargent, "Stocktaking after VE-Day," July 11, 1945, in *Documents on British Policy Overseas, Series 1, Volume 1: Conference at Potsdam, July–August*, ed. Rohan Butler and M. E. Pelly (London: Stationery Office, 1984), 182.

29. Quoted in Terry Anderson, *The United States, Britain, and the Cold War, 1944–1947* (Columbia: University of Missouri Press, 1981), 84.

30. For early U.S. optimism regarding British strength, however, see Richard A. Best Jr., "Approach to Alliance: British and American Defense Strategies, 1945–1948" (PhD diss., Georgetown University, 1983), 28–37.

31. Department of State, Memorandum by the Joint Chiefs of Staff to the Secretary of State, August 3, 1944, *Foreign Relations of the United States 1944, Volume 1: General* (Washington, DC: Government Printing Office, 1966), 701–2. Hereafter, volumes from the *Foreign Relations of the United States* series are given as *FRUS year:volume*.

32. Frederick S. Dunn, Edward M. Earle, William T. R. Fox, Grayson L. Kirk, David N. Rowe, Harold Sprout, and Arnold Wolfers, "A Security Policy for Postwar America," March 8, 1945, projects, RG 1.1, series 200.S, box 417, folder 4948, Rockefeller Archive Center, Rockefeller Foundation, Sleepy Hollow, New York. Thanks to David Ekbladh for supplying the document. On this document's origins and use, see Mark A. Stoler, *Allies and Adversaries: The Joint Chiefs of Staff, the Grand Alliance, and U.S Strategy in World War II* (Chapel Hill: University of North Carolina Press, 2003), 227–30.

33. British Plan for a Western European Bloc, June 28, 1945, *FRUS 1945: The Conference at Malta and Yalta*, part 1 (Washington, DC: Government Printing Office, 1955), 265.

34. British Plans for a Western European Bloc, undated, *FRUS 1945: The Conference of Berlin (Potsdam)* (Washington: Government Printing Office, 1960), 1:258. See also James L. Gormly, *The Collapse of the Grand Alliance, 1945–1948* (Baton Rouge: Louisiana State University Press, 1987), 11.

35. Joint Intelligence Staff, "Military Capabilities and Intentions of Great Britain," December 17, 1945, JIS 161/6, box 081, Geographic File 1942–1945, RG 218, National Archives and Record Administration II, College Park, MD (hereafter NARA); Joint Intelligence Staff, "Capabilities and Military of Soviet and Non-Soviet Powers in 1956," January 8, 1947, JIC 374/5, box 56, Geographic File 1946–1947, RG 218, NARA.

36. George Kennan, "Top Secret Supplement to the Report of the Policy Planning Staff of July 23, 1947 entitled: Certain Aspects of the European Recovery Program from the United States Standpoint," accessed October 25, 2017, https://www.state.gov/documents/organization/179131.pdf.

37. J. Coutts, "Effects of British Decline as a World Military Power on U.S. Security Interests," February 11, 1950, box 13, NSC File: Subject File, CIA Subseries, Harry S. Truman Presidential Library, Independence, MO.

38. Quoted in Vladimir O. Pechatnov, "The Big Three after World War II: New Documents on Soviet Thinking about Postwar Relations with the United States and Great Britain," May 1995, Working Paper 13, Cold War International History Project, Woodrow Wilson International Center for Scholars, Washington (hereafter CWIHP), 5.

39. Quoted in Pechatnov, "Big Three," 12–13. See also Silvio Pons, "In the Aftermath of the Age of Wars: The Impact of World War II on Soviet Security Policy," in *Russia in the Age of Wars, 1914–1945*, ed. Silvio Pons and Andrea Romano (Milan: Feltrinelli, 2000), 300–304.

40. Nikolai Novikov, "The Novikov Telegram: U.S. Foreign Policy in the Postwar Period, September 27, 1946," *Diplomatic History* 15, no. 4 (October 1993): 528.

41. Quoted in Geoffrey Roberts, "Moscow and the Marshall Plan: Politics, Ideology, and the Onset of the Cold War, 1947," *Europe-Asia Studies* 46, no. 8 (December 1994): 1375–76.

42. "Stenographic Record of a Speech by Comrade J.V. Stalin at a Special Session of the Politburo, March 14, 1948," in an archival collection compiled for the CWIHP conference "Stalin and the Cold War, 1945–1953," ed. Christian Ostermann, Yale University, New Haven, CT, September 23–26, 1999, 429–32.

43. For illustrative works, see Joseph M. Jones, *The Fifteen Weeks* (New York: Viking, 1955); Ritchie Ovendale, "Britain, the USA, and the European Cold War, 1945–1948," *History* 67, no. 220 (January 1982): 217–36; Barker, *British between the Superpowers*; Peter G. Boyle, "Britain, America and the Transition from Economic to Military Assistance," *Journal of Contemporary History* 22, no. 2 (July 1987): 521–38; Geir Lundestad, *The United States and Western Europe since 1945* (New York: Oxford University Press, 2003), 27–62. For Soviet aggrandizement, see Vojtech Mastny, *Russia's Road to the Cold War* (New York: Columbia University Press, 1979), 267–313.

44. John Lewis Gaddis, *The Cold War: A New History* (New York: Penguin, 2005), 27–34; John Lewis Gaddis, "Was the Truman Doctrine a Real Turning Point?," *Foreign Affairs* 52, no. 2 (January 1974): 386–402; Gormly, *Grand Alliance*, xi. Though acknowledging some Anglo-American differences in 1945–46, a similar discussion can be found in David Reynolds, *From World War to Cold War: Churchill, Roosevelt, and the International History of the 1940s* (New York: Oxford University Press, 2006), especially 312–13.

45. Raymond Dawson and Richard Rosecrance, "Theory and Reality in the Anglo-American Alliance," *World Politics* 19, no. 1 (October 1966): 48.

46. Anderson, *The United States, Britain, and the Cold War*, ix.

47. Suggesting this point is Mark Haas, *The Ideological Origins of Great Power Politics* (Ithaca, NY: Cornell University Press, 2005), 29.

48. For Anglo-American "liberal affinity," see Colin Kahl, "Constructing a Separate Peace: Constructivism, Collective Identity, and Democratic Peace," *Security Studies* 8, nos. 2–3 (Winter1998–Spring 1999): 120–29. On U.S. and U.K. liberalism, respectively, see Colin Dueck, *Reluctant Crusaders: Power, Culture, and Change in American Grand Strategy* (Princeton, NJ: Princeton University Press, 2006), 22–33; Keith Tribe, "Liberalism and Neoliberalism in Britain, 1930–1980," in *The Road from Mont Pelerin: The Making of the Neoliberal Thought Collective*, ed. Philip Mirowski and Dieter Plehwe (Cambridge, MA: Harvard University Press, 2009), 68–97.

49. Useful overviews of Soviet ideology can be found in Ted Hopf, *Reconstructing the Cold War: The Early Years, 1945–1958* (New York: Oxford University Press, 2012), 29–72; Werner G. Hahn, *Postwar Soviet Politics: The Fall of Zhdanov and the Defeat of Moderation, 1946–53* (Ithaca, NY: Cornell University Press, 1982).

50. Yoram Gorlizki and Oleg Khlevniuk, *Cold Peace: Stalin and the Soviet Ruling Circle, 1945–1953* (New York: Oxford University Press, 2004), 18. See also Mark Kramer, "Stalin, Soviet Policy, and the Establishment of a Communist Bloc in Eastern Europe," in *Imposing, Maintaining, and Tearing Open the Iron Curtain: The Cold War and East-Central Europe, 1945–1989*, ed. Mark Kramer and Vit Smetana (Lanham, MD: Lexington Books, 2014), 21–24.

51. Along these lines, see Richard A. Best Jr., *Co-operation with Like-Minded Peoples: British Influences on American Security Policy* (Westport, CT: Greenwood, 1986); Thomas Risse-Kappan, *Cooperation among Democracies: The European Influence on U.S. Foreign Policy* (Princeton, NJ: Princeton University Press, 1995), 31–32.

52. An escalating Anglo-Soviet insecurity spiral is implicit in Vladislav Zubok and Constantine Pleshakov, *Inside the Kremlin's Cold War: From Stalin to Khrushchev* (Cambridge, MA: Harvard University Press, 1996), 27–53; Jonathan Haslam, *Russia's Cold War: From the October Revolution to the Fall of the Wall* (New Haven, CT: Yale University Press, 2011), 29–89.

53. For similar arguments, see Benjamin O. Fordham, "Economic Interests, Party, and Ideology in Early Cold War Era U.S. Foreign Policy," *International Organization* 52, no. 2 (Spring 1998): 359–96; Michael J. Hogan, *A Cross of Iron: Harry S. Truman and the Origins of the National Security State, 1945–1954* (New York: Cambridge University Press, 1998).

54. Ovendale, *English-Speaking Alliance*, 18–19. Lend-Lease aid to the United Kingdom totaled $27 billion, equivalent to over two years' worth of British military production. See R. G. D. Allen, "Mutual Aid between the U.S. and the British Empire, 1941–1945," *Journal of the Royal Statistical Society* 109, no. 3 (January 1946): 252, table 5; Raymond W. Goldsmith, "The Power of Victory: Munitions Output in World War II," *Military Affairs* 10, no. 1 (Spring 1946): 75, table 2.

55. John Ruggie, "International Regimes, Transactions, and Change: Embedded Liberalism in the Postwar Economic Order," *International Organization* 36, no. 2 (Spring 1982): 393–405; G. John Ikenberry, "A World Economy Restored: Expert Consensus and the Anglo-American Postwar Settlement," *International Organization* 46, no. 1 (1992): 294–305. Though interdependence never operated as planners anticipated, economic exchange deepened compared to the interwar period. See Barry Eichengreen, *Globalizing Capital* (Princeton, NJ: Princeton University Press, 2008), 91–104. On the importance of the United Kingdom to U.S. postwar economic plans, see Curt Cardwell, *NSC 68 and the Political Economy of the Cold War* (New York: Cambridge University Press, 2011); Alan P. Dobson, *U.S. Wartime Aid to Britain, 1940–1946* (New York: St. Martin's, 1986).

56. Along similar lines, see Paul Papayoanou, "Economic Interdependence and the Balance of Power," *International Studies Quarterly* 41, no. 1 (March 1997): 134–35; Cardwell, *NSC 68*, especially 76–93, 128–93.

57. For details on Soviet-Western economic differences, see Robert Pollard, "Economic Security and the Origins of the Cold War: Bretton Woods, the Marshall Plan, and American Rearmament, 1944–1950," *Diplomatic History* 9, no. 3 (July 1985): 275–76; Scott D. Parrish and Mikhail M. Narinsky, "New Evidence on the Soviet Rejection of the Marshall Plan, 1947: Two Reports," March 1994, Working Paper 9, CWIHP; Roberts, "Moscow and the Marshall Plan," 1371–79. As Parrish and Roberts make clear, Moscow hoped to receive reconstruction assistance from the United States via the Marshall Plan but feared giving the United States influence over Soviet policy in the process.

58. On weakening U.S.-Soviet economic ties, see Dale C. Copeland, *Economic Interdependence and War* (Princeton, NJ: Princeton University Press, 2015), 258–70; George C. Herring, *Aid to Russia, 1941–1946* (New York: Columbia University Press, 1973).

59. Melvyn P. Leffler, *For the Soul of Mankind: The United States, the Soviet Union, and the Cold War*, Kindle ed. (New York: Hill and Wang, 2008), especially loc. 976–98; Gaddis, *Cold War*, 27–28. For general accounts of the Cold War as a security dilemma, see Robert Jervis, "Was the Cold War a Security Dilemma?," *Journal of Cold War Studies* 3, no. 1 (Winter 2001): 36–60; Melvyn P. Leffler, *A Preponderance of Power: National Security, the Truman Administration, and the Cold War* (Stanford, CA: Stanford University Press, 1992).

60. David Reynolds, "'A Special Relationship?' America, Britain, and the International Order since the Second World War," *International Affairs* 62, no. 1 (Winter 1985–86): 5.

61. Alan P. Dobson, *Anglo-American Relations in the Twentieth Century: Of Friendship, Conflict, and the Rise and Decline of Superpowers* (London: Routledge, 1995), 19–29.

62. Leffler, *Preponderance of Power*, 54. For Soviet insecurity as a driving force of the Cold War, see Vojtech Mastny, *The Cold War and Soviet Insecurity* (New York: Oxford University Press, 1996).

63. Keith Neilson, "'Pursued by a Bear:' British Estimates of Soviet Military Strength and Anglo-Soviet Relations, 1922–1939," *Canadian Journal of History* 28, no. 2 (August 1993): 189–221; Merrick, "Russia Committee," 456–61; Leffler, *For the Soul of Mankind*, loc. 714–24, 972–76.

64. On the importance of airpower and geography, see Geoffrey Warner, "From 'Ally' to Enemy: Britain's Relations with the Soviet Union in 1941–1948," in *The Soviet Union and Europe in the Cold War, 1945–1953*, ed. Francesca Gori and Silvio Pons (London: MacMillan, 1996), 303–4; Julian Lewis, *Changing Direction: British Military Planning for Postwar Strategic Defence, 1942–1947* (New York: Taylor and Francis, 2003), 2nd ed., chap. 6. As elaborated below, Britain at this time placed especially heavy emphasis on using long-range airpower to attack the Soviet Union. At least in theory, this situation gave the Soviet Union particular reason to worry about British intentions.

65. For the Soviet Union's evolving strategy, Britain's role therein, and Soviet insecurity, see Geoffrey Roberts, "Stalin's Wartime Vision of the Peace, 1939–1953," in *Stalin and Europe: Imitation and Domination, 1928–1953*, ed. Timothy Snyder and Mark Kramer (New York: Oxford University Press, 2014), 248–60.

66. Warren Kimball, *The Juggler: Franklin Roosevelt as Wartime Statesman* (Princeton, NJ: Princeton University Press, 1991), 100. See also Barker, *British between the Superpowers*, 26–27.

67. The quote is from the Private Secretary to British Foreign Minister Anthony Eden, quoted in John Charmley, *Churchill's Grand Alliance* (New York: Harcourt, 1995), 59. For details on U.S. policy, see Charmley, *Churchill's Grand Alliance*, chaps. 4–6, 8.

68. This is a central point in Hathaway, *Ambiguous Partnership*. See also D. Cameron Watt, *Succeeding John Bull: America in Britain's Place, 1900–1975* (New York: Cambridge University Press, 1984), 100–119.

69. Peter Ruggenthaler, *The Concept of Neutrality in Stalin's Foreign Policy, 1945–1953* (Lanham, MD: Lexington Books, 2015), 8.

70. Reynolds, *World War to Cold War*, 270.

71. Quoted in Gormly, *Grand Alliance*, 34. For an elaboration of this view, see Geoffrey Roberts, *Stalin's Wars: From World War to Cold War, 1939–1953* (New Haven, CT: Yale University Press, 2006), 228–53.

72. Christopher Layne, "The 'Poster Child for Offensive Realism': America as a Global Hegemon," *Security Studies* 12, no. 2 (2002–3): 143. See also John A. Thompson, *A Sense of Power: The Roots of America's Global Role* (Ithaca, NY: Cornell University Press, 2015), 223–26; Christopher Layne, *The Peace of Illusions: American Grand Strategy from 1940 to the Present* (Ithaca, NY: Cornell University Press, 2006), 47.

73. Christopher Layne, "The Unipolar Illusion Revisited: The Coming End of the United States' Unipolar Moment," *International Security* 31, no. 2 (Fall 2006): 30–32; Layne, *Peace of Illusions*, 34, 46–48, 86–97; Christopher Layne, comments to author, September 2015 and June 2016.

74. Roberts, "Moscow and the Marshall Plan," 1381; Roberts, *Stalin's Wars*, 228–53. See also Zubok and Pleshakov, *Inside the Kremlin's Cold War*, 28–35; Pons, "In the Aftermath," 303. For a review of related studies, see Melvyn Leffler, "The Cold War: What Do 'We Now Know?,'" *American Historical Review* 104, no. 2 (April 1999): 507–9.

75. For analogous argument that a hardening of Soviet identity vis-à-vis the West precipitated a competitive turn in Soviet policy in 1947, see Hopf, *Reconstructing the Cold War*, 72–117.

76. For the logic of Anglo-Soviet cooperation, see Aleksei M. Filitov, "Problems of Post-War Construction in Soviet Foreign Policy Conceptions during World War Two," in *The Soviet Union and Europe in the Cold War, 1943–53*, ed. Francesca Gori and Silvio Pons (London: Macmillan, 1996), 11–13; Zubok and Pleshakov, *Inside the Kremlin's Cold War*, 38–39; Roberts, *Stalin's Wars*, 229–37. For Soviet policy, see Vladimir O. Pechatnov, "The Soviet Union and the World, 1944–1953," in *The Cambridge History of the Cold War, Volume 1: Origins*, ed. Melvyn Leffler and Odd Arne Westad (New York: Cambridge University Press, 2010), 93–105.

77. Zubok and Pleshakov, *Inside the Kremlin's Cold War*, 50.

78. Pechatnov, "Big Three," 24–25; Pechatnov, "The Soviet Union and the World," 102–5.

79. David Reynolds, *The Creation of the Anglo-American Alliance, 1937–1941: A Study in Competitive Co-Operation* (Chapel Hill: University of North Carolina Press, 1982), 284–85.

80. Paul C. Avey, "Confronting Soviet Power: U.S. Policy during the Early Cold War," *International Security* 36, no. 4 (Spring 2012): 159–64.

81. Haslam, *Russia's Cold War*, 33–41; John Kent, "British Postwar Planning for Europe, 1942–1945," in *The Failure of Peace in Europe, 1943–1948*, ed. Antonio Varsori and Elena Calandri (New York: Palgrave, 2002), 44–47; Best, "Approach to Alliance," 28–35.

82. Anthony Adamthwaite, "Britain and the World, 1945–1949: The View from the Foreign Office," *International Affairs* 61, no. 2 (Spring 1985): 225–27; Reynolds, *Creation*, 285; Thompson, *A Sense of Power*, 244–45.

83. A French occupation zone in Germany was created from the U.S. and British sectors in mid-1945.

84. Henry Ryan, *The Vision of Anglo-America: The US-UK Alliance and the Emerging Cold War, 1943–1946* (New York: Cambridge University Press, 1987), 6–17; Leffler, *Preponderance of Power,* 55–68.

85. On the importance of Britain for U.S. military strategy in World War II, see Richard M. Leighton and Robert W. Coakley, *The United States Army in World War Two: Global Logistics and Strategy, 1940–1943* (Washington, DC: U.S. Army Center of Military History, 1995), 353–55. On similar U.S. postwar recognition of Britain's importance, see Steven T. Ross, *American War Plans, 1945–1950* (London: Frank Cass, 1996), 13–35.

86. Reynolds, *Creation,* 40–42, 110–13; Stoler, *Allies and Adversaries,* 16–34, 234–70; Joint Chiefs of Staff, "United States Assistance to Other Countries from the Standpoint of National Security," in *Containment: Documents on American Policy and Strategy, 1945–1950,* ed. Thomas Etzold and John Lewis Gaddis (New York: Columbia University Press, 1978), 70–74.

87. Pechatnov, "Big Three," 5–6, 10–15. Though not focused on assisting the Soviet Union, British policymakers considered protecting the maritime approaches a key mission. See Chiefs of Staff, "Future Defence Policy," May 1947, printed in Lewis, *Changing Direction,* 383–84.

88. Sean Greenwood, "Ernest Bevin, France, and 'Western Union': August 1945–February 1946," *European History Quarterly* 14, no. 3 (July 1984): 325; Jonathan Schneer, "Hopes Deferred or Shattered: The British Labour Left and the Third Force Movement," *Journal of Modern History* 56, no. 2 (June 1984): 197–226.

89. Bill Jones, *The Russia Complex: The British Labour Party and the Soviet Union* (Manchester: Manchester University Press, 1977), 103–146; Anderson, *The United States, Britain, and the Cold War,* 157–58.

90. Zubok and Pleshakov, *Inside the Kremlin's Cold War,* 50.

91. For Bevin's own changing attitudes, see Warner, "From 'Ally' to Enemy," 305.

92. Quoted in Geoffrey Warner, "Britain and Europe in 1948: The View from the Cabinet," in *Power in Europe? Great Britain, France, Italy, and Germany in a Postwar World, 1945–1950,* ed. Josef Becker and Franz Knipping (New York: de Gruyter, 1986), 28.

93. For a good overview of British defense policy, see Anthony Gorst, " 'We Must Cut Our Coat According to Our Cloth': The Making of British Defence Policy, 1945–8," in *British Intelligence, Strategy, and the Cold War, 1945–51,* ed. Richard Aldrich (London: Routledge, 1992), 143–65.

94. Gorst, " 'We Must Cut Our Coat,' " 145–54; Chiefs of Staff, "Strategic Position of the British Commonwealth," in *British Defence Policy since 1945,* ed. Ritchie Ovendale (Manchester, UK: Manchester University Press, 1994), 24–27.

95. On British guns-versus-butter debates in the immediate postwar period, see Jim Tomlinson, *Democratic Socialism and Economic Policy: The Attlee Years, 1945–1951* (New York: Cambridge University Press, 1997), 49–58. See also L. V. Scott, *Conscription and the Attlee Government* (New York: Clarendon Press, 1993), 51–54.

96. Cabinet Defence Committee, "Minutes of a Meeting held at No. 10 Downing Street on Monday, 21st January, 1946 at 3.0 P.M.," DO(46) 3rd Meeting, NA.

97. Michael R. Gordon, *Conflict and Consensus in Labour's Foreign Policy, 1914–1965* (Stanford, CA: Stanford University Press, 1969), 133. For debate in the British government on the necessity of protecting these areas, see Lewis, *Changing Direction,* 249–79.

98. Chiefs of Staff, "Size of the Armed Forces—30th June, 1946 and 31st December, 1946," and Annexes, February 13, 1946, DO(46) 20, NA; Chiefs of Staff, "Strength of the Armed Forces at 31st December, 1946 and 31st March, 1948," November 8, 1946, DO(46) 135, NA.

99. See the discussion of Army forces in Cabinet Defence Committee, "Minutes of a Meeting held at No. 10 Downing Street on Friday, 11th January, 1946 at 11.30 A.M.," DO(46) 1st Meeting, NA.

100. David French, *Army, Empire, and Cold War: The British Army and Military Policy, 1945–1971* (New York: Oxford University Press, 2012), 39–40; Paul Cornish, "Learning New Lessons: The British Army and the Strategic Debate, 1945–50," in *Big Wars and Small Wars: The British Army and the Lessons of War in the 20th Century,* ed. Hew Strachan (London: Routledge, 2006), 70; Chiefs of Staff, "Strength of the Armed Forces at 31st December, 1946 and 31st March, 1948;" Chiefs of Staff, "Call-Up of the Forces in the Transitional Period," May 10, 1946, DO(46) 66,

NA. The two Chiefs of Staff reports are important. Written in the middle of Britain's 1944–46 guns-versus-butter debates, both reports argue that proposed budget cuts would significantly impair British military power in the future—suggesting, in turn, that British forces *at the time* remained reasonably capable. For recruitment and retention efforts, see Cabinet Defence Committee, "Minutes of a Meeting held at No. 10 Downing Street on Friday, 15th February, 1946, at 11:30 A.M.," DO(46) 5th meeting, NA; Cabinet Defence Committee, "Minutes of a Meeting held at No. 10 Downing Street on Monday, 15th April, 1946 at 5:30 P.M.," DO(46) 12th meeting, NA; Chairman of the Manpower Committee, "Call Up of Forces in the Transitional Period," May 10, 1946, CP(46) 194, NA; Cabinet Defence Committee, "Minutes of a Meeting held at No. 10 Downing Street on Friday, 17th May, 1946 at 5:30 P.M.," DO(46) 16th meeting, NA; Secretary of State for War, "Size of the Army at 31st December 1946," July 15, 1946, DO(46) 91, NA; Scott, *Conscription*, 46–64.

101. Gorst, "'We Must Cut Our Coat,'" 144–54; French, *Army, Empire, and Cold War*, 40–50. For illustrative examples, see Air Ministry, "Call-Up of Forces in the Transitional Period," May 4, 1946, COS(46) 132(0), NA; Parliamentary Secretary of the Admiralty, "Size of the Navy" and Appendices, July 26, 1946, DO(46) 97, NA; Chiefs of Staff, "Strength of the Armed Forces at 31st December, 1946 and 31st March, 1948."

102. On what became known as Britain's "Three Pillars" strategy, see Lewis, *Changing Direction*, 294–334 and Appendix 7. On the continued importance of Europe in these arrangements, see Paul Cornish, *British Military Planning for the Defence of Germany, 1945–1950* (London: Palgrave Macmillan, 1996), 99–102; Ovendale, *English-Speaking Alliance*, 68–70; John Kent and John Young, "The 'Western Union' Concept and British Defence Policy, 1947–8," in *British Intelligence*, 168. For discussions of the strategy, see Scott, *Conscription and the Attlee Government*, chap. 4; Cornish, "Learning New Lessons," 58–61.

103. Chiefs of Staff Committee, "Size of the Armed Forces at 30th June, 1946," Annex III, January 8, 1946, COS(46) 5(0), NA; Chiefs of Staff Committee, "Size of the Armed Forces at 31st March, 1947" and Appendices, January 15, 1946, COS(46) 9(0) Revise, NA; Chiefs of Staff Committee, "Strength of the Royal Air Force," and Annex, February 7, 1946, COS(46) 36(0), NA; Lewis *Changing Direction*, 256–58 and 292. Contemporary American reports suggest Britain was disproportionately strong in bombers compared with the United States: despite having a significantly smaller industrial and military base than the U.S., reports into 1946 indicated that Britain would have a bomber force nearly half as large as that of the United States. See Joint War Plans Committee, "JWPC 432/3: Joint Basic Outline War Plan Short Title 'Pincher,'" Annex B to Appendix, April 27, 1946, in *America's Plans for War Against the Soviet Union, 1945–1950, Volume II: The Pincher Plans*, ed. Steven T. Ross and David Alan Rosenberg (New York: Garland, 1989), 37.

104. Donald C. Watt, "British Military Perceptions of the Soviet Union as a Strategic Threat, 1945–1950," in *Power in Europe?*, 331–33.

105. Chiefs of Staff Committee, "Strategic Position of the British Commonwealth," April 18, 1946, COS(46), NA; Chiefs of Staff, "Strength of the Armed Forces at 31st December, 1946 and 31st March, 1948"; Minister of Defence, "Preparations for Defence," August 19, 1948, DO(48) 55, NA. See also Barker, *British between the Superpowers*, 238–39; Lewis, *Changing Direction*, 263.

106. Cabinet Defence Committee, DO(46) 16th Meeting. Cautious but waning optimism regarding Britain's military options from 1945 through early 1947 is an underlying theme in Gorst, "'We Must Cut Our Coat,'" 145–57.

107. See the appendices to Chiefs of Staff, "Strength of the Armed Forces at 31st December, 1946 and 31st March, 1948." Also useful is Parliamentary Secretary of the Admiralty, "Size of the Navy."

108. Hence the focus on the Middle East, from which British bomber could attack Soviet oil production; Cornish, "Learning New Lessons," 58–59; Lewis, *Changing Direction*, 258–63.

109. Gorst, "'We Must Cut our Coat,'" 150. See also Chiefs of Staff Committee, "Call-Up of Forces in the Transitional Period: Note by the Air Ministry," May 4, 1946, COS(46) 132(0), NA. For early indications of the problem, see Lewis, *Changing Direction*, 251.

110. On calls to build the welfare state, see Rodney Lowe, "The Second World War Consensus, and the Foundations of the Welfare State," *Twentieth Century British History* 1, no. 2 (1990):

152–82. On the reallocation of resources from defense to social welfare, see the figures in John Baylis, *British Defence Policy: Striking the Right Balance* (New York: Palgrave, 1989), appendix 1.

111. Chancellor of the Exchequer, "Defence Estimates for 1947–1948," January 13, 1947, DO(47) 9, NA. Dalton's remark came in response to military estimates for 1947–1948; see Minister of Defence, "Defence Estimates 1947–1948," January 7, 1947, DO(47) 4, NA.

112. On the pressure for reductions, see Chancellor of the Exchequer, "Defence Estimates for 1947–1948;" Cabinet Defence Committee, "Conclusions of a Meeting of the Cabinet held at No. 10 Downing Street on Tuesday, 21 January, 1947 at 11 A.M.," CM(47) 10, NA. On opposition to reductions, see Cabinet Defence Committee, "Minutes of a Meeting Held at No. 10 Downing Street on Tuesday, 14th January, 1947 at 10.30 A.M.," DO(47) 2nd Meeting, NA; Cabinet, "Conclusions of a Meeting of the Cabinet held at No. 10 Downing Street on Friday, 17th January, 1947 at 2.30 P.M.," CM(47) 9th Conclusions, NA; Cabinet, "Conclusions of a Meeting of the Cabinet held at 10 Downing Street on Tuesday, 28th January, 1947, at 10.30 A.M.," January 28, 1947, CM(47) 13th Conclusions, NA.

113. Cabinet, "Conclusions of a Meeting of the Cabinet held at No. 10 Downing Street on Tuesday, 28th January, 1947, at 10.30 A.M."

114. Chancellor of the Exchequer, "Balance of Payments," July 30, 1947, CP(47) 221, NA; Minister of Defence, "Strength of the Armed Forces," and Annexes, August 2, 1947, DO(47) 63, NA. See also Cornish, *British Military Planning*, 41–42.

115. British defense spending totaled approximately $7 billion in 1946, versus $3.1 billion in 1948. See Richard Rosecrance, *Defense of the Realm: British Strategy in the Nuclear Epoch* (New York: Columbia University Press, 1968), table 1 (appendix).

116. Ovendale, *English-Speaking Alliance*, 48–60; Gorst, " 'We Must Cut Our Coat,' " 150–62.

117. Chiefs of Staff, "Strength of the Armed Forces at 31st December 1946 and 31st March 1948;" Cabinet, "Conclusions of a Meeting of the Cabinet held at No. 10 Downing Street on Friday, 17th January, 1947."

118. Chiefs of Staff, "Strength of the Armed Forces at 31st December 1946 and 31st March 1948;" Minister of Defence, "Defence Requirements," September 15, 1947, DO(47) 68, NA; Minister of Defence, "Defence Requirements," September 30, 1947, CP(47) 272, NA. For the inability to service commitments, see Cabinet Defence Committee, "Minutes of a Meeting Held at No. 10 Downing Street on Wednesday, 8th December, 1948, at 5.15 P.M.," DO(48) 23rd Meeting.

119. Minister of Defence, "Strength of the Armed Forces;" Chiefs of Staff, "Size and Shape of the Armed Forces," January 5, 1948, DO(48) 3, NA; Minister of Defence, "Draft Statement on Defence, 1949," February 3, 1949, DO(49) 4, NA.

120. Minister of Defence, "The Defence Position," and Annexes, July 26, 1948, DO(48) 46, NA; Chiefs of Staff, "Western European Defence—United Kingdom Commitment," June 17, 1949, DO(49) 45, NA.

121. Minister of Defence, "The Defence Position," and Annexes. See also Cabinet Defence Committee, "Minutes of a Meeting held at No. 10 Downing Street, on Tuesday, 14th January, 1947, at 10:30 A.M.," DO (47) 2nd meeting; Minister of Defence, "Defence Requirements," September 15, 1947.

122. Air Ministry, "Call-Up of Forces in the Transitional Period," May 4, 1946, COS(46) 132(0), NA; Minister of Defence, "The Defence Position," and Annex III. In 1949, the Minister of Defence reported that expected budget limits would leave the Royal Air Force with between one-third and one-half of the strength necessary to meet British commitments; see Minister of Defence, "The Requirements of National Defence: Size and Shape of the Armed Forces 1950–1953," October 18, 1949, DO(49) 66, NA.

123. For British military dilemmas at this time amid discussion of even more draconian financial limits, see Cabinet Defence Committee, "Size and Shape of the Armed Forces: Report of the Harwood Working Party," June 21, 1949, and enclosure, "Report of Inter-Service Working Party on Size and Shape of the Armed Forces," February 28, 1949, DO(49) 47, NA; Joint Secretary, "Size and Shape of the Armed Forces 1950/53," and Annexes, October 15, 1949, DO(49) 65, NA; Minister of Defence, "Requirements of National Defence."

124. Cornish, *British Military Planning*, 58–64; Joint Secretary, "Size and Shape of the Armed Forces 1950/53," and Annexes. For a clear statement of this problem, see Chiefs of Staff, "West-

ern European Defence—United Kingdom Commitment;" Chiefs of Staff, "Provision of Forces for Western Union," January 7, 1949, DO(49) 3, NA.

125. Chiefs of Staff, "The Man-Power Situation," and Annex, October 12, 1946, DO(46) 120, NA.

126. Minister of Defence, "National Service," November 7, 1949, DO(49) 70, NA; Minister of Defence, "Strength of the Armed Forces," and Annexes; Chiefs of Staff, "The Man-Power Situation," and Annex.

127. Even eighteen months was an increase from the twelve-month term of service contemplated in 1947–48.

128. Scott, *Conscription and the Attlee Government*, chaps. 5–6, 8.

129. French, *Army, Empire, and Cold War*, 39–43; Minister of Defence, "The Defence Position," and Annexes; Joint Planning Staff, "Position of Armed Forces—Summer 1947," and Annexes, July 8, 1947, JP(47) 97(Final), NA; Cabinet Defence Committee, "Size and Shape of the Armed Forces: The Harwood Report," and Annex, June 21, 1949, DO(49) 48, NA; Joint Secretary, "Size and Shape of the Armed Forces 1950/53," and Annexes.

130. Production Committee, "Production, Research, and Development Programmes, 1947–1948," January 7, 1947, DO(47) 5, NA; Minister of Defence, "Defence Estimates 1948–49," December 24, 1947, DO(47) 97, NA; Minister of Defence, "The Defence Position;" Minister of Defence, "Requirements of National Defence;" Joint Secretary, "Size and Shape of the Armed Forces 1950/53," and Annexes.

131. Minister of Defence, "Defence Requirements," September 15, 1947.

132. For general descriptions of the military's changing capabilities, see Scott, *Conscription and the Attlee Government*, 49–51, and French, *Army, Empire, and Cold War*, 51–53.

133. Minister of Defence, "Defence Position."

134. Chiefs of Staff, "Provision of Forces;" see also Minister of Defence, "Defence Position."

135. Churchill even ordered a study of a preventive attack on the Soviet Union in early 1945. See Reynolds, *World War to Cold War*, 250–51.

3. The U.S. and Soviet Response to Britain's Decline

1. Thanks go to John A. Thompson for help on this point.

2. Quoted in Ronald R. Krebs, *Narrative and the Making of U.S. National Security* (New York: Cambridge University Press, 2016), 194.

3. Melvyn P. Leffler, *For the Soul of Mankind: The United States, the Soviet Union, and the Cold War*, Kindle ed. (New York: Hill and Wang, 2008), loc. 536–98; James McAllister, *No Exit: America and the German Problem, 1943–1954* (Ithaca, NY: Cornell University Press, 2002), chaps. 1–2; Anne Deighton, "The 'Frozen Front': The Labour Government, the Division of Germany, and the Origins of the Cold War," *International Affairs* 63, no. 3 (Summer 1987): 450–57.

4. For detailed discussion of this point, see Marc Trachtenberg, *A Constructed Peace: The Making of the European Settlement, 1945–1963* (Princeton, NJ: Princeton University Press, 1999); John Baylis, "British Wartime Thinking About a Post-War European Security Group," *Review of International Studies* 9, no. 4 (October 1983): 273–78.

5. On the importance of airpower and geography, see Geoffrey Warner, "From 'Ally' to Enemy: Britain's Relations with the Soviet Union in 1941–1948," in *The Soviet Union and Europe in the Cold War, 1945–1953*, ed. Francesca Gori and Silvio Pons (London: MacMillan, 1996), 297–300.

6. Orme Sargent, "Stocktaking after VE-Day," July 11, 1945, in *The Foreign Office and the Kremlin*, ed. Graham Ross (New York: Cambridge University Press, 1984), 211.

7. Terry Anderson, *The United States, Great Britain, and the Cold War, 1944–1947* (Columbia: University of Missouri Press, 1981), 11–12.

8. John Lewis Gaddis, *The Cold War: A New History* (New York: Penguin, 2005), 17–18.

9. Quoted in Anderson, *The United States, Britain, and the Cold War*, 10.

10. Winston Churchill, "Iron Curtain Speech," Fulton, Missouri, March 5, 1946, https://www.cia.gov/library/readingroom/docs/1946-03-05.pdf.

11. Discussion of Anglo-American wartime arrangements, especially in military affairs, can be found in Mark A. Stoler, *Allies and Adversaries: The Joint Chiefs of Staff, the Grand Alliance, and U.S. Strategy in World War II* (Chapel Hill: University of North Carolina Press, 2003).

12. Robert M. Hathaway, *Ambiguous Partnership: Britain and America, 1944–1947* (New York: Columbia University Press, 1981), 46–47, 65–66; David Reynolds, *From World War to Cold War: Churchill, Roosevelt, and the International History of the 1940s* (New York: Oxford University Press, 2006), 58–59.

13. McAllister, *No Exit*, 44. An overview of British thinking on postwar great power relations can be found in Peter Boyle, "The British Foreign Office View of Soviet-American Relations, 1945–46," *Diplomatic History* 3, no. 3 (July 1979): 307–20.

14. Sean Greenwood, "Ernest Bevin, France, and 'Western Union': August 1945–February 1946," *European History Quarterly* 14, no. 3 (July 1984): 320–21; Baylis, "British Wartime Thinking," 277–78.

15. Baylis, "British Wartime Thinking," 265–81; D. Cameron Watt, *Succeeding John Bull: America in Britain's Place, 1900–1975* (New York: Cambridge University Press, 1984), 115.

16. Paul Nitze, "The Grand Strategy of Containment," in *NSC-68: Forging the Strategy of Containment*, ed. S. Nelson Drew (Washington, DC: National Defense University Press, 1994), 7.

17. On U.S. disengagement plans, see Mark S. Sheetz, "Exit Strategies: American Grand Designs for Postwar European Security," *Security Studies* 8, no. 4 (1999): 1–43.

18. McAllister, *No Exit*, 45–46.

19. Quoted in Sheetz, "Exit Strategies," 18.

20. According to John Thompson, Roosevelt "did not believe that it would be possible for the United States to assume responsibility for the enforcement of peace, at least by ground forces . . . yet he also did not wish to circumscribe the scope of the nation's interests"; see John A. Thompson, *A Sense of Power: The Roots of America's Global Role* (Ithaca, NY: Cornell University Press, 2015), 222. See also Melvyn P. Leffler, "The American Conception of National Security and the Beginning of the Cold War, 1945–1948," *American Historical Review* 89, no. 2 (April 1984): 346–81.

21. Sheetz, "Exit Strategies," 18–19; Trachtenberg, *A Constructed Peace*, especially 3–41; Randall Woods, *A Changing of the Guard: Anglo-American Relations, 1941–1946* (Chapel Hill: University of North Carolina Press, 1990), 256; Melvyn P. Leffler, *A Preponderance of Power: National Security, the Truman Administration, and the Cold War* (Stanford, CA: Stanford University Press, 1992), 77–78.

22. Reynolds, *World War to Cold War*, 270–72; John Lewis Gaddis, "Spheres of Influence: The United States and Europe, 1945–1949," in *The Long Peace: Inquiries into the History of the Cold War*, ed. John Lewis Gaddis (New York: Oxford University Press, 1987), 48–57; Trachtenberg, *A Constructed Peace*, 3–33.

23. Memorandum Prepared for the Secretary's Staff Committee, November 16, 1945, *Foreign Relations of the United States 1946, Volume 1: General, The United Nations* (Washington, DC: Government Printing Office, 1972), 1126. Hereafter, references to the *Foreign Relations of the United States* series are given as *FRUS year:volume*.

24. For both Leahy's initial advice and its subsequent delivery to Truman, see British Plans for a Western European Bloc, undated, *FRUS 1945: The Conference of Berlin (Potsdam)* (Washington, DC: Government Printing Office, 1960), 1: 256–66. Similarly, Harry Hopkins—a senior adviser to both Roosevelt and Truman—reportedly expressed the idea in mid-1945 that it was "highly desirable" to find a way to "dissipate the suspicion [in Soviet eyes] that we were 'ganging up' with the British versus the U.S.S.R." See Joseph Davies, Davies Journal, Entry for May 22, 1945 [1-16-54 revision], box 17, series 1, Joseph Davies Papers, Library of Congress, Washington, DC.

25. Eduard Mark, "American Policy toward Eastern Europe and the Origins of the Cold War, 1941–1946: An Alternative Explanation," *Journal of American History* 68, no. 2 (September 1981): 317–18.

26. British Plans for a Western European Bloc, *FRUS 1945: Potsdam*, 1:256.

27. The Chairman of the President's War Relief Council to the President, *FRUS 1945: Potsdam*, 1:77. See also William Leahy, *I Was There* (New York: McGraw-Hill, 1950), 379–81.

28. British Plans for a Western European Bloc, *FRUS 1945: Potsdam,* 1:256. See also Leffler, *Preponderance of Power,* 61–63.

29. Ritchie Ovendale, "Britain, the U.S.A., and the European Cold War, 1945–8," *History* 67, no. 220 (January 1982): 220–24.

30. Anne Deighton, *The Impossible Peace: Britain, the Division of Germany, and the Origins of the Cold War* (New York: Clarendon, 1993), 31–32; J. E. Farquharson, "Anglo-American Policy on German Reparations from Yalta to Potsdam," *English Historical Review* 112, no. 448 (September 1997): 904–26.

31. Deighton, *Impossible Peace,* 32–34.

32. British Plans for a Western European Bloc, *FRUS 1945: Potsdam,* 1:264.

33. On blocking Soviet involvement in West European discussions, see the discussion of policy toward Italy in James L. Gormly, *The Collapse of the Grand Alliance, 1945–1948* (Baton Rouge: Louisiana State University Press, 1987), 34–38.

34. Trachtenberg, *A Constructed Peace,* 25–30.

35. Hathaway, *Ambiguous Partnership,* 65–66, 84–85, 142–47.

36. Lord Keynes, "Our Overseas Financial Prospects," August 13, 1945, in *Documents on British Policy Overseas, Series 1, Volume 3: Britain and America: Negotiation of the United States Loan,* ed. R. Bullen and M.E. Pelly (London: Stationery Office, 1986), 27–37.

37. Will Clayton, *Selected Papers of Will Clayton,* ed. Fredrick Dobney (Baltimore, MD: Johns Hopkins Press, 1971), 147.

38. Harry S. Truman, *Memoirs, 1945: Year of Decisions* (New York: Konecky and Konecky, 1955), 478; Leffler, *Preponderance of Power,* 63.

39. Quoted in Hathaway, *Ambiguous Partnership,* 245. In fact, concerns—especially in Congress—that British financial weakness imperiled U.S. security had been growing throughout late 1945 and early 1946. For a survey of U.S. attitudes, see Woods, *Changing of the Guard,* 318–19, 331, 363–98.

40. Dean Acheson, *Present at the Creation* (New York: Norton, 1987), 122.

41. Woods, *Changing of the Guard,* 378. See also Acheson, *Present at the Creation,* 122.

42. Woods, *Changing of the Guard,* 340–42; Keynes, "Our Overseas Financial Prospects."

43. Richard N. Gardner, *Sterling-Dollar Diplomacy* (Oxford: Clarendon Press of Oxford University Press, 1956), 196–204. For U.S. estimates of British economic strength, see Joint Intelligence Staff (hereafter JIS), "British Economic Capabilities, 1945–1952," December 13, 1945, JIS 161/5, box 81, Records of the Joint Chiefs of Staff Geographic File 1942–1945, RG 218, National Archives and Record Administration II, College Park, MD (hereafter NARA).

44. Gardner, *Sterling-Dollar Diplomacy,* 202–4. For the evolving U.S. position, see Minutes of a Meeting of the United States Financial Committee, October 11, 1945, *FRUS 1945, Volume 6: The British Commonwealth, the Far East* (Washington, DC: Government Printing Office, 1969), 145–49.

45. Terms of the loan agreement are covered in Gardner, *Sterling-Dollar Diplomacy,* 202–4, 210–13. For shifts in U.S. and British positions, see, e.g., Minutes of a Meeting of United States Top Committee, November 7, 1945, *FRUS 1945:6,* 157–62; Minutes of a Meeting of the United States-United Kingdom Finance Committee, *FRUS 1945:6,* 162–67.

46. Gardner, *Sterling-Dollar Diplomacy,* 204.

47. Gardner, *Sterling-Dollar Diplomacy,* 208–9. See also Hathaway, *Ambiguous Partnership,* 196–97.

48. Minutes of a Meeting of the United States Financial Committee, October 11, 1945, *FRUS 1945:6,* 148. See also Secretary of State to the Ambassador in the United Kingdom, November 5, 1945, *FRUS 1945:6,* 154–56.

49. Second Plenary Session, Bohlen Minutes, February 5, 1945, *FRUS 1945: Conferences at Malta and Yalta* (Washington, DC: Government Printing Office, 1955), 617.

50. Steven T. Ross, *American War Plans: 1945–1950* (London: Frank Cass, 1996), 11; Cristann Gibson, "Patterns of Demobilization: The US and USSR after World War II" (Ph.D. diss., University of Denver, 1983), 82, 106; John C. Sparrow, *History of Personnel Demobilization in the United States Army* (Washington, DC: U.S. Army Center of Military History, 1952), 265–77, 320–21. Note that precise figures on U.S. military strength in Europe in 1946 are hard to obtain. Sparrow

reports that U.S. plans in early 1946 called for keeping 335,000 Army and Air Force personnel in Europe; Gibson notes that the United States retained 400,000 forces of all types at mid-1946 with demobilization ongoing. Meanwhile, as detailed in table 2.1, the assigned strength of U.S. forces in the European Theater in July 1946 stood at 330,000. Although the numbers vary, the United States seems to have kept a bit more than 300,000 troops in Europe at mid-1946.

51. Alan Bullock, *Ernest Bevin: Foreign Secretary, 1945–1951* (London: Oxford University Press, 1983), 124; Chairman of the President's War Relief Council to the President, *FRUS 1945: Potsdam*, 1:64–78.

52. Memorandum by the Acting Department of State Member to the State-War-Navy Coordinating Committee, April 1, 1946, *FRUS 1946:1*, 1170.

53. The phrase "political arrangements" is from British Plans for a Western European Bloc, *FRUS 1945: Potsdam*, 1:257. Although written in 1945, the basic theme was repeated in 1946 as U.S. leaders underscored the need to back British interests in geopolitically vital areas; see Memorandum by the Acting Department of State Member to the State-War-Navy Coordinating Committee, *FRUS 1946:1*, 1170.

54. Joseph Davies, Davies Journal, April 30, 1945, "First Talk with Truman," box 16, series 1, Davies Papers. See also Chairman of the President's War Relief Council to the President, *FRUS 1945: Potsdam*, 1:64–78, and the Hopkins discussion reported in Davies Journal, Entry for May 22, 1945 [1-16-54 revision].

55. Hathaway, *Ambiguous Partnership*, 137. See also Robert L. Messer, *The End of an Alliance: James F. Byrnes, Roosevelt, Truman, and the Origins of the Cold War* (Chapel Hill: University of North Carolina Press, 1982), 147.

56. JIS, "Military Capabilities and Intentions of Great Britain," December 17, 1945, JIS 161/6, box 81, Records of the Joint Chiefs of Staff Geographic File 1942–1945, RG 218, NARA.

57. Quoted in James Forrestal, *The Forrestal Diaries*, ed. Walter Millis (New York: Viking Press, 1951), 58.

58. JIS, "Estimate of British Post-War Capabilities and Intentions," December 28, 1945, JIS 161/8, box 81, Records of the Joint Chiefs of Staff Geographic File 1942–1945, RG 218, NARA.

59. United States Chiefs of Staff, "Combined Chiefs of Staff: Basic Objectives, Strategy, and Policies," July 21, 1945, in *Terminal Conference: July 1945*, ed. Office of the U.S. Secretary of the Combined Chiefs of Staff (Washington, DC: Office of the U.S. Secretary of the Combined Chiefs of Staff, 1945), 95.

60. Joint Staff Planners, "J.P.S. 789: Concept of Operations for 'Pincher,'" Enclosure B, in *America's Plans for War against the Soviet Union, 1945–1950, Volume II: The Pincher Plans*, ed. Steven T. Ross and David Alan Rosenberg (New York: Garland, 1989), 7.

61. Plans assumed that the United States would intervene six months after Britain went to war.

62. For the plans, see JPS 789, JPS 789/1, and JWPC 432/3, in *America's Plans for War, Volume II: The Pincher Plans*. For discussion of U.S. planning, see Ross, *American War Plans*, 26–54.

63. Elliott V. Converse III, *Circling the Earth: United States Plans for a Postwar Overseas Military Base System, 1942–1948* (Maxwell Air Force Base, AL: Air University Press, 2005), 113, 135–36. U.S. military leaders did seek permission to locate bombers at British bases in an emergency. However, Anglo-American negotiations in mid-1946 aimed only to produce what the historian Simon Duke terms a "temporary arrangement" that might never even be enacted; see Simon Duke, *U.S. Defence Bases in the United Kingdom: A Matter for Joint Decision?* (New York: St. Martin's, 1987), 20.

64. For a similar analysis, see McAllister, *No Exit*, 47–48.

65. For an appreciation of the British situation, see JIS, "British Economic Capabilities, 1945–1952."

66. Elisabeth Barker, *The British between the Superpowers, 1945–1950* (London: Macmillan, 1983), 27–28; John Baylis, "Exchanging Nuclear Secrets: Laying the Foundations of the Anglo-American Nuclear Relationship," *Diplomatic History* 25, no. 1 (Winter 2001): 35. Background on the British contribution to the Manhattan Project can be found in Margaret Gowing, *Britain and Atomic Energy, 1939–1945* (London: Macmillan, 1964).

67. Quoted in Hathaway, *Ambiguous Partnership*, 213.

68. Truman, *Memoirs, 1945*, 524, 535–36; Alfred Goldberg, "The Atomic Origins of the British Nuclear Deterrent," *International Affairs* 40, no. 3 (July 1964): 415.

69. President Truman to the British Prime Minister, April 20, 1946, *FRUS 1946:1*, 1235. See also Truman, *Memoirs, 1945*, 544.

70. Margaret Gowing and Lorna Arnold, *Independence and Deterrence: Britain and Atomic Energy, 1945–1952* (New York: St. Martin's, 1974), 1:76–123.

71. Barker, *British between the Superpowers*, 53. See also Goldberg, "Atomic Origins," 411–13; Alfred Grosser, *The Western Alliance: European-American Relations since 1945* (New York: Continuum, 1980), 15.

72. Barker, *British between the Superpowers*, 76; Goldberg, "Atomic Origins," 413–16.

73. Hathaway, *Ambiguous Partnership*, 215.

74. On worsening U.S. views of the Soviet Union, see Leffler, *Preponderance of Power*, 130–40.

75. Acheson, *Present at the Creation*, 194–200; Trachtenberg, *Constructed Peace*, 40.

76. Leffler, *Preponderance of Power*, 73–81.

77. Quoted in Walter S. Poole, "From Conciliation to Containment: The Joint Chiefs of Staff and the Coming of the Cold War, 1945–1946," *Military Affairs* 42, no. 1 (February 1978): 14.

78. Poole, "From Conciliation to Containment," 14.

79. Ritchie Ovendale, *The English-Speaking Alliance* (London: George Allen and Unwin, 1985), 41; Acting Secretary of State to the Secretary of State, August 17, 1946, *FRUS 1946, Volume 7: The Near East and Africa* (Washington, DC: Government Printing Office, 1969), 845; Memorandum of Conversation by the Acting Secretary of State, August 20, 1946, *FRUS 1946:7*, 849–50.

80. Bullock, *Ernest Bevin*, 234–37.

81. Memorandum by the Director of the Office of Near Eastern and African Affairs, October 21, 1946, *FRUS 1946: 7*, 896.

82. Quoted in Norman Graebner, "Yalta, Potsdam, and Beyond: The British and American Perspectives," in *The Rise and Fall of the Grand Alliance, 1941–1945*, ed. Ann Lane and Howard Temperley (New York: St. Martin's, 1995), 247. The report, which reflected the views of the Joint Chiefs of Staff, went out under Leahy's name; see Hathaway, *Ambiguous Partnership*, 307. For additional insight into military thinking at this time, see Stoler, *Allies and Adversaries*, 263–64.

83. Joint Staff Planners, "JWPC 432/7: Tentative Over-All Strategic Concept and Estimate of Initial Operations Short Title 'Pincher,'" June 18, 1946, in *America's Plans for War Volume II: The Pincher Plans*, 8.

84. Joint Staff Planners, "JWPC 432/7," 16. Protection of the United Kingdom was listed as the fourth of eight wartime priorities (blocking Soviet offensives on the Continent was lower still). Given that Britain was believed capable of defending itself with the military forces at its disposal, one gets the impression that U.S. planners did not intend to allocate significant forces to Britain's immediate defense. Although he overstates the U.S. commitment to Britain, a good discussion can be found in Ross, *American War Plans*, 31–33.

85. John Baylis, *The Diplomacy of Pragmatism: Britain and the Formation of NATO, 1942–1949* (Kent, OH: Kent State University Press, 1993), 82. For the inchoate nature of the talks and their limited impact, see Barker, *British between the Superpowers*, 55; John Baylis, *Anglo-American Defence Relations, 1939–84*, 2nd ed. (New York: Palgrave, 1984), 35–37.

86. Barker, *British between the Superpowers*, 55.

87. Deighton, *Impossible Peace*, 55; Robert W. Carden, "Before Bizonia: Britain's Economic Dilemma in Germany, 1945–46," *Journal of Contemporary History* 14, no. 3 (July 1979): 535–55.

88. Deighton, *Impossible Peace*, 74–75.

89. Hathaway, *Ambiguous Partnership*, 258–60.

90. Trachtenberg, *Constructed Peace*, 44–46.

91. Hathaway, *Ambiguous Partnership*, 259–60.

92. Memorandum by the Acting Department of State Member to the State-War-Navy Coordinating Committee, *FRUS 1946:1*, 1167–71.

93. Frederick S. Dunn, Edward M. Earle, William T.R. Fox, Grayson L. Kirk, David N. Rowe, Harold Sprout, and Arnold Wolfers, "A Security Policy for Postwar America," March 8, 1945, projects, RG 1.1, series 200.S, box 417, folder 4948, Rockefeller Archive Center, Rockefeller

Foundation, Sleepy Hollow, New York. On the document's subsequent classification, see Stoler, *Allies and Adversaries*, 227–30.

94. Memorandum by the Acting Department of State Member to the State-War-Navy Coordinating Committee, *FRUS 1946:1*, 1170.

95. Quoted in Anderson, *The United States, Britain, and the Cold War*, 153. Wallace's comment came in a September 1946 speech that received Truman's approval but which hastened Wallace's departure from office. Since the remainder of the speech contradicted contemporary U.S. policy, it remains unclear why Truman approved Wallace's remarks; see Messer, *End of an Alliance*, 205–6.

96. For the context, see Leffler, *Preponderance of Power*, 142–43.

97. James F. Schnabel, *History of the Joint Chiefs of Staff, Volume 1: The Joint Chiefs of Staff and National Policy, 1945–1947* (Washington, DC: Office of the Chairman of the Joint Chiefs of Staff, 1996), 59.

98. The Secretary of War to the Secretary of State, undated, *FRUS 1947, Volume 5: The Middle East and North Africa* (Washington, DC: Government Printing Office, 1971), 105–7.

99. Charles E. Bohlen, *The Transformation of American Foreign Policy* (New York: Norton, 1969), 86–87.

100. Minutes of the First Meeting of the Special Committee to Study Assistance to Greece and Turkey, February 24, 1947, *FRUS 1947:5*, 45.

101. John Lewis Gaddis, *The United States and the Origins of the Cold War: 1941–1947* (New York: Columbia University Press, 1972), 348; United States Representative on the Commission of Investigation to the Secretary of State, February 17, 1947, *FRUS 1947:5*, 23–25.

102. Minutes of the First Meeting of the Special Committee to Study Assistance to Greece and Turkey, *FRUS 1947:5*, 46.

103. Acheson, *Present at the Creation*, 219.

104. Thompson, *Sense of Power*, 244–45.

105. Memorandum of the Chairman of the Special Committee to Study Assistance to Greece and Turkey to the Under Secretary of State, undated, *FRUS 1947:5*, 47–52.

106. Memorandum of the Chairman of the Special Committee to Study Assistance to Greece and Turkey to the Under Secretary of State, *FRUS 1947:5*, 53. See also Memorandum by the Secretary of State to President Truman, February 26, 1947, *FRUS 1947:5*, 59; Robert G. Kaiser, *Cold Winter, Cold War* (New York: Stein and Day, 1974), 188–92.

107. Memorandum by the Secretary of State to President Truman, *FRUS 1947:5*, 58; Memorandum by the Secretary of State to President Truman, February 27, 1947, *FRUS 1947:5*, 60–62.

108. Harry S. Truman, "Address of the President of the United States before a Joint Session of the Senate and the House of Representatives Recommending Assistance to Greece and Turkey," March 12, 1947, http://avalon.law.yale.edu/20th_century/trudoc.asp. See also Timothy P. Ireland, *Creating the Entangling Alliance: The Origins of the North Atlantic Treaty Organization* (Westport, CT: Greenwood, 1981), 26–27.

109. See, for example, Memorandum of Conversation by the Secretary of State, March 22, 1947, *FRUS 1947:5*, 128–29; Acting Secretary of State to the Secretary of State, April 3, 1947, *FRUS 1947:5*, 137.

110. Acting Secretary of State to the Secretary of War, March 5, 1947, *FRUS 1947, Volume 3: The British Commonwealth; Europe* (Washington, DC: Government Printing Office, 1972), 197.

111. Ambassador in the United Kingdom to the Secretary of State, May 16, 1947, *FRUS 1947:3*, 13–14; Chancellor of the Exchequer to the Secretary of States May 23, 1947, *FRUS 1947:3*, 13–17; The British Embassy to the Department of State, *FRUS 1947:3*, 17–24; Ambassador in the United Kingdom to the Secretary of State, July 25, 1947, *FRUS 1947:3*, 43–44.

112. Bullock, *Ernest Bevin*, 452–53; Alec Cairncross, *Years of Recovery: British Economic Policy, 1945–51* (London: Methuen, 1985), 132–52.

113. Carden, "Before Bizonia," 550; Cairncross, *Years of Recovery*, 140.

114. Gardner, *Sterling-Dollar Diplomacy*, 323–24.

115. Ireland, *Creating the Entangling Alliance*, 35–37; Director of the Policy Planning Staff to the Under Secretary of State, May 23, 1947, *FRUS 1947:3*, 223–30; Memorandum by the Under Secretary of State for Economic Affairs, undated, *FRUS 1947:3*, 230–32.

116. Memorandum by the Director of the Policy Planning Staff, May 16, 1947, *FRUS 1947:3*, 220–23; Director of the Policy Planning Staff to the Under Secretary of State, *FRUS 1947:3*, 223–30; Secretary of State to the Consulate at Geneva, July 10, 1947, *FRUS 1947:3*, 324–26; Memorandum Prepared by the Policy Planning Staff, July, 21, 1947, *FRUS 1947:3*, 335–37; On Anglo-American talks, see *FRUS 1947:3*, 267–93. For British shaping of ERP aid, see, for example, Secretary of State to the Embassy in the United Kingdom, August 20, 1948, *FRUS 1948, Volume 3: Western Europe* (Washington, DC: Government Printing Office, 1974), 1117.

117. George Kennan, "Policy with Respect to American Aid to Western Europe," PPS/1, May 23, 1947, in *The State Department Policy Planning Staff Papers, Volume 1: 1947*, ed. Anna Kasten Nelson (New York: Garland, 1983), 4. On alerting Britain to U.S. plans, see Alan S. Milward, *The Reconstruction of Western Europe, 1945–51* (London: Routledge, 1992), 61.

118. Figures are from Grosser, *Western Alliance*, 79, table 1. See also Memorandum by the Secretary of State to the President, August 1, 1947, *FRUS 1947:3*, 48–49; Department of State Policy Statement: Great Britain, June 11, 1948, *FRUS 1948:3*, 3: 1091–1108.

119. Ovendale, *English-Speaking Alliance*, 63–65.

120. Memorandum of Conversation by the Secretary of State, July 28, 1947, *FRUS 1947:3*, 44–48.

121. Memorandum Prepared by the Policy Planning Staff, July, 21, 1947, *FRUS 1947:3*, 335–37. See also Ambassador in the United Kingdom to the Secretary of State, *FRUS 1947:3*, 43–44. As the U.S. Ambassador to Great Britain noted, British military strength rested on "delayed demobilization, plus peace-time conscription and heavy service appropriations;" see Ambassador in the United Kingdom to the Secretary of State, June 11, 1947, *FRUS 1947, Volume 1: General, The United Nations*, (Washington, DC: Government Printing Office, 1973), 752. All of these factors were in flux by early 1947.

122. Memorandum by the Joint Chiefs of Staff to the State-War-Navy Coordinating Committee, May 12, 1947, *FRUS 1947:1*, 739–40. See also Memorandum by the Counselor of the Department of State to the Under Secretary of State, September 2, 1947, *FRUS 1947:1*, 760–66.

123. Department of State Policy Statement: Great Britain, *FRUS 1948:3*, 1092.

124. Ambassador in the United Kingdom to the Secretary of State, April 2, 1948, *FRUS 1948:3*, 1080.

125. Department of State Policy Statement: Great Britain, *FRUS 1948:3*, 1093.

126. George F. Kennan, "Review of Current Trends: U.S. Foreign Policy," February 24, 1948, PPS/23, in *The State Department Policy Planning Staff Papers, Volume 2: 1948*, ed. Anna Kasten Nelson (New York: Garland, 1983), 104. Elsewhere in the report, Kennan elaborated that "If we wish to carry through with the main purpose of the ERP we must cordially and loyally support the British effort toward a Western European Union"; see Kennan, "Review of Current Trends, 106.

127. Quoted in Ireland, *Creating the Entangling Alliance*, 164–65.

128. Ambassador in the United Kingdom to the Secretary of State, *FRUS 1948:3*, 1080.

129. Ambassador in the United Kingdom to the Secretary of State, August 11, 1948, *FRUS 1948:3*, 1113.

130. Department of State Policy Statement: Great Britain, *FRUS 1948:3*, 1107.

131. Memorandum Prepared in the Department of State, undated, *FRUS 1947:5*, 488.

132. Memorandum Memorandum Prepared in the Department of State, undated, *FRUS 1947:5*, 489.

133. Memorandum by the Chief of the Division of South Asian Affairs, November 5, 1947, *FRUS 1947:5*, 577.

134. Memorandum Prepared in the Department of State, undated [circa fall 1947], *FRUS 1947:5*, 492.

135. Baylis, *Pragmatism*, 82. For background and consequences of the talks, see Kenneth W. Condit, *History of the Joint Chiefs of Staff, Volume 2: The Joint Chiefs of Staff and National Policy* (Washington, DC: Office of the Chairman of the Joint Chiefs of Staff, 1996), 15–16, 156; Steve L. Rearden, *History of the Office of the Secretary of Defense: The Formative Years, 1947–1950* (Washington, DC: Office of the Secretary of Defense, 1984), 460–65.

136. For British calls to expand on the 1947 talks to cover the defense of Europe, see British Ambassador to the Under Secretary of State, January 27, 1948, *FRUS 1948:3*, 15–16.

137. Ross, *American War Plans*, 89–91; Robert Alan Wampler, "Ambiguous Legacy: The United States, Great Britain, and the Foundations of NATO Strategy, 1948–1957" (PhD diss., Harvard University, 1991), 2–9.

138. Ross, *American War Plans*, 108–22; Wampler, "Ambiguous Legacy," 7–9; Condit, *History of the Joint Chiefs of Staff*, 159–62. The troop buildup involved forces already in existence that could be deployed in wartime, and long-term plans for mobilizing additional units.

139. Ross, *American War Plans*, 55; Duke, *U.S. Defence Bases*, 27–29.

140. Joint Chiefs of Staff, "Strategic Guidance for Industrial Mobilization Planning," JCS 1725/1 May 1, 1947, in Department of State, Policy Planning Staff, "Policy with Respect to American Aid to Western Europe," May 23, 1947, PPS 1 in *Containment: Documents on American Policy and Strategy, 1945–1950*, ed. Thomas Etzold and John L. Gaddis (New York: Columbia University Press, 1978), 304–5; Joint Chiefs of Staff, "Brief of Short Range Emergency War Plan (HALFMOON), JCS 1844/13, July 21, 1948 in *Containment*, 319; Ross, *American War Plans*, 115–16.

141. Memorandum of Conversation, by the Director of the Office of European Affairs, January 21, 1948, *FRUS 1948:3*, 10–11. See also Secretary of State to the British Ambassador, January 20, 1948, *FRUS 1948:3*, 8–9.

142. Quoted in Rearden, *Formative Years*, 460. See also Minutes of the First Meeting of the United States-United Kingdom-Canada Security Conversations, Held at Washington, March 22, 1948, *FRUS 1948:3*, 59–61; Report by the Policy Planning Staff Concerning Western Union and Related Problems, March 23, 1948, *FRUS 1948:3*, 61–64.

143. Joint Strategic Plans Committee, "Estimate of Probable Developments in the World Situation up to 1957," December 11, 1947, JSPC 814/3, in *Containment*, 292.

144. Joint Strategic Plans Committee, "Estimate of Probable Developments" in *Containment*, 290.

145. Memorandum by the Director of the Office of European Affairs to the Secretary of State, March 8, 1948, *FRUS 1948:3*, 40. See also Memorandum by the Secretary of State to President Truman, March 12, 1948, *FRUS 1948:3*, 49.

146. Ambassador in the United Kingdom to the Secretary of State, April 16, 1948, *FRUS 1948:3*, 89.

147. Joint Strategic Plans Committee, "Estimate of Probable Developments," 290.

148. Memorandum by George H. Butler of the Policy Planning Staff, March 19, 1948, *FRUS 1948:3*, 58–59.

149. Secretary of State to the British Ambassador, March 12, 1948, *FRUS 1948:3*, 48.

150. Harry S. Truman, "Special Message to the Congress on the Threat to the Freedom of Europe," March 17, 1948, http://trumanlibrary.org/publicpapers/index.php?pid=1417.

151. Rearden, *Formative Years*, 459–61; Minutes of the First Meeting of the United States-United Kingdom-Canada Security Conversations, March 22, 1948, *FRUS 1948:3*, 59–61. See also "Pentagon Paper," unsigned and undated [circa March–April, 1948], box 5, Records of the Office of European Regional Affairs, Records Relating to the North Atlantic Treaty Organization, 1947–1953, RG 59, NARA.

152. For background on the Brussels Pact, see John Baylis, "Britain, the Brussels Pact, and the Continental Commitment," *International Affairs* 60, no. 4 (Autumn 1984): 615–29; Lawrence S. Kaplan, *NATO 1948: The Birth of the Transatlantic Alliance* (Lanham, MD: Rowman and Littlefield, 2007), 59–61.

153. For British influence on alliance discussions, see Ireland, *Creating the Entangling Alliance*, 82–92; Wilson D. Miscamble, *George F. Kennan and the Making of American Foreign Policy, 1947–1950* (Princeton, NJ: Princeton University Press, 1992), 116–40.

154. Paraphrase of a Telegram from the British Secretary of State for Foreign Affairs on April 9th Regarding Recent Talks on North Atlantic Security Arrangements, *FRUS 1948:3*, 80.

155. Ireland, *Creating the Entangling Alliance*, 92–100; British Embassy to the Secretary of State, undated [circa May 14, 1948], *FRUS 1948:3*, 122; Enclosure from Bevin in Memorandum of Conversation by the Secretary of State, June 14, 1948, *FRUS 1948:3*, 138.

156. Memorandum by the Counselor of the Department of State to the Secretary of State and the Under Secretary of State, February 16, 1949, *FRUS 1949, Volume 4: Western Europe* (Washington, DC: Government Printing Office, 1975), 113–14.

157. Acting Secretary of State to the United States Special Representative, December 3, 1948, *FRUS 1948:3*, 304–5; Ambassador in the United Kingdom to the Secretary of State, March 2, 1949, *FRUS 1949:4*, 136–38; Memorandum by the Counselor of the Department of State to the Secretary of State, March 31, 1949, *FRUS 1949:4*, 255–57.

158. Ireland, *Creating the Entangling Alliance*, 110–12.

159. Robert T. Connery and Paul T. David, "The Mutual Defense Assistance Program," *American Political Science Review* 45, no. 2 (June 1951): 323–30; Rearden, *Formative Years*, 481–82; Wampler, "Ambiguous Legacy," 4–5.

160. Forrestal, *Forrestal Diaries*, 457.

161. Acting Secretary of State to the United States Special Representative, *FRUS 1948:3*, 303. See also Memorandum by Mr. Paul H. Nitze, Deputy to the Assistant Secretary of State for Economic Affairs, to the Foreign Assistance Steering Committee, January 31, 1949, *FRUS 1949:4*, 54–55.

162. For Britain as an American "spokesman," see Ambassador in the United Kingdom to the Secretary of State, July 14, 1949, *FRUS 1949:4*, 310. For British military strength and role vis-à-vis Germany, see, respectively, Memorandum by the Counselor of the Department of State to the Secretary of State, *FRUS 1949:4*, 255–56; George Kennan, "Outline: Study of U.S. Stance Toward Question of European Union," July 7, 1949, PPS/55, in *The State Department Policy Planning Staff Papers, Volume 3: 1949*, ed. Anna Kasten Nelson (New York: Garland, 1983), 82–100.

163. Secretary of State to the Embassy in the United Kingdom, October 24, 1949, *FRUS 1949:4*, 349.

164. Cairncross, *Years of Recovery*, 168–85.

165. Ambassador in the United Kingdom to the Acting Secretary of State, June 16, 1949, *FRUS 1949:4*, 785.

166. Ambassador in the United Kingdom to the Secretary of State, June 22, 1949, *FRUS 1949:4*, 787–88.

167. Chief of the Division of British Commonwealth Affairs to the Assistant Secretary of State for European Affairs, August 9, 1949, *FRUS 1949:4*, 805. See also Paper Prepared in the United States Embassy in the United Kingdom, August 18, 1949, *FRUS 1949:4*, 807; Memorandum by Mr. William H. Bray of the Office of the Coordinator for Foreign Military Assistance Programs to the Coordinator, September 3, 1949, *FRUS 1949:4*, 830–32.

168. Grosser, *Western Alliance*, 72.

169. J. Coutts, "Effects of British Decline as a World Military Power on U.S. Security Interests," February 11, 1950, box 13, NSC File: Subject File, CIA Subseries, Harry S. Truman Presidential Library, Independence, MO.

170. Norman Graebner, "Yalta, Potsdam, and Beyond: The British and American Perspectives," in *The Rise and Fall of the Grand Alliance, 1941–1945*, ed. Ann Lane and Howard Temperley (New York: St. Martin's, 1995), 233–34.

171. Vladimir O. Pechatnov, "The Big Three after World War II: New Documents on Soviet Thinking about Postwar Relations with the United States and Great Britain," May 1995, Working Paper 13, Cold War International History Project, Woodrow Wilson International Center for Scholars, Washington, DC.

172. For further discussion of the Soviet Union's hopes for postwar cooperation, see Vladislav Zubok and Constantine Pleshakov, *Inside the Kremlin's Cold War: From Stalin to Khrushchev* (Cambridge, MA: Harvard University Press, 1996), 29–35; Scott D. Parrish, "The USSR and the Security Dilemma: Explaining Soviet Self-Encirclement" (PhD diss., Columbia University, 1993), 117–32; Geoffrey Roberts, "Stalin's Vision of the Postwar Peace, 1939–1945," in *Stalin and Europe: Imitation and Domination, 1928–1953*, ed. Timothy Snyder and Ray Brandon (New York: Oxford University Press, 2014), 254.

173. Quoted in Pechatnov, "Big Three," 4. See also Alexei Filitov, "Problems of Post-War Reconstruction in Soviet Foreign Policy Conceptions during World War II," in *The Soviet Union and Europe in the Cold War, 1943–53*, ed. Francesca Gori and Silvio Pons (London: Macmillan, 1996), 11–12.

174. Quoted in Pechatnov, "Big Three," 10. See also Anna Di Biagio, "The Marshall Plan and the Founding of the Cominform, June-September 1947," in *The Soviet Union and Europe in the Cold War*, 213.

175. Quoted in Filitov, "Problems," 12.

176. Pechatnov, "Big Three," 3.

177. Filitov, "Problems," 13.

178. Quoted in Vladimir O. Pechatnov and C. Earl Edmondson, "The Russian Perspective," in *Debating the Origins of the Cold War: American and Russian Perspectives*, ed. Ralph D. Levering, Vladimir O. Pechatnov, Verena Botzenhart-Viehe, and C. Earl Edmondson (Lanham, MD: Rowman and Littlefield, 2001), 100.

179. Filitov, "Problems," 13.

180. Silvio Pons, "In the Aftermath of the Age of Wars: The Impact of World War II on Soviet Security Policy," in *Russia in the Age of Wars, 1914–1945*, ed. Silvio Pons and Andrea Romano (Milan: Feltrinelli, 2000), 300.

181. Pechatnov, "Big Three," 14.

182. For the effects of the Soviet domestic crackdown on Soviet foreign policy in general, see Pechatnov and Edmondson, "Russian Perspective," 123–24.

183. Zubok and Pleshakov, *Inside the Kremlin's Cold War*, 38.

184. Quoted in Pechatnov and Edmondson, "Russian Perspective," 97.

185. Geoffrey Roberts, *Stalin's Wars: From World War to Cold War, 1939–1953* (New Haven, CT: Yale University Press, 2006), 217–25.

186. Roberts, *Stalin's Wars*, 235.

187. Quoted in Roberts, *Stalin's Wars*, 221. See also Jonathan Haslam, *Russia's Cold War: From the October Revolution to the Fall of the Wall* (New Haven, CT: Yale University Press, 2011), 25–26.

188. Quoted in Roberts, *Stalin's Wars*, 235. See also Gerhard Wettig, *Stalin and the Cold War in Europe: The Emergence and Development of East-West Conflict, 1939–1953* (Lanham, MD: Rowman and Littlefield, 2008), 52.

189. Quoted in Roberts, *Stalin's Wars*, 235.

190. Zubok and Pleshakov, *Inside the Kremlin's Cold War*, 29–31; Pechatnov, "Big Three," 11–15.

191. Roberts, *Stalin's Wars*, 317–18; Di Biagio, "Marshall Plan," 209–10. Scholars disagree on whether the Comintern's wartime disbandment was meant as a show of cooperation with the West. Calls for its postwar reinstatement, however, likely reflected the desire to exercise more control over European Communist parties so as to focus their efforts against the West—after all, Soviet control over Western European Communist parties (in particular) had atrophied during and immediately after World War II. Hence, delaying the resumption of the Comintern presented Britain with less of a threat than would otherwise be the case. See Roberts, *Stalin's Wars*, 172, 317; Fridrikh I. Firsov, Harvey Klehr, and John Earl Haynes, *Secret Cables of the Comintern, 1933–1943* (New Haven, CT: Yale University Press, 2014), 243–44; Anna Di Biagio, "The Cominform as the Soviet Response to the Marshall Plan," in *The Failure of Peace in Europe, 1943–48*, ed. Antonio Varsori and Elena Calandri (New York: Palgrave, 2002), 299–300.

192. Elena Aga-Rossi and Victor Zaslavsky, "The Soviet Union and the Italian Communist Party, 1944–1948," in *The Soviet Union and Europe in the Cold War*, 162–64; Silvio Pons, "Stalin, Togliatti, and the Origins of the Cold War in Europe," *Journal of Cold War Studies* 3, no. 2 (Spring 2001): 6–14; Douglas J. Macdonald, "Communist Bloc Expansion in the Early Cold War: Challenging Realism, Refuting Revisionism," *International Security* 20, no. 3 (Winter 1995–96): 164. See also Wettig, *Cold War in Europe*, 111, for Soviet criticism of insufficient Communist efforts to compromise with non-Communist groups in Western Europe.

193. Eduard Mark, "Revolution by Degrees: Stalin's National-Front Strategy for Europe, 1941–1947," Cold War International History Project Working Paper 31, February 2001, 35. See also Wettig, *Cold War in Europe*, 31–38; Roberts, *Stalin's Wars*, 222; Zubok and Pleshakov, *Inside the Kremlin's Cold War*, 45. For Soviet efforts in Germany, see Vladislav Zubok, *A Failed Empire: The Soviet Union in the Cold War from Stalin to Gorbachev* (Chapel Hill: University of North Carolina Press, 2007), 72.

194. Zubok and Pleshakov, *Inside the Kremlin's Cold War*, 45.

195. Nikolai Novikov, "The Novikov Telegram Washington, September 27, 1946," *Diplomatic History* 15, no. 4 (Fall 1991): 535.

196. Pechatnov, "Big Three," 6, 11–12; Pechatnov and Edmondson, "Russian Perspective," 106–9.

197. Mark, "Revolution by Degrees."

198. Trachtenberg, *Constructed Peace*, 40–55.

199. For continued Soviet interest in cooperation with Britain (and the United States) over Germany, see Trachtenberg, *Constructed Peace*, 53; Wettig, *Cold War in Europe*, 106–8. For the evolution of Soviet control in Eastern Germany and Soviet efforts in Germany as a whole, see Vladimir O. Pechatnov, "The Soviet Union and the World, 1944–1953," in *The Cambridge History of the Cold War, Volume 1: Origins*, ed. Melvyn Leffler and Odd Arne Westad (New York: Cambridge University Press, 2010), 103; Hans-Peter Schwarz, "The Division of Germany, 1945–1949," in *Cambridge History of the Cold War, Volume 1*, 133–53; Wettig, *Cold War in Europe*, 108–9; V. Pechatnov, "Exercise in Frustration: Soviet Foreign Propaganda in the Early Cold War, 1945–1947," *Cold War History* 1, no. 2 (January 2001): 4–6; Alfred Rieber, *Stalin and the Struggle for Supremacy in Eurasia* (Cambridge: Cambridge University Press, 2015), 309–10. For the lengthy and fraught process of consolidating the Soviet occupation zone under Communist rule, see Norman M. Naimark, *The Russians in Germany: A History of the Soviet Zone of Occupation, 1945–1949* (Cambridge, MA: Belknap Press, 1995).

200. John Gimbel, *The Origins of the Marshall Plan* (Stanford, CA: Stanford University Press, 1976), 97–140; Geoffrey Roberts, *Molotov: Stalin's Cold Warrior* (Washington, DC: Potomac Books, 2011), 110–13.

201. For a similar analysis, see Caroline Kennedy-Pipe, *Stalin's Cold War: Soviet Strategies in Europe, 1943 to 1956* (Manchester, UK: Manchester University Press, 1995), 93–110.

202. Gibson, "Patterns of Demobilization," 209.

203. Gibson, "Patterns of Demobilization," 200, 212–13.

204. Phillip A. Karber and Jerald A. Combs, "The United States, NATO, and the Soviet Threat to Western Europe: Military Estimates and Policy Options, 1945–1963," *Diplomatic History* 22, no. 3 (Summer 1998): 413.

205. Gibson, "Patterns of Demobilization," 209–11; Matthew Evangelista, "Stalin's Postwar Army Reappraised," *International Security* 7, no. 3 (Winter 1982): 112–14.

206. Matthew Evangelista, "The 'Soviet Threat': Intentions, Capabilities, and Context," *Diplomatic History* 22, no. 3 (Summer 1998): 444.

207. Pechatnov and Edmondson, "Russian Perspective," 124. See also Pechatnov, "Soviet Union and the World," 103–4.

208. Pechatnov and Edmondson, "Russian Perspective," 111. See also Zubok, *Failed Empire*, 36–50.

209. Melvyn P. Leffler, "Strategy, Diplomacy, and the Cold War: The United States, Turkey, and NATO, 1945–1952," *Journal of American History* 71, no. 4 (March 1985): 807–25; Gaddis, *Origins of the Cold War*, 336–37. The Soviet Union also initially demanded the return of provinces ceded to Turkey after the Russian Revolution, but these demands were subsequently dropped.

210. Acheson, *Present at the Creation*, 195–96; Eduard Mark, "The War Scare of 1946 and Its Consequences," *Diplomatic History* 21, no. 3 (Summer 1997): 383–415.

211. Mark, "War Scare."

212. Leffler, "Strategy, Diplomacy, and the Cold War," 809.

213. Leffler, "Strategy, Diplomacy, and the Cold War," 809–11.

214. For U.S. discussion—albeit in confused form—of the military implications of Soviet bases in Turkey, see Secretary of War and the Acting Secretary of the Navy to the Acting Secretary of State, August 28, 1946, *FRUS 1946:7*, 856–58. Although more concerned with the potential for Soviet forces operating from Turkish bases to threaten the Eastern Mediterranean, British officials reached similar findings. Note, too, that British analyses indicated that a Soviet military threat to the area could also come from other bases in Southeastern Europe (e.g., Bulgaria), implying that Soviet bases in Turkey would hardly be decisive in affecting Britain's military position; see Julian Lewis, *Changing Direction: British Military Planning for Postwar Strategic Defence, 1942–1947* (New York: Taylor and Francis, 2003), 56–58.

215. Roberts, *Stalin's Wars*, 310–11.

216. Eduard M. Mark, "Allied Relations in Iran, 1941–1947: The Origins of a Cold War Crisis," *Wisconsin Magazine of History* 59, no. 1 (October 1975): 51–63; Gaddis, *Origins of the Cold War*, 309–12.

217. Louise Fawcett, "Revisiting the Iranian Crisis of 1946: How Much More Do We Know?," *Iranian Studies* 47, no. 3 (March 2014): 384–90.

218. For British war plans, see Lewis, *Changing Directions*, 58–63; Chiefs of Staff, "Strategic Position of the British Commonwealth," April 2, 1946, DO(46) 47, National Archives, Kew (hereafter NA). The analysis is my own: control over northern Iran could give the Soviet Union a separate source of oil that Britain would be unable to disrupt without intervening in Iran, or offer the Soviets defense in depth against British bombers approaching the Soviet Union.

219. Zubok, *Failed Empire*, 41–45.

220. Roberts, *Stalin's Wars*, 311.

221. For the text of Stalin's letter, see Roberts, *Stalin's Wars*, 309.

222. "The Novikov Report, September 27, 1946," in *Debating the Origins of the Cold War*, 160–62.

223. "Answers to the Questions of Mr. H. Bailey, President of the American Agency of the 'United Press,' October 26, 1946," in an archival collection compiled for the CWIHP conference "Stalin and the Cold War, 1945–1953," ed. Christian Ostermann, Yale University, New Haven, CT, September 23–26, 1999, 343.

224. "Record of the Conversation of Comrade I.V. Stalin with Rasmussen, Denmark Minister of Foreign Affairs, and Prince Axel, Chief of the Trade Delegation, June 6, 1946," in "Stalin and the Cold War, 1945–1953," 323–24.

225. Indeed, as noted above, U.S. strategists worried into mid-1947 that Britain might bandwagon with the Soviet Union, with even Bevin warning that Britain and the Soviets might end up making common cause.

226. There is no satisfactory study of prospects for postwar Anglo-Soviet cooperation. For British interest in Anglo-Soviet relations that were at least as warm as Anglo-American relations—and the relationship of Soviet policy to this objective—see Jonathan Schneer, "Hopes Deferred or Shattered: The British Labour Left and the Third Force Movement," *Journal of Modern History* 56, no. 2 (June 1984): 197–226.

227. "Report of the Labour Party on Its Goodwill Mission to the USSR, August 7, 1946," in *Stalin and the Cold War*, 330.

228. Background on intra-Labour Party disputes over British foreign policy can be found in Wayne Knight, "Labourite Britain: America's 'Sure Friend?' The Anglo-Soviet Treaty Issue, 1947," *Diplomatic History* 7, no. 4 (October 1983): 267–72. Note, however, that Knight's study overstates the extent of contemporary Anglo-American cooperation.

229. Quoted in Haslam, *Russia's Cold War*, 76.

230. "Answers to Questions Posed by A. Werth, Moscow Correspondent for the *Sunday Times*, September 17, 1946," in *Stalin and the Cold War*, 340.

231. Knight, "Labourite Britain," 274–75; Hathaway, *Ambiguous Partnership*, 264–72; John Baylis, "Britain and the Dunkirk Treaty: The Origins of NATO," *Journal of Strategic Studies* 5, no. 2 (1982): 236–47. Anglo-American staff talks in late 1946 were officially focused on technical military matters.

232. Cabinet Defence Committee, "The Anglo-Soviet Treaty, the Question of an Anglo-Soviet Military Alliance; and Anglo-American Standardisation, Memorandum by the Secretary of State for Foreign Affairs" and enclosed annexes, January 30, 1947, DO(47) 18, NA.

233. Cabinet Defence Committee, "Anglo-Soviet Treaty." See also Cabinet Defence Committee, "Confidential Annex," January 31, 1947, DO(47) 4th meeting, NA; Bullock, *Ernest Bevin*, 371.

234. Cabinet Defence Committee, "Confidential Annex."

235. Cabinet, "Revision of the Anglo-Soviet Treaty: Memorandum by the Prime Minister," March 16, 1947, CP(47) 93, NA. See also Cabinet Defence Committee, "Minutes of a Meeting Held at No. 10 Downing Street, on Wednesday, 12th February, 1947 at 3:45 P.M.," DO(47) 5th meeting, NA.

236. Quoted in Baylis, "Britain and the Dunkirk Treaty," 244.

237. Cabinet, "Conclusions of a Meeting the Cabinet Held at 10 Downing Street on Monday, 3rd February 1947 at 11 A.M.," CM(47) 15th Conclusions, NA. Hinting at broader spillover from warm Anglo-Soviet relations, this meeting also raised the possibility of Anglo-Soviet economic collaboration in developing Middle Eastern oil reserves.

238. Cabinet, "Revision of the Anglo-Soviet Treaty: Memorandum by the Prime Minister," Appendix B, April 20, 1947, CP(47) 129, NA.

239. Cabinet, "Conclusions of a Meeting of the Cabinet Held at 10 Downing Street, on Thursday, 17th April, 1947 at 11 A.M.," CM(47) 37th Conclusions, NA.

240. Cabinet, "Revision of the Anglo-Soviet Treaty: Memorandum by the Prime Minister," April 20, 1947, CP(47) 129, NA.

241. For more on Anglo-Soviet discord, see Warner, "From 'Ally' to Enemy," 305.

242. Cabinet, "Conclusions of a Meeting of the Cabinet Held at 10 Downing Street, on Tuesday, 22nd April, 1947 at 11 A.M., CM(47) 38th Conclusions, NA.

243. Knight, "Labourite Britain," 279–81.

244. Bullock, *Ernest Bevin*, 357–92; Philip Zelikow, "George C. Marshall and the Moscow CFM Meeting of 1947," *Diplomacy and Statecraft* 8, no. 2 (July 1997): 97–124.

245. Bullock, *Ernest Bevin*, 385.

246. Quoted in Pechatnov and Edmondson, "The Russian Perspective," 125.

247. Scott D. Parrish, "The Turn to Confrontation: The Soviet Reaction to the Marshall Plan, 1947," March 1994, Working Paper 9, Cold War International History Project, Woodrow Wilson International Center for Scholars, Washington, DC, 5–13; Geoffrey Roberts, "Moscow and the Marshall Plan: Politics, Ideology and the Onset of the Cold War, 1947," *Europe-Asia Studies* 46, no. 8 (December 1994): 1373–74.

248. Parrish, "Turn to Confrontation," 13–22, 25; Roberts, "Moscow and the Marshall Plan," 1374–75.

249. For British policies before the ERP negotiations, see William C. Cromwell, "The Marshall Plan, Britain, and the Cold War," *Review of International Studies* 8, no. 4 (October 1982): 233–49.

250. Roberts, "Moscow and the Marshall Plan," 1374–76; Parrish, "Turn to Confrontation," 27.

251. Quoted in Galina Takhenko, "Anatomy of a Political Decision: Notes on the Marshall Plan," *International Affairs* (Moscow), July 1992, 116. See also Roberts, "Moscow and the Marshall Plan," 1374.

252. Mikhail M. Narinsky, "The Soviet Union and the Marshall Plan," in Parrish, "Turn to Confrontation," 45.

253. Quoted in Roberts, "Moscow and the Marshall Plan," 1376. See also Parrish, "Turn to Confrontation," 26–28.

254. Quoted in Narinsky, "Marshall Plan," 46.

255. Quoted in Pechatnov and Edmondson, "Russian Perspective," 128.

256. Knight, "Labourite Britain," 280–81; Rhiannon Vickers, *The Labour Party and the World, Volume 1: The Evolution of Labour's Foreign Policy, 1900–51* (Manchester, UK: Manchester University Press, 2003), 171–72.

257. Sue Onslow, *Backbench Debate within the Conservative Party and Its Influence on British Foreign Policy, 1948–57* (New York: St. Martin's, 1997), 12–32.

258. Quoted in Di Biagio, "Marshall Plan," 213.

259. Andrei Zhdanov, "Report on the International Situation on the Cominform," September 22, 1947, http://www.csun.edu/~twd61312/342%202014/Zhdanov.pdf. On Zhdanov's editing of initial reports, see Di Biagio, "Marshall Plan," 213–21; Anna Di Biagio, "The Establishment of the Cominform," in *The Cominform: Minutes of Three Conferences 1947/1948/1949*, ed. G. Procacci (Milan: Feltrinelli Editore, 1994), 20–25.

260. Quoted in Di Biagio, "Marshall Plan," 215.

261. Di Biagio, "Marshall Plan," 215.

262. Roberts, *Molotov*, 115; Grant Adibekov, "How the First Conference of the Cominform Came About," in *Cominform*, 3–4.

263. Parrish, "USSR and the Security Dilemma," 222–23.

264. Zubok, *Failed Empire*, 73–75; Mark Kramer, "Stalin, Soviet Policy, and the Establishment of a Communist Bloc in Eastern Europe, 1941–1948," in *Stalin and Europe: Imitation and Domination,*

1928–1953, ed. Timothy Snyder and Ray Brandon (New York: Oxford University Press, 2014), 284.

265. Quoted in Parrish, "USSR and the Security Dilemma," 220–21.

266. Quoted in Wettig, *Cold War in Europe*, 141.

267. Wettig, *Cold War in Europe*, 160–66.

268. Kennedy-Pipe, *Stalin's Cold War*, 125–26.

269. Vojtech Mastny, "NATO in the Beholder's Eye: Soviet Perceptions and Policies, 1949–56," March 2002, Working Paper 35, Cold War International History Project, Woodrow Wilson International Center for Scholars, Washington, DC, 8–10.

270. Kennedy-Pipe, *Stalin's Cold War*, 122–23.

271. Pechatnov and Edmondson, "Russian Perspective," 137.

272. Mastny, "NATO in the Beholder's Eye," 6; Zubok, *Failed Empire*, 75.

273. Quoted in Zubok, *Failed Empire*, 75.

274. Quoted in Zubok, *Failed Empire*, 76. See also Silvio Pons, "A Challenge Let Drop: Soviet Foreign Policy, the Cominform, and the Italian Communist Party, 1947–1948," in *The Soviet Union and Europe in the Cold War*, 257.

275. "Stenographic Record of a Speech by Comrade J.V. Stalin at a Special Session of the Politburo, March 14, 1948," in *Stalin and the Cold War*, 430–31.

276. Roberts, *Stalin's Wars*, 361. See also Mastny, "NATO in the Beholder's Eye," 13.

277. Quoted in Kennedy-Pipe, *Stalin's Cold War*, 149.

278. Roberts, *Stalin's Wars*, 355.

279. Zubok, *Failed Empire*, 78.

280. Pechatnov and Edmondson, "Russian Perspective," 144–45.

4. Watching the Soviet Union Decline

1. Saki Dockrill, *The End of the Cold War Era* (New York: Oxford University Press, 2005), 11.

2. "U.S. Relations with the USSR (Draft)," unsigned and undated [cover memo dated October 27, 1982], box 91278, NSC Executive Secretariat: NSDD Files, Ronald Reagan Presidential Library, Simi Valley, California (hereafter RRPL).

3. Charles Krauthammer, "The Unipolar Moment," *Foreign Affairs* 70, no. 1 (January/February 1990): 23–33.

4. Jack F. Matlock, *Reagan and Gorbachev: How the Cold War Ended* (New York: Random House, 2004), 11–14; George P. Shultz, "A Perspective from Washington," in *Turning Points in Ending the Cold War*, ed. Kiron Skinner (Stanford, CA: Hoover Institution Press, 2008), xx. Although the book is not focused on U.S. decline relative to the Soviet Union, a general sense of contemporary U.S. concerns can be found in Paul Kennedy, *The Rise and Fall of the Great Powers: Economic Change and Military Conflict from 1500 to 2000* (New York: Random House, 1987). For fears about U.S. decline throughout the Cold War, see Robert J. Lieber, *Power and Willpower in the American Future: Why the United States Is Not Destined to Decline* (New York: Cambridge University Press, 2012), 81–84.

5. On U.S. growth, see Michael J. Boskin, "Tax Policy and Economic Growth: Lessons from the 1980s," *Journal of Economic Perspectives* 2, no. 4 (Fall 1988): 71–97; Barry R. Posen and Stephen Van Evera, "Defense Policy and the Reagan Administration: Departure from Containment," *International Security* 8, no. 1 (Summer 1983): 3–45; Hal Brands, *Making the Unipolar Moment: U.S. Foreign Policy and the Rise of the Post–Cold War Order* (Ithaca, NY: Cornell University Press, 2016), especially chaps. 1–2.

6. "Agenda for Briefing of President-elect Reagan," unsigned, December 11 1980, http://www.foia.cia.gov/sites/default/files/document_conversions/17/19801211.pdf; Richard Allen, "CIA Special National Intelligence Estimate," November 21, 1981, and enclosure, Special National Intelligence Estimate, "Dependence of Soviet Military Power on Economic Relations with the West," SNIE 3/11-4-81, http://www.foia.cia.gov/sites/default/files/document_conversions/17/19811117.pdf.

7. Marc Trachtenberg, "Assessing Soviet Economic Performance during the Cold War: A Failure of Intelligence?," October 9, 2014, unpublished paper, http://cisac.fsi.stanford.edu /sites/default/files/soviet_economic_performance_marctrachtenberg_.pdf.

8. William Clark, "The Prospects for Progress in US-Soviet Relations," February 4, 1983, box 8, Clark Files, RRPL. That said, few officials, at least until 1990–1991, expected the Soviet Union to dissolve as a sovereign actor in the near future. I thank Brent Scowcroft for underscoring the unanticipated nature of the Soviet dissolution; author interview with Brent Scowcroft, August 3, 2011.

9. William Easterly and Stanley Fischer, "The Soviet Economic Decline," *World Bank Economic Review* 9, no. 3 (September 1995): 341–71, especially table 4.

10. Central Intelligence Agency (hereafter CIA), *The Soviet Economy in a Global Perspective*, March 1989, https://www.cia.gov/library/readingroom/docs/19890301.pdf, 19.

11. Mark Galeotti, *Gorbachev and His Revolution* (New York: St. Martin's, 1997), 16–17.

12. For Gorbachev's attitude immediately before coming to office, see Robert English, "Sources, Methods, and Competing Perspectives on the End of the Cold War," *Diplomatic History* 21, no. 2 (April 1997): 289–90.

13. Philip Hanson, *The Rise and Fall of the Soviet Economy: An Economic History of the USSR from 1945* (London: Longman, 2003), 178–85; Chris Miller, *The Struggle to Save the Soviet Economy: Mikhail Gorbachev and the Collapse of the USSR* (Chapel Hill: University of North Carolina Press, 2016), 60–62.

14. Hanson, *Rise and Fall of the Soviet Economy*, 195–97; Raymond L. Garthoff, *The Great Transition: American-Soviet Relations and the End of the Cold War* (Washington, DC: Brookings Institution, 1994), 302–5. See also Miller, *Struggle to Save the Soviet Economy*.

15. Unless otherwise noted, I use the terms "Central-Eastern Europe" and "Eastern Europe" interchangeably to describe the area from the inner-German border to the Soviet border with Poland, Hungary, Czechoslovakia, and Romania in which Soviet influence predominated.

16. Gerard Snel, "'A (More) Defensive Strategy': The Reconceptualisation of Soviet Conventional Strategy in the 1980s," *Europe-Asia Studies* 50, no. 2 (March 1998): 205–39; Vladislav Zubok, *A Failed Empire: The Soviet Union in the Cold War from Stalin to Gorbachev* (Chapel Hill: University of North Carolina Press, 2007), 322–30.

17. International Monetary Fund (hereafter IMF), *The Economy of the USSR: Summary and Recommendations* (Washington, DC: IMF, 1991); IMF, *A Study of the Soviet Economy* (Washington, DC: IMF, 1991), 2:62–64.

18. Archie Brown, *Seven Years That Changed the World: Perestroika in Perspective* (Oxford: Oxford University Press, 2007), 82–96; Randall L. Schweller and William C. Wohlforth, "Power Test: Evaluating Realism in Response to the End of the Cold War," *Security Studies* 9, no. 3 (Spring 2000): 88–91; CIA and Defense Intelligence Agency (hereafter DIA), "Gorbachev's Economic Program: Problems Emerge," in Joint Economic Committee, Congress of the United States, Subcommittee on National Security Economics, *Allocation of Resources in the Soviet Union and China, 1987* (Washington, DC: Government Printing Office, 1989), 23–25, 34–38; CIA, "Gorbachev's Strategy for Managing the Defense Burden," April 1989, SOV 89-10036, http://www.foia.cia.gov /sites/default/files/document_conversions/89801/DOC_0000499116.pdf.

19. For intra-Soviet disagreements and U.S. assessment of these debates, see University of Virginia Miller Center, "Interview with Robert M. Gates," July 23–24, 2000, 36–38, http://web1 .millercenter.org/poh/transcripts/ohp_2000_0723_gates.pdf.

20. "Agenda for Briefing of President-elect Reagan."

21. Allen, "CIA Special National Intelligence Estimate," and SNIE 3/11-4-81.

22. President's Assistant for National Security Affairs to President Reagan, November 18, 1981, *Foreign Relations of the United States 1981–1988, Volume 3: Soviet Union, 1981–1983* (Washington, DC: Government Printing Office, 2016), 361. Subsequent volumes from the *Foreign Relations of the United States* series are given as *FRUS year:volume*.

23. National Security Council (hereafter NSC) minutes, "Review of Soviet Sanctions," May 24, 1982, and NSC minutes, "NSSD 1-82," April 16, 1982, in *The Reagan Files*, ed. Jason Saltoun-Ebin (self-published, 2010), 144, 164.

24. Matlock, *Reagan and Gorbachev*, 11–13; author interviews with Matlock, August 3, 2011, and Richard Pipes, July 8, 2011; Charles S. Maier, " 'Malaise': The Crisis of Capitalism in the 1970s," in *The Shock of the Global: The 1970s in Perspective*, ed. Niall Ferguson, Charles S. Maier, Erez Manela, and Daniel J. Sargent (Cambridge, MA: Harvard University Press, 2010), 25–48. Interestingly, Soviet policymakers apparently also believed that the United States was declining in the late 1970s and early 1980s; see Miller, *Struggle to Save the Soviet Economy*, 20–23.

25. Henry R. Nau, "Charges of Foreign Policy Disarray," November 25, 1981, box 39, Matlock Files, RRPL.

26. Simon Miles, "Engaging the 'Evil Empire': East-West Relations in the Second Cold War" (PhD diss., University of Texas at Austin, 2017), chap. 3; "U.S.-Soviet Relations Executive Summary," unsigned and undated [included with a January 10, 1983 packet], box 91306, NSC Executive Secretariat Files, RRPL.

27. Henry Nau, *Conservative Internationalism: Armed Diplomacy under Jefferson, Polk, Truman and Reagan*, Kindle ed. (Princeton, NJ: Princeton University Press, 2013), 181, 290 note 69.

28. Clark, "The Prospects for Progress in U.S.-Soviet Relations."

29. George P. Shultz, "USG-Soviet Relations—Where Do We Want To Be and How Do We Get There?" March 3, 1983, box 8, Clark Files, RRPL. For further discussion of the link between U.S. relative strength and bargaining with the Soviet Union, see Hal Brands, *What Good Is Grand Strategy?*, Kindle ed. (Ithaca, NY: Cornell University Press, 2014), 108–11.

30. See, for instance, Paper Prepared in the Central Intelligence Agency, December 13, 1982, *FRUS 1981–88*:3, 825–31.

31. "U.S.-Soviet Relations: The Next Year," unsigned and undated [included with documents from January–February 1984], box 34, Matlock Files, RRPL.

32. Jack Matlock, enclosures to "Poindexter Tasking on U.S.-Soviet Relations," May 29, 1986, box 44, Matlock Files, RRPL.

33. Frank Carlucci, "Scope Paper on December US-Soviet Summit," undated [circa November 1987], box 92305, Jameson Files, RRPL.

34. Robert Gates, "Gorbachev's Gameplan: The Long View," November 24, 1987, http://www.foia.cia.gov/sites/default/files/document_conversions/17/19871124.pdf. See also Colin Powell, "Your Meetings with Gorbachev," December 2, 1987, box 4, Duberstein Files, RRPL; George P. Shultz, "The Washington Summit," December 1, 1987, box 4, Duberstein Files, RRPL.

35. James A. Baker annotations on "U.S.-Soviet Relations," February 10, 1989, box 108, Baker Papers, Seeley Mudd Manuscript Library, Princeton University, Princeton, New Jersey (hereafter BP).

36. George H. W. Bush, "National Security Review 3: Comprehensive Review of US-Soviet Relations," February 15, 1989, http://bushlibrary.tamu.edu/research/pdfs/nsr/nsr3.pdf.

37. "JAB personal notes from 2/6/89 mtg w/POTUS & Others, WDC," box 108, BP.

38. In addition to those cited below, standard treatments include Garthoff, *Great Transition*; James Mann, *The Rebellion of Ronald Reagan: A History of the End of the Cold War* (New York: Viking, 2009); Matlock, *Reagan and Gorbachev*; James Graham Wilson, *The Triumph of Improvisation: Gorbachev's Adaptability, Reagan's Engagement, and the End of the Cold War* (Ithaca, NY: Cornell University Press, 2014); Beth A. Fischer, "Toeing the Hardline? The Reagan Administration and the Ending of the Cold War," *Political Science Quarterly* 112, no. 3 (Autumn 1997): 477–96.

39. G. John Ikenberry, *After Victory: Institutions, Strategic Restraint, and the Rebuilding of Power after Major Wars* (Princeton, NJ: Princeton University Press, 2001), chap. 7.

40. Thomas Risse-Kappen, "Ideas Do Not Float Freely: Transnational Coalitions, Domestic Structures, and the End of the Cold War," *International Organization* 48, no. 2 (Spring 1994): 185. See also Richard Ned Lebow, "The Search for Accommodation: Gorbachev in Comparative Perspective," in *International Relations Theory and the End of the Cold War*, ed. Thomas Risse-Kappen and Richard Ned Lebow (New York: Columbia University Press, 1995), 178.

41. For overviews of initial tensions, see Brands, *What Good Is Grand Strategy?*, chap. 3; Melvyn P. Leffler, *For the Soul of Mankind: The United States, the Soviet Union, and the Cold War*, Kindle ed. (New York: Hill and Wang, 2008), loc. 6378–63; Wilson, *The Triumph of Improvisation*, chaps. 1–3.

42. Robert D. English, " 'Merely an Above-Average Product of the Soviet Nomenklatura'? Assessing Leadership in the Cold War's End," *International Politics* 48, nos. 4–5 (June 2011): 607–26; George Breslauer and Richard Ned Lebow, "Leadership and the End of the Cold War: A Counterfactual Thought Experiment," in *Ending the Cold War: Interpretations, Causation, and the Study of International Relations*, ed. Richard Hermann and Richard Ned Lebow (New York: Palgrave MacMillan, 2004), 161–88.

43. Andrew Kydd, "Trust, Reassurance, and Cooperation," *International Organization* 54, no. 2 (Spring 2000): 325–57; Keren Yarhi-Milo, *Knowing the Adversary: Leaders, Intelligence, and Assessment of Intentions in International Relations* (Princeton, NJ: Princeton University Press, 2014), 192–223.

44. James Goldgeier and Derek Chollet, "Once Burned, Twice Shy? The Pause of 1989," in *Cold War Endgame: Oral History, Analysis, Debates*, ed. William C. Wohlforth (University Park: Pennsylvania State University Press, 2003), 141–73.

45. Daniel Deudney and G. John Ikenberry, "The Unraveling of the Cold War Settlement," *Survival* 51, no. 6 (December 2009): 47; Ikenberry, *After Victory*, 215–56.

46. This seems to be the view not only of scholars such as Ikenberry, but also of many former policymakers. See Philip Zelikow and Condoleezza Rice, *Germany Unified and Europe Transformed* (Cambridge, MA: Harvard University Press, 1995) as well as comments by James Baker, Brent Scowcroft, and Robert Zoellick in "The Unification of Germany" [transcript], in *Cold War Endgame*, 49–75.

47. Andrew Kydd, *Trust and Mistrust in International Politics* (Princeton, NJ: Princeton University Press, 2005), chap. 8; Yarhi-Milo, *Knowing the Adversary*, 192–223.

48. Kenneth Oye, "Explaining the End of the Cold War: Behavioral and Morphological Adaptations to the Nuclear Peace," in *International Relations Theory and the End of the Cold War*, 57–84.

49. Kydd, *Trust and Mistrust*, 227–37; Yarhi-Milo, *Knowing the Adversary*, 206–21.

50. Details on Soviet reforms can be found in Garthoff, *Great Transition*, 300–307, 360–65. For contemporary monitoring of Soviet reforms and their interpretation, see Jack F. Matlock, *Autopsy of an Empire: The American Ambassador's Account of the Collapse of the Soviet Union* (New York: Random House, 1995), 121–22, 153–54; Matlock, *Reagan and Gorbachev*, 295–312, 320.

51. Mark L. Haas, "The United States and the End of the Cold War: Reactions to Shifts in Soviet Power, Policies, or Domestic Politics?," *International Organization* 61, no. 1 (January 2007): 145–79; G. John Ikenberry, *Liberal Leviathan: The Origins, Crisis, and Transformation of the American World Order* (Princeton, NJ: Princeton University Press, 2012), 226. For a related argument, see Thomas Risse, " 'Let's Argue!': Communicative Action in World Politics," *International Organization* 54, no. 1 (Winter 2000): 23–28.

52. On U.S. support for an open economic order, see Michael A. Bailey, Judith Goldstein, and Barry Weingast, "The Institutional Roots of American Trade Policy: Politics, Coalitions, and International Trade," *World Politics* 49, no. 3 (April 1997): 309–38; John G. Ruggie, "International Regimes, Transactions, and Change: Embedded Liberalism in the Postwar Economic Order," *International Organization* 36, no. 2 (Spring 1982): 379–415.

53. Dale Copeland, "Trade Expectations and the Outbreak of Peace: Detente 1970–74 and the End of the Cold War 1985–91," *Security Studies* 9, nos. 1–2 (Fall 1999): especially 43–56. On domestic politics and Soviet reforms, see Jack L. Snyder, "International Leverage on Soviet Domestic Change," *World Politics* 42, no. 1 (October 1989): 1–30.

54. Dale Copeland, *Economic Interdependence and War* (Princeton, NJ: Princeton University Press, 2015), 315. See also Copeland, "Trade Expectations," 47–56.

55. Members of the Reagan administration have long promoted this interpretation, but it is only in the last decade or so that their views have gained wide scholarly attention. See Richard Pipes, "Misinterpreting the Cold War: The Hardliners Were Right," *Foreign Affairs* 74, no. 1 (February 1995): 154–60; Norman Bailey, *The Strategic Plan That Won the Cold War: National Security Decision Directive 75* (McLean, VA: Potomac Foundation, 1998); author interview with Roger W. Robinson, August 9, 2011. For earlier scholarship, see Fareed Zakaria, "The Reagan Strategy of Containment," *Political Science Quarterly* 105, no. 3 (October 1990): 373–95.

56. The extreme version of this argument claims that U.S. policy caused the decline of the Soviet Union. See Peter Schweizer, *Victory: The Reagan Administration's Secret Strategy That Hastened the Collapse of the Soviet Union* (New York: Atlantic Monthly Press, 1994).

57. Francis Marlo, *Planning Reagan's War: Conservative Strategists and America's Cold War Victory* (Washington, DC: Potomac Books, 2012), 26.

58. Steven Hayward, *The Age of Reagan: The Conservative Counterrevolution, 1980–1989* (New York: Crown Publishing, 2009).

59. John Prados, *How the Cold War Ended: Debating and Doing History* (Washington, DC: Potomac Books, 2011), 186.

60. John Lewis Gaddis, *Strategies of Containment*, rev. ed (New York: Oxford University Press, 2005), 350–79.

61. Colin Dueck, *Hard Line: The Republican Party and U.S. Foreign Policy since World War Two*, Kindle ed. (Princeton, NJ: Princeton University Press, 2010), loc. 2374–75, 2793–98.

62. Nau, *Conservative Internationalism*, especially 172–82. See also William Inboden, "Ronald Reagan, Exemplar of Conservative Internationalism?," *Orbis* 62, no. 1 (Winter 2018): 43–55.

63. Quoted in Timothy Naftali, *George H. W. Bush* (New York: Holt, 2007), 92.

64. Dueck, *Hard Line*, chap. 7.

65. Christopher Layne, *The Peace of Illusions: American Grand Strategy from 1940 to the Present* (Ithaca, NY: Cornell University Press, 2006), 110.

66. Layne, *Peace of Illusions*, 96, 110.

67. Leffler, *For the Soul of Mankind*, loc. 6227–8368.

68. In the period 1965–89, the CIA estimated that Soviet and U.S. military expenditures totaled $6.3 and $6.1 trillion, respectively, in 1988 dollars; see Noel Firth and James Noren, *Soviet Defense Spending: A History of CIA Estimates, 1950–1990* (College Station: Texas A&M University Press, 1998), 116, figure 5.8. By comparison, West Germany spent approximately $813 billion and the United Kingdom $667 billion over the same period; see Stockholm International Peace Research Institute, "SIPRI Military Expenditure Database," 2015, http://www.sipri.org/research /armaments/milex/milex_database.Dollar conversion is according to the U.S. Bureau of Labor Statistics, Consumer Price Index Calculator, 2015, https://www.bls.gov/data/inflation _calculator.htm.

69. John Duffield, *Power Rules: The Evolution of NATO's Conventional Force Posture* (Stanford, CA: Stanford University Press, 1995); Valerie Bunce, "The Empire Strikes Back: The Evolution of the Eastern Bloc from a Soviet Asset to a Soviet Liability," *International Organization* 39, no. 1 (Winter 1985): 1–46; Layne, *Peace of Illusions*, 95–96.

70. Quoted in Gaddis, *Strategies of Containment*, 29.

71. Troop withdrawals announced in December 1988 promised to lengthen the period before the Soviet Union could launch an offensive but did not preclude an attack. See Director of Central Intelligence, *Warning of War in Europe: Changing Warsaw Pact Planning and Forces*, September 1989, NIE 4-1-84, https://www.cia.gov/library/readingroom/docs/DOC_0000265626 .pdf.

72. International Institute for Strategic Studies (hereafter IISS), *The Military Balance, 1988– 1989* (London: IISS, 1989), 28–42 and inset.

73. Vojtech Mastny, "The Warsaw Pact as History," in *A Cardboard Castle? An Inside History of the Warsaw Pact, 1955–1991*, ed. Vojtech Mastny and Malcolm Byrne (Budapest: Central European University Press, 2005), 53.

74. Joshua M. Epstein, *Conventional Force Reductions: A Dynamic Assessment* (Washington, DC: Brookings Institution, 1990); Dale R. Herspring and Ivan Volgyes, "Political Reliability in the Eastern European Warsaw Pact Armies," *Armed Forces and Society* 6, no. 2 (January 1980): 270–96.

75. Robert Jervis, *The Meaning of the Nuclear Revolution: Statecraft and the Prospect of Armageddon* (Ithaca, NY: Cornell University Press, 1989); Charles Glaser, *Analyzing Strategic Nuclear Policy* (Princeton, NJ: Princeton University Press, 1990), chap. 2.

76. Senator Strom Thurmond captured this distinction, arguing that "It is clear that the conventional threat in Europe has diminished, and the Warsaw Pact may no longer function as a military alliance. At the same time, however, we need to remind ourselves that the Soviet strategic capability has not diminished"; see Senate Armed Services Committee, *Department of Defense Authorization for Appropriations for Fiscal Year 1991*, 101st Cong., 2nd sess., February 1, 1990, 209.

77. By late 1989, for example, mobilized East German citizens were confronting GDR security forces; see Mary Sarotte, *The Collapse: The Accidental Opening of the Berlin Wall* (New York: Basic Books, 2014), 42–96.

78. Bernard E. Trainor, "Upheaval in the East: With Reform, Tough Times for the Warsaw Pact," *New York Times*, December 20, 1989.

79. There is an extensive literature covering the reforms of the East European military and security services. For illustration of the reform processes, see AmEmbassy Sofia, "Communist Party Cells removed from the Army and Police," January 30, 1990, available through foia.state .gov; Kieran Williams, "The StB in Czechoslovakia, 1945–89," in *Security Intelligence Services in New Democracies: The Czech Republic, Slovakia and Romania*, ed. Kieran Williams and Dennis Deletant (New York: Palgrave, 2001), 57–58; Thomas Szayna, *The Military in Post-Communist Czechoslovakia* (Santa Monica, CA: RAND Corporation, 1992), especially 21–43; Thomas Szayna, *The Military in a Post-Communist Poland* (Santa Monica, CA: RAND Corporation, 1991); Dale R. Herspring, "Civil-Military Relations in Post-Communist Eastern Europe: The Potential for Praetorianism," *Studies in Comparative Communism* 25, no. 2 (June 1992): 114; Dale R. Herspring, *Requiem for an Army: The Demise of the East German Military* (Lanham, MD: Rowman and Littlefield, 1998), 88–90; Andrezj Grajewski, "Poland: Continuity and Change," *Demokratizatsiya* 12, no. 3 (Summer 2004): 453–54; John Koehler, "East Germany: The Stasi and De-Stasification," *Demokratizatsiya* 12, no. 3 (Summer 2004): 387–89; Charles S. Maier, *Dissolution: The Crisis of Communism and the End of East Germany* (Princeton, NJ: Princeton University Press, 1997), 178; Marina Caparini, "Internal Security Reform in Post-Communist Europe: A Study of Democratisation in the Czech Republic, Hungary, and Romania," (PhD diss., King's College London, 2010), chap. 3.

80. For illustration of collapsing morale in the East German military—considered one of the best in the Pact—see Herspring, *Requiem for an Army*, 55–56, 95; Marc Fisher, "E. German Military Reforming; Prospect of Unity Prompts Unease," *Washington Post*, February 13, 1990.

81. Director of Central Intelligence, *The Future of Eastern Europe (Key Judgments)*, April 26, 1990, NIE 12-90, https://www.cia.gov/library/readingroom/docs/DOC_0000265644.pdf.

82. Thanks go to Dr. Robert Hutchings for clarifying my thinking on this matter.

83. Director of Central Intelligence, *Outlook for Eastern Europe in 1990*, January 4, 1990, Interagency Intelligence Memorandum 90-10001, http://www.foia.cia.gov/sites/default/files /document_conversions/89801/DOC_0000265642.pdf.

84. Testimony by CIA Director William Webster and Defense Intelligence Agency (DIA) Director Harry Soyster, Senate Armed Services Committee, *Threats Facing the United States and Its Allies*, 101st Cong., 2nd sess., January 23, 1990, 58–63.

85. Raymond L. Garthoff, "The Warsaw Pact Today—And Tomorrow?," *Brookings Review* 8, no. 3 (June 1990): 37–38; R. Jeffrey Smith, "Non-Communists to Get Role in Setting Warsaw Pact Policy; Full Revision Seen for Command Structure," *Washington Post*, January 18, 1990; R. J. Smith, "Warsaw Pact—Endgame; In Eastern Europe, the Military Alliance Is Dead," *Washington Post*, February 4, 1990. See also Soyster Testimony, *Threats Facing*, 63.

86. National Intelligence Council (hereafter NIC), "The Direction of Change in the Warsaw Pact," April 1990, NIC M 90-10002, https://www.cia.gov/library/center-for-the-study-of -intelligence/csi-publications/books-and-monographs/at-cold-wars-end-us-intelligence-on -the-soviet-union-and-eastern-europe-1989-1991/16526pdffiles/NIC90-10002.pdf.

87. NIC, "Direction of Change." See also the exchange between Secretary of Defense Richard Cheney and Chairman of the Joint Chiefs of Staff Colin Powell with Senator Al Gore in Senate Armed Services Committee, *Department of Defense Authorization for Appropriations for Fiscal Year 1991*, 101st Cong., 2nd sess., February 1, 1990, 200–202.

88. Garthoff, *Great Transition*, 618.

89. Comments by Soviet Chief of Staff Moiseyev in Office of the Chairman of the Joint Chiefs of Staff, Memorandum for Record, "Discussion with Soviet Chief of Staff General Moiseyev, 16–17 January 1990," CF00719, Rice Files, George Bush Presidential Library, College Station, Texas (hereafter GBPL).

90. Reuters, "Soviets Say Cutback in Military Spending Will Be 8.2% in '90," *New York Times*, December 16, 1989; Memorandum of Conversation, "Meeting with President François Mitterand

of France," December 16, 1989, https://bush41library.tamu.edu/files/memcons-telcons/1989 -12-16—Mitterrand.pdf.

91. Alan Riding, "Hungary Seeks Withdrawal of Soviet Forces in Two Years," *New York Times*, January 19, 1990; Foreign Broadcast Information Service (hereafter FBIS), "Dobrovsky: Soviet Troop Withdrawal in 1990," January 9, 1990, "Officials on Temelin, Soviet Withdrawal, Germans," January 11, 1990, "Nemeth on CEMA Reform, Kaifu Visit," January 13, 1990, "Dienstbier Ends Visit, Gives News Conference," January 15, 1990, and "Calfa Discusses Economy, Soviet Withdrawal," January 27–28, 1990; Reuters, "Hungary, Poland Join Call for Pullout of Soviet Troops," January 19, 1990.

92. "Czechoslovak Report on a Meeting at the Soviet General Staff, January 29, 1990," in *A Cardboard Castle?*, 666–67; Jacques Lévesque, *The Enigma of 1989: The USSR and the Liberation of Eastern Europe* (Berkeley: University of California Press, 1997), 240–43.

93. Note that Polish leaders in early 1990 were divided on the wisdom of pushing for an immediate Soviet withdrawal owing to ongoing diplomatic negotiations with Germany over the future (i.e., post-reunification) location of the German-Polish border. Nevertheless, they seem to have accepted that an eventual Soviet military withdrawal was desirable. For East European pressure for Soviet military withdrawals, see Garthoff, *Great Transition*, 413n11; Richard Falkenrath, *Shaping Europe's Military Order: The Origins and Consequences of the CFE Treaty* (Cambridge, MA: MIT Press, 1995), 55–57; Joanna A. Gorska, *Dealing with a Juggernaut: Analyzing Poland's Policy toward Russia, 1989–2009* (Lanham, MD: Lexington Books, 2010), 31–44; Dale R. Herspring, "Reassessing the Warsaw Pact Threat: The East European Militaries," *Arms Control Today* 20, no. 2 (March 1990): 9. Concurrently, a U.S.-Soviet agreement on February 13 limited both sides to 195,000 troops in Central Europe and required the Soviet Union to withdraw "a couple hundred thousand" troops from the area; see FBIS, "Moiseyev Comments on Reduction of Troops," February 14, 1990.

94. A good overview of the changing military situation is in Herspring, "Reassessing the Warsaw Pact Threat," 8–12.

95. Quoted in Mark Kramer, "The Demise of the Soviet Bloc," in *Imposing, Maintaining, and Tearing Open the Iron Curtain: The Cold War and East-Central Europe, 1945–1989*, ed. Vit Smetana and Mark Kramer (New York: Lexington Books, 2013), 414.

96. James D. Marchio, "Risking General War in Pursuit of Limited Objectives: U.S. Military Contingency Planning in the Wake of the 1956 Hungarian Uprising," *Journal of Military History* 66, no. 3 (July 2002): 783–812; John G. McGinn, "The Politics of Collective Inaction: NATO's Response to the Prague Spring," *Journal of Cold War Studies* 1, no. 3 (Fall 1999): 111–38.

97. For related discussion, see Rey Koslowski and Friedrich V. Kratochwil, "Understanding Change in International Politics: The Soviet Empire's Demise and the International System," *International Organization* 48, no. 2 (Spring 1994): 215.

98. Testimony by General John R. Galvin, Commander in Chief, European Command, Senate Armed Services Committee, *Military Strategy and Operational Requirements for NATO Defense*, 101st Cong., 2nd sess., February 7, 1990, 413–14.

99. Director of Central Intelligence, *The Deepening Crisis in the USSR: Prospects for the Next Year*, November 1990, NIE 11-8-90, iii, https://www.cia.gov/library/readingroom/docs/19901101.pdf; Condoleezza Rice and Timothy Deal to Brent Scowcroft, "IMF/World Bank Report on the Soviet Economy," December 17, 1990, CF00715, Rice Files, GBPL.

100. Serhii Plokhy, *The Last Empire* (New York: Basic Books, 2014); Mark R. Beissinger, *Nationalist Violence and the Collapse of the Soviet State* (Cambridge: Cambridge University Press); Director of Central Intelligence, *Deepening Crisis*, NIE 11-8-90, 7–10.

101. Condoleezza Rice, "Senior Small Group Meeting on Soviet Contingencies," December 18, 1990, and enclosure "Soviet Crisis Contingencies," Burns Files, CF01536, GBPL; Condoleezza Rice, "The Disintegration of the Soviet Union and U.S. Policy," August 13, 1990, and enclosure "Turmoil in the Soviet Union and U.S. Policy," August 18, 1990, 91118, Scowcroft Files, GBPL.

102. See, for example, National Intelligence Officer/USSR, "The Gathering Storm," October 24, 1991, CF01498, Burns Files, GBPL; "The Debate over a Successor (or Successors) to the USSR: Possible Outcomes, U.S. Influence over Those Outcomes, and Contingent Responses," unsigned, October 7, 1991, CF01599, Burns and Hewett Files, GBPL.

103. Numbers are from Louise Shelley, "The Ministry of Internal Affairs," in *Executive Power and Soviet Politics: The Rise and Decline of the Soviet State*, ed. Eugene Huskey (New York: M. E. Sharpe, 1992), 211.

104. Director of Central Intelligence, *Deepening Crisis*, NIE 11-8-90, 17; CIA, "The Soviet Cauldron," April 25, 1991, SOV 91-20177, 4–5, https://www.cia.gov/library/center-for-the-study -of-intelligence/csi-publications/books-and-monographs/at-cold-wars-end-us-intelligence -on-the-soviet-union-and-eastern-europe-1989-1991/16526pdffiles/SOV91-20177.pdf.

105. Director of Central Intelligence, *Implications of Alternative Soviet Futures*, June 1991, NIE 11-8-91, especially 7–8, http://www.foia.cia.gov/sites/default/files/document_conversions /89801/DOC_0000265647.pdf.

106. For the Soviet ability to intervene and/or use force within its borders, see Condoleezza Rice, "Dealing with the 'Lull' in the Baltics Crisis," January 15, 1991, CF00718, Rice Files, GBPL; Condoleezza Rice, "Responding to Moscow," January 21, 1991, CF00718, Rice Files, GBPL; James A. Baker III, "Letter from Secretary Baker to Lithuanian President Landsbergis," March 18, 1991, CF01487, Burns Files, GBPL.

107. Director of Central Intelligence, *Soviet Forces and Capabilities for Strategic Nuclear Conflict through the Year 2000*, August 8, 1991, NIE 11-3/8-91W, http://www.foia.cia.gov/sites/default /files/document_conversions/89801/DOC_0000265648.pdf.

5. U.S. Strategy and the Decline of the Soviet Union

1. Brent Scowcroft, "The Soviets and the German Question," November 29, 1989, 91116, Scowcroft Files, George Bush Presidential Library, College Station, Texas (hereafter GBPL).

2. James Graham Wilson, *The Triumph of Improvisation: Gorbachev's Adaptability, Reagan's Engagement, and the End of the Cold War* (Ithaca, NY: Cornell University Press, 2014), 14–36.

3. Hal Brands, *What Good Is Grand Strategy? Power and Purpose in American Grand Strategy from Harry S. Truman to George W. Bush* (Ithaca, NY: Cornell University Press, 2014), 106–9. Thanks go to James Wilson for clarifying this point.

4. Quoted in *What Good Is Grand Strategy?*, 107. On overstated U.S. military concerns, see Barry R. Posen and Stephen Van Evera, "Defense Policy and the Reagan Administration: Departure from Containment," *International Security* 8, no. 1 (Summer 1983): 11–23.

5. Brands, *What Good Is Grand Strategy?*, 107–8. See also "Decision Memorandum on East-West Relations," enclosed with L. Paul Bremer, "Memorandum for Mr. Richard V. Allen, The White House," July 14, 1981, box 91278, NSC Executive Secretariat: NSDD Files, Ronald Reagan Presidential Library, Simi Valley, California (hereafter RRPL).

6. Minutes of an Interagency Coordinating Committee for U.S.-Soviet Affairs, March 17, 1981, *Foreign Relations of the United States 1981–1988, Volume 3: Soviet Union, 1981–1983* (Washington, DC: Government Printing Office, 2016), 77–81; Memorandum from Secretary of State Haig to President Reagan, March 17, 1982, *FRUS 1981–88:3*, 502–3. Volumes from the *Foreign Relations of the United States* series are given as *FRUS year:volume*.

7. Ronald Reagan, "The President's News Conference," January 29, 1981, in Gerhard Peters and John T. Woolley, "The American Presidency Project," http://www.presidency.ucsb.edu /ws/index.php?pid=44101&st=&st1=.

8. Robert C. McFarlane and Zofia Smardz, *Special Trust* (New York: Cadell and Davies, 1994), 201–2. See also the discussions in the National Security Council (NSC) meetings on December 10 and December 22, 1981, in *The Reagan Files: The Untold Story of Reagan's Top-Secret Efforts to Win the Cold War*, ed. Jason Saltoun-Ebin (self-published, 2010), 81–85, 101–11.

9. Steve Coll, *Ghost Wars: The Secret History of the CIA, Afghanistan, and Bin Laden, from the Soviet Invasion to September 10, 2001*, Kindle ed. (New York: Penguin), chap. 3.

10. Memorandum from Secretary of State Haig to President Reagan, July 8, 1981, *FRUS 1981– 88:3*, 204–7; Minutes of a National Security Council Meeting, July 9, 1981, *FRUS 1981–88:3*, 208–18.

11. Calculations based on Office of Management and Budget, Historical Tables, "Table 4.1—Outlays by Agency: 1962–2021," accessed July 10, 2016, https://www.whitehouse .gov/omb/budget/Historicals.

12. NSC Meeting, "NSSD 1–82," April 16, 1982, in *The Reagan Files*, 144. See also "U.S. National Security Strategy," April 1982, box 4, NSC System II Files, RRPL; author interview with Thomas Reed, March 10, 2011.

13. On U.S. priorities and strategy at the start of 1983, see George Shultz, *Turmoil and Triumph: My Years as Secretary of State* (New York: Macmillan, 1993), 154–56.

14. NSC Meeting, "NSSD 1–82," April 16, 1982, in *The Reagan Files*, 142. On fears of conflict, see Brands, *What Good Is Grand Strategy?*, 122–25; Wilson, *Triumph of Improvisation*, 66–67; George Shultz, "USG-Soviet Relations—Where Do We Want to Be and How Do We Get There?," March 3, 1983, box 8, Clark Files, RRPL.

15. Quoted in Wilson, *Triumph of Improvisation*, 67.

16. Memorandum of Conversation (Haig-Gromyko), June 18, 1982, *FRUS 1981–88:3*, 585; see also Memorandum of Conversation (Shultz-Gromyko), September 28, 1982, *FRUS 1981–88:3*, 719–20.

17. I thank Dr. Simon Miles for sharing his research on U.S.-Soviet tensions in 1982–83 and clarifying this point. Along similar lines, see Memorandum of Conversation, "U.S.-Soviet Relations: Jack F. Matlock, Sergei Vishevsky," October 11, 1983, https://nsarchive2.gwu.edu/NSAEBB/NSAEBB426/docs/18.US-Soviet%20Relations-October%2011,%201983.pdf.

18. Quoted in James Mann, *The Rebellion of Ronald Reagan* (New York: Penguin, 2009), 79; see also 73–79. The quote is Reagan's from late 1983 but, as noted above, U.S. concerns had been growing since at least 1982.

19. Jack F. Matlock, *Reagan and Gorbachev: How the Cold War Ended* (New York: Random House, 2004), 75–77.

20. "Response to NSSD 11–82—U.S. Relations with the Soviet Union," unsigned, December 6, 1982, NSC Executive Secretariat: NSC Meeting Files, box 91285, RRPL.

21. "U.S.-Soviet Relations Executive Summary," unsigned and undated, enclosed with William P. Clark, "NSPG Meeting," January 10, 1983, box 91306, NSC Executive Secretariat: NSPG Meetings, RRPL.

22. Shultz, *Turmoil and Triumph*, 267–68; Raymond L. Garthoff, *The Great Transition: American-Soviet Relations and the End of the Cold War* (Washington, DC: Brookings Institution, 1994), 45, 103–5; Wilson, *Triumph of Improvisation*, 67–69.

23. George Shultz, "US-Soviet Relations in 1983," January 19, 1983, box 8, Clark Files, RRPL; Robert McFarlane to William Clark, "Next Steps in US-Soviet Relations," May 21, 1983, box 8, Clark Files, RRPL.

24. Shultz, "US-Soviet Relations in 1983." See also Shultz, *Turmoil and Triumph*, 267.

25. Wilson, *Triumph of Improvisation*, chaps. 3–5; also Frances Fitzgerald, *Way Out There in the Blue: Reagan, Star Wars, and the End of the Cold War* (New York: Simon and Schuster, 2000), 222–25.

26. "U.S.-Soviet Relations Executive Summary."

27. Henry Nau, *Conservative Internationalism: Armed Diplomacy under Jefferson, Polk, Truman, and Reagan*, Kindle ed. (Princeton, NJ: Princeton University Press, 2013), 190–94; author interview with Reed.

28. Brands, *What Good Is Grand Strategy?*, 123.

29. Shultz, "USG-Soviet Relations." See also Jack Matlock, "Hartman-Gromyko Meeting," October 28, 1983 and enclosure, AmEmbassy Moscow "Ambassador's Call on Gromyko October 19," box 2, Matlock Files, RRPL.

30. Shultz, "US-Soviet Relations in 1983."

31. William Clark, "The Prospects for Progress in U.S.-Soviet Relations," February 4, 1983, box 8, Clark Files, RRPL. See also William P. Clark, "NSPG Meeting," January 13, 1983, box 91306, NSC Executive Secretariat: NSPG Files, RRPL.

32. For the importance of arms control, see, for instance, Steven F. Hayward, *The Age of Reagan: The Conservative Counterrevolution, 1980–1989*, Kindle ed. (New York: Crown Forum, 2009), 427–39; Brands, *What Good Is Grand Strategy?*, 116–19.

33. Hayward, *Age of Reagan*, 219–20. Background on U.S. policy can be found in Clark, "NSPG Meeting," and enclosed briefing papers from the State and Defense Departments, box 91306, NSC Executive Secretariat: NSPG Files, RRPL.

34. Ronald Reagan, "National Security Decision Directive 33: U.S. Approach to START Negotiations," May 14, 1982, http://fas.org/irp/offdocs/nsdd/nsdd-33.pdf. See also Memorandum from the Under Secretary of State for Political Affairs to Secretary of State Shultz, September 12, 1982, *FRUS 1981–88:3*, 691–96. For the United States' focus on eliminating Soviet advantages, especially in "heavy" missiles, see Kerry M. Kartchner, *Negotiating START: Strategic Arms Reduction Talks and the Quest for Strategic Stability* (New Brunswick, NJ: Transaction Publishers, 1992); Richard Burt, "Basic Considerations for US SALT Policy: Executive Summary," undated [cover memo dated September 23, 1981], box 34, Matlock Files, RRPL.

35. Minutes of a National Security Council Meeting, October 13, 1981, *FRUS 1981–88:3*, 309–16; Memorandum from the President's Assistant for National Security Affairs (Clark) to President Reagan: Al Haig's Memorandum "U.S.-Soviet Relations over the Near Term," undated, *FRUS 1981–88:3*, 527–28.

36. "U.S.-Soviet Relations: The Next Year," unsigned and undated [circa January 28, 1984], box 34, Matlock Files, RRPL.

37. Kartctner, *Negotiating START*, 34.

38. William P. Clark, "National Security Decision Directive (NSDD-106): U.S. Approach to START Negotiations—VII," October 5, 1983, https://fas.org/irp/offdocs/nsdd/nsdd-106.htm.

39. Sven Kraemer, *Inside the Cold War, From Marx to Reagan* (Lanham, MD: University Press of America, 2015), 278–80.

40. Austin Long and Brendan Rittenhouse Green, "Stalking the Secure Second Strike: Intelligence, Counterforce, and Nuclear Strategy," *Journal of Strategic Studies* 38, nos. 1–2 (January 2015): 38–73; John J. Mearsheimer, "Nuclear Weapons and Deterrence in Europe," *International Security* 9, no. 3 (Winter 1984–85): 29–30; Richard K. Betts, "Conventional Deterrence: Predictive Uncertainty and Policy Confidence," *World Politics* 37, no. 2 (January 1985): 172–77; Fareed Zakaria, "The Reagan Strategy of Containment," *Political Science Quarterly* 105, no. 3 (Autumn 1990): 384–85; William R. Richardson, "FM 100-5: The AirLand Battle in 1986," *Military Review* 66, no. 3 (March 1986): 6–10.

41. McFarlane and Smardz, *Special Trust*, 225–27; author interview with Robert McFarlane, June 28, 2011.

42. Brands, *What Good Is Grand Strategy?*, 121; Archie Brown, *The Gorbachev Factor* (New York: Oxford University Press, 1996), 225–27.

43. For signaling that the United States did not want war in spite of taking these steps, see Robert McFarlane, untitled note to Reagan, December 18, 1983, box 5, McFarlane Files, RRPL; SecState, "Gromyko Meeting," January 16, 1984, available through http://foia.state.gov

44. "Key Summit Economic Themes," unsigned and undated [circa June 1984], box 8, Clark Files, RRPL.

45. Beverly Crawford, *Economic Vulnerability in International Relations: The Case of East-West Trade, Investment, and Finance* (New York: Columbia University Press, 1993), 135–36; Michael Mastanduono, "CoCom and American Export Control Policy: The Experience of the Reagan Administration," in *East-West Trade and the Atlantic Alliance*, ed. Helen Milner, David Baldwin, and Martha Chinouya (New York: St. Martin's, 1990), 195–96.

46. Beverly Crawford, "Western Control of East-West Trade Finance: The Role of U.S. Power and the International Regime," in *Controlling East-West Trade and Technology Transfer: Power, Politics, and Policies*, ed. Gary K. Bertsch (Durham, NC: Duke University Press, 1988), 309.

47. "U.S. Relations with the USSR," unsigned and undated, enclosed with Michael O. Wheeler, "NSSD 11-82: NSC Meeting to Review Draft NSDD, Thursday, December 16, 1982—2:00 P.M.—The Cabinet Room," December 14, 1982, box 91287, NSC Executive Secretariat: NSDD File, RRPL.

48. Shultz, *Turmoil and Triumph*, 477–79.

49. Jack Matlock, "U.S.-Soviet Relations in 1984: A Program of Action," undated [circa January 1984], box 34, Matlock Files, RRPL; "U.S.-Soviet Relations: The Next Year."

50. See NSC meetings of November 30 and December 5, 1984, in *The Reagan Files*, 242–50.

51. Shultz, *Turmoil and Triumph*, 375.

52. Robert McFarlane, "Papers for the NSPG on the Geneva Arms Control Talks—Monday, December 10, 2:00–3:00 P.M.," December 9, 1984, and enclosure, "Alternative Negotiating Formats," December 8, 1984, box 91307, NSC Executive Secretariat: NSPG Records, RRPL.

53. Herb Meyer, "What Should We Do about the Russians?," June 21, 1984, box 9, Clark Files, RRPL. See also Matlock, *Reagan and Gorbachev*, 112.

54. "Alternative Negotiating Formats," December 8, 1984; Fitzgerald, *Way Out There*, 257.

55. Shultz, *Turmoil and Triumph*, 516. See also Fitzgerald, *Way Out There*, 257.

56. Vladislav Zubok, *A Failed Empire: The Soviet Union in the Cold War from Stalin to Gorbachev* (Chapel Hill: University of North Carolina Press, 2007), 278–87; Wilson, *Triumph of Improvisation*, 91–93.

57. This conclusion is found in an untitled note from 1985–86. Matlock deemed the assessment sufficiently important that he kept it in a file for his successor on the NSC. See Jack Matlock, untitled and undated notes, box 27, Matlock Files, RRPL.

58. Jack Matlock, "Talking Points for President, Meeting with Shultz, Weinberger, Casey, Poindexter," undated [submitted as part of a briefing packet on April 10, 1986], box 44, Matlock Files, RRPL.

59. Shultz, *Turmoil and Triumph*, 564.

60. Fitzgerald, *Way Out There*, 290, 302. See also Shultz, *Turmoil and Triumph*, 576–98.

61. National Security Planning Group Meeting, "U.S.-Soviet Relations," June 12, 1986, box 91308, NSC Executive Secretariat: NSPG Files, RRPL.

62. Shultz, *Turmoil and Triumph*, 690, 704–6, 716.

63. Fitzgerald, *Way Out There*, 323–24.

64. Jack Matlock, "NSPG Meeting June 6—Draft Outline Talking Points for President," undated [cover memo dated May 29, 1986], box 44, Matlock Files, RRPL.

65. Fitzgerald, *Way Out There*, 325–26.

66. Soviet missiles were also becoming increasingly vulnerable to U.S. counterforce options. Reducing the number of Soviet missiles and/or warheads exacerbated the problem. For Soviet dilemmas, see Long and Green, "Stalking"; Brendan R. Green and Austin Long, "The MAD Who Wasn't There: Soviet Reactions to the Late Cold War Nuclear Balance," *Security Studies* 26, no. 4 (October 2017): 606–41; Keir A. Lieber and Daryl G. Press, "The New Era of Counterforce: Technological Change and the Future of Nuclear Deterrence," *International Security* 41, no. 4 (Spring 2017): 9–49.

67. Fitzgerald, *Way Out There*, 337–39; see also Matlock, *Reagan and Gorbachev*, 184. There is some confusion over whether the U.S. offer focused on all strategic delivery systems or just ballistic missiles. The text of the letter clarifies that the 50 percent reduction offer centered on ballistic missiles (more precisely, missile warheads), although Reagan also allowed that some interim reductions in delivery systems such as bomber aircraft and cruise missiles might be tolerated. See Ronald Reagan, "National Security Decision Directive 233: Consultations on a Response to General Secretary Gorbachev," July 31, 1986, http://fas.org/irp/offdocs/nsdd/nsdd-233.htm. For the U.S. focus on Soviet ballistic missiles when advancing this offer, see Shultz, *Turmoil and Triumph*, 718–24.

68. Shultz, *Turmoil and Triumph*, 773–74.

69. George Shultz, "Strategy for the Soviets," November 14, 1986, http://endofcoldwarforum.org/sites/default/files/docs/reagan/STY-1986-11-14.pdf.

70. Garthoff, *Great Transition*, 199, 249, 268.

71. Gregory Domber, *Empowering Revolution: America, Poland, and the End of the Cold War* (Chapel Hill: University of North Carolina Press, 2014), 110, 188, 319n132.

72. Domber, *Empowering Revolution*, 123–30; Shultz, *Turmoil and Triumph*, 873; John C. Whitehead, *A Life in Leadership* (New York: Basic Books, 2005), 169–71; author interview with John C. Whitehead, August 8, 2011.

73. Quoted in Domber, *Empowering Revolution*, 177.

74. Robert M. Gates, *From the Shadows* (New York: Simon and Schuster, 2007), 348–50.

75. "How to Maximize Your Leverage," unsigned, October 2, 1986, box 90907, NSC European and Soviet Affairs Directorate Files, RRPL.

76. Memorandum of Conversation (hereafter Memcon) between George Shultz and Eduard Shevardnadze, July 31, 1985, http://nsarchive.gwu.edu/NSAEBB/NSAEBB481/docs/Document%203.pdf. See also Memcon, "The Secretary's Initial Meeting with Shevardnadze," April 21, 1988, http://nsarchive.gwu.edu/NSAEBB/NSAEBB481/docs/Document%205.pdf.

77. Shultz, *Turmoil and Triumph*, 888.

78. State Department, "Soviet Image of the United States," undated [submitted to Reagan on November 5, 1985], box 7, Series I: Subject File, Regan Files, RRPL.

79. Jack Matlock, "Next Steps in U.S.-Soviet Relations," October 17, 1986, and enclosure to the President, "U.S.-Soviet Relations: Where Do We Go from Here?," box 91639, Keel Files, RRPL; "Shultz Recommended Next Steps Post Reykjavik," October 13, 1986, box 91639, Keel Files, RRPL.

80. Frank Carlucci, "Scope Paper on December US-Soviet Summit," circa November 1987, box 92305, Jameson Files, RRPL. A related planning document described the Soviet Union as holding a "hegemonical [sic], subversive, and imperial approach to other nations," resulting in "continuing Cold War;" see "Key Issues for the Summit," unsigned and undated [included as part of a briefing book to Reagan delivered circa late November 1987], box 92158, Ledsky Files, RRPL.

81. Non-Paper Prepared by Secretary of State Shultz, November 18, 1987, *FRUS 1981–1988, Volume 6: Soviet Union, October 1986–January 1989* (Washington, DC: Government Printing Office, 2016), 530–31.

82. Elizabeth Charles, "Gorbachev and the Decision to Decouple the Arms Control Package: How the Breakdown of the Reykjavik Summit Led to the Elimination of the Euromissiles," in *The Euromissile Crisis and the End of the Cold War*, ed. Leopoldo Nuti, Frederic Bozo, Marie-Pierre Rey, Bernd Rother (Stanford, CA: Stanford University Press, 2015), 66–84; Shultz, *Turmoil and Triumph*, 876.

83. Shultz, *Turmoil and Triumph*, 894. Even before the Reykjavik Summit, Soviet officials complained of the hard-line U.S. position with, for instance, the Soviet ambassador arguing in mid-1986 that "the U.S. side had not taken a single step toward the Soviet position. . . . The U.S. seemed to have an 'all or nothing' position;" see Memcon, "Secretary Shultz's Meeting with CPSU Secretary Dobrynin," April 9, 1986, box 44, Matlock Files, RRPL.

84. On tracking Soviet forces, see Long and Green, "Stalking." See also START," unsigned and undated [included with Background Book for Moscow Summit, May 29–June 2, 1988], box 92187, Cobb Files, RRPL.

85. Owen R. Cote Jr., *The Third Battle: Innovation in the U.S. Navy's Silent Cold War Struggle with Soviet Submarines*, Naval War College Newport Papers No. 16 (Newport, RI: Naval War College Press, 2003), 69–78.

86. Thanks go to Austin Long and Brendan Green for background on this point. On efforts to use arms control to restructure Soviet nuclear forces, see National Security Council, "National Security Planning Group Meeting," October 14, 1987, http://www.thereaganfiles.com/871014.pdf.

87. National Security Council, "National Security Council Planning Group Meeting," February 9, 1988, http://www.thereaganfiles.com/880209.pdf.

88. For efforts to structure deals to the U.S. advantage, see George Shultz, "Preparing for the Summit," undated [circa early November 1987], box 2, Howard Baker Files, RRPL; National Security Council, "National Security Planning Group Meeting," May 23, 1988, http://www.thereaganfiles.com/19880523-nspg-190.pdf.

89. Zubok, *Failed Empire*, 289–311.

90. Domber, *Empowering Revolution*, 200–213; Svetlana Savranskaya and Thomas Blanton, "The Moscow Summit, 1988," in *The Last Superpower Summits: Gorbachev, Reagan, and Bush*, ed. Svetlana Savranskaya and Thomas Blanton (New York: Central European University Press, 2016), 368–69.

91. State Department Briefing Paper, "US-Soviet Trade," undated [included with State Department Background Book for Moscow Summit, May 29–June 2, 1988], enclosed in "President Reagan's Meetings with General Secretary Gorbachev, May 29–June 2, 1988: Background Book," NSA: http://nsarchive.gwu.edu/NSAEBB/NSAEBB251/10.pdf.

92. Memcon, "President's Second One-on-One Meeting with General Secretary Gorbachev," May 31, 1988, http://nsarchive.gwu.edu/NSAEBB/NSAEBB251/20.pdf.

93. Carlucci, "Scope Paper."

94. Carlucci, "Scope Paper." See also Colin Powell, "Your Meetings with Gorbachev," December 2, 1987, box 4, Duberstein Files, RRPL; George Shultz, "The Washington Summit," December 1, 1987, December 2, 1987, box 4, Duberstein Files, RRPL. Both memos were included in a briefing book prepared for the December 1987 Washington Summit.

95. James Baker, *The Politics of Diplomacy* (New York: G. P. Putnam's Sons, 1995), 70; Derek H. Chollet and James M. Goldgeier, "Once Burned, Twice Shy? The Pause of 1989," in *Cold War Endgame: Oral History, Analysis, Debates*, ed. William C. Wohlforth (University Park: Penn State University Press, 2003), 152–53. See also Norman A. Graebner, Richard Dean Burns, and Joseph Siracusa, *Reagan, Bush, and Gorbachev: Revisiting the End of the Cold War*, Kindle ed. (Westport, CT: Praeger, 2008), loc. 1624–45.

96. Brent Scowcroft, "The NATO Summit," March 20, 1989, CF00779, Kanter Files, GBPL.

97. Michael R. Beschloss and Strobe Talbott, *At the Highest Levels: The Inside Story of the End of the Cold War* (Boston: Little, Brown, and Company, 1993), 17. See also author interviews with Brent Scowcroft, August 3, 2011; Philip Zelikow, August 18, 2011; and an anonymous NSC official, July 20, 2012.

98. Beschloss and Talbott, *Highest Levels*, 22–25, 99.

99. Quoted in Saki Dockrill, *The End of the Cold War Era* (New York: Oxford University Press, 2005), 12.

100. Brent Scowcroft, "Getting Ahead of Gorbachev," March 1, 1989, CF91117, Scowcroft Files, GBPL; James Baker, "Proposed Agenda for Meeting with the President," March 8, 1989, box 115, Baker Papers, Seeley Mudd Manuscript Library, Princeton University, Princeton, New Jersey (hereafter BP).

101. Jack Matlock, "The Soviet Union over the Next Four Years," in *Masterpieces of History: The Peaceful End of the Cold War in Europe, 1989*, ed. Svetlana Savranskaya, Thomas Blanton, and Vladislav Zubok (Budapest: Central European University Press, 2010), 390–96.

102. Scowcroft, "Getting Ahead of Gorbachev"; "JAB [James A. Baker] Personal Notes from 2/10–2/17/89 NATO Trip," box 108, BP.

103. Brent Scowcroft, "Scope Paper—Your Trip to Europe and Participation in the NATO Summit," May 25, 1989, 91120, Scowcroft Files, GBPL. See also Author interview with Scowcroft, August 3, 2011; Philip Zelikow, "NATO Summit," April 13, 1989, CF00779, Kanter Files, GBPL.

104. Beschloss and Talbott, *At the Highest Levels*, 37.

105. Beschloss and Talbott, *At the Highest Levels*, 36–37; "JAB personal notes from 2/6/89 mtg w/POTUS & Others, WDC," box 108, BP; George Bush and Brent Scowcroft, *A World Transformed* (New York: Knopf, 1998), 56–71; "JAB notes from 4/24/89 mtg w/FRG FM Genscher & DM Stoltenberg, WDCs," box 108, BP.

106. Scowcroft, "The NATO Summit"; Zelikow, "NATO Summit"; "JAB notes from 5/15/89 re: possible initiatives for NATO summit," box 108, BP; "JAB notes from 5/19/89 mtg w/FRG DM Stoltenberg - & notes from conversation w/POTUS," box 108, BP.

107. Richard Falkenrath, *Shaping Europe's Military Order: The Origins and Consequences of the CFE Treaty* (Cambridge, MA: MIT Press, 1995), 47–48.

108. "Reaction to Shevardnadze Speech [at Ministerial Meeting in Vienna on CFE]," March 1989, box 108, BP.

109. Falkenrath, *Shaping Europe's Military Order*, 47–48.

110. For the quote, see the enclosed letters to foreign heads of state that accompany Arnold Kanter, "NATO Summit CFE Proposal—President Letters," May 24, 1989, CF00779, Kanter Files, GBPL. See also Bush and Scowcroft, *World Transformed*, 73–74; Scowcroft, "Scope Paper—Your Trip to Europe."

111. Barry R. Posen, "Measuring the European Conventional Balance: Coping with Complexity in Threat Assessment," *International Security* 9, no. 3 (December 1984): 47–88.

112. Scowcroft, "Scope Paper—Your Trip to Europe." See also Bush and Scowcroft, *World Transformed*, 64–66; Baker, *Politics of Diplomacy*, 92.

NOTES TO PAGES 131–133

113. Baker, *Politics of Diplomacy*, 93. See also Robert Hutchings, *American Diplomacy and the End of the Cold War* (Washington, DC: Woodrow Wilson Center Press, 1997), 54.

114. Quotes are from Bush and Scowcroft, *World Transformed*, 38–39 and 43, respectively.

115. Gates, *From the Shadows*, 464. See also Scowcroft, "Scope Paper—Your Trip to Europe"; University of Virginia Miller Center, "Interview with Robert M. Gates," July 23–24, 2000, 24, https://millercenter.org/the-presidency/presidential-oral-histories/robert-m-gates-deputy-director-central.

116. Hutchings, *American Diplomacy*, 36–37.

117. Scowcroft, "Getting Ahead of Gorbachev."

118. Bush and Scowcroft, *World Transformed*, 39. See also "JAB personal notes from 2/10/89 mtg w/POTUS & Canada PM Mulroney, Ottawa, Canada," box 108, BP.

119. University of Virginia Miller Center, "Interview with Brent Scowcroft," November 12-13, 1999, 51, https://millercenter.org/the-presidency/presidential-oral-histories/brent-scowcroft-oral-history-national-security-advisor. See also George Bush, "National Security Review 3: Comprehensive Review of U.S.-Soviet Relations," February 15, 1989, https://bush41library.tamu.edu/archives/nsr.

120. Igor Lukes, "Central Europe Has Joined NATO: The Continuing Search for a More Perfect Habsburg Empire," *SAIS Review* 19, no. 2 (Summer–Fall 1999): 53–54. Transcripts of Kissinger's conversations with Soviet leaders are in *Masterpieces of History*, 341–46.

121. Quoted in Thomas Friedman, "Baker, Outlining World View, Assesses Plan for Soviet Bloc," *New York Times*, March 28, 1989. See also Beschloss and Talbott, *Highest Levels*, 19–20; Peter Rodman, " 'Kissinger Plan' for Central Europe," March 14, 1989, 91124, Scowcroft Files, GBPL.

122. Robert Hutchings, "National Security Council Meeting on Western Europe and Eastern Europe, April 4, 2:45 P.M.–4:15 P.M., Cabinet Room," April 3, 1989, box 90000, NSC Meeting Files, GBPL; Domber, *Empowering Revolution*, 225–26; Walter Isaacson, *Kissinger: A Biography* (New York: Simon & Schuster, 1992), 727–28.

123. Wiktor Osiatynski, "The Roundtable Talks in Poland," in *The Roundtable Talks and the Breakdown of Communism*, ed. Jon Elster (Chicago: University of Chicago Press, 1996), 21–68; Rudolf L. Tökés, *Hungary's Negotiated Revolution: Economic Reform, Social Change and Political Succession* (Cambridge: Cambridge University Press, 1996), 305–29. A good discussion of the Hungarian and Polish reforms can be found in Gale Stokes, *The Walls Came Tumbling Down: The Collapse of Communism in Eastern Europe* (New York: Oxford University Press, 1993).

124. The White House considered several versions of a statement to respond to the Roundtable Accords. See "Presidential Statement Supporting Democracy in Poland Option 1: Forward Looking" and "Presidential Statement Supporting Democracy in Poland Option 1I: Moderate," both unsigned and undated, CF00716, Rice Files, GBPL. For the final version, see Robert Blackwill and Peter Rodman, "Presidential Pronouncements on Poland and Eastern Europe," April 4, 1990, and accompanying statements, CF00206, Rodman Files, GBPL.

125. George Bush, "The President's News Conference," April 7, 1989, in Peters and Woolley, "The American Presidency Project," http://www.presidency.ucsb.edu/ws/index.php?pid=16894&st=Poland&st1.

126. Bush and Scowcroft, *World Transformed*, 52. See also "JAB notes from 5/15/89 re: possible initiatives for NATO summit."

127. USMission USNATO, "Presentation by DAS Simon at April 13 NAC on Poland," April 14, 1989, box 35, Soviet Flashpoints Collection, National Security Archive, George Washington University, Washington, DC (hereafter Soviet Flashpoints, NSA).

128. Brent Scowcroft, "Letter from General Jaruzelski," July 8, 1989, and enclosure from Wojtech Jaruzelski, June 30, 1989, 91124, Scowcroft Files, GBPL; John Tagliabue, "Poland to Seek Debt Aid in Wake of Bush Pledge," *New York Times*, April 24, 1989; "Issue Paper—Poland: Economic Problems and Prospects," unsigned and undated [circa July 1989], CF00189, Deal Files, GBPL; "Issue Paper—The Hungarian Economy: Problems & Prospects," unsigned and undated [circa July 1989], CF00189, Deal Files, GBPL.

129. Memcon, Conversation with Prime Minister Mulroney of Canada, July 6, 1989, https://bush41library.tamu.edu/files/memcons-telcons/1989-07-06—Mulroney.pdf.

130. "Proposed Agenda for Meeting with the President," June 7, 1989, box 115, BP; "Proposed Agenda for Meeting with the President," June 21, 1989, box 115, BP; The President's News Conference with Journalists from the Economic Summit Countries, July 6, 1989, https://bush41library.tamu.edu/archives/public-papers/637; Henry Kamm, "Bush Extends Support for Hungary and Offers Modest Aid," *New York Times*, July 13, 1989. The United States also expressed support for Polish debt restructuring, but there was no movement on this issue into the fall of 1989; Robert Blackwill, "Strategy toward Poland and Hungary," September 19, 1989 and enclosure, "Key Elements of a Successful US Program for Poland," 91124, Scowcroft Files, GBPL.

131. Bush and Scowcroft, *World Transformed*, 114. See also Peter Rodman, "Eastern Europe: Why Is Gorbachev Permitting This?," August 8, 1989, 91124, Scowcroft Files, GBPL.

132. Amembassy Warsaw, "Poland Looks to President Bush," June 27, 1989, box 34, Soviet Flashpoints, NSA.

133. Domber, *Empowering Revolution*, 235–36.

134. Domber, *Empowering Revolution*, 236–37. For the connection between domestic events in Pact member states and Soviet policy, see Brent Scowcroft, "Repudiating the Brezhnev Doctrine," June 20, 1989, 91117, Scowcroft Files, GBPL.

135. For Poland's political fragility, strategic importance, and receptivity to U.S. initiatives, see Amembassy Warsaw, "Poland Looks to President Bush."

136. Gregory F. Domber, "Skepticism and Stability: Reevaluating U.S. Policy during Poland's Democratic Transformation in 1989," *Journal of Cold War Studies* 13, no. 3 (Summer 2011): 70–71. See also Amembassy Warsaw, "How to Elect Jaruzelski without Voting for Him, and Will He Run?," June 23, 1989, http://www.gwu.edu/~nsarchiv/NSAEBB/NSAEBB42/.

137. Bush and Scowcroft, *World Transformed*, 117.

138. Memcon, "Bilateral Meeting with Wojciech Jaruzelski, Chairman of Poland," July 10, 1989, https://bush41library.tamu.edu/files/memcons-telcons/1989-07-10—Jaruzelski.pdf.

139. Amembassy Warsaw, "Conversation with General Kiszcak," August 11, 1989, http://www.gwu.edu/~nsarchiv/NSAEBB/NSAEBB42/Doc6.pdf; SecState, "Solidarity-Government Dialogue," August 12, 1989, http://www.gwu.edu/~nsarchiv/NSAEBB/NSAEBB42/Doc7.pdf.

140. Domber, "Skepticism and Stability," 75.

141. Author interviews with an anonymous NSC official, July 12, 2012, and Raymond Seitz, October 27, 2011.

142. Quoted in Bush and Scowcroft, *World Transformed*, 115.

143. Robert Blackwell, "July Warning and Forecast Report," July 21, 1989, CF00206, Rodman Files, GBPL.

144. Peter Rodman, "Why Is Gorbachev Permitting This?," July 28, 1989, 91124, Scowcroft Files, GBPL.

145. Author interview with Scowcroft, August 3, 2011. See also author interview with Seitz, October 27, 2011; Hutchings, *American Diplomacy*, 60–61.

146. George Bush, "The President's News Conference with Journalists from the Economic Summit Countries," July 6, 1989, in Peters and Woolley, "The American Presidency Project," http://www.presidency.ucsb.edu/ws/index.php?pid=17246.

147. Memcon, "Meeting with Jaruzelski," July 10, 1989.

148. Memcon, "Meeting with Francois Mitterrand, President of France," July 13, 1989, https://bush41library.tamu.edu/files/memcons-telcons/1989-07-13—Mitterrand.pdf.

149. Bush and Scowcroft, *World Transformed*, 137.

150. Raymond Seitz, "The Future of Germany in a Fast Changing Europe," October 10, 1990, box 38, Soviet Flashpoints, NSA.

151. For the importance of the German question earlier in the Cold War, see Marc Trachtenberg, *A Constructed Peace: The Making of the European Settlement, 1945–1963* (Princeton, NJ: Princeton University Press, 1999); James McAllister, *No Exit: America and the German Problem, 1943–1954* (Ithaca, NY: Cornell University Press, 2002).

152. Scowcroft, "Scope Paper—Your Trip to Europe."

153. "JAB notes from 5/15/89 re: possible initiatives for NATO summit."

154. "JAB notes from 5/15/89 re: possible initiatives for NATO summit." See also Brent Scowcroft, "Dealing with the Germans," August 7, 1989, CF01354, Zelikow Files, GBPL.

155. Philip Zelikow and Condoleezza Rice, *Germany Unified and Europe Transformed* (Cambridge, MA: Harvard University Press, 1995), 87–88.

156. Mary Sarotte, *1989: The Struggle to Create Post–Cold War Europe* (Princeton, NJ: Princeton University Press, 2009), 35–47.

157. Seitz, "The Future of Germany."

158. Miller Center, "Interview with Scowcroft," 81; see also Bush and Scowcroft, *World Transformed*, 147–48; Gates, *From the Shadows*, 483–84.

159. Seitz, "The Future of Germany."

160. See, for example, George Bush, "The President's News Conference," October 31, 1989, in Peters and Woolley, "The American Presidency Project," http://www.presidency.ucsb.edu /ws/index.php?pid=17724&st=Germany&st1=, and "The President's News Conference," November 7, 1989, in Peters and Woolley, "The American Presidency Project," http://www .presidency.ucsb.edu/ws/?pid=17762.

161. Seitz, "The Future of Germany;" CIA, "German Reunification: What Would Have to Happen?," October 11, 1989, box 38, Soviet Flashpoints, NSA.

162. Hutchings, *American Diplomacy*, 97. See also Robert Hutchings, "The German Question," November 20, 1989, and enclosure, "Handling the German Question at Malta and Beyond," CF00717, Rice Files, GBPL.

163. Zelikow and Rice, *Germany Unified and Europe Transformed*, 404n32. See also Robert Hutchings, "Paper on German Reunification," November 11, 1989, supplied via GBPL.

164. Hutchings, "German Question," enclosure.

165. The Four Powers refer to the four European victors in World War II: the United States, the Soviet Union, the United Kingdom, and France. Wartime agreements gave the Four Powers formal oversight over German security.

166. See Hutchings, "German Question," enclosure.

167. Quote is from Hutchings, "German Question," enclosure. On rejection of Four Power talks, see Sarotte, *1989*, 66–68.

168. "Head of State Correspondence—Summary" and enclosed letter, November 13, 1989, 91116, Scowcroft Files, GBPL.

169. "GDR Crisis Contingencies," unsigned [forwarded by Robert Blackwill], November 6–7, 1989, CF00182, Blackwill Files, GBPL. Author conversations with Seitz, Dobbins, Hutchings, and Scowcroft reinforced this perspective.

170. Bush and Scowcroft, *World Transformed*, 149.

171. Bush and Scowcroft, *World Transformed*, 190.

172. Hutchings, "German Question," enclosure.

173. Sarotte, *1989*, 72–75.

174. Bush and Scowcroft, *World Transformed*, 196–97; Brent Scowcroft, "Scope Paper—Your Bilateral with Chancellor Kohl," November 29, 1989, 91116, Scowcroft Files, GBPL.

175. Scowcroft, "Soviets and the German Question."

176. Joshua R. Itzkowitz Shifrinson, "The Malta Summit and US-Soviet Relations: Testing the Waters amidst Stormy Seas," Cold War International History Project e-Dossier 40, July 2013, https://www.wilsoncenter.org/publication/the-malta-summit-and-us-soviet-relations -testing-the-waters-amidst-stormy-seas.

177. Scowcroft, "Soviets and the German Question." Similarly, the CIA concluded that pressure for GDR reforms could result in "anti-Soviet violence . . . that might force [the Soviet Union] to intervene militarily." See Directorate of Intelligence, "The German Question and Soviet Policy," November 27, 1989, https://www.cia.gov/library/readingroom/docs/DOC_0000515565.pdf.

178. James A. Baker III, "Your December Meeting with Gorbachev," November 29, 1989, http://www.gwu.edu/~nsarchiv/NSAEBB/NSAEBB298/Document%206.pdf. Although the United States had long espoused the principle of reunification, it had also avoided specific commitments on the timing and operationalization of this goal; see Seitz, "Future of Germany."

179. Memcon, "First Restricted Bilateral Session with Chairman Gorbachev of the Soviet Union," December 2, 1989, C00769, Kanter Files, GBPL.

180. Brent Scowcroft, "The Future of Perestroika and the European Order," undated [circa December 1, 1989, CF00717, Rice Files, GBPL.

181. Memcon, "Meeting with Helmut Kohl, Chancellor of the Federal Republic of Germany," December 3, 1989, https://bush41library.tamu.edu/files/memcons-telcons/1989-12-03—Kohl .pdf.

182. Zelikow and Rice, *Germany Unified and Europe Transformed*, 132–33; "President's Afternoon Intervention on the Future of Europe," unsigned, December 4, 1989, CF00770, Kanter Files, GBPL.

183. Alexander Moens, "American Diplomacy and German Unification," *Survival* 33, no. 6 (November 1991): 533–36.

184. Zelikow and Rice, *Germany Unified and Europe Transformed*, 133–34.

185. Zelikow and Rice, *Germany Unified and Europe Transformed*, 136.

186. Quote is from Hutchings, *American Diplomacy*, 101. See also Zelikow and Rice, *Germany Unified and Europe Transformed*, 135.

187. Zelikow and Rice, *Germany Unified and Europe Transformed*, 140; Hutchings, *American Diplomacy*, 102–3; Bush and Scowcroft, *World Transformed*, 202.

188. Scowcroft, "Soviets and the German Question."

189. Sarotte, *1989*, 80–81.

190. USMission Berlin, "Four-Power Talks on Berlin Initiative," December 11, 1989, CF00206, Rodman Files, GBPL.

191. Brent Scowcroft, "U.S. Diplomacy for the New Europe," December 22, 1989, 91116, Scowcroft Files, GBPL.

192. Harvey Sicherman, "Disquieting Signs in U.S. Policy," January 4, 1990, box 176, BP. See also Robert Blackwill, "1990," January 19, 1990, CF00182, Blackwill Files, GBPL.

193. Author interview with James Dobbins, November 14, 2011.

194. Robert Hutchings, "Responding to a Soviet Call for a Peace Conference" and enclosure, "Responding to a Soviet Call for a Peace Conference," undated, CF01414, Hutchings Files, GBPL. For dating of the document, see Hutchings, *American Diplomacy*, 385n56; Zelikow and Rice, *Germany Unified and Europe Transformed*, 415n9.

195. This is not intended to minimize other elements in U.S.-Soviet relations, but to acknowledge that issues related to arms control and other aspects of U.S.-Soviet diplomacy were means to reinforce the deals surrounding German reunification. See Brent Scowcroft, "Objectives for U.S.-Soviet Relations in 1990," January 13, 1990, 30547, Blackwill Files, GBPL; Zelikow and Rice, *Germany Unified and Europe Transformed*, 168–72; Bush and Scowcroft, *World Transformed*, 206–11.

196. CIA, "Special Analysis: Four Power Talks and Reunification," January 5, 1990, box 35, Soviet Flashpoints, NSA.

197. In mid-January, for example, Kohl announced plans to accelerate the pace of reunification and called for early GDR elections that were expected to return a pro-reunification government. See Sarotte, *1989*, 99–100; Douglas Mulholland, "German Unity: Kohl Escalates His Demands," January 22, 1990, box 35, Soviet Flashpoints, NSA.

198. Zelikow and Rice, *Germany Unified and Europe Transformed*, 159–60; Hutchings, *American Diplomacy*, 107–8.

199. "Meeting of the National Security Council," January 16, 1990, NSC Meeting Files, 90001, GBPL.

200. Robert Hutchings, "Your Breakfast with Kissinger: Managing the German Question," January 26, 1990, CF00182, Blackwill Files, GBPL.

201. Scowcroft, "Objectives."

202. For Cheney's comment, see "Meeting of the National Security Council," January 16, 1990. Bush noted in the same meeting that American arms control initiatives needed to better account for "the political pressures in Eastern Europe to reduce" Soviet forces.

203. Scowcroft, "Objectives."

204. Quoted in Zelikow and Rice, *Germany Unified and Europe Transformed*, 160.

205. Condoleezza Rice, "Showdown in Moscow?," February 1, 1990, CF00719, Rice Files, GBPL.

206. Hutchings, "Your Breakfast with Kissinger." For possible Soviet intervention, see Hutchings, "Responding to a Soviet Call" and enclosure; CIA, "East/West Germany: What Could Derail Reunification?," January 30, 1990, supplied to author by GBPL.

207. Rice, "Showdown in Moscow?"

208. Scowcroft, "Objectives."

209. Robert Blackwill, "Germany," January 30, 1990, and enclosure, "A Strategy for German Unification," 900092, NSC PA Files, GBPL; Hutchings, "Your Breakfast with Kissinger."

210. National Intelligence Council (hereafter NIC), "Main Soviet Objectives for the Moscow Summit," NIC 0116/90, February 2, 1990, https://www.cia.gov/library/readingroom/docs/DOC_0001325093.pdf; Vladislav Zubok, "With his Back against the Wall: Gorbachev, Soviet Demise, and German Reunification," *Cold War History* 14, no. 4 (October 2014): 629–30; Zelikow and Rice, *Germany Unified and Europe Transformed*, 150–51, 204–5.

211. Scowcroft, "Strategy for German Unification."

212. Memcon, "Secretary Baker, President Gorbachev, Eduard Shevardnadze," February 9, 1990, box 38, Soviet Flashpoints, NSA.

213. Memcon, "Telephone Call to Chancellor Helmut Kohl of the Federal Republic of Germany," February 13, 1990 (3 P.M. conversation), https://bush41library.tamu.edu/files/memcons-telcons/1990-02-13—Kohl%20[2].pdf.

214. Brent Scowcroft, "Preparing for the Six Power German Peace Conference," undated [circa February 14, 1990], CF00716, Rice Files, GBPL. For the origins and dating of the document, see Condoleezza Rice, "Preparing for the German Peace Conference," February 14, 1990, CF00182, Blackwill Files, GBPL.

215. Robert Zoellick, "Two Plus Four: Advantages, Possible Concerns, and Rebuttal Points," February 21, 1990, box 38, Soviet Flashpoints, NSA.

216. Frederic Bozo, *Mitterrand, the End of the Cold War, and German Unification*, trans. Susan Emanuel (New York: Berghahn, 2009), 174–76. For British policy, see *Documents on British Policy Overseas, Series 3, Volume 7: German Unification, 1989–1990*, ed. Patrick Salmon, Keith Hamilton, and Stephen R. Twigge (London: Routledge, 2010).

217. Brent Scowcroft, "Meetings with German Chancellor Helmut Kohl," February 24–25, 1990, CF00774, Kanter Files, GBPL.

218. Scowcroft, "Meetings with Kohl."

219. Memcon, "Meeting with Helmut Kohl, Chancellor of the Federal Republic of Germany," February 24, 1990, https://bush41library.tamu.edu/files/memcons-telcons/1990-02-24—Kohl.pdf.

220. Zelikow and Rice, *Germany Unified and Europe Transformed*, 214–15; Zoellick, "Two Plus Four."

221. Zelikow and Rice, *Germany Unified and Europe Transformed*, 223–30, 246–47; Robert Zoellick, "Quad Meeting Discussion of German Unification and Two-Plus-Four," undated [circa March 13, 1990], CF00721, Rice Files, GBPL; Philip Zelikow, "Readout on March 13 Meeting between US, UK, French, and FRG Representatives for March 14 Two Plus Four Discussion," March 13, 1990, CF00721, Rice Files, GBPL; B. P. Hall, "Security Issues in the Two-Plus-Four," April 5, 1990, CF00182, Blackwill Files, GBPL. For the U.S. focus on maintaining Western unity, see Brent Scowcroft, "The First Round of Two Plus Four Deliberations on German Unification," undated [circa March 14, 1990], CF00721, Rice Files, GBPL. For more on delaying the Two Plus Four discussions, see Robert Blackwill, "State Department Paper on Two Plus Four Talks," February 23, 1990 and enclosure, "Managing 'Two-Plus-Four' Consultations on German Unification," undated, CF00182, Blackwill Files, GBPL; Philip Zelikow, "Discussions with State on Plans for Two Plus Four Meeting on March 14," March 9, 1990, CF00182, Blackwill Files, GBPL; SecState, "Two Plus Four—Soviets Look to Ministerial and Summit; Bondarenko Takes Lead in Berlin," April 27, 1990, available via www.foia.state.gov.

222. Zelikow and Rice, *Germany Unified and Europe Transformed*, 246.

223. "Points to Be Made for Telephone Conversation with Prime Minister Thatcher of the United Kingdom," undated [before the February meeting with Kohl], 91116, Scowcroft Files, GBPL.

224. Hall, "Security Issues in the Two-Plus-Four."

225. Philip Zelikow, "The Two Plus Four Agenda," March 12, 1990, Doc. No. 9001938, NSC PA Files, GBPL; Roger George, "The Two-Plus-Four Tightrope," March 12, 1990, CF00712, Rice Files, GBPL.

226. Memcon, "Meeting with Prime Minister Margaret Thatcher of Great Britain," April 13, 1990, https://bush41library.tamu.edu/files/memcons-telcons/1990-04-13—Thatcher.pdf. For more on efforts to limit the Two Plus Four mandate, see Zelikow, "Readout on the March 13, Meeting"; Condoleezza Rice, "Memorandum for the President on On the One Plus Three Officials Level Meeting," April 18, 1990, and enclosure, "Officials-Level Meeting of the 'One Plus Three' on German Unification," undated, CF00721, Rice Files, GBPL.

227. Harvey Sicherman, "Our European Strategy: Next Steps," March 12, 1990, box 176, BP.

228. Seitz, "Future of Germany."

229. Scowcroft, "Preparing for the Six Power German Peace Conference."

230. Robert Blackwill, "The Beginning of the Big Game," February 7, 1990, CF00182, Blackwill Files, GBPL.

231. Memcon, "Meeting with Douglas Hurd, Foreign Secretary of the United Kingdom," January 29, 1990, https://bush41library.tamu.edu/files/memcons-telcons/1990-01-29—Hurd.pdf.

232. This quote is found in a draft of a letter from Bush to Kohl, enclosed with Robert Blackwill, "Message to Kohl," February 8, 1990, CF00182, Blackwill Files, GBPL. See also Memcon, "Second One-on-One, the Secretary, Eduard Shevardnadze," February 9, 1990, box 38, Soviet Flashpoints, NSA.

233. Bush letter to Kohl, February 8. See also Memcon, "Telephone Conversation with Brian Mulroney, Prime Minister of Canada," February 24, 1990, https://bush41library.tamu.edu/files/memcons-telcons/1990-02-24—Mulroney.pdf.

234. George Bush, "Address before a Joint Session of the Congress on the State of the Union," January 31, 1990, in Peters and Woolley, "The American Presidency Project," http://www.presidency.ucsb.edu/ws/index.php?pid=18095. For background on the cuts and their logic, see Gates, *From the Shadows*, 486–88; "Meeting of the National Security Council," January 16, 1990; "Meeting with Douglas Hurd," January 29, 1990; Memcon, "Telephone Call with Chancellor Helmut Kohl of the Federal Republic of Germany," January 26, 1990, https://bush41library.tamu.edu/files/memcons-telcons/1990-01-26—Kohl.pdf.

235. Falkenrath, *Shaping Europe's Military Order*, 63–64.

236. Sicherman, "Our European Strategy."

237. This analysis is my own. For discussions along these lines, see Scowcroft, "Preparing for the Six Power Peace Conference" and "Meetings with Kohl."

238. Zelikow and Rice, *Germany Unified and Europe Transformed*, 174–75; Scowcroft, "Strategy for German Unification."

239. Joshua R. Itzkowitz Shifrinson, "Deal or No Deal? The End of the Cold War and the U.S. Offer to Limit NATO Enlargement," *International Security* 40, no. 4 (Spring 2016): 22–24.

240. Itzkowitz Shifrinson, "Deal or No Deal?," 23–25.

241. Department of State, Press Release, "Press Conference of James Baker III Following U.S.-USSR Ministerial Meetings, Moscow, USSR, February 9, 1990," PR No. 14, February 16, 1990, box 161, BP. See also Zelikow and Rice, *Germany Unified and Europe Transformed*, 184.

242. For iterations of the "special military status" offer, see Itzkowitz Shifrinson, "Deal or No Deal?," 25–27.

243. Memcon, "Telephone Conversation with Brian Mulroney, Prime Minister of Canada," February 24, 1990, https://bush41library.tamu.edu/files/memcons-telcons/1990-02-24—Mulroney.pdf.

244. "Points to be Made in Telephone Calls with Foreign Leaders," unsigned and undated, enclosed with Philip Zelikow, "Talking Points for Presidential Calls to Foreign Leaders about His Meetings with Chancellor Kohl," February 26, 1990, CF00182, Blackwill Files, GBPL. See also Memcon, "Meeting with Kohl," February 24, 1990; Memcon, "Meeting with Helmut Kohl, Chancellor of the Federal Republic of Germany," February 25, 1990, https://bush41library.tamu.edu/files/memcons-telcons/1990-02-25—Kohl.pdf.

245. Scowcroft, "Meetings with Kohl."

246. Memcon, "Meeting with Kohl," February 25, 1990. Nonetheless, the United States continued to suggest that NATO non-expansion remained on the table in talks with the Soviets; see Itzkowitz Shifrinson, "Deal or No Deal?"

247. Itzkowitz Shifrinson, "Deal or No Deal?," 37–39.

248. Memcon, "Meeting with Kohl," February 24, 1990.

249. USDel Secretary Namibia, "My Meeting with Soviet Foreign Minister Shevardnadze," March 20, 1990, available via http://foia.state.gov; Baker, *Politics of Diplomacy*, 235–36; Raymond Seitz, "CSCE 'Institutionalization and the U.S.-Soviet and NATO Summits," May 16, 1990, box 38, Soviet Flashpoints, NSA; CIA, "USSR: Developing a Game Plan for Six-Power Meetings on German Unification," SOV 90-10014, March 1990, https://www.cia.gov/library/readingroom/docs/DOC_0000499179.

250. Shevardnadze's comments were routed by Robert Blackwill to Robert Gates and Brent Scowcroft; see "Shevardnadze Intervention at Two-Plus-Four Ministerial, May 5, 1990," CF01354, Zelikow Files, GBPL. See also NIC, "Primary Soviet Objectives for the Summit," NIC 00562/90, May 24, 1990, https://www.cia.gov/library/readingroom/docs/DOC_0001325087.pdf.

251. Zelikow and Rice, *Germany Unified and Europe Transformed*, 242–46.

252. "Talking Points on Ministerial for Cabinet Meeting," April 9, 1990, box 108, BP.

253. Baker, *Politics of Diplomacy*, 248–54. See also SecState, "Message to Foreign Minister Genscher," May 9, 1990, available through http://foia.state.gov; "Shevardnadze Intervention," May 5, 1990; Zelikow and Rice, *Germany Unified and Europe Transformed*, 248–54.

254. James Dobbins, "The Kohl-Genscher Visit," May 18, 1990, CF00721, Rice Files, GBPL.

255. See, for example, G. John Ikenberry, *After Victory: Institutions, Strategic Restraint, and the Rebuilding of Power after Major Wars* (Princeton, NJ: Princeton University Press, 2001), 230; Andrew Kydd, *Trust and Mistrust in International Politics* (Princeton, NJ: Princeton University Press, 2005), 237–38.

256. F. Miles, "Evolving Soviet Position on Germany," June 13, 1990 [included with briefing book for Baker dated June 20-23], CF01010, NSC European and Soviet Directorate Files, GBPL.

257. Even U.S. pledges to help develop German-Soviet economic relations involved minimal U.S. costs, as U.S. officials assiduously avoided incurring any economic commitments to the Soviet Union. See Memcon, "Meeting with Kohn," February 24; Memcon (draft), "President's Meeting and Dinner with Chancellor Kohl on June 8," CF01413, Hutchings Files, GBPL.

258. Baker's marginalia on Zoellick, "Two Plus Four." See also comments by Zoellick, Baker, and Seitz in "Notes from Jim Cicconi re: 7/3/90 pre-NATO Summit briefing at Kennebunkport," box 109, BP. For U.S. ambivalence regarding Soviet concerns and U.S. strategy, see also Robert Zoellick, "German Unification—Two Plus Four Process," May 25, 1990, CF01414, Hutchings Files, GBPL.

259. Memcon, "Secretary Baker, Mikhail Gorbachev, Eduard Shevardnadze," May 18, 1990, 91127, Scowcroft Files, GBPL.

260. Sarotte, *1989*, 167.

261. Bush and Scowcroft, *World Transformed*, 273, 276–77. See also NIC, "Primary Soviet Objectives"; Douglas P. Mulholland, "Gorbachev's Summit Agenda: Looking Ahead," May 23, 1990, available through http://foia.state.gov.

262. "Economic Aid for the USSR—The $20 Billion Question," unsigned, May 25, 1990, CF01309, Burns Files, GBPL. This document appears to have been part of a late May 1990 briefing for Bush and his top advisors regarding aid to the Soviet Union; see Brent Scowcroft, "Briefing on Strategic Choices," May 29, 1990, CF01309, Burns Files, GBPL.

263. Zelikow and Rice, *Germany Unified and Europe Transformed*, 300. See also Memcon, "Baker, Gorbachev, Shevardnadze," May 18, 1990.

264. Brent Scowcroft, "The President's Meeting with Congressional Leaders on June 5, at 9:00 A.M.," and enclosure, "Points to be Made on US-Soviet Summit for Meeting with Congressional Leaders," June 5, 1990, 91118, Scowcroft Files, GBPL; George Bush, "Remarks on the Waiver of Jackson-Vanik Amendment and on Economic Assistance to the Soviet Union," December 12, 1990, in Peters and Woolley, "The American Presidency Project," http://www.presidency.ucsb.edu/ws/?pid=19152; "White House Fact Sheet on the Waiver of the Jackson-Vanik Amendment," December 12, 1990, in Peters and Woolley, "The American Presidency Project," http://www.presidency.ucsb.edu/ws/?pid=19153. Although some lending restrictions were eventually lifted in December 1990, total lending was capped at $300 million.

265. Memcon, "Telephone Call from Chancellor Helmut Kohl of the Federal Republic of Germany," May 30, 1990, https://bush41library.tamu.edu/files/memcons-telcons/1990-05

-30—Kohl.pdf; Memcon, "Bilateral Meeting with German Chancellor Helmut Kohl," July 9, 1990, https://bush41library.tamu.edu/files/memcons-telcons/1990-07-09—Kohl.pdf.

266. Memcon, "First Main Plenary Session of the 16th Economic Summit of Industrialized Nations," July 10 1990, https://bush41library.tamu.edu/files/memcons-telcons/1990-07-10—Mitterrand%20[1].pdf. See also "Aid to USSR," unsigned [appear to be Baker's personal notes], July 9, 1990, box 109, BP.

267. Brent Scowcroft, "Points to be made on NATO and Economic Summits at Bipartisan Congressional Leadership Meeting, June [sic] 12, 1990," July 11, 1990, 91120, Scowcroft Files, GBPL. That said, the Kohl government had agreed earlier that spring to help the Soviet Union obtain West German financial credits in order to expedite German reunification; Bush's efforts focused on blocking additional assistance to the Soviet Union. For the West German-Soviet deal, see Sarotte, *1989*, 154–60.

268. Hutchings, *American Diplomacy*, 137–39; Sarotte, *1989*, 177–86.

269. Zeikow and Rice, *Germany Unified and Europe Transformed*, 343.

270. Sarotte, *1989*, 190–91; Zelikow and Rice, *Germany Unified and Europe Transformed*, 356; Robert Hutchings, "German Unification: New Problems at End-Game," August 27, 1990, CF01414, Hutchings Files, GBPL.

271. Sarotte, *1989*, 190–94.

272. Gates, *From the Shadows*, 501–2.

273. Bush, "Waiver of Jackson-Vanik"; James A. Baker III, "U.S. Economic Support-Assistance for the Soviet Union," December 7, 1990, 91119, Scowcroft Files, GBPL.

274. Bush and Scowcroft, *World Transformed*, 502–3.

275. On calls for U.S. intervention, see Gates, *From the Shadows*, 501–4; Jack F. Matlock, *Autopsy on an Empire: The American Ambassador's Account of the Collapse of the Soviet Union* (New York: Random House, 1995), 449–522. Yeltsin became President of the Russian Socialist Republic in July 1991.

276. Bush and Scowcroft, *World Transformed*, 500. See also Memcon, "Meeting with Francois Mitterrand, President of France," March 14, 1991, https://bush41library.tamu.edu/files/memcons-telcons/1991-03-14—Mitterrand.pdf; Condoleezza Rice, "Responding to Moscow," January 21, 1991, CF00718, Rice Files, GBPL. For discussion of constraining U.S. involvement in Soviet internal politics later in 1991, see Matlock, *Autopsy on an Empire*, 562–71; "Points to be Made for Meeting with Ukrainian Chairman Leonid Kravchuk," unsigned and undated [included with briefing packet for Bush's visit to the Soviet Union in July-August 1991], CF01308, Burns Files, GBPL.

277. Condoleezza Rice, "Coping with the Soviet Union's Internal Turmoil," and enclosure to The President, undated [routing slip dated March 7, 1991], 91119, Scowcroft Files, GBPL. See also Gates, *From the Shadows*, 502.

278. Rice, "Coping," enclosure. For a similar argument on the need to continue conducting business with the Soviet central government despite Soviet internal unrest, see Rice, "Responding to Moscow."

279. "Contingency Group Workplan," unsigned [likely Ed Hewett] and undated, Burns and Hewett Files, CF01599, "Policy Group Meetings 1991 [1]," GBPL. The report's content indicates that it originated circa October–November 1991.

280. For U.S. efforts to communicate conditions, see "JAB Notes from 10/2/91 mtg w/Gen. Scowcroft, Sec. Cheney, The White House," October 2, 1991, box 110, BP; Arnie [Kanter] to the Secretary [of State], October 1, 1991, untitled letter on nuclear initiatives found on the back of a document titled, "JAB Notes from 9/27/91 mtgs. w/UK, France, Germany; Soviet FM Pankin; NATO, Japan, Republic of Korea, Australia re: POTUS speech on Defense Strategy," October 1, 1991, box 110, BP; "The Debate over a Successor (or Successors) to the USSR: Possible Outcomes, U.S. Influence over Those Outcomes, and Contingent Responses (Draft 1)," unsigned, October 7, 1991, CF01599, Burns and Hewett Files, GBPL; Baker, *Politics of Diplomacy*, 525, 531–36, 560–64; "JAB Notes from 11/15/91 Meetings with PRC Officials," box 110, BP. See also Charles Stewart Kennedy, "Interview with Ambassador Thomas M. T. Niles," June 5, 1998, Association for Diplomatic Studies and Training Foreign Affairs Oral History Project, 246–50, http://www.adst.org/OH%20TOCs/Niles,%20Thomas%20M.T.toc.pdf.

281. Quoted in Gates, *From the Shadows*, 530.

282. Gates, *From the Shadows*, 529. For a related discussion, see James Goldgeier and Michael McFaul, *Power and Purpose: U.S. Policy toward Russia after the Cold War* (Washington, DC: Brookings Institution Press, 2003), 34–36. For more on nuclear issues and U.S. principles related to the Soviet breakup, see "JAB Items used during 12/13/91 briefing for WH Press Corps—Washington, D.C.," box 110, BP.

283. For an overview of Soviet requests and the U.S. response in 1991, see Jeffrey Engel, *When the World Seemed New: George H. W. Bush and the End of the Cold War* (New York: Houghton Mifflin Harcourt, 2017), 446–49.

284. "JAB Notes from 6/3/91 NSC Principals mtg on US Economic Relationship w/USSR," box 110, BP; Beschloss and Talbott, *Highest Levels*, 380–91.

285. Memorandum for the Files, "Meeting on U.S.-Soviet Economic Relations, 1:30–2:30 P.M., June 3, 1991, White House Situation Room," CF01407, Burns and Hewett Files, GBPL. For more on U.S. assistance policy at this time, see James Baker, "Proposed Agenda for Meeting with the President, June 26, 1991," box 115, BP.

286. Bush and Scowcroft, *World Transformed*, 540–41; Baker, *Politics of Diplomacy*, 527; Ed A. Hewett and Timothy E. Deal, "Proposed Presidential Letters to the London Summit Participants Concerning the Meeting with Gorbachev," July 3, 1991 and enclosed letters to G-7 leaders, CF01407, Burns and Hewett Files, GBPL; Ed A. Hewett, "Proposed Letter to President Gorbachev on the G-7 Meeting," July 10, 1991, and enclosed letter to Gorbachev, CF01407, Burns and Hewett Files, GBPL.

287. The Warsaw Pact formally dissolved in July 1991. As should be clear from the analysis, however, it had ceased functioning as a military alliance over one year prior.

288. Lorna S. Jaffe, *The Development of the Base Force, 1989–1992* (Washington, DC: Joint History Office, Office of the Chairman of the Joint Chiefs of Staff, 1993); Paul Wolfowitz, "Shaping the Future: Planning at the Pentagon, 1989–1992," in *In Uncertain Times: American Foreign Policy after the Berlin Wall and 9/11*, ed. Melvyn P. Leffler and Jeffrey Legro (Ithaca, NY: Cornell University Press, 2011), 44–62; Alexandra Homolar, "How to Last Alone at the Top: US Strategic Planning for the Unipolar Era," *Journal of Strategic Studies* 34, no. 2 (April 2011): 199–204.

289. Dale A. Vesser, "First Draft of [Defense Planning Guidance]," September 3, 1991, https://nsarchive2.gwu.edu/nukevault/ebb245/doc02.pdf.

290. Bush and Scowcroft, *World Transformed*, 543–545; Susan Koch, *The Presidential Nuclear Initiatives of 1991–1992* (Washington, DC: National Defense University, 2012).

291. Bush and Scowcroft, *World Transformed*, 544.

292. Bush and Scowcroft, *World Transformed*, 499.

293. Baker, *Politics of Diplomacy*, 475.

294. Memorandum, "Meeting on U.S.-Soviet Economic Relations."

295. Quote is from "The U.S. Response to the New Soviet Pluralism," unsigned and undated, enclosed with Brent Scowcroft, "Meeting with Secretaries Baker, Brady, Cheney RE U.S.-Soviet Relations," June 13, 1991, CF01407, Burns and Hewett Files, GBPL.

296. Bush and Scowcroft, *World Transformed*, 543. See also Lawrence Eagleburger, "Your Visit to the USSR," July 25, 1991, CF01308, Burns Files, GBPL.

297. Vesser, "First Draft."

298. Eagleburger, "Your Visit to the USSR."

299. Eagleburger aptly captured the issue, writing Bush in July 1991 that "the outcome of this internal struggle of the [Soviet Union's] political and economic fate has become our dominant foreign policy concern." See Eagleburger, "Your Visit to the USSR."

300. Gates, *From the Shadows*, 528.

301. CIA Directorate of Intelligence, "The Gorbachev Succession," April 29, 1991, CF01486, Burns Files, GBPL. For the NSC's commissioning of and reactions to the report, see David Gompert and Ed Hewett, "The Gorbachev Succession," April 10, 1991, CF01486, Burns Files, GBPL; Nicholas Burns, "Report on Gorbachev Succession," April 30, 1991, CF01486, Burns Files, GBPL. For previous assessments, see Rice, "Coping"; Brent Scowcroft, Responding to the Toughening Line in Moscow," December 21, 1990, 91119, Scowcroft Files, GBPL.

302. Quotes are from, respectively, Gates, *From the Shadows*, 528, and "JAB Notes from 9/4/91 Cabinet Meeting w/GB, The White House, Washington, DC," September 4, 1991, box 110, BP.

See also Bush and Scowcroft, *World Transformed*, 541–43. On hard-liners' prospects in a conflict, see Rice, "Coping."

303. Gates, *From the Shadows*, 521.

304. Gates, *From the Shadows*, 529. My conversations with Bob Hutchings and Nicholas Burns reinforced this assessment. See also "JAB Notes from 9/4/91 Cabinet Meeting;" Marginalia on the NSC copy of National Intelligence Officer/USSR, "The Gathering Storm," October 24, 1991, CF01498, Burns Files, GBPL; "Debate over a Successor (or Successors) to the USSR;" Kennedy, "Interview with Niles," 234–35. Note, too, that U.S. policy by September–October 1991 was also influenced by questions over whether prospective successor states to the Soviet Union could be entrusted with nuclear weapons.

305. CIA, "Yel'tsin's Game Plan," August 31, 1991, https://www.cia.gov/library/readingroom/docs/DOC_0000588091.pdf; CIA, "Breakup of the Empire," August 26, 1991, https://www.cia.gov/library/readingroom/docs/DOC_0000588090.pdf; Serhii Plokhy, *The Last Empire* (New York: Basic Books, 2014), 323–24.

306. CIA, *Handbook of International Economic Statistics, 1992* (Washington, DC: Government Printing Office, 1992), 59, table 31; Plokhy, *Last Empire*, 295–343.

307. Bush and Scowcroft, *World Transformed*, 542–59; Gates, *From the Shadows*, 529–31.

308. "JAB Notes from 11/15/91 meetings with PRC officials."

309. Memorandum for the Files, "Meeting on U.S.-Soviet Economic Relations, 1:30–2:30 P.M., June 3, 1991, White House Situation Room," CF01407, Burns and Hewett Files, GBPL; Memorandum, "Meeting on U.S.-Soviet Economic Relations, June 3, 1991."

Conclusion

1. For discussion of the Open Door thesis and the Reagan administration's hawkish anti-Communism, see chapters 2 and 4.

2. I use "Austria" and "Austria-Hungary" interchangeably.

3. The literature on the consequences of shifting power among Germany, Russia, and Britain is extensive. For overviews, see Paul M. Kennedy, *The Rise and Fall of the Great Powers: Economic Change and Military Conflict from 1500 to 2000* (New York: Random House, 1987); Paul M. Kennedy, *The Rise of the Anglo-German Antagonism, 1860–1914* (London: Allen and Unwin, 1980); Dale C. Copeland, *The Origins of Major War* (Ithaca, NY: Cornell University Press, 2000).

4. See, for example, W. E. Mosse, *The European Powers and the German Question, 1848–71* (New York: Octagon Books, 1958).

5. William L. Langer, *European Alliances and Alignments, 1871–1890* (New York: Vintage, 1964); A. J. P. Taylor, *The Struggle for Mastery in Europe, 1848–1918* (Oxford: Clarendon Press, 1954), 255.

6. For a recent treatment along these lines, see Jonathan Steinberg, *Bismarck: A Life* (New York: Oxford University Press, 2011).

7. Nicholas Der Bagdasarian, *The Austro-German Rapprochement: From the Battle of Sedan to the Dual Alliance* (London: Associated University Presses, 1976), 28–41.

8. Good discussions of the military balance are in Geoffrey Wawro, *The Austro-Prussian War: Austria's War with Prussia and Italy in 1866* (New York: Cambridge University Press, 1996); Michael Howard, *The Franco-Prussian War: The German Invasion of France, 1870–1871* (New York: Macmillan, 1961).

9. Wawro, *Austro-Prussian War*, 39–44; D. G. Williamson, *Bismarck and Germany: 1862–1890*, 3rd ed. (New York: Routledge, 2011), 33–35.

10. Quoted in Mosse, *European Powers*, 130.

11. Gordon A. Craig, *Germany, 1866–1945* (Oxford: Clarendon Press, 1978), 4–6; Otto Pflanze, *Bismarck and the Development of Germany: The Period of Unification, 1815–1871*, Kindle ed. (Princeton, NJ: Princeton University Press, 1971), loc. 5086–94.

12. Allan Mitchell, *Bismarck and the French Nation, 1848–1890* (New York: Pegasus, 1971), 30–61; Langer, *European Alliances and Alignments*, 3–10; Pflanze, *Bismarck*, loc. 6278–86, 6421–33.

13. Pflanze, *Bismarck*, loc. 6041–54, 6292–99.

14. Taylor, *Struggle*, 217–18, especially 217n3; W. R. Fryer, "The Republic and the Iron Chancellor: The Pattern of Franco-German Relations, 1871–1890," *Transactions of the Royal Historical Society* 29 (December 1979): 171–73.

15. Quoted in Joseph V. Fuller, "The War Scare of 1875," *American Historical Review* 24, no. 2 (January 1919): 198. See also Immanuel Geiss, *German Foreign Policy, 1871–1914* (Boston: Routledge, 1976), 18.

16. For Austrian policy in this period, see F. R. Bridge, *The Habsburg Monarchy among the Great Powers* (New York: Berg, 1990), chaps. 3–4.

17. Quoted in Mosse, *European Powers*, 227.

18. Quoted in Mosse, *European Powers*, 323.

19. Quoted in, respectively, Richard Millman, *British Foreign Policy and the Coming of the Franco-Prussian War* (New York: Oxford University Press, 1965), 20–21 note 8, and Mosse, *European Powers*, 330.

20. Quoted in T. G. Otte, *The Foreign Office Mind: The Making of British Foreign Policy, 1865–1914* (New York: Cambridge University Press, 2011), 39. See also Mosse, *European Powers*, 321–24. For expectations that the Austro-Prussian and Franco-Prussian conflicts would be costly struggles between near-equal powers, see Mosse, *European Powers*, 231, 238–40, 314–30; Millman, *British Foreign Policy*, 22–23.

21. Quoted in Langer, *European Alliances and Alignments*, 48.

22. George F. Kennan, *The Decline of Bismarck's European Order: Franco-Russian Relations, 1875–1890* (Princeton, NJ: Princeton University Press, 1979), 18–21. See also Langer, *European Alliances and Alignments*, 48–49.

23. Kennedy, *Rise and Fall*, 185–87, 215–24.

24. For an overview of Austrian problems, see A. J. P. Taylor, *The Habsburg Monarchy, 1809–1918* (Chicago: University of Chicago Press, 1976); Pieter M. Judson, *The Habsburg Empire: A New History* (Cambridge, MA: Belknap Press, 2016).

25. Bridge, *Habsburg Monarchy*, chaps. 4–6.

26. Gunther Rothenberg, *The Army of Francis Joseph* (West Lafayette, IN: Purdue University Press, 1976), 80–122. For problems after the 1880s–1890s, see Rothenberg, *Army of Francis Joseph*, 126–27. Likewise, F. R. Bridge notes that Austrian military problems only began to tell in the 1890s—meaning that the force was good enough for Austria's foreign and security needs beforehand; see F. R. Bridge, *From Sadowa to Sarajevo: The Foreign Policy of Austria-Hungary, 1866–1914* (London: Routledge, 1972), 255.

27. For French domestic politics and foreign policy, see Kennan, *Decline*; Christopher M. Andrew, *Théophile Delcassé and the Making of the Entente Cordiale: A Reappraisal of French Foreign Policy, 1898–1905* (London: Macmillan, 1968), especially chaps. 2–6.

28. On the French reforms, see Allan Mitchell, *Victors and Vanquished: The German Influence on Army and Church in France after 1870* (Chapel Hill: University of North Carolina Press, 1984), chaps. 2–4; Douglas Porch, *The March to the Marne: The French Army, 1871–1914* (New York: Cambridge University Press, 1981), chaps. 1–3; David B. Ralston, *The Army of the Republic: The Place of the Military in the Political Evolution of France, 1871–1914* (Cambridge, MA: MIT Press, 1967), 87–200. Mitchell, Porch, and Ralston all note the often incomplete nature of French reforms and France's general inability to match Germany—as the strongest European power—in all aspects of military affairs. Nevertheless, the analyses show that the reforms afforded France's leaders with a potent instrument of statecraft that, at a minimum, required other great powers to pay careful attention to French behavior. For illustration of France's influence on the other powers at this time, see Kennan, *Decline*, 247.

29. Bridge, *From Sadowa to Sarajevo*, 67–107. On the background to the alliance, see Langer, *European Alliances and Alignments*, 110.

30. Patricia Weitsman, "Intimate Enemies: The Politics of Peacetime Alliances," *Security Studies* 7, no. 1 (Autumn 1997): 171–73; Norman Stone, "Moltke-Conrad: Relations between the Austro-Hungarian and German General Staffs, 1909–1914," *Historical Journal* 9, no. 2 (January 1966): 202–3.

31. Bridge, *From Sadowa to Sarajevo*, 106–21.

32. Kennan, *Decline*, 277.

33. Langer, *European Alliances and Alignments*, 23–24, 92–93, 198–211; Bridge, *From Sadowa to Sarajevo*, 231–33; Barbara Jelavich, *Russia's Balkan Entanglements, 1806–1914* (New York: Cambridge University Press), 212–13. See also Bridge, *From Sadowa to Sarajecvo*, 243–88, for Austrian and Russian efforts to carry out the agreement.

34. Bridge, *From Sadowa to Sarajevo*, 90; Langer, *European Alliances and Alignments*, 130–37.

35. W. N. Medlicott, "The Mediterranean Agreements of 1887," *Slavonic Review* 5, no. 13 (June 1926): 73, 85–87; Frederick D. R. Shipton, "British Diplomatic Relations with Austria-Hungary and British Attitudes towards It in the Years 1885–1918," (PhD diss., University of Sussex, 2012), 66–67.

36. Bridge, *From Sadowa to Sarajevo*, 166–67.

37. Quoted in Shipton, "British Diplomatic Relations," 73.

38. F. R. Bridge, *Great Britain and Austria-Hungary, 1906–1914: A Diplomatic History* (London: London School of Economics, 1972), 2–3.

39. Quoted in Nathan N. Orgill, "Between Coercion and Conciliation: Franco-German Relations in the Bismarck Era, 1871–1890," in *A History of Franco-German Relations in Europe*, ed. Carine Germond and Henning Turk (New York: Palgrave-Macmillan, 2008), 53. See also Taylor, *Struggle*, 221–25.

40. Orgill, "Between Coercion and Conciliation," 53–57; Taylor, *Struggle*, 221–25, 260–61, 278–80, 316–17.

41. Geiss, *German Foreign Policy*, 68–71; Mark Hewitson, "Germany and France before the First World War: A Reassessment of Wilhelmine Foreign Policy," *English Historical Review* 115, no. 462 (June 2000): 578.

42. Kennan, *Decline*, 156–57, 188, 240.

43. Langer, *European Alliances and Alignments*, 385–86.

44. Quoted in Kennan, *Decline*, 156. See also V. I. Boykin "The Franco-Russian Alliance," *History* 64, no. 210 (Winter 1979): 22–23.

45. William L. Langer, "The Franco-Russian Alliance (1890–1894)," *Slavonic Review* 3, no. 9 (March 1925): 565–75; Barbara Jelavich, *A Century of Russian Foreign Policy, 1814–1914* (Philadelphia, PA: J.B. Lippincott, 1964), 213–24. Regular Franco-Russian military planning did not begin until the early 1900s. See David G. Hermann, *The Arming of Europe and the Making of the First World War* (Princeton, NJ: Princeton University Press, 1996), 60.

46. Taylor, *Struggle*, 281–303, 342–53, 379–82; T. G. Otte, "From 'War-in-Sight' to Nearly War: Anglo-French Relations in the Age of High Imperialism," *Diplomacy & Statecraft* 17, no. 6 (December 2006): 698–703; Aaron L. Friedberg, *The Weary Titan: Britain and the Experience of Relative Decline, 1895–1905* (Princeton, NJ: Princeton University Press, 1988), 146–52.

47. Joseph V. Fuller, *Bismarck's Diplomacy at Its Zenith* (Cambridge, MA: Harvard University Press, 1922), 137–42; Langer, *European Alliances and Alignments*, 385.

48. See, for example, Thomas J. Christensen and Jack Snyder, "Chain Gangs and Passed Bucks: Predicting Alliance Patterns in Multipolarity," *International Organization* 44, no. 2 (Spring 1990): 137–68.

49. See Kennedy, *Rise and Fall*, 185–87, 215–24; Taylor, *Habsburg Monarchy*; Judson, *Habsburg Empire*.

50. Bridge, *From Sadowa to Sarajevo*, 290–91, 322–23; Taylor, *Habsburg Monarchy*, 204–6, 220–30. Though there is debate regarding when the German-Austrian relationship became indispensable to Austrian policy, Bridge and Taylor both suggest that the turning point came in 1905–8.

51. Taylor, *Struggle*, 413; Andrew, *Théophile Delcassé*, chaps. 9–10.

52. Bridge, *From Sadowa to Sarajevo*, 255; Rothenberg, *Army of Francis Joseph*, 126–27.

53. Geoffrey Wawro, *A Mad Catastrophe: The Outbreak of World War I and the Collapse of the Habsburg Empire*, Kindle ed. (New York: Basic Books, 2014), 29.

54. Graydon A. Tunstall, *Planning for War against Russia and Serbia: Austro-Hungarian and German Military Strategies, 1871–1914* (Boulder, CO: Social Science Monographs, 1993), chaps. 3–4; Rothenberg, *Army of Francis Joseph*, 155–60; Tim Hadley, "Military Diplomacy in the Dual Alliance:

German Military Attaché Reporting from Vienna, 1906–1914," *War in History* 17, no. 3 (July 2010): 294–312.

55. Wawro, *Mad Catastrophe*, 16–50; Rothenberg, *Army of Francis Joseph*, 128; Hadley, "Military Diplomacy."

56. Wawro, *Mad Catastrophe*, 8.

57. Ralston, *Army of the Republic*, 134–35.

58. Work on military fortifications, for instance, slowed to a crawl after the 1890s; see Mitchell, *Victors and Vanquished*, 111–16. For other acquisition problems, see Hermann, *Arming of Europe*, 46–47, 90–91, 150–51; Allan Mitchell, " 'A Situation of Inferiority': French Military Reorganization after the Defeat of 1870," *American Historical Review* 86, no. 1 (February 1981): 54–55.

59. Hermann, *Arming of Europe*, 81–83; Mitchell, " 'A Situation of Inferiority,' " 55–57.

60. Ralston, *Army of the Republic*, chaps. 5–6.

61. Hermann, *Arming of Europe*, 30–31, 60; Ralston, *Army of the Republic*, 312–13.

62. See Robert A. Doughty, "France," in *War Planning 1914*, ed. Richard F. Hamilton and Holger H. Herwig (New York: Cambridge University Press, 2010), 143–74; Annika Mombauer, "German War Plans," in *War Planning 1914*, 48–79; Jack Snyder, "Civil-Military Relations and the Cult of the Offensive, 1914 and 1984," *International Security* 9, no. 1 (Summer 1984): 133. See also Samuel J. Williamson Jr., *The Politics of Grand Strategy: Britain and France Prepare for War, 1904–1914* (Cambridge, MA: Harvard University Press, 1969).

63. Hermann, *Arming of Europe*, 115–21.

64. Geiss, *German Foreign Policy*, 114–18, 139–45, 150–59.

65. Quoted in Geiss, *German Foreign Policy*, 141.

66. On the German concerns, see Copeland, *Origins of Major War*, chaps. 3–4.

67. Tunstall, *Planning for War*, 64–75, 81–107; Stone, "Moltke-Conrad," 207–10.

68. William Mulligan, *The Origins of the First World War* (New York: Cambridge University Press, 2010), 62–84. See also Andrew Rossos, *Russia and the Balkans: Inter-Balkan Rivalries and Russian Foreign Policy, 1908–1914* (Toronto: University of Toronto Press, 1981), 5–46; Jelavich, *Russia's Balkan Entanglements*, 216–50; Samuel R. Williamson Jr., "German Perceptions of the Triple Entente after 1911: Their Mounting Apprehensions Reconsidered," *Foreign Policy Analysis* 7, no. 2 (April 2011): 209–10.

69. Serbia's desire to unify Southeastern Europe's Slavs presented a particular challenge. See Bridge, *Habsburg Monarchy*, 297–327.

70. Quoted in Hermann, *Arming of Europe*, 130.

71. Hermann, *Arming of Europe*, 130–31.

72. Paul Schroeder, "World War I as Galloping Gertie: A Reply to Joachim Remak," *Journal of Modern History* 44, no. 3 (September 1972): 337–38.

73. Hermann, *Arming of Europe*, 122, 127.

74. For an example, see Rossos, *Russia and the Balkans*, 95–96.

75. Shipton, "British Diplomatic Relations," 93–94, 110–14.

76. Schroeder, "Galloping Gertie," 339–41. See also Shipton, "British Diplomatic Relations," 152–55, 160–68, 177–81.

77. Shipton, "British Diplomatic Relations," 183–85.

78. See for instance, German worries about British and Russian aid to France during the Second Moroccan Crisis (1911); Hermann, *Arming of Europe*, 158–59.

79. Quoted in Hewitson, "Germany and France," 577.

80. L. C. F. Turner, "The Significance of the Schlieffen Plan," in *The War Plans of the Great Powers, 1880–1914*, ed. Paul M. Kennedy (New York: Routledge, 1979), 199–207.

81. Geiss, *German Foreign Policy*, 132–35; Jack Snyder, *Myths of Empire: Domestic Politics and International Ambition* (Ithaca, NY: Cornell University Press, 1991), 78.

82. Hermann, *Arming of Europe*, 37–40; Hewitson, "Germany and France," 585–96; Taylor, *Struggle*, 466–67.

83. Williamson, *Politics of Grand Strategy*, 208–23; Doughty, "France," 146–47.

84. D. W. Spring, "Russia and the Franco-Russian Alliance, 1905–1914: Dependence or Independence?," *Slavonic and East European Review* 66, no. 4 (October 1988): 583–90; Bernadotte E.

Smith, "Triple Alliance and Triple Entente, 1902–1914," *American Historical Review* 29, no. 3 (April 1924): 453–58.

85. Fiona K. Tomaszewski, *A Great Russia: Russia and the Triple Entente* (Westport, CT: Praeger, 2002), 30, 79–80.

86. Christopher Andrew, "The Entente Cordiale from Its Origins to 1914," in *Troubled Neighbors: Franco-British Relations in the Twentieth Century*, ed. Neville Waites (London: Weidenfeld and Nicolson, 1971), 11–39; Williamson, *Grand Strategy*, 2–29.

87. Quoted in T. G. Otte, "The Elusive Balance: British Foreign Policy and the French Entente before the First World War," in *Anglo-French Relations in Twentieth Century: Rivalry and Cooperation*, ed. Alan Sharp and Glyn Stone (London: Routledge, 2000), 17.

88. John W. Coogan and Peter F. Coogan, "The British Cabinet and the Anglo-French Staff Talks: Who Knew What and When Did He Know It?," *Journal of British Studies* 24, no. 1 (January 1985): 110–31. British policymakers never formally committed to the British military's deployment, but they sanctioned increasingly extensive Anglo-French military talks and signaled to their French counterparts that intervention was likely. For the evolution of Anglo-French plans and discussions, see Williamson, *Grand Strategy*.

89. For the 1906 discussion, see T. G. Otte, "'Almost a Law of Nature'? Sir Edward Grey, the Foreign Office, and the Balance of Power in Europe, 1905–1912," *Diplomacy and Statecraft* 14, no. 2 (June 2003): 86. For Britain's subsequent efforts to signal its support for France, see Smith, "Triple Alliance and Triple Entente," 459–61; Otte, "'Almost a Law of Nature'?," 87, 103–6; Taylor, *Struggle*, 458–82.

90. Quoted in Otte, "Elusive Balance," 24.

91. Quoted in K. M. Wilson, "To the Western Front: British War Plans and the 'Military Entente' with France before the First World War," *British Journal of International Studies* 3, no. 2 (July 1977): 156.

92. See, for example, William C. Wohlforth, "Realism and the End of the Cold War," *International Security* 19, no. 3 (Winter 1994–95): 91–129; Kennedy, *Rise and Fall*, chaps. 6–7.

93. Aaron L. Friedberg, "The Future of U.S.-China Relations: Is Conflict Inevitable?," *International Security* 30, no. 2 (Fall 2005): 8–9.

94. For overviews of defensive and offensive realist theories, see Barry R. Posen, "The Best Defense," *National Interest*, no. 67 (Spring 2002): 119–26; Stephen G. Brooks, "Dueling Realisms," *International Organization* 51, no. 3 (Summer 1997): 445–77. The foundational statements of each are, respectively, Kenneth N. Waltz, *Theory of International Politics* (Reading, MA: Addison-Wesley, 1979), and John J. Mearsheimer, *The Tragedy of Great Power Politics* (New York: Norton, 2001).

95. Joshua R. Itzkowitz Shifrinson and Michael Beckley, "Correspondence: Debating China's Rise and U.S. Decline," *International Security* 37, no. 3 (Winter 2012–13): 172–81.

96. David Edelstein, *Over the Horizon: Time, Uncertainty, and the Rise of Great Powers* (Ithaca, NY: Cornell University Press, 2017); Michael A. Glosny, "The Grand Strategies of Rising Powers: Reassurance, Coercion, and Balancing Responses" (PhD diss., Massachusetts Institute of Technology, 2012).

97. Avi Shlaim, *The Iron Wall: Israel and the Arab World* (New York: Norton, 2001).

98. See, for example, Joao Resende-Santos, "The Origins of Security Cooperation in the Southern Cone," *Latin American Politics and Society* 44, no. 4 (2002): 89–126.

99. Barak Barfi, "The Real Reason Why Iran Backs Syria," *National Interest*, January 24, 2016, http://nationalinterest.org/feature/the-real-reason-why-iran-backs-syria-14999; Stephen Kinzer, "Europe, Backing Germans, Accepts Yugoslav Breakup," *New York Times*, January 16, 1992.

100. Graham Allison, "The Thucydides Trap: Are the U.S. and China Headed for War?," *Atlantic*, September 24, 2015, https://www.theatlantic.com/international/archive/2015/09/united-states-china-war-thucydides-trap/406756/.

101. Harry Harding, "Has U.S. China Policy Failed?," *Washington Quarterly* 38, no. 3 (Fall 2015): 95–122; Thomas J. Christensen, "Fostering Stability or Creating a Monster? The Rise of China and U.S. Policy toward East Asia," *International Security* 31, no. 1 (Summer 2006): 81–126.

102. Takeo Hoshi and Anil K. Kashyap, "Japan's Financial Crisis and Economic Stagnation," *Journal of Economic Perspectives* 18, no. 1 (Winter 2004): 3–26; "China Overtakes Japan as World's Second-Biggest Economy," *BBCNews.com*, February 14, 2011, http://www.bbc.com/news/business-12427321.

103. In 2016, the United States' GDP was approximately $16.1 trillion, China's GDP was $8.3 trillion, and Japan's was $5.9 trillion. All figures (in 2010 U.S. dollars) are from World Bank, DataBank: World Development Indicators, accessed July 2017, http://databank.worldbank.org/data/reports.aspx?source=world-development-indicators.

104. Friedberg, "Future of U.S.-China Relations," 16–24; John J. Mearsheimer, "The Gathering Storm: China's Challenge to U.S. Power in Asia," *Chinese Journal of International Politics* 3, no. 4 (December 2010): 381–96.

105. Allison, "Thucydides Trap"; Christopher Layne, "The Shadow of the Past: Why the Sino-American Relationship Resembles the Pre-1914 Anglo-German Antagonism," unpublished manuscript, accessed November 4, 2017, https://politicalscience.nd.edu/assets/230753/nobel_revision_final.pdf.

106. Barry R. Posen, "Command of the Commons: The Military Foundations of U.S. Hegemony," *International Security* 28, no. 1 (Summer 2003): 5–46; Eric Heginbotham, Michael Nixon, Forrest Morgan, Jacob Helm, Jeff Hagen, Sheng Li, Jeffrey Engstrom, Martin Libicki, Paul DeLuca, David Shlapak, David Frelinger, Burgess Laird, Kyle Brady, and Lyle Morris, *The U.S.-China Military Scorecard: Forces, Geography, and the Evolving Balance of Power, 1996–2017* (Santa Monica, CA: Rand Corporation, 2015).

107. Heginbotham et al., *U.S.-China Military Scorecard*, xxx. For a similar analysis, see Stephen Biddle and Ivan Oelrich, "Future Warfare in the Western Pacific," *International Security* 41, no. 1 (Summer 2016): 7–48; U.S-China Economic and Security Commission, *2016 Report to Congress* (Washington, DC: U.S.-China Economic and Security Review Commission, 2016), 273.

108. Kenneth Pyle, *Japan Rising: The Resurgence and Promise of Japanese Power and Purpose* (New York: Public Affairs, 2007), chap. 1.

109. My figures (in 2010 U.S. dollars) are based on data from World Bank, DataBank: World Development Indicators, accessed July 2017, http://databank.worldbank.org/data/reports.aspx?source=world-development-indicators.

110. Jake Douglas, "The U.S. Will Defend Japan: The Question Is How?," *The Diplomat*, August 25, 2014, http://thediplomat.com/2014/08/the-us-will-defend-japan-the-question-is-how/; Ayumi Teraoka, "Adhering, Distancing, or Waffling? Understanding a New Dilemma in the U.S.-Japan Alliance," *Georgetown Journal of Asian Affairs* 2, no. 1 (Spring/Summer 2015), 67–97; Richard C. Bush, *The Perils of Proximity: China-Japan Security Relations* (Washington, DC: Brookings Institution Press, 2010), 270–72; Emma Chanlett-Avery and Ian E. Rinehart, *The U.S.-Japan Alliance*, Congressional Research Service Report RL33740, February 9, 2016, https://fas.org/sgp/crs/row/RL33740.pdf.

111. Bjorn Elias Mikalsen Gronning, "Japan's Shifting Military Priorities: Counterbalancing China's Rise," *Asian Security* 10, no. 1 (March 2014): 3–9; Richard C. Bush, "China-Japan Tensions, 1995–2006: Why They Happened, What to Do," Brookings Policy Paper no. 16, June 2009, https://www.brookings.edu/wp-content/uploads/2016/06/06_china_japan_bush.pdf, 9–11.

112. Jennifer Lind, "Japan's Security Evolution," Cato Institute, Policy Analysis no. 788, February 25, 2016, https://www.cato.org/publications/policy-analysis/japans-security-evolution.

113. For overviews of PRC-Japanese relations, see Bush, *Perils of Proximity*; Ming Wan, *Sino-Japanese Relations: Interaction, Logic, and Transformation* (Washington, DC: Wilson Center Press, 2006). See also Alastair Iain Johnston, "How New and Assertive Is China's New Assertiveness?," *International Security* 37, no. 4 (Spring 2013): 7–48.

114. On Japan's current concerns, see Bryce Wakefield, ed., *A Time for Change? Japan's "Peace" Constitution at 65* (Washington, DC: Wilson Center Press, 2012); Lind, "Japan's Security Evolution."

Appendix 1

1. Paul Kennedy, *The Rise and Fall of the Great Powers: Economic Change and Military Conflict from 1500 to 2000* (New York: Random House, 1987; Paul K. MacDonald and Joseph Parent, "Graceful Decline? The Surprising Success of Great Power Retrenchment," *International Security* 35, no. 4 (Spring 2011): 7–44.

2. Kennedy, *Rise and Fall*, 158–59.

3. Paul Bairoch, "Europe's Gross National Product: 1800–1975," *Journal of European Economic History* 5, no. 2 (Fall 1976): 281 table 4.

4. Kennedy, *Rise and Fall*, 203–6.

5. Kennedy, *Rise and Fall*, 202–49. Kennedy also includes the United States and Japan in his list, but acknowledges that these two states were absent from European politics in this period.

6. MacDonald and Parent, "Graceful Decline?," 23 note 46, 28. The authors' non-European great powers include China, Japan, and the United States.

Index

Page numbers in *italics* indicate tables and charts.

The **Essential** Buyer's Guide

LOTUS
EUROPA

Series 1, Series 2, Twin Cam and Twin Cam Special
1966-1975

Your marque expert:
Matthew Vale

VELOCE PUBLISHING
THE PUBLISHER OF FINE AUTOMOTIVE BOOKS

Essential Buyer's Guide Series

Alfa Romeo Alfasud (Metcalfe)
Alfa Romeo Alfetta: all saloon/sedan models 1972 to 1984 & coupé models 1974 to 1987 (Metcalfe)
Alfa Romeo Giulia GT Coupé (Booker)
Alfa Romeo Giulia Spider (Booker)
Audi TT (Davies)
Audi TT Mk2 2006 to 2014 (Durnan)
Austin-Healey Big Healeys (Trummel)
BMW Boxer Twins (Henshaw)
BMW E30 3 Series 1981 to 1994 (Hosier)
BMW GS (Henshaw)
BMW X5 (Saunders)
BMW Z3 Roadster (Fishwick)
BMW Z4: E85 Roadster and E86 Coupe including M and Alpina 2003 to 2009 (Smitheram)
BSA 350, 441 & 500 Singles (Henshaw)
BSA 500 & 650 Twins (Henshaw)
BSA Bantam (Henshaw)
Choosing, Using & Maintaining Your Electric Bicycle (Henshaw)
Citroën 2CV (Paxton)
Citroën ID & DS (Heilig)
Cobra Replicas (Ayre)
Corvette C2 Sting Ray 1963-1967 (Falconer)
Datsun 240Z 1969 to 1973 (Newlyn)
DeLorean DMC-12 1981 to 1983 (Williams)
Ducati Bevel Twins (Falloon)
Ducati Desmodue Twins (Falloon)
Ducati Desmoquattro Twins – 851, 888, 916, 996, 998, ST4 1988 to 2004 (Falloon)
Fiat 500 & 600 (Bobbitt)
Ford Capri (Paxton)
Ford Escort Mk1 & Mk2 (Williamson)
Ford Model A – All Models 1927 to 1931 (Buckley)
Ford Model T – All models 1909 to 1927 (Barker)
Ford Mustang – First Generation 1964 to 1973 (Cook)
Ford Mustang (Cook)
Ford RS Cosworth Sierra & Escort (Williamson)
Harley-Davidson Big Twins (Henshaw)
Hillman Imp (Morgan)
Hinckley Triumph triples & fours 750, 900, 955, 1000, 1050, 1200 – 1991-2009 (Henshaw)
Honda CBR FireBlade (Henshaw)
Honda CBR600 Hurricane (Henshaw)
Honda SOHC Fours 1969-1984 (Henshaw)
Jaguar E-Type 3.8 & 4.2 litre (Crespin)
Jaguar E-type V12 5.3 litre (Crespin)
Jaguar Mark 1 & 2 (All models including Daimler 2.5-litre V8) 1955 to 1969 (Thorley)
Jaguar New XK 2005-2014 (Thorley)
Jaguar S-Type – 1999 to 2007 (Thorley)
Jaguar X-Type – 2001 to 2009 (Thorley)
Jaguar XJ-S (Crespin)
Jaguar XJ6, XJ8 & XJR (Thorley)
Jaguar XK 120, 140 & 150 (Thorley)
Jaguar XK8 & XKR (1996-2005) (Thorley)
Jaguar/Daimler XJ 1994-2003 (Crespin)
Jaguar/Daimler XJ40 (Crespin)
Jaguar/Daimler XJ6, XJ12 & Sovereign (Crespin)
Kawasaki Z1 & Z900 (Orritt)
Land Rover Discovery Series 1 (1989-1998) (Taylor)

Land Rover Discovery Series II (1998-2004) (Taylor)
Land Rover Series I, II & IIA (Thurman)
Land Rover Series III (Thurman)
Lotus Seven replicas & Caterham 7: 1973-2013 (Hawkins)
Mazda MX-5 Miata (Mk1 1989-97 & Mk2 98-2001) (Crook)
Mazda RX-8 (Parish)
Mercedes Benz Pagoda 230SL, 250SL & 280SL roadsters & coupés (Bass)
Mercedes-Benz 190: all 190 models (W201 series) 1982 to 1993 (Parish)
Mercedes-Benz 280-560SL & SLC (Bass)
Mercedes-Benz SL R129-series 1989 to 2001 (Parish)
Mercedes-Benz SLK (Bass)
Mercedes-Benz W123 (Parish)
Mercedes-Benz W124 – All models 1984-1997 (Zoporowski)
MG Midget & A-H Sprite (Horler)
MG TD, TF & TF1500 (Jones)
MGA 1955-1962 (Crosier)
MGB & MGB GT (Williams)
MGF & MG TF (Hawkins)
Mini (Paxton)
Morris Minor & 1000 (Newell)
Moto Guzzi 2-valve big twins (Falloon)
New Mini (Collins)
Norton Commando (Henshaw)
Peugeot 205 GTI (Blackburn)
Piaggio Scooters – all modern two-stroke & four-stroke automatic models 1991 to 2016 (Willis)
Porsche 911 (964) (Streather)
Porsche 911 (993) (Streather)
Porsche 911 (996) (Streather)
Porsche 911 (997) – Model years 2004 to 2009 (Streather)
Porsche 911 (997) – Second generation models 2009 to 2012 (Streather)
Porsche 911 Carrera 3.2 (Streather)
Porsche 911SC (Streather)
Porsche 924 – All models 1976 to 1988 (Hodgkins)
Porsche 928 (Hemmings)
Porsche 930 Turbo & 911 (930) Turbo (Streather)
Porsche 944 (Higgins)
Porsche 981 Boxster & Cayman (Streather)
Porsche 986 Boxster (Streather)
Porsche 987 Boxster and Cayman 1st generation (2005-2009) (Streather)
Porsche 987 Boxster and Cayman 2nd generation (2009-2012) (Streather)
Range Rover – First Generation models 1970 to 1996 (Taylor)
Rolls-Royce Silver Shadow & Bentley T-Series (Bobbitt)
Royal Enfield Bullet (Henshaw)
Subaru Impreza (Hobbs)
Sunbeam Alpine (Barker)
Triumph 350 & 500 Twins (Henshaw)
Triumph Bonneville (Henshaw)
Triumph Stag (Mort)
Triumph Thunderbird, Trophy & Tiger (Henshaw)
Triumph TR6 (Williams)
Triumph TR7 & TR8 (Williams)
Velocette 350 & 500 Singles 1946 to 1970 (Henshaw)
Vespa Scooters – Classic 2-stroke models 1960-2008 (Paxton)
Volkswagen Bus (Copping)
Volvo 700/900 Series (Beavis)
Volvo P1800/1800S, E & ES 1961 to 1973 (Murray)
VW Beetle (Copping)
VW Golf GTI (Copping)

www.veloce.co.uk

First published in September 2018 by Veloce Publishing Limited, Veloce House, Parkway Farm Business Park, Middle Farm Way, Poundbury, Dorchester, DT1 3AR, England. Tel +44 (0)1305 260068 / Fax 01305 250479 / e-mail info@veloce.co.uk / web www.veloce.co.uk or www.velocebooks.com.
ISBN: 978-1-787112-87-2 UPC: 6-36847-01287-8.